MULTILEVEL DYNAMICS IN DEVELOPMENTAL PSYCHOPATHOLOGY: PATHWAYS TO THE FUTURE

The Minnesota Symposia on Child Psychology

Volume 34

MULTILEVEL DYNAMICS IN DEVELOPMENTAL PSYCHOPATHOLOGY: PATHWAYS TO THE FUTURE

The Minnesota Symposia on Child Psychology

Volume 34

Edited by

ANN S. MASTEN
University of Minnesota, Twin Cities

LEA
LAWRENCE ERLBAUM ASSOCIATES, PUBLISHERS
2007   Mahwah, New Jersey   London

Copyright © 2007 by Lawrence Erlbaum Associates, Inc.

Lawrence Erlbaum Associates, Inc., Publishers
10 Industrial Avenue
Mahwah, New Jersey 07430
www.erlbaum.com

Cover design by Tomai Maridou

Library of Congress Cataloging-in-Publication Data

Minnesota Symposium on Child Psychology (34th : 2004 :
University of Minnesota)
  Multilevel dynamics in developmental psychopathology :
pathways to the future / edited by Ann S. Masten.
     p. ;   cm. — (The Minnesota symposia on child psychology ; v. 34)
     Includes bibliographical references and index.
     ISBN 0–8058–6162–9 (cloth : alk. paper)
     1. Child development—Congresses. 2. Child psychology—Congresses.
  3. Psychology, Pathological—Congresses. I. Masten, Ann S. II. Title.
  III. Series: Minnesota symposia on child psychology (Series) ; v. 34.
     [DNLM: 1. Child Development—Congresses. 2. Psychopathology—
  Congresses. 3. Adolescent Development—Congresses. 4. Mental Disorders—
  etiology—Congresses. W3 MI607 v.34 2007 / WS 350 M665m 2007]
  RJ499.M495   2004
  618.92'89—dc22   2006010901

Books published by Lawrence Erlbaum Associates are printed on acid-
free paper, and their bindings are chosen for strength and durability.

Printed in the United States of America
10 9 8 7 6 5 4 3 2 1

In memory of

IRVING B. HARRIS,

*exemplary philanthropist
and champion for children*

Contents

Preface

Developmental psychopathology emerged in the 1970s with an ambitious agenda aimed at integrating sciences concerned with human development and mental health (Cicchetti, 2006; Masten, 2006). The mission of this integrated science was to understand and eventually to influence the processes leading toward and away from behavioral problems and disorders over the life course, including the pathways to mental health and positive development. Scientists were optimistic that integration across disciplines and levels of analysis, from molecules to media or neurons to neighborhoods, would yield better strategies for promoting healthy development and preventing or ameliorating the suffering and costs inflicted by psychopathology on individuals, families, and societies. Initially, however, there was considerable preliminary work needed to develop the basic tools for research, communication, and collaboration across disciplines and levels of analysis, as well as the knowledge base required to move this challenging agenda forward. Progress could be noted, but the promise of developmental psychopathology seemed elusive or distant.

Then a series of dramatic advances in technologies for identifying, assessing, and analyzing key components and processes of human behavior and development began to transform virtually all of the fields engaged in developmental psychopathology. Intensive work on the human genome, gene expression, gene–environment interaction, brain imaging, brain development, stress, the statistics of growth and change, animal models of human behavior, and social networks, for example, began to change the prospects for an integrated approach to development and psychopathology. New possibilities for integration across multiple levels of analysis were rapidly becoming a reality.

When it was time to plan the 34th Minnesota Symposium on Child Psychology, the faculty of the Institute of Child Development decided to focus on developmental psychopathology for the first time. We wanted a theme that would reflect the most exciting work of the present and future, and quickly settled on the topic of multilevel dynamics in developmental psychopathology. The chapters of this volume represent the presentations at this symposium, which was held in October, 2004, on the campus of the University of Minnesota. Of course, no single conference could capture the profound and broad transformations underway. It was our goal to provide a sample of integrative thinking and empirical work across levels of analysis and disciplines by a group of leading investigators in developmental psychopathology.

The importance of conceptualizing multiple levels of analysis and understanding the dynamic processes that connect these levels had been recognized for a long time in the history of psychiatry, psychology, and developmental science, as noted in multiple chapters of this volume. Many of the most influential ideas and theories about normal and abnormal development of the 20th century addressed the theme of multilevel dynamics, including, for example: Waddington's (1957) epigenetic landscape; Weiss's (1959) model of cellular dynamics; multilevel transactional models (Gottlieb, 1998; Sameroff, 2000a, b; Sameroff & Chandler, 1975), Bronfenbrenner's ecological systems model (1977); the organizational theory of development (Cicchetti, 1990; Sroufe, 1979, 1997); and general developmental systems theory (Ford & Lerner, 1992; Thelen & Smith, 1998).

What is new, as we enter the 21st century, is the focus on how these processes linking levels actually work, more precise measurement at each level of analysis, and attempts to directly assess dynamic interaction itself, as well as strategies to analyze joint effects and interactions over time and to capture the complexity of multilevel dynamics in practical research designs. These advances are giving dynamic models new traction, accompanied by a growing appreciation for the bidirectional nature of multilevel interactions. Genes now can be identified and shown to moderate the influences of experience, while experiences can be shown to alter gene expression through specific processes.

It is also clear that these advances are transforming the possibilities for intervention and prevention. It is now conceivable to consider specific changes in the context or experiences of children, in their education or families or peer interactions, that have the aim of altering biological vulnerability or brain development, reprogramming adaptive systems, or in other ways fostering healthier development through a better understanding of how multilevel dynamics work. With these possibilities come many ethical considerations, not only in terms of when, how, and whether to intervene, but also in terms of the moral significance of societal failures to protect child development.

The first three chapters of this volume highlight the interactions of biology and context in development, invoking metaphors of "dances" and "symphonies" to capture the complexity and dynamic nature of the interactions that produce coherent patterns of development. In the first chapter, Michael Rutter delineates the principles and processes guiding contemporary work on how genes and environments shape development. He outlines core principles of current biomedical models that integrate biological, medical, and psychological approaches across levels of analysis and disciplines. These principles bear a striking resemblance to the principles of developmental psychopathology as articulated by Cicchetti, Masten, Sameroff, Sroufe, and others, emphasizing development, multiple causes, probabilistic pathways, and related themes (Cicchetti, 1984, 2006; Masten, 2006; Sameroff, 2000a, b; Sroufe, 1997; Sroufe & Rutter, 1984). Rutter underscores the rejection of dualistic approaches to brain and mind, or physical and mental disorder, as well as the demise of simplistic reductionism, where causal explanations are limited to a single (e.g., molecular) level. Rutter reviews concepts and findings from quantitative genetics, research on gene–environment correlation and interaction, and molecular genetics, in order to highlight progress in understanding how genes and environments work to influence each other, each manifesting pervasive effects on normal and abnormal development.

In chapter 2, Daniel Hanson and Irving Gottesman also consider the interplay of genes and environments and highlight the role of chance in development, elaborating the dynamic processes of adaptation reflected in evolution and individual development, the plasticity of the human brain, and epigenetic processes. They present a thought-provoking analysis of how highly patterned, yet improvisational and complex "dances" of human behavior, including psychopathology, might arise arise from many interactions and combinations of common genes and experiences. Hanson and Gottesman focus on the central issue of epigenesis, how multiple genes and environments interacting become integrated in development at multiple levels. Their analysis leads to some surprising conclusions about the "causes" of psychopathology, how to categorize disorders, and how to think about intervention.

The theme of biology-context dynamics is further explored in chapter 3, by Thomas Boyce, who argues that virtually all human disease and disorder arises from the interplay of biological susceptibilities and exposures to pathogenic contexts. He advances three claims, supported by his and other research on biology–environment interactions: (a) that stress reactivity should be reconceptualized as biological sensitivity to context, which enhances the effects of bad or good environments; (b) that this sensitivity itself is the result of reciprocal influences of biology and experience in concert; and (c) that biological sensitivity to context may account for "SES gradients," the pervasive association of economic and social disadvantage with health problems (physical and psychological), achievement gaps, and morbidities of many kinds. Based on the "biology of misfortune" he describes,

Boyce makes a persuasive case for the moral imperative of societies to protect development by reducing the harmful circumstances of disadvantaged
children.

The next three chapters focus on the dynamics of individual, family, and
peer interactions in the social worlds of children. Recent research on interpersonal dynamics within and across levels of analysis has demonstrated
the potential of individual, sibling, family, and peer systems to coregulate
and moderate each other (Masten, 2005; Masten & Shaffer, 2006; Steinberg et al., 2006). Families, friends, and individuals interact in many ways
to influence the course of development, with families and peers potentially
serving a variety of protective or regulatory functions for individuals and
vice versa. The chapters of this volume sound this theme in multiple ways.

In chapter 4, Byron Egeland draws on findings from the Minnesota Longitudinal Study of Parents and Children to discuss processes of resilience and
psychopathology, with a particular focus on dynamics related to attachment
and caregiving systems and the development of competence. He describes
the historical context of this now-classic study spanning three decades,
which closely parallels the history of developmental psychopathology at
Minnesota. Pathways toward (and away from) externalizing problems, anxiety disorders, and dissociative symptoms are highlighted as Egeland examines the role of relationships, parenting, and a child's own competence in
the development of psychopathology or resilience. He discusses implications of such research for policies and preventive interventions designed
to alter the developmental course through change in the key relationships
and interactions of children in the multiple ecologies important at different periods of their lives.

In chapter 5, Barbara Fiese and Mary Spagnola delve into the dynamics of family systems as a context of child development, analyzing the processes by which individual development interacts with the "whole family
processes" of family life. From the perspectives of outside-the-family perspectives and inside-the-family perceptions, these investigators focus on
family narratives, routines, and rituals and how the sense of connectedness,
meaning, and cohesion afforded by these processes may work to protect,
support, or change the lives of children. Their work provides a rich examination of family life and the way families promote or fail to protect their
children in relation to socialization in the family and stressful experiences
arising outside the family. Such family–child dynamics may serve to regulate behavior and emotion, and thereby support the development of competence. These authors describe their recent work on understanding how
such family processes work to promote competence of individual children
in risky circumstances, particularly in families with a chronically ill child.

Thomas Dishion and Timothy Piehler focus on peer dynamics across
multiple levels of analysis in chapter 6, including peer social network for-

mation, friendship formation and peer deviancy training, and the role of individual self-regulation skills as a moderator of peer influences. These investigators and their colleagues have conducted ground-breaking work on the microsocial processes by which peers influence each other, developing powerful strategies for measuring the social dynamics across smaller and larger groups. They have documented the iatrogenic effects of well-intended interventions that inadvertently increase deviance by grouping deviant peers together. Their work also demonstrates the potential protective effects of good monitoring by parents and good self-regulation skills against the influences of deviant peers.

Peer dynamics, positive and negative, have numerous implications for prevention, school policies, and other kinds of intervention discussed by Dishion and Piehler. Some may focus on preventing formation of deviant networks and friendships, whereas others focus on strengthening the regulatory skills of family or individual, after deviant peer connections have already become established.

The final two chapters of this 34th Symposium volume illustrate the challenges and benefits of encompassing multiple levels of analysis in a single research program. In chapter 7, Judy Garber describes the complexities of a bio-psycho-social perspective on depression, one of the most common forms of psychopathology, and one with dramatic patterns of change over the course of adolescence. Garber describes her longitudinal research study to understand the interplay of vulnerability, context, stress, and cognition in the development of depression. Though her project focused on psychological and social processes, Garber's conceptual framework assumed that many other levels were operating. Her chapter illustrates the progress and also the formidable challenges inherent in the goal of understanding the developmental pathways of depression across levels of analysis.

Dante Cicchetti, in collaboration with Kristin Valentino in chapter 8, describes a comprehensive, multiple-levels research program to understand developmental pathways in relation to child maltreatment, focusing on a particular class of risk or threat to human development, rather than a particular form of psychopathology. This research program embodies the principles of developmental psychopathology and provides a paradigmatic example of programmatic research designed to address and integrate multiple levels of analysis and multiple systems of interaction within level. Cicchetti has been instrumental in formulating and advancing the agenda of developmental psychopathology for more than three decades, beginning as a student at the University of Minnesota, and his profound influence on his peers, teachers, and students is evident throughout this volume.

One of Cicchetti's teachers, Alan Sroufe, provided the overall discussion and closing remarks at the Symposium. Sroufe has mentored, collaborated with, and inspired many of the scientists who shaped this symposium. He has taught a graduate course on developmental psychopathology for well over three decades. In his closing commentary, Sroufe offers his reflections on all the chapters, highlighting and extending the integrative theme that unites all the levels of analysis discussed here, all of the chapters, as well as every other symposium in this series and developmental psychopathology itself, which is *development*.

This volume provides a tantalizing preview of the future of developmental psychopathology, illuminating potential pathways to more integrated and effective sciences of normal and abnormal development and their applications in prevention and treatment. Repeated themes emerge across the pages, promising fine music and dancing in years to come.

The 34th Symposium was dedicated to the memory of Irving B. Harris (1910–2004), who died the week of the symposium. Harris contributed in many ways to the Institute of Child Development, establishing the Irving B. Harris Center for Infant and Toddler Development, sponsoring numerous training programs, and endowing two professorships in developmental science, one held by Alan Sroufe and the other held by Byron Egeland. This great philanthropist also made many contributions over many decades to developmental programs across the United States, with the goal of improving child welfare and the kind of science that would inform policies and practices supporting healthy development.

On behalf of the Institute of Child Development, I want to thank all of the participants in this Symposium for their ideas, energy, interactions, and generosity in creating a memorable experience that shaped this volume in many ways. These participants included the speakers, the incredible students of the Institute who helped organize and host the symposium, an enthusiastic audience of multidisciplinary faculty, administrators, and students past and present, visiting scholars and diverse professionals invested in child development. I also thank my faculty co-organizers, Byron Egeland and Alan Sroufe, as well as the department's executive administrators at the time, Signe Bobbitt and John Schepers, all of whom contributed in numerous ways throughout the symposium. Staff support for the symposium and the preparation of this volume was provided by Danielle Bordeleau, Dolly Britzman, Jeanne Cowan, Wendy McCormick, and Liz Plunkett.

Financial sponsorship for this symposium was provided by the Marian Radke-Yarrow and Leon Yarrow Endowment for Research on Social Development and Relationships, the College of Education and Human Development, and the Institute of Child Development at the University of Minnesota. In addition, contributions for special symposium events were provided by the Departments of Family Social Science, Psychiatry, Psychology, and Sociology, as well as the Life Course Center, all at the University of Minnesota.

REFERENCES

Bronfenbrenner, U. (1979). *The ecology of human development: Experiments by nature and design.* Cambridge, MA: Harvard University Press.

Cicchetti, D. (1984). The emergence of developmental psychopathology. *Child Development, 55,* 1–7.

Cicchetti, D. (1990). The organization and coherence of socioemotional, cognitive, and representational development: Illustrations through a developmental psychopathology perspective on Down syndrome and child maltreatment. In R. Thompson (Ed.), *Socioemotional development: Nebraska symposium on motivation* (Vol. 36, pp. 259–366). Lincoln, NE: University of Nebraska Press.

Cicchetti, D. (2006). Development and psychopathology. In D. Cicchetti & D. Cohen (Eds.), *Developmental psychopathology: Vol. 1. Theory and method* (2nd ed., 1–23). New York: Wiley.

Ford, D. H., & Lerner, R. M. (1992). *Developmental systems theory: An integrative approach.* Newbury Park, CA: Sage.

Gottlieb, G. (1998). The significance of biology for human development: A developmental psychobiological systems view. In W. Damon & R. M. Lerner (Eds.), *Handbook of child psychology* (5th ed.; Vol. 1, pp. 233–273). New York: John Wiley & Sons.

Masten, A. S. (2005). Peer relationships and psychopathology in developmental perspective: Reflections on progress and promise. *Journal of Clinical Child and Adolescent Psychology, 34,* 87–92.

Masten, A. S. (2006). Developmental psychopathology: Pathways to the future. *International Journal of Behavioral Development, 31,* 46–53.

Masten, A. S., & Shaffer, A. (2006). How families matter in child development: Reflections from research on risk and resilience. In A. Clarke-Stewart & J. Dunn (Eds.), *Families count: Effects on child and adolescent development* (pp. 5–25). New York: Cambridge University Press.

Sameroff, A. J. (2000a). Developmental systems and psychopathology. *Development and Psychopathology, 12,* 297–312.

Sameroff, A. J. (2000b). Dialectical processes in developmental psychopathology. In A. J. Sameroff, M. Lewis, & S. M. Miller (Eds.), *Handbook of developmental psychopathology* (2nd ed., pp. 23–40). New York: Kluwer Academic/Plenum.

Sameroff, A. J., & Chandler, M. J. (1975). Reproductive risk and the continuum of caretaking casualty. *Review of Child Development Research, 4,* 187–244.

Sroufe, L. A. (1979). The coherence of individual development: Early care, attachment, and subsequent developmental issues. *American Psychologist, 34,* 834–841.

Sroufe, L. A. (1997). Psychopathology as an outcome of development. *Development and Psychopathology, 9,* 251–268.

Sroufe, L. A., & Rutter, M. (1984). The domain of developmental psychopathology. *Child Development, 55,* 17–29.

Steinberg, L., Dahl, R., Keating, D., Kupfer, D., Masten, A., & Pine, D. (2006). Psychopathology in adolescence: Integrating affective neuroscience with the study of context. In D. Cicchetti & D. Cohen (Eds.), *Developmental psychopathology: Vol. 2. Developmental neuroscience* (2nd ed., pp. 710–741). New York: Wiley.

Thelen, E., & Smith, L. (1998). Dynamic systems theories. In R. M. Lerner (Ed.), *Handbook of child psychology: Vol. 1. Theoretical models of human development* (5th ed., pp. 563–634). New York: Wiley.

Waddington, C. H. (1957). *The strategy of genes.* London: Allen & Unwin.

Weiss, P. (1959). Cellular dynamics. *Review of Modern Physics, 31,* 11–20.

Chapter 1

Gene–Environment Interplay and Developmental Psychopathology

Michael Rutter
Kings College, London

The general notion that genes might influence behavior has proved surprisingly controversial (Rutter, 2006a). Some of the concerns expressed have focused on methodological issues in relation to behavior genetics, some on the excessive claims of some genetic evangelists, some on a supposedly implied biological determinism, some on the problems in studying genetic influences on socially defined behaviors, and some on the negative messages about the possibility of making preventive or therapeutic interventions effective. However, many psychosocial researchers have been quite reluctant to accept the reality of genetic effects on individual differences, and some have seemed to want to place developmental psychology outside of both biology and medicine. This wish to separate off psychology is, however, based on a misunderstanding of what is entailed in a biomedical approach. Accordingly, it is necessary to outline some of the main biomedical principles before turning to the specifics of genetic concepts and findings. This is essential because any adequate understanding of the processes of normal and abnormal development must be based on these principles.

BIOMEDICAL PRINCIPLES

In order to emphasize the close links between psychology and both biology and medicine, the principles are illustrated first by giving medical examples and then by turning to psychological ones.

Developmental Approaches Are Fundamental

It has long been recognized that any adequate understanding of the origins of disease must recognize the necessity of taking a developmental approach (Rutter & Sroufe, 2000). For example, the multiphase precancerous developments that precede the development of overt cancer constitute an essential element in the study of cancer. This is not just a matter of early diagnosis of tumors, but rather an appreciation that the development of cancer is preceded by changes that are benign in themselves but that predispose to a course of development that ultimately ends up with the growth of malignant tumors. A quite different example is provided by the evidence of the increased risk of heart disease in adult life that stems from impaired physical growth in the neonatal period (Barker, 1997, 1999; Bateson et al., 2004). The finding is of particular developmental interest because it is subnormal weight in infancy that predisposes to later heart disease, whereas in adult life, it is excessive weight that constitutes the risk factor. Herpes zoster, commonly known as shingles, constitutes a third, rather different, sort of example. This disease is due to a reactivation of the latent virus that will have caused chicken pox in childhood. Although shingles is most common in the elderly, its origins lie in the childhood infection of chicken pox.

Psychopathological examples are provided by schizophrenia, depression, and antisocial behavior. Schizophrenia used to be regarded as an adult-onset psychosis, but it is now clear that in a high proportion of cases it is a neurodevelopmental disorder that is first evident in childhood (Keshavan, Kennedy, & Murray, 2004). With respect to depression, it is important that prepubertal anxiety is a characteristic precursor of depression that begins only postpubertally (Eaves, Silberg, & Erklani, 2003). Life-course-persistent antisocial behavior, manifest in adulthood as antisocial personality disorder, typically begins in early childhood, usually in association with hyperactivity Moffitt, 1993; Moffitt, Caspi, Rutter, & Silva, 2001).

Many Disease Processes Are Dimensional

A second key biomedical principle is that many disease processes are dimensional in nature, with continuity between normality and pathology (Rutter, 2003). With respect to internal medicine, this is shown in the childhood origins of atheroma, the continuity in liability to allergies, and the continuity in liability to late-onset diabetes. There are clinically important transition points when the stage in the disease process is accompanied by an acute and pressing need for treatment, but the disease process itself is dimensional.

With respect to psychopathology, there are comparable continuities with respect to depression, antisocial behavior, and in the genetic liability to hyperactivity/inattention. Categorical distinctions are needed with respect to clinical decision making, but the psychopathological concept is clearly dimensional.

Many Risk Factors for Disease Are Dimensional

Most of the key risk factors for somatic disease are dimensional rather than categorical. Thus, for example, a raised cholesterol level, an increased clotting tendency of the blood, an increased blood pressure, and heavy smoking are all well-demonstrated risk factors for coronary artery disease. The same applies in the field of psychopathology. This is evident with respect to the intrauterine exposure to alcohol or smoking and the development of attention deficit disorder with hyperactivity (Linnet et al., 2003; Thapar et al., 2003). It is also evident in the consistent finding of an association between the number and severity of psychosocial risks and most types of mental disorder (Rutter, 2006b; Sameroff, 2006). Single risks, when experienced in isolation, tend to carry rather low risks but the cumulative effect of multiple risk factors is great.

There Are Multiple Causal Pathways
to the Same Disease Endpoint

There are numerous examples of multiple causal pathways in internal medicine; one example illustrates the point (Rutter, 1997). Smoking, infections of the lung, and asthma all serve as pathways to obstructive lung disease. The initial phase in the causal pathway is quite different in each case— an irritant in the case of smoking, infection in the second pathway, and allergy in the third. With respect to psychopathology, ADHD may be used as an example in which prenatal alcohol exposure, prolonged institutional care in infancy, and neurodevelopmental impairment, all serve as causal pathways (Sandberg, 2002). The mechanisms at the beginning of the pathway are quite different, but the endpoints of different pathways look quite similar.

Risk Factors May Influence Several Different Outcomes

The converse also applies; that is to say, the same risk factor may influence the development of several quite different outcomes, although not necessarily through the same mechanism. Thus, smoking predisposes to lung cancer, coronary artery disease, osteoporosis, and wrinkling of the skin. In this case, we know that the causal mechanisms are quite different and the multiple endpoints arise because what is supposedly a single risk factor, namely smoking, actually encompasses a rather diverse range of risks including carcinogenic tars, carbon monoxide, and nicotinic effects on blood vessels. In the field of psychopathology, early parental loss has been shown to predispose to adult depression, alcoholism, and personality disorder (Maughan & McCarthy, 1997). In this case, we do not know whether the mechanisms for each of these outcomes is the same or different. However, it may be expected that, quite often, the mechanisms are disparate. For example, maltreatment in childhood is a risk factor for both antisocial behavior and for depressive disorders, but the evidence on gene–environment interactions suggests that the causal pathways are probably different (Caspi et al., 2002, 2003; Moffitt, Caspi, & Rutter, 2005).

Social Context Influences Risk

The evidence on social context effects is actually stronger in the field of internal medicine than it is in the field of mental disorders, although it is present for both (Rutter, 1999). Thus, there is much evidence that social inequality is a substantial risk factor for numerous diseases (Marmot & Wilkinson, 1999). The point here is that it is not the absolute level of affluence or poverty that matters, but rather the degree of inequality within the society in which the individual grows up. Similarly, there is substantial evidence that a lack of job autonomy is a pervasive risk factor for physical disease. The evidence suggests that it is not the work requirements of the job itself that matter, but rather the degree of control that the individual has over his work situation. In the field of psychopathology, the risk for antisocial behavior associated with social disorganization in communities (Brooks-Gunn, Duncan, & Aber, 1997; Sampson, Raudenbush, & Earls, 1997) and the role of the school ethos (Rutter, Maughan, Mortimore, & Ouston with Smith, 1979; Rutter & Maughan, 2002) as a risk factor for childhood disorders constitute parallel examples.

Rejection of Dualism

It is clear from a large body of evidence that there is a two-way interplay between soma and psyche, and it makes no sense to regard one as in any sense more basic than the other. For example, it has been well demonstrated in both humans and animals that testosterone has significant effects on dominance but, equally, it has been shown that defeat in sporting combat leads to a drop in testosterone levels (Booth, Shelley, Mazur, Tharp, & Kittock, 1989; Mazur, Booth, & Dabbs, 1992). This is not a consequence of exercise because the effects are as evident with chess as they are with tennis. A rather different sort of example is provided by the effects of psychological treatments on brain imaging findings. The intervention is psychological but the effects are evident in brain functioning. Sometimes the effects of pharmacological treatments and psychological treatments are similar

(Baxter, Schwartz, Bergman, Szuba, Guze, et al., 1992) and sometimes they are different (Goldapple, Segal, Garson, Lau, Bieling, et al., 2004). A third example is provided by the effects of learning in adult life on brain structure—as shown, for example, by studies of London taxicab drivers and by studies of violin players (see Huttenlocher, 2002; Rutter, 2002). Elbert, Pantev, Wienbruch, Rockstroh, & Taub (1995), using magnetic resonance imaging (MRI), found that the cortical representation of the digits of the left hand in violinists and other string players was larger than that in controls and that the amount of cortical reorganization in the representation of the fingering digits was correlated with the age at which the person had begun to play. Maguire, Gadian, Johnsrude, Good, Ashburner, et al. (2000), also using structural MRI, found that the posterior hippocampi of London taxi drivers (who are required to gain an extensive knowledge of routes all over London—a process called gaining "the knowledge," which usually takes place over 2 to 3 years) was significantly larger than that of controls. Hippocampal volume was correlated with the amount of time spent as a taxi driver. Both studies suggest that the brain has the capacity in later childhood or adult life to change in structure in response to environmental demands.

All workings of the mind have to be based on the functioning of the brain. That does not mean, of course, that the thought processes are caused by some neural feature, but it does mean that there has to be a neural accompaniment of any mental operation. A subdivision of mental disorders into those that are "medical" and those that are "social" is totally meaningless.

Identification of Physiological and Pathophysiological Pathways

A further biomedical principle is that there is a unifying concern to identify the physiological and pathophysiological pathways that are involved in any outcome that may be studied. This is so whether the starting point is an intrinsic or extrinsic risk factor. This is characteristic of the whole of medicine and biology, including psychopathology. For quite a while in psychology, there was a tendency to assume that it was somehow disloyal to the discipline to want to invoke physiology but, fortunately, that is now a thing of the past. It is crucially important to identify mental mechanisms, but it is equally important to determine the pathways involved and the physiological basis.

Rejection of Disproven Theories

A central feature of biomedical principles is the commitment to rejecting favored theories when the empirical data indicate that this is necessary.

Thus, for a very long time peptic ulcer was thought to be due to stress, but it is now clear that it is actually the result of an infection. Much attention used to be paid to the effects of diet on cholesterol levels, but it came to be recognized that cholesterol levels were mainly influenced by liver metabolism and not by diet, although diet does have a minor effect (particularly in individuals who are genetically susceptible). A third example is the appreciation that the physical disease risks associated with employment are due to a subservient job situation rather than executive stress (Marmot & Wilkinson, 1999).

Aversion to Nonexplanatory Jargon

The tenth principle is an aversion to nonexplanatory jargon terms and meaningless soapbox prejudices that can ignore the realities. The accusations that this finding or that one constitutes "medicalization" is one example of that kind, and another would be the accusation of "biological determinism."

Reductionism

Critics of genetics frequently raise the charge of biological reductionism (Rose, 1995, 1998). It is important to recognize that there are both acceptable and unacceptable varieties of reductionism. The unacceptable variety constitutes a forcing of all causal processes into explanations only at the molecular level. This is unacceptable because it ignores the evolutionary development of the abilities to think back, to plan ahead, and thereby to influence events (Dennett, 2003). It is also unacceptable because biological organisms involve hierarchies of systems and, to an important extent, these systems operate as a whole and not just as the sum of separate independent components (Kendler, 2005; Morange, 2001; Rutter, 2006a). What is acceptable, however, is the seeking of unifying, simplifying principles for complex phenomena plus the search for an integrating organization and system. This should be combined with an attempt to account for high-level functions on the basis of lower level features when that is possible. It is not that there is one "correct" level of explanation, and it is not that all complex phenomena can be explained on a simple basis. Rather, it is a recognition that biology works on a structured, organized basis and that it is a frequent experience in biology to find that what appears complex today is actually explicable on the basis of a much simpler principle once that has been demonstrated and understood. Genetics includes several examples of that kind, as illustrated by the intergenerational expansion of trinucleotide repeats, by genomic imprinting, and by the role of environmental influences on gene expression (Rutter, 2006a).

Biology Functions on a Probabilistic Basis

The last general point to make is that biology, including genetics, functions on a probabilistic basis. Development is genetically programmed with respect to an overall pattern and not in terms of a precise specification of what each and every cell does. Examples that illustrate this probabilistic specification are provided by the corrective process of neuronal pruning (in which an initial overproduction of neurons allows a selective pruning in order to fine-tune functioning (Goodman, 1994; Nelson & Bloom, 1997), and experience-adaptive biological programming in which development is tailored to meet the needs of the particular environment in which the organism develops (Bateson et al., 2004; Rutter, 2005).

What all of this amounts to is that it is likely that there is no kind of somatic development free of genetic influence but, equally, no kind is likely to be free of an environmental influence. Similarly, no aspect of psychological functioning is independent from brain function. Having attempted to set the scene in terms of the biological background, let me now turn to concepts and findings with respect to behavioral, and psychiatric, genetics.

QUANTITATIVE GENETICS

Quantitative genetics is concerned with determining the relative strength of the effects of genes and of the environment as influences on the population variance of some particular trait. Nongeneticists tend to focus on the heritability quotient as the basic output from the quantitative genetic research. However, although that might have applied to the early days of behavioral genetics, it certainly does not apply to modern behavioral genetics (Rutter, 2004; Rutter, 2006a). To begin with, there is an appreciation that, in addition to the main effect of genes and the main effects of environment, it is essential to take account of gene–environment correlations and gene–environment interactions (Rutter & Silberg, 2002; Rutter, Moffitt & Caspi, 2006). Also, distinctions are drawn between additive genetic effects and genetic effects that involve synergistic interplay among genes (or among different alleles of the same gene). In the same way, quantitative genetic strategies could be used to differentiate between environmental effects that tend to make siblings more similar (so-called shared effects) and those that make them more different (so-called nonshared effects). But, beyond all of that, quantitative genetic analyses can be hugely informative in investigating mediating developmental mechanisms of one kind or another.

Traditionally, quantitative genetics analyses ignored the effects of gene–environment correlations and gene–environment interactions, both of which would be largely encompassed in the term for genetic influences.

It is now clear that neither gene–environment correlations nor interactions can be ignored, and there are ways in which these can be separated from the main effects of genes that are independent of the environment (see Eaves et al., 2003; Purcell & Sham, 2002). In other words, it has become evident that variance cannot be wholly attributed to the sum of the effects of genes and the effects of environments because some of the effects require the coaction of the two.

For the most part, quantitative genetics relies on the use of a variety of twin, and of adoption, strategies that provide various means of separating the effects of genes and environment. However, family studies are also informative. Although they cannot clearly separate the effects of genes and environment, it is possible to determine the extent to which the degree of biological relatedness is associated with familial liability. Also, family studies are crucial for the examination of patterns of inheritance.

All of the research strategies involve a range of crucial assumptions of one kind or another (Rutter, Bolton, Harrington, Le Coutier, Macdonald, et al., 1990; Rutter, Pickles, Murray, & Eaves, 2001; Rutter, Silberg, O'Connor, & Simonoff, 1999). In the past, these tended to be pushed to one side in a rather cavalier way, but modern quantitative genetics research has taken these seriously and has attempted to assess the degree to which the assumptions are met in practice. Clearly, that is essential. Some behavioral geneticists tend to emphasize particular advantages of studying separated twins and using adoption designs. They do indeed have their own interest but, for a variety of reasons (particularly concerned with sampling), in my view they are less satisfactory than twin strategies. It should be added that twin strategies involve more possibilities than simply comparing monozygotic and dizygotic pairs. For example, there have been recent developments in the use of the Children of Twins strategy (D'Onofrio, Turkheimer, Eaves, Corey, Berg, et al., 2003; Silberg & Eaves, 2004).

Quantitative Genetics Findings

Let me now turn to the findings from quantitative genetic research (Rutter, 2004; Rutter, 2006a). To begin with, there are some disorders for which there is good evidence of strong genetic influences, meaning that in the populations studied, they account for a majority of the population variance. This would apply to conditions such as autism and schizophrenia and probably also to bipolar affective disorders and to ADHD. There is, too, a much larger number of traits for which there is consistent evidence of an important, but not predominant, genetic effect. That would probably be the case with respect to ordinary varieties of unipolar depression, of antisocial behavior, and of intelligence, in all of which the effects of genes and of environment are of roughly equal magnitude. Then there are a variety of traits in which it is clear that there is a genetic influence, but one that accounts for only a small proportion of the variance. This would apply to some psychological traits, but it would also apply to life experiences such as divorce or family negativity or life events that are outside the person's own control.

The findings on all three groups may be summarized in terms of the conclusion that there are significant genetic effects, of varying strength, on virtually all human behaviors. This includes the likelihood of experiencing positive and negative life events insofar as such events are open to the effects of people's own behavior in shaping and selecting environments. Sometimes, nongeneticists have wanted to equate genetic influences with effects on medical diseases or disorders, but that involves a total misunderstanding of how genes operate. Genetic effects apply to all behaviors that have any kind of basis in the structure and functioning of the brain, and that applies to virtually all behaviors. Genetic effects are far from confined to disorders and diseases; on the contrary, they are all-pervasive with respect to behavior.

Before accepting that conclusion, we need to ask, however, how confident we can be on these reported heritabilities (Rutter, 2006a). There are three main tests that may be used to assess the validity of quantitative genetics findings. First, there is the consistency of findings across studies. Second, there is the question of whether the highest quality studies with respect to sampling, measurement, and the meeting of assumptions produce broadly comparable findings. Third, there is the consistency of the findings across research strategies (the different varieties of twin, adoptee, and family strategies). The conclusions on heritability that I have summarized stand up well to these tests. There can be reasonable confidence that the figures are approximately correct.

When quantitative genetic findings are assessed in this sort of way, the conclusion is that the findings are reasonably robust. Critics are inclined to point to the methodological limitations of particular studies (Joseph, 2003), but that really is not an appropriate way of considering the evidence. In the whole of science, not just in quantitative genetics, all studies have their imperfections. That is why it is the golden rule in science that replications by independent groups using independent samples are crucial. There are admitted imperfections in some of the key studies in the literature, and it has to be accepted that some studies have serious flaws. Nevertheless, the overall consistency of findings from the best studies is impressive. Moreover, it is important to ask whether nongenetic mechanisms could provide a more satisfactory explanation of the same phenomena. Clearly, they cannot. However, it is important for people to appreciate that there is not much point in arguing whether the "true" heritability is actually 30% rather than 50%, or any other difference that you care to mention. That is partly because variations in heritability within quite a broad range are of no theoretical or practical consequence.

However, we do need to note five crucial features of heritability estimates. First, they are specific to particular populations at a particular time period. That may seem a bit of scientific pedantry, but it is actually much more than that. There is some indication that heritability estimates may be substantially higher in socially advantaged populations than in socially disadvantaged ones (Rowe, Jacobson, & van den Oord, 1999; Turkheimer, Haley, Waldron, D'Onofrio, & Gottesman, 2003). The data are too limited to be at all sure how far this finding (reported from two independent studies) is a general one (see Rutter et al., 2006), but what is clear is that if either environments change in a major way, or gene distributions change substantially, heritabilities will alter.

Second, although heritabilities do provide useful information on the relative importance of genetic and nongenetic influences on population variance, they do not provide information on how the genetic influences operate. That is an important qualification because the genetic effects on either normal or abnormal psychological features may well operate through some intervening variable, rather than through any effect on the psychological feature as such (see Gottesman & Hanson, 2005).

Third, heritability figures include the effects of gene–environment correlations and interactions and, hence, they incorporate the coaction of genes and environments and not just the independent main effect of genes.

Fourth, the findings are strictly confined to variables that differ among individuals. Thus, for example, there will be zero heritability for characteristics such as the ability to develop spoken language or the ability to walk upright because, in the absence of disease, these are a universal part of the human heritage. They are due to genetic influences, but they are ones that have come to be present in all human beings as a result of evolutionary change.

Fifth, because quantitative genetics is concerned with individual differences within particular populations, the findings will often not be informative on differences between populations, either as reflected in differences over time or geographical variations. Thus, despite the demonstrated high heritability of both height and intelligence, genetic factors are unlikely to account for the great increase in the average height of individuals that has taken place over the last century (van Wieringen, 1986; Weir, 1952), or the increase in levels of IQ during the last 50 years or so (Flynn, 1987, 2000), or the marked reduction in infantile mortality and the increase in life expectancy. The same applies to the rise in the frequency of suicide among young males over the last half century, during a period when suicide rates in older people were falling (Rutter & Smith, 1995), or the rise in the rate of disorders involving either emotional disturbance or behavioral disruption (Collishaw, Maughan, Goodman, & Pickles, 2004). So far as geographical variations were concerned, most striking is the hugely higher level of the rate of homicide in the United States as compared with all European countries (Rutter, Giller, & Hagell, 1998). The evidence indicates that the availability of guns accounts for most of this difference. Within the field of psychopathology, the much higher rate of schizophrenia (and to a lesser extent of other psychoses) among people of Afro-Caribbean background living in the United Kingdom or the Netherlands, as compared to indigenous Whites living in these countries, and as compared with people of the same ethnic background living in the West Indies, constitutes a population difference of considerable public health importance that must be attributed to some type of nongenetic influence (Jones & Fung, 2005). It is unfortunate that so many people in behavioral genetics have ignored these major differences in frequency or level and have written and acted as if individual differences within particular populations comprised the only question of interest. It does not.

Nevertheless, even bearing in mind these important cautions, it is clear that virtually all mental disorders show a significant genetic contribution to individual variations in liability, with heritabilities in the 20% to 40% range. The same applies to normal psychological traits. In addition, it is noteworthy and important that there is a significant genetic effect on people's likelihood of experiencing stressful life events and on individual differences in the rearing environments that they provide for their children. This arises because environments are not randomly distributed and because people, through their behavior, to some extent select and shape the environments that they experience (Rutter, Dunn, Plomin, Simonoff, Pickles, et al., 1997; Scarr, 1992). In other words, genetic effects are on people's behavior, and not on the environments as such but, because of the behavioral effects on the selecting and shaping of environments, there is an important indirect effect on individual differences in environmental risk exposure.

Objections to the Heritability of Socially Defined and Socially Influenced Phenomena

Critics of behavioral genetics have cast scorn on the evidence that features such as antisocial behavior or divorce show a substantial heritability (see Rutter, 2006a). They pose the question of how on earth there could be a gene for crime or a gene for divorce. Of course, the answer is that there are no such genes. On the other hand, the behaviors that make it more likely that someone will engage in antisocial behavior or that they will have a repeated breakdown in love relationships will be genetically influenced. The need, as ever, is to identify the key mediators of the influences.

Similarly, the critics have suggested that it was patently ridiculous to argue that life events such as the experience of family negativity, or rebuffs by friends, or a lack of social support, could be due to genes. Once more, the answer is that, of course, the events themselves cannot be the result of genes; there is no DNA in the environment. On the other hand, it is obvious from a large body of research that environments are not randomly distributed across the population. Some people have a horrendous, never-ending series of awful things happening to them and other people have scarcely any experiences of this kind. The point is that, to an important extent, people's experiences are shaped by their own behavior and, insofar as that is the case, the likelihood of experiencing risky, or protective, environments is likely to be genetically influenced.

Longitudinal studies have shown repeatedly that people's behavior, as measured in childhood, is quite a strong predictor of the likelihood that they will have negative life experiences in adult life. For example, this was shown in a dramatic fashion in the classical follow-up study by Robins (1966), in which it was found that antisocial behavior in childhood was accompanied by a much increased risk of multiple divorces, unemployment, and lack of social support in adult life many years later. Similarly, Champion, Goodall, and Rutter (1995) showed that conduct problems at age 10 were associated with a more than doubling of the likelihood of experiencing major negative life events some 18 years later. Emotional disturbance at age 10 was also associated with an increase in negative life events, although the effect was not as strong.

GENE–ENVIRONMENT CORRELATIONS

Genetic effects on individual differences in environmental experiences come about through gene–environment correlations (Plomin, DeFries, & Loehlin, 1977; Rutter et al., 1997; Rutter & Silberg, 2002; Rutter et al., 2006). These are most conveniently subdivided into what are called passive, active, and evocative correlations. Passive correlations mean that the parents who pass on genes carrying psychopathological risk are more likely than other parents also to provide environments carrying psychopathological risk. The genetic mediator in this case involves the parents' genes insofar as they are influencing parental behavior relevant to the rearing environments that they provide. Thus, some years ago, we found that mentally ill parents were much more likely than other parents to have families exhibiting marked discord and conflict (Rutter & Quinton, 1984). They were more likely to show hostility focused on particular children in the family. Active gene–environment correlations reflect people's behavior in shaping and selecting their own environments. Thus, whether or not a child chooses to spend time reading rather than playing football with his friends, or going to museums, or playing the piano, will be influenced by their own interests (as well as the influence of their parents). Insofar as it is their own behavior, the genes that are relevant are their own, rather than the genes of their parents. Evocative gene–environment correlations reflect the fact that people's behavior influences the responses that they elicit from other people. Thus, quarrels with, and rebuffs from, friends are determined in part by the person's own behavior as well as by the behavior of the other person.

The findings from twin and adoptee studies show the reality of these gene–environment correlations. For example, O'Connor, Deater-Deckard, Fulker, Rutter, and Plomin (1998) showed that children who had an anti-social parent but who had been adopted in early life and brought up by adoptive parents were more likely to elicit negativity from their adoptive parents. The mediating factor was found to be the child's own disruptive behavior, and the finding reminds us, as pointed out by Bell nearly four decades ago (Bell, 1968), that children influence parents just as parents influence their offspring.

The conclusion is that genetic effects on exposure to risky and protective environments are pervasive and important, although it is necessary to add that the genetic effects are of only moderate strength in most instances.

GENE–ENVIRONMENT INTERACTIONS

Gene–environment interactions are concerned with a different issue— namely, people's vulnerability or susceptibility to risk environments, rather than the likelihood that they will experience such environments. For a long time, the reality and importance of gene–environment interactions was dis-missed by both psychosocial researchers and behavioral geneticists. Psycho-social researchers were reluctant to accept that the environmental effects that they were studying were not "pure." Somehow, bringing in genetics seemed to take away from the importance of the environment. It has to be said that this was a foolish and completely misguided way of thinking about nature–nurture interplay. It is all very well to focus on the importance of environmental influences, but it is necessary also to take on board the fact that with environmental hazards of all types, there is huge heterogene-ity in response. That has been shown experimentally as well as naturalisti-cally, and it applies to all environmental influences that have been studied (Rutter, 2006b; Sandberg & Rutter, 2002). It is in those individual differ-ences that genes may be operating. Behavioral geneticists dismissed gene–environment interactions on rather different grounds (Plomin, DeFries, & Fulker, 1988; Plomin & Hershberger, 1991). They drew attention to the rarity with which gene–environment interactions were found in quantitative genetic analyses. However, what they were looking for was a significant statistical interaction between the totality of anonymous genes and the totality of anonymous environments. The notion that gene–environment interactions would work in this way was patently ridiculous because all of the known gene–environment interactions apply to much more specific effects. Also, behavioral geneticists were reluctant to acknowledge that there was more than one concept of interaction (Rutter, 1983; Rutter & Pickles, 1991), and that a statistically significant interaction requires variance in both the genes and the environment. In biology, of course, there are many examples in which there is not appreciable variation in the environment, despite the existence of a hugely important gene–environment interaction. The example of phenylketonuria (PKU) is the best-known illustration. In this case, the effects of the genetic mutation in leading to the outcome of mental retardation are entirely dependent on the person having a diet including phenylalanines. Ordinarily, there is no appreciable dietary variation because all ordinary human diets include substantial levels of phenylalanines. The importance of the diet, of course, is shown by the hugely beneficial effects of putting individuals with PKU on a low-phenylalanine diet.

There are three main reasons for expecting gene–environment interactions to be both common and important (Rutter, 2006a). First, to suppose that sensitivity to the environment is free of genetic influence would mean that this would have to be the one unique function that is uninfluenced by genes. How could it be that genes influence all other aspects of functioning but not sensitivity to the environment? The very idea is absurd. Second, genetically influenced adaptation to the environment is known to constitute the main mechanism for evolutionary change. The evolutionary change comes about because genetic propensities work better in the individual's adaptation to particular environments. Note, however, that the adaptive quality is specific to particular environments and is not a general characteristic that applies to all environments. The third reason is the one already mentioned, namely, that there is huge individual variation in response to all types of environmental risk. That is so with even the most severe environmental hazards (Rutter, 2006b). It may be concluded that there are very strong biological reasons for expecting gene–environment interactions to be both common and important. Nevertheless, the matter cannot be left there; we need to go on to ask whether the empirical research findings are in line with the expectation.

Let me start with the evidence from quantitative genetics. Relevant findings are available from both twin and adoptee studies. Kendler et al. (1995) argued that patterns of concordance within monozygotic and dizygotic twin pairs could be used to infer genetic liability. Thus, in relation to major depression, genetic liability was likely to be highest when dealing with a monzygotic pair in which both twins had experienced a major depressive disorder. Conversely, genetic liability was likely to be at its lowest when only one twin in a monozygotic pair had experienced major depression. The logic here is that if genetic liability was high, one would expect both twins in an MZ pair to have experienced depression and, if only one did so, this implied that the liability derived from nongenetic factors to an important extent. Dizygotic pairs would be expected to be somewhere in the middle with respect to genetic liability. What was found was that the likelihood that an individual adult would develop a new major depressive disorder was higher in those with high genetic liability than in those with low genetic liability. The implication is that although the onset of the depression was provoked by the life event, the susceptibility to that provoking effect was influenced by genes. Jaffee and her colleagues (2005) used the same design to examine the effects of maltreatment in childhood on the development of antisocial behavior and, again, a significant interaction was found.

The adoptee design works in a somewhat different way. The rationale here is that the genetic risk is indexed by the behavior shown by the biological parent who played no part in the upbringing of the child, and that the environmental risk is indexed by features in the adoptive home environment. The gene–environment interaction applies when the risk of some outcome is greater when the genetic risk and the environmental risk coincide than when this is not the case. Cadoret and his colleagues (Cadoret, Yates, Troughton, Woodworth, & Stewart, 1995) showed that this was what was found in the case of antisocial behavior, and Tienari et al. (2004) showed the same for schizophrenia.

Behavioral geneticists have also used modeling approaches to identify the various alternative pathways by which genetic factors may influence the likelihood that someone will experience a particular psychopathological outcome. Thus, Eaves and colleagues (2003) did this with respect to the development of postpubertal depression in adolescent girls. The findings showed that there were three main routes by which genetic factors operated. First, there was a so-called main effect of genes on prepubertal anxiety that, in turn, predisposed to postpubertal depression. This route was relatively independent of the environment. The other two routes both involved coaction with the environment. The first of these other routes involved genetic influences on exposure to risk environments and the second involved genetic influences on susceptibility to risk environments.

Kendler, Gardner, and Prescott (2002) used somewhat different statistical approaches to the same end when dealing with major depressive disorder in adult life. It was found that there was a genetic route that operated through anxiety disorders and neuroticism, which then predisposed to depression. In addition, there was a genetic influence that seemed to operate more directly on depression, rather than through anxiety. There was a third route that operated through genetic influences on disruptive behavior and that, in turn, predisposed to depression. And there was a fourth route that operated primarily on differences in exposure to risk environments in early life which, in turn, predisposed to risk environments in later life, which then played a role in the development of depression. For a whole variety of reasons, it is not at all straightforward, and indeed not particularly useful, to try to quantify the relative importance of these causal pathways (which will in any case vary according to circumstances), but what is clear is that although some genetic effects operate relatively independently of the environment, many do not. Gene–environment correlations and gene–environment interactions are hugely important.

MOLECULAR GENETIC STUDIES

The fact that genetic liabilities in quantitative behavioral genetics can only be inferred provides a major limitation. The situation is quite different with molecular genetics because the actual susceptibility genes can be identified and the genetic liability thereby studied at an individual level. In essence, there are two main molecular genetic strategies (Rutter, 2004; Rutter, 2006a; Rutter et al., 1999). The first, involving linkage methods, is based on co-inheritance. That is, genes are identified on the basis that there is a significant sharing of the genetic transmission of particular gene loci (and within that, with particular genes) and the inheritance of the disorder or behavior being studied. Association methods are based on a quite different principle—namely, the comparison of the particular allelic patterns shown by individuals with the trait being investigated and by appropriate controls. Each of these strategies has a different pattern of strengths and weaknesses, and usually it desirable to combine the two approaches. This is not the place to deal with the many crucially important details of the use of molecular genetic strategies. I simply note that there are many methodological hazards, and it has proved extremely difficult to replicate positive findings. Nevertheless, replicated findings are now beginning to be found, and there is every reason to suppose that molecular genetics research over the decades to come will succeed in identifying susceptibility genes for many of the mental disorders and psychological traits that are of interest. In the meanwhile, positive findings are beginning to be found and confirmed by other investigators and by other research methods.

Thus, for example, there are now at least four genes that appear to be implicated in the susceptibility to schizophrenia (Harrison & Owen, 2003). Not only are the findings ones that have been confirmed across studies but, in most cases, they have been confirmed in animal models. What is

of particular interest in these findings is that each of the genes is implicated with one or more neurotransmitters that have been thought likely to
be involved in the development of schizophrenia. We are still quite a long
way from understanding how all of this comes together in a causal pathway,
and it is important to note that the effects of each of these susceptibility
genes is quite weak. Nevertheless, they provide important leads. Attention
deficit disorder with hyperactivity (ADHD) constitutes a different example
(Thapar, 2002). The evidence here is not quite so strong, but it is highly
suggestive because the findings have held up in meta-analyses that have
combined the results of multiple studies and because, as with schizophrenia, the genes are ones involved with neurotransmitters thought to play a
role in the development of ADHD. The one genome-wide scan gave rise to
negative findings, and it is not yet clear why that was so. However, it is evident that much more research is required and also it may well be that the
search for susceptibility genes has been hampered by not taking account of
gene–environment interactions.

GENE–ENVIRONMENT INTERACTIONS
WITH IDENTIFIED GENES

Three important findings from the Dunedin Longitudinal Study have provided the first decisive evidence on the interaction between identified
genes and measured specific environments. In the first study, it was hypothesized that a functional polymorphism in the promoter region of the gene
encoding the neurotransmitter-metabolizing enzyme monoamine oxidase
A (MAOA) would moderate the effect of child maltreatment in predispos-
ing to antisocial behavior. The findings showed that maltreatment in children whose genotype led to low levels of MAOA expression more often
developed conduct disorder, antisocial personality, and adult violent crime,
than children with a high activity MAOA genotype (Caspi et al., 2002), and
these have now been replicated by the genetics group in Richmond, Virginia, using a different sample and measures that differed in detail but kept
the same basic constructs (Foley et al., 2004).

In the second study, it was hypothesized that a functional polymorphism
in the promoter region of the serotonin transporter gene would moderate the influence of both maltreatment and stressful life events on depression. It was found that individuals with one or two copies of the short allele
of this gene exhibited more depressive symptoms, diagnosable depression, and suicidality than individuals who were homozygous for the long
allele. That is, they had two copies. Again, the findings have been replicated several times (see Rutter et al., 2006). Three aspects of these findings
are particularly noteworthy. First, there was no main effect of the gene in

the absence of the environmental hazards. There was a small main effect of the environmental hazards, but much the largest effect was evident with the co-occurrence of the susceptibility gene and the adverse environmental experience. The implication is that the two genes were not susceptibility genes for these outcomes as such but, rather, operated on susceptibility to adverse environments.

Second, the genetic effects were not specific to a particular type of environmental hazard. That is, in the case of depression, they applied to both early child maltreatment and more recent acute life stressors. In other words, insofar as the genes affected environmental vulnerability, it was not a vulnerability specific to one particular type of environmental hazard, nor did it apply to just one age period.

Third, although neither gene can sensibly be viewed as a gene that caused a particular adverse outcome, nevertheless the effects were outcome-specific. That is to say, the MAOA gene had no effect on responsivity to maltreatment in relation to the outcome of depression. Conversely, the serotonin transporter gene had no effect on responsivity to maltreatment in relation to the outcome of antisocial behavior. The implication is that both of the genes and the environments were operating on a specific pathophysiological causal pathway and, moreover, it was likely to be the same pathway for both genetic and environmental effects.

The third example, from the Dunedin Study, concerned the question of why early exposure to heavy cannabis use provokes schizophrenic psychosis in some users but not others. The COMT gene, shown to be associated with schizophrenia, was hypothesized to moderate the risk from adolescent cannabis use of developing adult psychosis. The findings showed that cannabis users with the valine allelic variant of that gene were more likely to develop psychotic symptoms and more likely to develop schizophreniform disorder, whereas cannabis use had no such influence on individuals with other allelic variants of that gene (Caspi et al., 2005). Again, there is the implication that both the genetic susceptibility and the cannabis effect operate through the same pathophysiological pathway. The evidence with respect to schizophrenia suggests that this is likely to involve glutamate metabolism. Taken in conjunction with the epidemiological evidence (Arseneault, Cannon, Witton, & Murray, 2004), there are implications for how the environmental risks might operate. What is striking is that the risks for schizophrenia are derived from cannabis and not from stronger drugs such as heroin and cocaine, and that the effects are confined to heavy early use rather than later sporadic use. Putting all of that together, it would seem to imply that the risk operates through biochemical pathways rather than through social stressors and peer group pressures or stigma, both of which would be likely to be greater with drugs other than cannabis.

It may be concluded, therefore, that the identification of interactions between specific identified genes and specific measured environments is going to be informative not only about the indirect effects of genetic influences that operate in coaction with the environment, but also it will cast light on the effects of risk environments on the organism and the likely pathways by which such effects lead to disorder. Critics are sometimes worried that genetic research will lead to a neglect of the environment, but, actually, the evidence suggests that the findings may bring renewed vigor to environmental research and cast important light on how environmental risk factors may operate.

HOW GENES WORK

Before considering some of the causal pathways involved in this interplay between nature and nurture, something must be said about how genes work (Rutter, 2006a). Much of the popular writing on genetics tends to imply that there is a single entity that can be called a gene and that that single entity has a unitary effect that leads to a particular trait or disorder. However, that constitutes a quite serious misrepresentation of how genes actually work. Three main points need to be made. First, although DNA provides the particulate genes that are handed on from one generation to the next, it is not the DNA as such that directly affects the outcome. DNA specifies the RNA that is involved in the production of polypeptides, which are then transformed into proteins, which then undergo a process of protein folding. The basic biological effects derive from the folded proteins, but there is a much longer causal chain involved in the effects of the proteins on the outcome of interest.

Second, the genetic action derives from gene expression, which tends to be tissue-specific and developmental phase-specific. The processes involved in gene expression are quite complex, but the main consideration that is relevant here is that a variety of other genes are involved in the mechanisms leading to gene expression. These other genes do not themselves lead to proteins, but they play a crucial role in determining whether the genes that do affect proteins are expressed in particular tissues at particular times, and thereby they have a powerful role in effects. At one time, it was argued that each gene affected just one enzyme. However, that is an oversimplification. To begin with, not all effects are on enzymes, and also each gene may affect several proteins as a result of the way in which the splicing of genes takes place. In addition, many biochemical pathways are influenced by more than one gene.

Environmental Influences on Gene Expression

The third point is that these epigenetic processes that affect gene expression (but that do not affect the sequence of the gene) are also influenced by environments—including diet, hormones, toxins, and psychosocial experiences. These processes comprise what has come to be called epigenetics. This means processes that do not alter the DNA sequence (and therefore are not genetic) but do bring about potentially heritable (but potentially reversible) alterations in gene expression (as a result of methylation and other related chemical processes). What this means, among other things, is that environments affect genes. The process of methylation can only meaningfully be studied in the tissues where there is gene expression. For practical purposes, so far as mental disorders are concerned, this means that the relevant research can only be undertaken in animals or on postmortem specimens. However, there has been a series of rigorous, well-controlled experiments by Michael Meaney and his colleagues (Cameron et al., 2005; Champagne et al., 2004; Weaver et al., 2004) that provide a clear demonstration of methylation effects as a result of rearing experiences. The use of a cross-fostering design made it possible to be sure that the effects did indeed derive from the environmental influences, rather than the genes. What all of this means is that the traditional neat and tidy subdivision into genetic effects and environmental effects has broken down. Of course, it is possible to isolate the effects of each, but the main message is that many of the most important effects derive from the coaction of genes and environment.

CONCLUSIONS

As we have seen, there are several rather different pathways that may be involved in nature–nurture interplay. There are the epigenetic processes that involve environmental influences on gene expression, that may be thought of in terms of environmental effects on genes. Second, there are genetic effects on the likelihood of exposure to risk environments. Gene–environment correlations mean that genes play a contributory role in individual differences in behavior that are instrumental in a person's shaping and selecting of environments. This may be thought of in terms of genetic influences on the environment. In these circumstances, the proximal causal effect may be environmentally mediated, but the fact that the risk environment is operating at all has been influenced by genes. Third, there are genetic effects on individual susceptibility to risk environments, a mechanism that comes about as a result of gene–environment interaction. With this pathway, it makes little sense to argue whether the effect is genetic or environmental because the end result is crucially dependent on their both acting together in synergistic fashion.

Fourth, genes may play a role in pathways that predispose to phenotypes that, according to circumstances, can have varying effects on particular forms of psychopathology. In other words, genes are playing a contributory role in the multifactorial determination of traits such as neuroticism or sensation seeking that do not, in themselves, represent psychopathology. However, according to circumstances, they may have pathophysiological effects. Note, however, that the same dimensional feature may act as either a risk factor or a protective influence. For example, behavioral inhibition is a risk factor for anxiety disorders, but it is a protective factor against antisocial behavior.

Fifth, there may be genetic involvement in pathophysiological pathways that predispose to disorder in ways that are relatively independent of the environment. Clearly, this is the case with Mendelian conditions, but it is possible that it may also apply to some forms of multifactorial disorder.

Put another way, the evidence is clear in indicating that genes are pervasive in their effects. They have an influence on biological development, on neurotransmitter functions that involve liability to psychopathology, on the likelihood of exposure to environmental influences, on the degree of susceptibility to specific environmental features, and may act as a mechanism for the persistence of environmental effects.

But the evidence is equally clear-cut that environments are also pervasively influential (Rutter, 2005). There are effects on the neuroendocrine system, on biological programming of the brain, on gene expression, and on neural structure and function as well as on cognitive/affective sets and models, and on interpersonal interactions. The challenge for the future concerns the determination of the mechanisms involved in the interplay between nature and nurture over the course of normal and abnormal development as it affects the impact of both genes and environment on the organism, thereby influencing the pathways leading to psychological outcomes of interest and importance (Nelson et al., 2002). Most people nowadays pay lip service to a rejection of the dualism that separates brain from mind and the dualism that separates nature and nurture. However, lip service is not enough. Rather, the need is to accept that rejection of the dualism necessarily means the imperative to study the interconnections between brain and mind and between nature and nurture. The means to make these interconnections are beginning to be available, and it is essential that our concepts, our empirical research, and our recommendations to policymakers and practitioners reflect this integration. The need with respect to both research and clinical practice is to bring about an effective integration among social, genetic, and developmental perspectives and strategies (Rutter & McGuffin, 2004).

REFERENCES

Arseneault, L., Cannon, M., Witton, J., & Murray, R. (2004). Causal association between cannabis and psychosis: Examination of the evidence. *British Journal of Psychiatry, 184,* 110–117.

Barker, D. J. (1997). Fetal nutrition and cardiovascular disease in later life. *British Medical Bulletin, 53*, 96–108.

Barker, D. J. P. (1999). Fetal programming and public health. In P. M. S. O'Brien, T. Wheeler,& D. J. P. Barker (Eds.), *Fetal programming: Influences on development and disease in later life.* London: RCOG Press, 3–11.

Bateson, P., Barker, D., Clutton-Brock, T., Deb, D., D'Udine, B., Foley, R. A., et al. (2004). Developmental plasticity and human health. *Nature, 430*, 419–421.

Baxter, L. R., Schwartz, J. M., Bergman, K. S., Szuba, M. P., Guze, B. H., Mazziotla, J. C., et al. (1992). Caudate glucose metabolic rate changes with both drug and behavior therapy for obsessive–compulsive disorder. *Archives of General Psychiatry, 49*, 681–689.

Bell, R. Q. (1968). A reinterpretation of the direction of effects in studies of socialization. *Psychological Review, 75*, 81–95.

Booth, A., Shelley, G., Mazur, A., Tharp, G., & Kittok, R. (1989). Testosterone, and winning and losing in human competition. *Hormones and Behavior, 23*, 556–571.

Brooks-Gunn, J., Duncan, G. J., & Aber, J. L. (1997) *Neighborhood poverty, Vol. 1: Context and consequences for children.* New York: Russell Sage Foundation.

Cadoret, R. J., Yates, W. R., Troughton, E., Woodworth, G., & Stewart, M. A. S. (1995). Genetic–environmental interaction in the genesis of aggressivity and conduct disorders. *Archives of General Psychiatry, 52*, 916–924.

Cameron, N. M., Parent, C., Champagne, F. A., Fish, E. W., Ozaki-Kuroda, K., & Meaney, M. J. (2005). The programming of individual differences in defensive responses and reproductive strategies in the rat through variations in maternal care. *Neuroscience & Biobehavioral Reviews, 29*, 843–865.

Caspi, A., McClay, J., Moffitt, T. E., Mill, J., Martin, J., Craig, I. W., et al. (2002). Role of genotype in the cycle of violence in maltreated children. *Science, 297*, 851–854.

Caspi, A., Moffitt, T. E., Cannon, M., McClay, J., Murray, R., Harrington, H., et al. (2005). Moderation of the effect of adolescent-onset cannabis use on adult psychosis by a functional polymorphism in the catechol-O-methyltransferase gene: Longitudinal evidence of a gene X environment interaction. *Biological Psychiatry, 57*, 1117–1127.

Caspi, A., Sugden, K., Moffitt, T. E., Taylor, A., Craig, I. W., Harrington, H. L., et al. (2003). Influence of life stress on depression: Moderation by a polymorphism in the 5-HTT gene. *Science, 301*, 386–389.

Champagne, F. A., Chretien, P., Stevenson, C. W., Zhang, T. Y., Gratton, A., & Meaney, M. J. (2004). Variations in nucleus accumbens dopamine associated with individual differences in maternal behavior in the rat. *Journal of Neuroscience, 24*, 4113–4123.

Champion, L. A., Goodall, G. M., & Rutter, M. (1995). Behaviour problems in childhood and stressors in early adult life. I. A 20- year follow-up of London school children. *Psychological Medicine, 25*, 231–246.

Collishaw, S., Maughan, B., Goodman, R., & Pickles, A. (2004) Time trends in adolescent mental health. *Journal of Child Psychology and Psychiatry, 45*, 1350–1362.

Dennett, D.C. (2003). *Freedom evolves.* London: Allen Lane, The Penguin Press.

D'Onofrio, B., Turkheimer, E., Eaves, L., Corey, L. A., Berg, K., Solaas, M. H., et al. (2003). The role of the Children of Twins design in elucidating causal relations between parent characteristics and child outcomes. *Journal of Child Psychology and Psychiatry, 44*, 1130–1144.

Eaves, L., Silberg, J., & Erkanli, A. (2003) Resolving multiple epigenetic pathways to adolescent depression. *Journal of Child Psychology and Psychiatry, 44*, 1006–1014.

Elbert, T., Pantev, C., Wienbruch, C., Rockstroh, B., & Taub, E. (1995). Increased cortical representation of the fingers of the left hand in string players. *Science, 270*, 305–307.

Flynn, J. R. (1987). Massive IQ gains in 14 nations: What IQ tests really measure. *Psychological Bulletin, 101*, 171–191.

Flynn, J. R. (2000). IQ gains, WISC subtests and fluid g: g theory and the relevance of Spearman's hypothesis to race. In G. R. Bock J. A. Goode, & K. Webb (Eds.), *The Nature of Intelligence. Novartis Foundation Symposium 233* (pp. 202–216). Chichester: Wiley.

Foley, D. L., Eaves, L. J., Wormley, B., Silberg, J. L., Maes, H. H., Kuhn, J., et al. (2004). Childhood adversity, monoamine oxidase A genotype, and risk for conduct disorder. *Archives of General Psychiatry, 61,* 738–744.

Goldapple, K., Segal, Z., Garson, C., Lau, M., Bieling, P., Kennedy, S., et al. (2004). Modulation of cortical-limbic pathways in major depression: Treatment-specific effects of Cognitive Behavior Therapy. *Archives of General Psychiatry, 61,* 34–41.

Goodman, R. (1994) Brain development. In M. Rutter & D. Hay (Eds.), *Development through life: A handbook for clinicians (pp.* 49–78). Oxford: Blackwell Scientific Publications.

Gottesman, I. I., & Hanson, D. R. (2005) Human development: Biological and genetic processes. *Annual Review of Psychology, 56,* 263–286.

Harrison, P., & Owen, M. (2003). Genes for schizophrenia: Recent findings and their pathophysiological implications. *The Lancet, 361,* 417–419.

Huttenlocher, P. R. (2002) *Neural plasticity: The effects of environment on the development of the cerebral cortex.* Cambridge, MA: Harvard University Press.

Jaffee, S., Caspi, A., Moffitt, T. E., Dodge, K. A., Rutter, M., Taylor, A., et al. (2005). Nature x nurture: Genetic vulnerabilities interact with physical maltreatment to promote conduct problems. *Development and Psychopathology, 17,* 67–84.

Jones, P. B., & Fung, W. L. A. (2005). Ethnicity and mental health: The example of schizophrenia in the African-Caribbean population in Europe. In M. Rutter & M. Tienda (Eds.), *Ethnicity and causal mechanisms* (pp. 227–261). New York: Cambridge University Press.

Joseph, J. (2003). *The Gene Illusion: Genetic research in psychiatry and psychology under the microscope.* Ross on Wye: PCCS Books.

Kendler, K. S. (2005) "A gene for . . ." The nature of gene action in psychiatric disorders. *American Journal of Psychiatry, 162,* 1243–1252.

Kendler, K. S., Gardner, C. O., & Prescott, C. A. (2002). Toward a comprehensive developmental model for major depression in women. *American Journal of Psychiatry, 159,* 1133–1145.

Kendler, K. S., Kessler, R. C., Walters, E. E., MacLean, C., Neale, M., Heath, A. C., et al. (1995). Stressful life events, genetic liability and onset of an episode of major depression in women. *American Journal of Psychiatry, 152,* 833–842.

Keshavan, M. S., Kennedy, J. L. & Murray, R. M. (Eds.). (2004). *Neurodevelopment and schizophrenia.* London & New York: Cambridge University Press.

Linnet, K. M., Dalsgaard, S., Obel, C., Wisborg, K., Henriksen, T. B., Rodriguez, A., et al. (2003). Maternal lifestyle factors in pregnancy risk of Attention Deficit Hyperactivity Disorder and associated behaviors: Review of the current evidence. *American Journal of Psychiatry,* 160, 1028–1040.

Maguire, E. A., Gadian, D. G., Johnsrude, I. S., Good, C. D., Ashburner, J., Frackowiak, R. S., et al. (2000). Navigation-related structural change in the hippocampi of taxi drivers. *Proceedings of the National Academy of Sciences of USA, 97,* 4398–4403.

Marmot, M., & Wilkinson, R. G. (1999). *Social determinants of health.* Oxford: Oxford University Press.

Maughan, B., & McCarthy, G. (1997). Childhood adversities and psychosocial disorders. *British Medical Bulletin, 53,* 156–169.

Mazur, A., Booth, A., & Dabbs, J. M. (1992). Testosterone and chess competition. *Social Psychology Quarterly, 55,* 70–77.

Moffitt, T. E. (1993). Adolescence-limited and life-course-persistent antisocial behavior: A developmental taxonomy. *Psychological Review, 100,* 674–701.

Moffitt, T. E., Caspi, A., Rutter, M., & Silva, P. A. (2001). *Sex differences in antisocial behavior: Conduct disorder, delinquency, and violence in the Dunedin Longitudinal Study.* Cambridge, UK: Cambridge University Press.

Moffitt, T. E., Caspi, A., & Rutter, M. (2005). Strategy for investigating interactions between measured genes and measured environments. *Archives of General Psychiatry, 62*, 473–481.

Morange, M. (2001) *The misunderstood gene.* Cambridge, MA & London: Harvard University Press.

Nelson, C. A., & Bloom, F. E. (1997). Child development and neuroscience. *Child Development, 68*, 970–987.

Nelson, C. A., Bloom, F. E., Cameron, J. L., Amaral, D., Dahl, R. E., & Pine, D. (2002). An integrative, multidisciplinary approach to the study of brain-behavior relations in the context of typical and atypical development. *Development and Psychopathology, 14*, 499–520.

O'Connor, T. G., Deater-Deckard, K., Fulker, D., Rutter, M., & Plomin, R. (1998). Genotype–environment correlations in late childhood and early adolescence: Antisocial behavioral problems and coercive parenting. *Developmental Psychology, 34*, 970–981.

Plomin, R., DeFries, J. C., & Fulker, D. W. (1988). *Nature and nurture during infancy and early childhood.* New York: Cambridge University Press.

Plomin, R., DeFries, J. C., & Loehlin, J. C. (1977). Genotype–environment interaction and correlation in the analysis of human behavior. *Psychological Bulletin, 84*, 309–322.

Plomin, R., & Hershberger, S. (1991). Genotype–environment interaction. In T. D. Wachs & R. Plomin (Eds.), *Conceptualization and measurement of organism–environment interaction* (pp. 29–43). Washington, DC: American Psychological Association.

Purcell, S., & Sham, P. (2002). Variance components models for gene–environment interaction in quantitative trait locus linkage analysis. *Twin Research, 5*, 572–576.

Robins, L. (1966). *Deviant children grown up: A sociological and psychiatric study of sociopathic personality.* Baltimore: Williams & Wilkins.

Rose, S. (1995). The rise of neurogenetic determinism. *Nature, 373*, 380–382.

Rose, S. (1998). *Lifelines: Biology, freedom, determinism.* Harmondsworth, U.K.: Penguin.

Rowe, D. C., Jacobson, K. C., & van den Oord, E. J. C. G. (1999). Genetic and environmental influences on vocabulary IQ: Parental education level as moderator. *Child Development, 70*, 1151–1162.

Rutter, M. (1983) Statistical and personal interactions: Facets and perspectives. In D. Magnusson & V. Allen (Eds.), *Human development: An interactional perspective* (pp. 295–319). New York: Academic Press.

Rutter, M. (1997). Comorbidity: Concepts, claims and choices. *Criminal Behaviour and Mental Health, 7*, 265–286.

Rutter, M. (1999). Social context: Meanings, measures ands mechanisms. *European Review, 7*, 139–149.

Rutter, M. (2002). Nature, nurture, and development: From evangelism through science toward policy and practice. *Child Development, 73*, 1–21.

Rutter, M. (2003). Categories, dimensions, and the mental health of children and adolescents. In J. A. King, C. F. Ferris, & I. I. Lederhendler (Eds.), *Roots of mental illness in children* (pp. 11–21). New York: The New York Academy of Sciences.

Rutter, M. (2004) Pathways of genetic influences on psychopathology. *European Review, 12*, 19–33.

Rutter, M. (2005). Environmentally mediated risks for psychopathology: Research strategies and findings. *Journal of the American Academy of Child and Adolescent Psychiatry, 44*, 3–18.

Rutter, M. (2006a). *Genes and behavior: Nature–nurture interplay explained.* Oxford: Blackwell.

Rutter, M. (2006b). The promotion of resilience in the face of adversity. In A. Clarke-Stewart & J. Dunn (Eds.), *Families count: Effects on child and adolescent development* (pp. 26–52). New York & Cambridge: Cambridge University Press.

Rutter, M., Bolton, P., Harrington, R., Le Couteur, A., Macdonald, H., & Simonoff, A. (1990). Genetic factors in child psychiatric disorders: I. A review of research strategies. *Journal of Child Psychology & Psychiatry, 31*, 3–37.

Rutter, M., Dunn, J., Plomin, R., Simonoff, E., Pickles, A., Maughan, B., et al. (1997). Integrating nature and nurture: Implications of person–environment correlations and interactions for developmental psychology. *Development and Psychopathology, 9,* 335–364.

Rutter, M., Giller, H., & Hagell, A. (1998). *Antisocial behavior by young people.* New York: Cambridge University Press.

Rutter, M. & Maughan, B. (2002). School effectiveness findings 1979–2002. *Journal of School Psychology, 40,* 451–475.

Rutter, M., Maughan, B., Mortimore, P., & Ouston, J. (with Smith, A.) (1979). *Fifteen thousand hours: Secondary schools and their effects on children.* London: Open Books; Cambridge, Mass: Harvard University Press.

Rutter, M., & McGuffin, P. (2004). The Social, Genetic and Developmental Psychiatry Centre: Its origins, conception and initial accomplishments. *Psychological Medicine, 34,* 933–947.

Rutter, M., Moffitt, T., & Caspi, A. (2006). Gene–environment interplay and psychopathology: Multiple varieties but real effects. *Journal of Child Psychology and Psychiatry, 47,* 226–261.

Rutter, M., & Pickles, A. (1991). Person–environment interactions: Concepts, mechanisms, and implications for data analysis. In T. D. Wachs & R. Plomin (Eds.), *Conceptualization and measurement of organism–environment interaction* (pp. 105–141). Washington DC: American Psychological Association.

Rutter, M., Pickles, A., Murray, R., & Eaves, L. (2001). Testing hypotheses on specific environmental causal effects on behavior. *Psychological Bulletin, 127,* 291–324.

Rutter, M., & Quinton, D. (1984). Parental psychiatric disorder: Effects on children. *Psychological Medicine, 14,* 853–880.

Rutter, M., & Silberg, J. (2002). Gene–environment interplay in relation to emotional and behavioral disturbance. *Annual Review of Psychology, 53,* 463–490.

Rutter, M., Silberg, J., O'Connor, T., & Simonoff, E. (1999). Genetics and child psychiatry: I. Advances in quantitative and molecular genetics. *Journal of Child Psychology and Psychiatry, 40,* 3–18.

Rutter, M., & Smith, D. (1995). *Psychosocial disorders in young people: Time trends and their causes.* Chichester: Wiley.

Rutter, M., & Sroufe, L.A. (2000). Developmental psychopathology: Concepts and challenges. *Development and Psychopathology, 12,* 265–296.

Sameroff, A. (2006). Identifying risk and protective factors for healthy child development. In A. Clarke-Stewart & J. Dunn (Eds.), *Families count: Effects on child and adolescent development* (pp. 53–78). Cambridge and New York: Cambridge University Press.

Sampson, R. J., Raudenbush, S. W., & Earls, F. (1997). Neighborhoods and violent crime: A multilevel study of collective efficacy. *Science, 277,* 918–924.

Sandberg, S. (Ed.). (2002). *Hyperactivity and attention disorders of childhood.* Cambridge: Cambridge University Press.

Sandberg, S., & Rutter, M. (2002). The role of acute life stresses. In M. Rutter & E. Taylor, (Eds.), *Child and adolescent psychiatry* (pp. 287–298). Oxford: Blackwell Scientific.

Scarr, S. (1992). Developmental theories for the 1990s: Development and individual differences. *Child Development, 63,* 1–19.

Silberg, J. L., & Eaves, L. J. (2004). Analysing the contributions of genes and parent–child interaction to childhood behavioural and emotional problems: A model for the children of twins. *Psychological Medicine, 34,* 347–356.

Thapar, A. (2002). Attention Deficit Hyperactivity Disorder: New genetic findings, new directions. In R. Plomin, J. C. DeFries, I. Craig, & P. McGuffin (Eds.), *Behavioural genetics in the postgenomic era* (pp. 445–462). Washington, DC.: American Psychological Association.

Thapar, A., Fowler, T., Rice, F., Scourfield, J., van den Bree, M., Thomas, et al. (2003). Maternal smoking during pregnancy and attention deficit hyperactivity disorder symptoms in offspring. *American Journal of Psychiatry, 160,* 1985–1989.

Tienari, P., Wynne, L. C., Sorri, A., Lahti, I., Laksy, K., Moring, J., et al. (2004). Genotype–environment interaction in schizophrenia-spectrum disorder: Long-term follow-up study of Finnish adoptees. *British Journal of Psychiatry, 184*, 216–222.

Turkheimer, E., Haley, A., Waldron, M., D'Onofrio, B., & Gottesman, I. I. (2003). Socioeconomic status modifies heritability of IQ in young children. *Psychological Science, 14*, 623–628, 2003.

van Wieringen, J. C. (1986). Secular growth changes. In F. Falkner & J. M. Tanner (Eds.), *Human growth: Vol. 3. Methodology* (2nd ed., pp. 307–331). New York: Plenum Press.

Weaver, I. C. G., Cervoni, N., Champagne, F. A., D'Alessio, A. C., Charma, S., Seckl, J., et al. (2004). Epigenetic programming by maternal behavior. *Nature Neuroscience, 7*, 847–854.

Weir, J. B. (1952). The assessment of the growth of schoolchildren with special reference to secular changes. *British Journal of Nutrition, 6*, 19–33.

Chapter 2

Choreographing Genetic, Epigenetic, and Stochastic Steps in the Dances of Developmental Psychopathology

Daniel R. Hanson
Irving I. Gottesman
University of Minnesota

INTRODUCTION: A CONCEPTUAL METAPHOR

Conceptualizing human development as starting with a blank slate on which experience writes the story of a person is a metaphor from John Locke for explaining much about human behavior. However, without conceding that Steven Pinker (Blackburn, 2002) has expunged Locke's slate, we believe a more complete understanding can be obtained by understanding the properties of the slate itself, and then getting on with the task of choreographing the dances of developmental psychopathology. After all, nothing can be "written" without acknowledging the slate's existence. We must then ask: Will the slate take the chalk (or chisel) well? Is the slate durable or will it crumble? Is the slate protected from the elements or will the story wash away with the next rain? For human stories, the slate is the brain (Nelson & Gottesman, 2005). Weighing in at about three pounds, the adult brain, like other organs, is the product of evolution. Hopefully, over the course of a person's life, the stories on the slate will not be prematurely wiped away by defects in the slate (dementing illness) or unfortunate experiences (head injury, abusing alcohol). Because of our interest in the slate itself, we choose a different metaphor.

Normal development is at once a highly choreographed and surprisingly improvised dance among biology, environment, and chance. The dance is an endurance event lasting decades, if one avoids wars and automobile accidents. The sequence of steps appears complex in length of step, rhythm of step, direction of step, and interaction between partners, but this complexity is created from very simple elements, for a step, after all, is common and ordinary. And, although common and ordinary, a step, in itself, is a remarkable assembly of bone, muscle, and tendon integrated by neurons and perfected with practice. In the final analysis, the outcome of the dance will be a product of genetically guided anatomy and talents combined with teaching and training plus the impact of luck either for good or for bad. Unpredictable events influence the roll of the genetic dice and influence much of life experience—Hamlet's ". . . slings and arrows of outrageous fortune."

COMBINING GENES AND ENVIRONMENT: MOVING ON TO EPIGENESIS

There are various ways of conceptualizing the intermingling of genetic and environmental factors (cf. Rutter, chapter 1, this volume; Carey, 2003; and also Gottesman, 1974, for a take on Waddington's epigenetic landscape). The phrase *gene environment interaction* is often used to indicate that both genes and environment make a difference for the development of a trait. Height is a common example; a person's height depends on genes promoting height as well as a healthy diet. But, no matter what the genotype, good nutrition always works in the same direction to enhance height. This may be thought of as co-action, but it is not G × E interaction as used by quantitative geneticists.

The origins of a more precise G × E interaction concept can be traced back to early plant and animal agricultural genetics (Falconer, 1960) and represent, in a strict sense, an interaction effect in an analysis of variance. As such, G × E interaction means that different genotypes respond differently to different environments. Children homozygous for the gene for phenylketonuria (PKU) develop mental retardation if raised on a normal diet but do quite well on a low phenylalanine diet. By contrast, children free of the phenylketonuria genes would be damaged if raised on a diet missing the essential amino acid phenylalanine. In this example, the nutritional factor (phenylalanine) works in different directions (conferring health or damaging the brain), depending on the genotype. The fact that a diet healthy for one individual may be damaging to another individual indicates there is an interaction between diet and genotype.

The concept of gene–environment interaction, however defined, is difficult to apply in studies of developmental psychopathology (Caspi et al.,

2002; Caspi et al., 2003; Gunnar, 2003; Kagan, 2003). We cannot (fortunately!) manipulate environmental and genetic factors as done so readily by plant breeders. Furthermore, simple additive models that suggest that the phenotype is the sum of environmental and genetic effects do not conform to biological realities of complex adaptive systems (Holland, 1995, 1998; Meaney, 2001). An instructive example of nonadditivity comes from Turkheimer's demonstration(Turkheimer, Haley, Waldron, D'Onofrio, & Gottesman, 2003) that socioeconomic status modified the heritability of IQ in a nonlinear fashion such that, in impoverished families, 60% of the variance in IQ was attributed to shared environment, whereas genetic effects were negligible. The reverse, traditional finding of appreciable heritability was true in affluent families.

A further limitation of simple G × E interaction models arises from the fact that gene expression is dynamic over time. For example, when mice were placed on restricted diets, there was a rapid change in the expression of genes associated with longevity, including genes mediating metabolism, signal transduction, stress response, and inflammation (Dhahbi, Kim, Note, Beaver, & Spindler, 2004). Moving on to the concept of epigenesis allows us to introduce a dimension of time into models of development that can incorporate changes in the environment and the expressed genotype. We say more about epigenesis later, but to set the stage for that discussion, we need to step back to view a big picture of biological systems.

ADAPTATION AND ENERGY

In the mental health field, we pay a lot of attention to a person's degree of contact with reality. This is a tricky business because reality changes continuously. With age, the realities of our body change. Over time, the status of our health, finances, relationships, or geographic locale (to name just a few) will all change. For those of us living in the United States, especially in New York City, our reality changed on September 11, 2001. Children get new teachers, parents divorce, a sibling gets sick, a new sibling is born, someone in the family wins the lottery. Change is never-ending and universal and many changes are stochastic. We cannot prophesy life trajectories. As Popper (1957) stated,

> . . . although we may assume that any actual succession of phenomena proceeds according to the laws of nature, it is important to realize that practically *no sequence of, say, three or more causally connected concrete events proceeds according to any single law of nature.* If the wind shakes a tree and Newton's apple falls to the ground, nobody will deny that these events can be described in terms of causal laws. But there is no single law . . . nor even a single definite set of laws, to describe the actual or concrete succession of causally connected events;

apart from gravity, we should have to consider the laws explaining wind pressure; the jerking movement of the branches; the tension in the apple's stalk
.... The idea that any concrete sequence of succession of events ... can be
described or explained by any one law or by any one definite set of laws is
simply mistaken. (p. 117)

Given that the environment is constantly changing, and is doing so in
ways that may not be predictable, living creatures must have some mechanism for adjusting to these changes—an ability to adapt. Adaptation is a key
organizing principle in biology. We define adaptation as change in function
or behavior by which a species (over evolutionary time) or an individual
(over the life span) improves its condition in relationship to the environment. Whether we are talking about nervous systems or genetic systems, the
purpose (if you will) of these systems is to confer adaptability. By "purpose"
we do not imply that there must be any intelligence, planning, or mystical
force at work. We use purpose in the way we might say the purpose of the
eye is to process light signals and the purpose of the foot is ambulation.
Nobel laureate Jacques Monod (1971) described purpose, or *teleonomy*, as

> ... one of the fundamental characteristics common to all living beings with-
> out exception: that of being objects endowed with a purpose or project which
> at the same time they show in their structure and execute through their per-
> formances ... it must be recognized as essential to the very definition of living
> beings. (p. 20; See Pross, 2003, for further discussion.)

So, if the purpose of the DNA and of the central nervous system (CNS)
is to facilitate adaptation, we would expect these systems to be sensitive to
environmental input and able to change in response. Knowing that our
genomes have been "designed" by evolution to maximize adaptability, we
could not conclude that genetically mediated traits are fixed and immuta-
ble. On the contrary, we would expect genetic factors to play an important
role in adaptive change even within the individual and over short time intervals. The idea that genetic factors are fixed stems from the study of "broken" genes as found in human genetic diseases such as the inborn errors
of metabolism and chromosomal anomalies. These examples of genetic
errors cannot be generalized to characterize intact genetic systems functioning via feedback loops connecting an individual's physiology with his or
her external environments.

Just as observations of broken genes lead to the erroneous conclusion
that genetic effects are not modifiable, the observations that broken brains
(e.g., stroke, trauma) do not repair has led to the mistaken belief that the
CNS is a fixed structure. To the contrary, the intact brain is quite plastic.
Synaptic connections and neuronal circuits are continuously reshaped by
time and experience (Thompson et al., 2004). Plastic changes are associ-

ated with learning/memory, skill acquisition, recovery from injury, and even addiction. Brain plasticity is influenced by many factors including pre- and postnatal experience, genes, drugs, hormones, maturation/aging, diet, disease, stress, and trauma. Psychopathology can be viewed, in part, as diminished adaptive capacity. Maladaptive reactions to stress, including the development of depression and posttraumatic stress disorder, are attributed to failures in CNS plasticity, more so in predisposed persons. Chronic stress is implicated in disrupting CNS signal transduction cascades that normally allow neuronal plasticity. Chronic stress damages a wide variety of plasticity modulators and, at the biochemical level, causes a reduction in expression of genes associated with synaptic plasticity, resulting in diminished frontal cortical activity (Kuipers, Trentani, Den Boar, & Ter Host, 2003). The interested reader is referred to Grossman et al., 2003; Hodge & Boakye, 2001; Johansson, 2000; Shonkoff, 2003; and Thompson & Nelson, 2001 for further discussions of molecular as well as political intricacies.

The process of adaptation requires energy, with the second law of thermodynamics coming into play. One statement of the second law is that all organized systems require a constant input of energy to remain organized. In the absence of energy, the system unravels to chaos. Think about your kitchen counter. Without a constant input of energy, the counter is quickly cluttered and, if neglected long enough, the mess may well reach chaotic proportions. The same principal applies to human development. The sources of energy are not only physical (nutrition, clothing, shelter), but also psychological in the form of nurturing, caring, bonding/attachment, teaching, training, and so on. Thus, failures of adaptation occur when there is not enough energy to fuel the adaptive process. In human terms, a child is at risk if parents/caretakers are too fatigued, depressed, sociopathic, stressed, or stoned to channel positive energy into the child. A child is at risk if the community does not channel energy (often in the form of tax dollars) into education, social programs, sanitation, peacekeeping, and medical care. This brings us close to a political digression that we will not pursue here. Instead, our intent is to reinforce the notion of adaptation as a dynamic process in which genetic factors respond to the environment in ways that enhance an individual's well being, and this process requires a constant input of energy, both molar and molecular. The outcome of the process depends on the nature of the environmental changes, the genetic resources, and the energy devoted to the system—all three components may vary systematically or by chance. Chemists think of bonds between molecules as a form of energy. Likewise, the bonds between caretaker and child or between culture and child are forms of energy that promote adaptive growth and mental health when sufficient. When deficient, the child's trajectory is tilted toward chaos that often takes the form of behavioral disturbances.

EPIGENESIS

Human development is more than an interaction term in an analysis of genetic and environmental variances. To better understand the process, we prefer the concept of epigenesis. The term *epigenesis* originated with embryological theories suggesting that complex organisms originate from undifferentiated cells, and the term has been broadly defined to include all the forces that lead to the phenotypic expression of an individual's genotype (Petronis, 2004, 2003; Waddington, 1957). Gottesman and Shields (1972) transduced this concept of epigenesis into human behavioral genetics in the early 1970s, with later elaboration (Gottesman, Shields, & Hanson, 1982). The definition of *epigenetics* continues to evolve and, to many molecular biologists, the term refers to the mechanisms by which cells change form or function and then transmit that form or function to future cells in that cell line (Jablonka & Lamb, 2002; Jaenisch & Bird, 2003; Morange, 2002). Examples include transformation of an undifferentiated embryo cell into a liver cell or transformation of a normal liver cell into a cancerous cell. Once a cell type acquires a new form through selective gene expression and environmental influences, that cell, through cell division, transmits that acquired characteristic to future cells in the lineage. The previously spurned concept of the inheritance of acquired characteristics is resurfacing at the molecular level (Varmuza, 2003) but now based on credible data.

The best studied mechanisms for the epigenetic regulation of mammalian gene expression involves the addition of a methyl group to cytosine that, along with adenine, thiamine, and guanine, form the four-letter alphabet of DNA (Petronis, 2003; Petronis et al., 2003). This methylation of cytosine changes the configuration of the DNA such that the genetic information encoded in that area cannot be read and is nullified (Jaenisch & Bird, 2003; Jones & Takai, 2001) — the gene is essentially turned off. Conversely, removing DNA methylation allows the gene to be expressed. The variety of factors that influence DNA methylation is huge and includes such things as developmental processes, diet, viral infections, aging, and chance. Failure of methylation systems leads to clinical syndromes such as Rett Syndrome, which involves mental retardation, autistic-like behaviors, and other neurodevelopmental anomalies in girls (Shahbazian & Huda, 2002). The impact of prenatal and early postnatal nutrition on adult development of Type 2 diabetes, cardiovascular disease, obesity, and cancer are also thought to be mediated by epigenetic factors mediated by DNA methylation (Waterland & Jirtle, 2004). Such epigenetic mechanisms may account for why, in a rodent model, maternal behavior toward young offspring affects the size of the offspring's hippocampus in adulthood, depending on the offspring's genotype (Weaver, Grant, & Meaney, 2002). These investigators further observed a wide range in the intensity of nurturing behaviors among the rodent mothers. Some mothers showed high levels of licking and grooming their pups and had high levels of what is called "arched back nursing." Pups of these mothers differed from the pups of mothers with limited nurturing behaviors in DNA methylation patterns associated with brain development, and these brain changes were followed by changes in the hypothalamic–pituitary–adrenal systems that respond to stress. The nurturing-induced effects on brain development and stress response persisted into maturity (Sapolsky, 2004; Weaver et al., 2004). It is tempting to speculate about the power of such findings to help explain the long-lasting impact of human attachment behaviors described by several authors in this volume. Even more speculatively, epigenetic theorizing is being applied to the development of schizophrenia (Petronis et al., 2003) and depression (Caspi et al., 2003; Charney & Manji, 2004). Although not approaching a biochemical analysis, even traits such as specific talents are being rethought in epigenetic terms (Simonton, 1999).

Epigenetic perspectives grapple with complexities of how multiple genetic factors and multiple environmental factors become integrated over time through dynamic, often nonlinear, sometimes irreversible, processes to produce behaviorally relevant endophenotypes and phenotypes. How an embryonic cell differentiates into a liver cell whereas a genetically identical cell in the same embryo develops into a neuron is an epigenetic question. Identical twins discordant for a given trait or disease provide other examples of epigenetic processes (Cannon et al., 2002; Pol et al., 2004; van Erp et al., 2004)

Diverse reviews of epigenetic concepts relevant to human development are available (Gottesman & Gould, 2003; Nijhout, 2003; Petronis, 2003; Sing, Stengard, & Kardia, 2003). A stellar example of a systems biology approach to studying epigenesis can be found in the research mapping the developmental sequences in the sea urchin from fertilized egg onward (Davidson et al., 2002). Epigenetic thinking builds on the notion that only a small fraction of our DNA codes for structures (proteins, enzymes, etc.) whereas, in keeping with our central theme of adaptation, the majority of the DNA codes for regulatory processes and thus falls outside the purview of the new dogma about a 30K limit on the number of human genes (as the latter produce proteins, not regulatory signals). In response to transduced environmental stimuli, genes are turned on or turned off as the organism proceeds through life.

At any time, any one genotype may have a wide array of potential phenotypes referred to as a "reaction range" (Turkheimer, Goldsmith, & Gottesman, 1995). The actual phenotype depends on the influence of the individual's other genes and on the specific contexts of environments experienced among a wide array of possible environments. Which environment is experienced may be stochastic (chance) or may be a function of the individual's past phenotypes. Indeed, an individual's phenotype (which is partially a result of their genotype) may lead him or her to select environments, thereby establishing a correlation between genotype and environment (Carey, 2003). Choices made in selecting environments promote or detract from adaptation. Thus, we find the epigenetic process of adaptation useful therapeutically by helping people learn to avoid previous maladaptive habits and environments and to learn new adaptive strategies. We also find the concepts to be philosophically meaningful, as the adaptive process places the individual in an active role in his or her own development rather than being the passive recipient of influences imposed by G or by E.

The array of possible outcomes for any developmental process could, in theory, be plotted in multidimensional space as functions of genotypes, environments, and time. The plot would produce an undulating surface that would represent the phenotype for that unique combination of genotype, environment, and time. Such a surface has been referred to as a *reaction surface* (Gottesman & Gould, 2003; Sing et al., 2003) or *phenotypic surface* (Nijhout, 2003), and these articles provide informative graphics. Figure 2.1 (updated to 2005) provides such an example (Manji, Gottesman, & Gould, 2003) applied to the ontogenesis of schizophrenia with provision for the changing reaction surface and a threshold, suggested endophenotypes, some already connected to candidate genes, and a dimension of environmental inputs (harmful vs. protective), all "bathed" in epigenetic influences.

EVEN RARE DISORDERS DEVELOP
FROM COMMON FACTORS

One of the first actions in teasing out the putative causes of psychopathology is to try to clarify whether we are looking for rare/abnormal genetic or environmental factors, or common and ordinary events, cumulatively toxic. We can start this process by obtaining the population frequency of the disorder (the "base rate"; see Meehl & Rosen, 1955, for a discussion of the importance of this simple number). Second, we know that for almost all common psychopathologies there is evidence implicating multifactorial causes. Schizophrenia provides a good example where there is strong evidence for genetic factors, yet the concordance rate for schizophrenia in identical twins is only about 50%. Thus, there must be something genetic *and* something environmental about the causes of this disorder. Let us assume just two risk factors (one G and one E) and assume these risk factors are independent of each other. If so, the joint probability of acquiring both risk factors is the product of their population frequencies and,

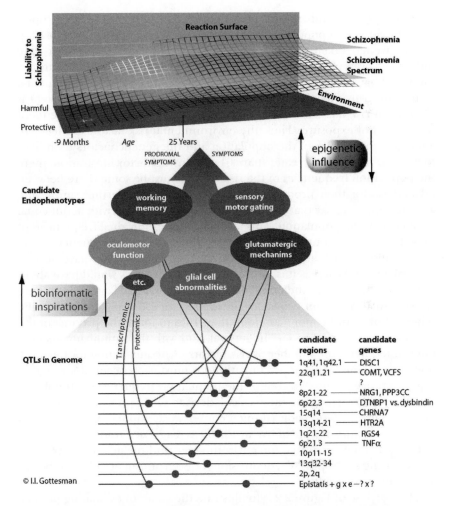

Figure 2.1.   Illustration of a systems biology approach toward explaining complex behavior incorporating dynamic interplay among candidate genes and gene regions, endophenotypes, and pre- and postnatal environmental and epigenetic influences (protective or harmful) over the course of development. Question marks indicate gaps in our knowledge. Two planes intersect the reaction surface for the liability to developing schizophrenia over time, indicating levels above which clinical diagnoses are manifest (cf. Gottesman & Gould, 2003, and Manji et al., 2003, for details). Copyright 2005 by I. I. Gottesman (used with permission).

35

for schizophrenia, this product must equal about .01 or 1%, the proportion of people in a population who will at some time in their lives develop schizophrenia. Taken to the limit, if the environmental contributor were universally present (frequency = 1.0), then the frequency of the genetic factor would have to be at least .01. However, it is unlikely that environmental factors are truly universal in trait-relevant "doses." Exposure to sunlight is a universal risk factor for skin cancer, but actual risk is highly dependent on amount of exposure. Thus, the environmental risk factors are likely to affect less than 100% of the population and the genetic factors then have to be present at a rate greater than .01. In our two-factor illustration, then, the population frequencies of the risk factors must be somewhere between .01 and 1.0 for their product to equal .01. To make a further simplifying assumption, let us say that the two risk factors are present with about equal frequency in the population. This means that the individual frequencies of these factors are about the square root of the population frequency of 1%. That would mean that about 10% of the population would have at least one risk factor. Whereas it is unlikely that all risk factors would have about the same frequency in the population, every time a risk factor's frequency is less than 10% (in our two-factor illustration for schizophrenia), then the other factor must be more common than 10% to make the product of the two frequencies equal to 1%. In general, and with the simplifying assumptions noted here, the number of risk factors (N) contributing to the development of some forms of psychopathology must each occur at a rate that is in the range of the Nth root of the population frequency for the illness (see Figure 2.2). Applying these calculations to schizophrenia (population rate 1%), major depression (using a conservative population lifetime risk of 10%), and autism (rate of five in 10,000 as diagnosed traditionally) leads to the surprising result that the environmental and the genetic risk factors for acquiring schizophrenia, depression, or even autism are likely to be relatively common events.

The purpose of Figure 2.2 is to illustrate the issues of estimating population frequency of risk factors and it is not intended as a rigorous epidemiological model. However, it serves as a point of departure in thinking about whether we are looking for rare pathogens or normal variation with uncommon accumulations. Using this illustration, if autism results from the independent contribution of, say, five risk factors, then we would expect any one of these factors to be present in about 20% of us ($.2 \times .2 \times .2 \times .2 \times .2 = 5/10,000$). Somewhere along the curves in Figure 2.2, we would stop thinking of the risk factors as rare pathological events and start thinking of them as common individual differences within the normal range. Thompson and Esposito (1999), arguing from a molecular perspective about the causes of complex diseases, arrive at a similar conclusion. And, if our assumption that the risk factors are independent of each other holds, then the

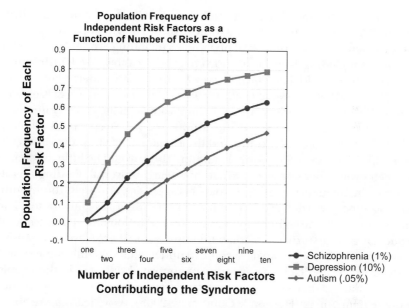

Figure 2.2. Possible relationships between the number of factors that contribute to the development of depression, schizophrenia, or autism and the frequency of causal factors in the general population. The numbers in parentheses in the legend indicate the base rate of each disorder in the general population. This illustration provides a guess as to how common the causal factors could be in the general population assuming each factor is independent of the others and that all factors are about equally common (see worked example in the text). We do not intend to suggest that the factors that predispose to, say, schizophrenia, are the same factors that cause the other disorders.

co-occurrence of several factors in one affected individual may simply be rotten luck.

WHERE TO PLACE OUR BETS
IN THE GENOMIC ERA

The possibility that the developmental causes of psychopathology are common events creates a conundrum for researchers using null hypothesis designs: Key etiological contributors, examined one at a time, may be found at high rates in both pathological and control groups, leading to erroneously discarding important causal clues. PANDAS (*p*ediatric *a*utoimmune *n*eurological *d*isorder *a*ssociated with *s*treptococcal infections) provides a useful example. PANDAS syndrome often includes an acute onset obsessive–compulsive disorder in children shortly after acquiring a strep throat. PANDAS syndrome and a variety of other psychopathologies are also associated with streptococcal pharyngitis including Syndenham chorea, motor tics including Tourette's syndrome, and, possibly, ADHD (Asbahr et al., 1998; Bottas & Richer, 2002; Garvey & Swedo, 1998; Mercadante et al., 2000; Moore, 1996; S. Swedo et al., 1989; S. E. Swedo, Leonard, & Kiessling, 1994). Psychotic disorders are also implicated (Hanson & Gottesman, 2005). If an investigator tested the hypothesis that strep throat played a role in PANDAS and then compared the frequency of strep throat in children with PANDAS and in normal children, there would be little difference between groups because strep throats are nearly universal. Finding no differences in frequency of strep throats between sick and well, the hypothesis might be discarded even though strep throat is a key contributor. The importance of the strep infection was discovered by looking at the temporal sequencing (strep throat immediately before onset of obsessive–compulsive disorder). Furthermore, we have come to understand that only some strains of streptococci are likely to engender an abnormal response in the people infected and, furthermore, genetic factors render some people more susceptible than others (Hanson & Gottesman, 2005). As we learn more about how genes and environments lead to psychopathology, we are forced to discard old ways of thinking. In the PANDAS scenario, realizing that genetic factors play a major role affecting host susceptibility and response to infection, we can then start to think about infectious diseases as having a heritable component (Hanson, 2004).

Turning our attention to schizophrenia, there is a large mass of data implicating both genetics and environmental contributors. From the discussion here, we also realize that contributing factors may be very common. How do we select a place to start to the riddle? Figure 2.3 provides the clues. The many postulated contributors such as prenatal infections, obstetric complications, and living in lower social classes, add minimally to the risk for schizophrenia and are dwarfed by the 10-fold increased risk to a sibling of a person with a schizophrenia-related psychosis (SRP), and even more dramatically, by the 50-fold increased risk to an identical twin of a person with schizophrenia. Data such as these tell us that for schizophrenia, we should focus on the high-impact genetic contributors. Similar analyses for other disorders will point to the research paths that have the greatest likelihood for a payoff.

WHAT DOES IT ALL MEAN?

The inherent plasticity of the nervous system and of genetic regulatory systems requires us to rethink our strategies as we try to find solutions to the

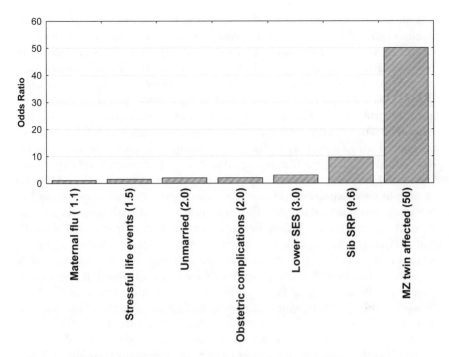

Figure 2.3.   Relative "potency" of factors associated with an increased rate of schizophrenia. On the low end of the scale, children exposed in utero to maternal influenza have a slightly increased risk compared to the general population (odds ratio = 1.1). At the other extreme, individuals with an affected identical twin have a vastly increased risk (odds ratio = 50). SRP = schizophrenia related psychosis.

causes of psychopathologies (Gottesman & Hanson, 2005). The chain of reasoning outlined here leads us to several conclusions. There may be no genes, per se, for a specific form of psychopathology even when there is evidence of strong genetic factors. As with the PANDAS syndrome, genetic factors appear important in shaping an individual's reaction to streptococcal infection. However, these are not genes for obsessive–compulsive disorder. Instead, these genes are more likely to be involved in the immune response system or in some form of genetic resistance. A cascade of many physiological reactions, including immune modulation and tissue response, leads eventually to altered function in, most probably, the basal ganglia, which in turn results in obsessive–compulsive behaviors. If the crucial genetic factors are in the immune system, then this example also shows us that the genetic factors leading to a behavioral disorder may not be in the brain; recall that the inherited enzyme abnormality leading to PKU and mental retardation is in the liver.

Our line of reasoning also tells us that the factors (genetic and/or environmental) contributing to a behavioral abnormality may, themselves, be common and therefore normal. Another way of saying this is that many purported contributing agents lack specificity for the disorder, given that many people may experience one or more of the contributing agents but do not develop psychopathology. Again, using schizophrenia as an example and returning to Figure 2.3, we see that being unmarried or experiencing complications at birth or living in lower socioeconomic conditions are all associated with an increased risk for schizophrenia. However, we hope no one would ever suggest that being unmarried, or poor, or even experiencing some kind of birth complication are pathological events per se. Millions of people have experienced these phenomena and the vast majority, by far, are totally normal and healthy. Our interpretation of such nonspecific and typically normal factors is that they have very little specific etiological significance. Instead, they are likely consequences of the psychopathology or are nonspecific wherein any form of stress might contribute to the expression of psychopathology in those people who are so predisposed. If these common and typically normal factors do have any specific contributing role, it must be in conjunction with other contributing factors (multifactorial causation), and the co-occurrence of these multiple factors is likely a matter of chance. We suggest, therefore, that our research efforts and dollars be focused on the factors with greatest impact and greatest specificity as determined by analyses of the kind illustrated in Figure 2.3.

We hope this essay leads the reader to shift some paradigms. We need to discard the historic strategies for categorizing disorders or traits into groupings such as infectious, inherited, traumatic, genetic, environmental, and so forth. Ulcer disease appears highly heritable from twin studies, but bacteria are known now to be a major contributor, the latter finding leading to a 2005 Nobel Prize. Depression is highly heritable, but targeted searches for the impact of life stress on depression have paid off by demonstrating the impact of stress on the liability to develop depression (Caspi et al., 2003). Debates about nature versus nurture are not helpful. Instead, we need new metaphors to understand how genes respond to environmental signals that, in turn, lead to improvements or detriments in adaptation (cf. Rutter, chapter 1, this volume). We need to understand that environmental and genetic factors that lead to maladjustment are not necessarily abnormal in themselves, but may represent unfortunate (in place or time) combinations of otherwise totally normal or common phenomena. We need to accept the fact that to some degree, bad luck happens. To the extent that stochastic events lead to psychopathology, there will always be a need for resources devoted to repair and rehabilitation while, at the same time, we strive to pour energy into primary prevention of the psychopathologies that so devastate individuals and impose huge costs on our societies. Ready to dance?

REFERENCES

Asbahr, F., Negrao, A., Gentil, V., Zanetta, D., da Paz, J., Marques-Dias, M., et al. (1998). Obsessive compulsive and related syndromes in children and adolescents with rheumatic fever with and without chorea: A prospective 6-month study. *American Journal of Psychiatry, 155,* 1122–1124.

Blackburn, S. (2002). Meet the Flintstones. *New Republic, 227,* 28–34.

Bottas, A., & Richer, M. A. (2002). Pediatric autoimmune neuropsychiatric disorders associated with streptococcal infections (PANDAS). *Pediatric Infectious Disease Journal, 21,* 67–71.

Cannon, T., Thompson, P., van Erp, T., Toga, A., Poutanen, V., Huttunen, M., et al. (2002). Cortex mapping reveals regionally specific patterns of genetic and disease-specific gray-matter deficits in twins discordant for schizophrenia. *Proceedings of the National Academy of Science, 99*(5), 3228–3233.

Carey, G. (2003). *Human genetics for the social sciences.* Thousand Oaks, CA: Sage.

Caspi, A., McClay, J., Moffitt, T., Mill, J., Martin, J., Craig, I., et al. (2002). Role of genotype in the cycle of violence in maltreated children. *Science, 297,* 851–854.

Caspi, A., Sugden, K., Moffitt, T., Taylor, A., Craig, I., Harrington, H., et al. (2003). Influence of life stress on depression: Moderation by a polymorphism in the 5-HTT gene. *Science, 301,* 386–389.

Charney, D., & Manji, H. (2004). Life stress, genes, and depression: Multiple pathways lead to increased risk and new opportunities for depression. *Science's STKE, 225,* 5.

Davidson, E., Rast, J., Oliveri, P., Ransick, A., Calestani, C., Yuh, C-H., et al. (2002). A genomic regulatory network for development. *Science, 295,* 1669–1678.

Dhahbi, J., Kim, H-J., Note, P., Beaver, R., & Spindler, S. (2004). Temporal linkage between the phenotypic and genomic responses to caloric restriction. *Proceedings of the National Academy of Science, 101*(15), 5524–5529.

Falconer, D. (1960). *Introduction to quantitative genetics.* New York: Ronald Press Co.

Garvey, M. A., & Swedo, S. E. (1998). PANDAS: The search for environmental triggers of pediatric neuropsychiatric disorders. Lessons from rheumatic fever. *Journal of Child Neurology, 13,* 413–423.

Gottesman, I., & Gould, T. (2003). The endophenotype concept in psychiatry: Etymology and strategic intentions. *American Journal of Psychiatry, 160*(4), 1–10.

Gottesman, I., Shields, J., & Hanson, D. (1982). *Schizophrenia: The epigenetic puzzle.* Cambridge: Cambridge University Press.

Gottesman, I. I. (1974). Developmental genetics and ontogenetic psychology: Overdue detente and propositions from a matchmaker. In A. Pick (Ed.), *Minnesota Symposium on Child Psychology* (pp. 55–80). Minneapolis: University of Minnesota Press.

Gottesman, I. I., & Hanson, D. (2005). Human development: Biological and genetic processes. *Annual Review of Psychology, 56,* 263–286.

Gottesman, I. I., & Shields, J. (1972). *Schizophrenia and genetics: A twin study vantage point.* New York: Academic Press.

Grossman, A., Churchill, J., McKinney, B., Kodish, I., Otte, S., & Greenough, W. (2003). Experience effects on brain development: Possible contributions to psychopathology. *Journal of Child Psychology and Psychiatry, 44*(1), 33–63.

Gunnar, M. (2003). Integrating neuroscience and the psychological approaches in the study of early experience. *Annals of the New York Academy of Sciences, 1008,* 238–247.

Hanson, D. (2004). Getting the bugs into our genetic theories of schizophrenia. In L. DiLalla (Ed.), *Behavior genetics principles: Perspective in development, personality and psychopathology* (pp. 205–216). Washington, DC: American Psychological Press.

Hanson, D., & Gottesman, I. (2005). Theories of schizophrenia: A genetic-inflammatory-vascular synthesis. *BMC Med Gen, 6*(7). http://www.biomedcentral.com/1471–2350/6/7

Hodge, C., & Boakye, M. (2001). Biological plasticity: The future of science in neurosurgery. *Neurosurgery, 48*(1), 2–16.

Holland, J. (1995). *Hidden order: How adaptation builds on complexity.* Cambridge, MA: Perseus Books.

Holland, J. (1998). *Emergence.* Cambridge, MA: Perseus Books.

Jablonka, E., & Lamb, M. (2002). The changing concept of epigenetics. *Annals of the New York Academy of Sciences, 981*(Dec), 82–96.

Jaenisch, R., & Bird, A. (2003). Epigenetic regulation of gene expression: How the genome integrates intrinsic and environmental signals. *Nature Genetics, 33 Suppl*(Mar), 245–254.

Johansson, B. (2000). Brain plasticity and stroke rehabilitation: the Willis Lecture. *Stroke, 31*(1), 223–230.

Jones, P., & Takai, D. (2001). The role of DNA methylation in mammalian epigenetics. *Science, 263,* 1068–1070.

Kagan, J. (2003). Biology, context, and developmental inquiry. *Annual Review of Psychology, 54,* 1–3.

Kuipers, S., Trentani, A., Den Boar, J., & Ter Host, G. (2003). Molecular correlates of impaired prefrontal plasticity in response to chronic stress. *Journal of Neurochemistry, 85,* 1312–1323.

Manji, H., Gottesman, I., & Gould, T. (2003). Signal transduction and genes-to-behaviors pathways in psychiatric diseases. *Sci STKE, 207,* 49.

Meaney, M. (2001). Nature, nurture, and the disunity of knowledge. *Annals of the New York Academy of Sciences, 935,* 50–61.

Meehl, P., & Rosen, A. (1955). Antecedent probability and the efficiency of psychometric signs, patterns, or cutting scores. *Psychology Bulletin, 52,* 194–216.

Mercadante, M., Busatto, G. F., Lombroso, P., Prado, L., Rosario-Campos, M., do Valle, R., et al. (2000). The psychiatric symptoms of rheumatic fever. *American Journal of Psychiatry, 157,* 2036–2038.

Monod, J. (1971). *Chance and necessity* (A. Wainhouse, Trans.). Glasgow: William Collins and Sons.

Moore, D. (1996). Neuropsychiatric aspects of Sydenham's Chorea. *Journal of Clinical Psychiatry, 57,* 407–414.

Morange, M. (2002). The relations between genetics and epigenetics: A historical point of view. *Annals of the New York Academy of Sciences, 981*(Dec), 50–60.

Nelson, C., & Gottesman, I. I. (2005). A piece of a neuroscientist's mind. *Science, 307*(25 Feb), 1204.

Nijhout, H. (2003). The importance of context in genetics. *American Scientist, 91,* 416–423.

Petronis, A. (2004). The origins of schizophrenia: Genetic thesis, epigenetic antithesis, and resolving synthesis. *Biological Psychiatry, 55*(10), 965–970.

Petronis, A. (Ed.). (2003). *Epigenetics: Influence on behavioral disorders.* London: Nature Publishing Group.

Petronis, A., Gottesman, I., Kan, P.X., Kennedy, J., Basile, V., Paterson, A., et al. (2003). Monozygotic twins exhibit numerous epigenetic differences: Clues to twin discordance. *Schizophrenia Bulletin, 29*(1), 169–178.

Pol, H., Brans, R., van Haren, N., Schnack, H., Langen, M., Baare, W., et al. (2004). Gray and white mater volume abnormalities in monozygotic and same-gender dizygotic twins discordant for schizophrenia. *Biological Psychiatry, 55,* 126–130.

Popper, K. (1957). *The poverty of historicism.* London: Routledge & Kegan Paul.

Pross, A. (2003). The driving force for life's emergence: Kinetic and thermodynamic considerations. *Journal of Theoretical Biology, 220,* 393–406.

Sapolsky, R. (2004). Mothering style and methylation. *Nature Neuroscience, 7*(8), 791–792.

Shahbazian, M., & Huda, Y. (2002). Rett syndrome and the MeCP2: Linking epigenetics and neuronal function. *American Journal of Human Genetics, 71,* 1259–1272.

Shonkoff, J. (2003). From neurons to neighborhoods: Old and new challenges for developmental and behavioral pediatrics. *Developmental and Behavioral Pediatrics, 24*(1), 70–76.

Simonton, D. (1999). Talent and its development: An emergenic and epigenetic model. *Psychological Review, 106*(3), 435–457.

Sing, C., Stengard, J., & Kardia, S. (2003). Genes, environment, and cardiovascular disease. *Arteriosclerosis, Thrombosis, and Vascular Biology, 23,* 1190–1196.

Swedo, S. E., Rapoport, J. L., Cheslow, D. L., Leonard, H. L., Ayoub, E. M., Hosier, D. M., et al. (1989). High prevalence of obsessive–compulsive symptoms in patients with Sydenham's Chorea. *American Journal of Psychiatry, 146,* 246–249.

Swedo, S. E., Leonard, H. L., & Kiessling, L. S. (1994). Speculations on antineuronal antibody-mediated neuropsychiatric disorders of childhood. *Pediatrics, 93,* 323–326.

Thompson, G., & Esposito, M. (1999). The genetics of complex diseases. *Trends in Cell Biology, 9*(12), M17–M20.

Thompson, P., Hayashi, K., Swoell, E., Gogtay, N., Giedd, J., Rapoport, J., et al. (2004). Mapping cortical change in Alzheimer's disease, brain development, and schizophrenia. *Neuroimage, 23*(Supp. 1), S2–S18.

Thompson, R., & Nelson, C. (2001). Developmental science and the media: Early brain development. *American Psychologist, 56*(1), 5–15.

Turkheimer, E., Goldsmith, H., & Gottesman, I. I. (1995). Commentary—Some conceptual deficiencies in "developmental" behavior genetics. *Human Development, 38,* 142–153.

Turkheimer, E., Haley, A., Waldron, M., D'Onofrio, B., & Gottesman, I. I. (2003). Socioeconomic status modifies heritability of IQ in young children. *Psychological Science, 14*(6), 623–628.

van Erp, T., Seleh, P., Huttunen, M., Lonnqvist, J., Kaprio, J., Salonen, O., et al. (2004). Hippocampal volumes in schizophrenic twins. *Archives of General Psychiatry, 61*(4), 346–353.

Varmuza, S. (2003). Epigenetics and the renaissance of heresy. *Genome, 46*(6), 963–967.

Waddington, C. (1957). *The strategy of the genes.* London: George Allen & Unwin Ltd.

Waterland, R., & Jirtle, R. (2004). Early nutrition, epigenetic changes at transposons and imprinted genes, and enhanced susceptibility to adult chronic diseases. *Nutrition, 20*(1), 63–68.

Weaver, I., Cervoni, N., Champagne, F., D'Alessio, A., Sharma, S., Seckl, J., et al. (2004). Epigenetic programming by maternal behavior. *Nature Neuroscience, 7*(8), 847–854.

Weaver, I., Grant, R., & Meaney, M. (2002). Maternal behavior regulates long-term hippocampal expression of BAX and apoptosis in the offspring. *Journal of Neurochemistry, 82,* 998–1002.

Chapter 3

A Biology of Misfortune: Stress Reactivity, Social Context, and the Ontogeny of Psychopathology in Early Life

W. Thomas Boyce
University of California, Berkeley

> *Do not forget the lives of your afflicted people forever.* —Psalm 74:19

INTRODUCTION: UNEVEN MISFORTUNE

Decades of research—and centuries of thought, reflection, and specula-tion—have been devoted to describing and understanding the dramatically uneven distributions of disease and misfortune within human populations. In every country, region, community, and sample in which it has been stud-ied, the most broadly and well-replicated findings of health services research is that 15% to 20% of the population—approximately one in five individu-als—sustains over half of the population-level morbidity and is responsible for the majority of health care visits (Boyce & Keating, 2004; Starfield et al., 1985). This maldistribution of morbidity is found in both adults (White, Williams, & Greenberg, 1961) and children (Boyce, 1992; Starfield et al., 1984), is present in both wealthy (Smedley & Syme, 2000) and impover-ished (Black, Morris, & Bryce, 2003) nations, and was as characteristic of ancient civilizations (Krieger, 2001) as it is of contemporary, postmodern societies (Syme, 1998). Inequalities in the distribution of disorders apply to "physical"/biomedical and mental illnesses as well as to problems in development and behavior. In the Cleveland Family Study (Dingle, Badger, & Jordan, 1964), for example, one third of the individual family members sustained over half of the common respiratory illnesses. The work of Starfield and colleagues (Starfield, 1991; Starfield et al., 1984) further documented the clustering of pediatric morbidities within relatively small subgroups of childhood populations and the high likelihood that children with multiple forms of ill health will carry such problems on into young adulthood. Research such as that by Rutter and Sroufe (2000) similarly indicates that disorders of mental health cluster within small groups of children, manifest—in some—continuities over time, and tend to occur with greater frequency and intensity in adverse early environments. Presyndromal behavior problems (e.g., Zahn-Waxler, Klimes-Dougan, & Slattery, 2000) and developmental disorders (e.g., Fombonne, Simmons, Ford, Meltzer, & Goodman, 2001) are also known to occur and persist (Verhulst & Van der Ende, 1995) within relatively small subsets of childhood populations. Furthermore, physical, mental, and developmental difficulties converge within such children, further burdening them with comorbidities that cross diagnostic and taxonomic categories (Bardone et al., 1998; Cohen, Pine, Must, Kasen, & Brook, 1998; Spady, Schopflocher, Svenson, & Thompson, 2005; Wells, Golding, & Burnam, 1988). Children with chronic biomedical diseases are more likely to develop psychiatric disorders, such as depression and anxiety, and those with mental disorders bear increased risks of chronic physical disease.

The single most potent and reliable environmental predictor of disproportionate health burdens remains socioeconomic status (SES): the educational, economic, and social class into which a child is delivered by birth (Adler et al., 1994; Adler, Boyce, Chesney, Folkman, & Syme, 1993; Chen, Matthews, & Boyce, 2002; Syme, 2005). Not only do children living in poverty incur systematically higher risks for virtually all forms of biomedical and psychiatric disorders, but children at every level of social class bear higher rates of disease and disorder than children lying just above them on a scale of social position. The SES–health association is thus a graded, continuous relation in which even those near the top sustain higher incidences of morbidity and mortality than those at the very top. As Adler et al. (1994) pointed out, the recognition of a gradient between SES and health outcomes fundamentally changes the conversation: the SES–health association becomes an issue not only of poverty, but rather of how social position influences risks to health across the spectra of class, wealth and education. Furthermore, although access to health care, diet, and exercise account for a portion of SES effects, a substantial percentage of the variance in health outcomes remains unexplained after controlling for these and other conventional explanations and mediators (Haan, Kaplan, & Syme, 1989; Marmot, Bosma, Hemingway, Brunner, & Stansfeld, 1997; Syme, 2005). Indeed, evidence from countries with universal health care access suggests that access reduces, but does not eliminate, health inequalities between the children of low and high SES families (Sin, Svenson, Cowie, & Man, 2003).

Misfortunes of health are unevenly distributed not only in North America, but within global childhood populations, as well. A recent study commissioned by UNICEF concluded that over one billion children, more than half the children from developing countries of the world, suffer severe deprivations of food, shelter, safe water, sanitation, health care, and/or education (Bellamy & UNICEF, 2005). As a consequence of these deprivations, almost 11 million of the world's children under 5 years of age die annually, and nearly all of these deaths occur in the poorest nations of sub-Saharan Africa (Bhutta, 2004). Whereas the life expectancy of a Japanese infant today is 82 years, a newborn in Zambia has a life expectancy of 33 years, and 82,000 Zambian children die annually before reaching their fifth birthday (Bellamy & UNICEF, 2005). The proportion of children under 5 years of age who are severely underweight is 8% and 16% in Africa and South Asia, respectively, and those incompletely immunized in the developing world range from 15% to 25% of the childhood population. It is estimated that 2.2 million children's lives could be saved each year with routine immunization alone, a preventive care modality with proven efficacy and safety. Around the world, 15 million children under the age of 18 have been orphaned by the AIDS epidemic, 80% of whom live in sub-Saharan Africa. UNICEF estimates that by 2010, 18 million African children will have lost one or both parents to HIV/AIDS (Bellamy & UNICEF, 2005). Much of this inequity in childhood mortality and morbidity is attributable to the economic crippling of developing countries with the burdens of debt, stagnant economies, and growing economic gaps between poor and rich nations (Bhutta, 2004). Indeed, as Sir Shridath Ramphal, the former Secretary General of the Commonwealth, has noted, "debt has a child's face" (Ramphal, 1999). Bhutta (2004), in a summary paper on global child health, concludes: ". . . without addressing the core issue of social justice, equity, and pragmatic poverty reduction strategies, sustainable improvement in child health in poor countries is impossible."

Inequalities in health and development are thus a pervasive, internationally epidemic phenomenon: recognized in virtually every human society, appearing throughout recorded history, in every age group and every demographic subset.The health effects of socioeconomic stratification, moreover, offer the single most powerful and parsimonious account for the maldistribution of affliction and morbidity within human groups.

HOW BIOLOGY AND CONTEXT CODETERMINE INEQUALITIES IN HEALTH

In considering the origins of disproportionate ill health among lower SES children, this chapter addresses the interplay between biology and context and advances three claims about the nature of pathogenic and health-protective interactions among biologically derived vulnerabilities and the character of social contexts:

1. Stress reactivity—conventionally viewed as a neuroendocrine risk factor for stress-related illness—should be reconceptualized as *biological sensitivity to context,* that is, a biologically embedded susceptibility to both pathogenic and protective aspects of the ambient social environment.

2. Biological sensitivity to context is itself the product of heritable genetic variation and adaptive signaling by early social and physical environments.

3. Biological sensitivity to context may offer an account for the great variability in SES influences on child and adult health endpoints.

Before developing the specific empirical grounds for these claims, I first argue that the uneven distribution of illness and disorder within human populations—including populations of children—is due to the joint, interactive operation of inherent, individual susceptibilities to environmental influence and the health-endangering aspects of the experienced social world.

Such an account is a not unfamiliar form of causal attribution, even outside the domains of health and development. The final, NASA-commissioned report on the 2003 Space Shuttle Columbia disaster, for example, ascribed the break-up of the shuttle and the loss of the crew to the collision of a 3-square-foot section of insulating foam from an external fuel tank with the leading edge of the left wing, causing a breach in the thermal protection system, destruction of the aluminum substructure of the left wing on atmospheric reentry, and the disintegration of the shuttle (Columbia Accident Investigation Board, 2003). The accident was thus the interactive product of an inherent, structural vulnerability in the shuttle itself and the impact of an external object derived from the craft's immediate physical environment at launch. Disaster, like disease, often (perhaps always) involves a confluence of inner vulnerability and outer threat.

Recent observations of the interplay between genetic susceptibilities and stressful environments in the etiologies of recurrent or persistent morbidities are also commensurate with the view that biology–context interactions are fundamental to the pathogenesis of human disease (Boyce, 2006; Rutter, 2002, 2005). Interactions between genetic polymorphisms and early social conditions have recently been shown, for example, to predict psychopathology in adult life. Caspi and colleagues (Caspi et al., 2002; Caspi et al., 2003) employed data from the Dunedin Multidisciplinary Health and Development Study to demonstrate that children with polymorphisms conveying enhanced susceptibility (low monoamine oxidase A activity and an s/s allele in the promoter region of the serotonin transporter gene) had strikingly higher rates of mental health disturbances under conditions of adversity (child maltreatment in the case of one analysis, and stressful life events in the other). As summarized by Boyce (2006), the growing inventory of interactions between biological vulnerabilities and aversive social contexts forms a "symphonic" view of disease causation in which regularities in the character of such interactions can be sought, cataloged, and eventually elucidated. In pursuit of such a symphonic account of developmental psychopathology, I now examine: (a) SES-partitioned sources of social stress and adversity, and (b) the neurobiological response systems that subserve reactivity to such stressors.

THE SOCIOECONOMIC PARTITIONING OF ADVERSITY IN CONTEXT

As noted previously, the powerful, pervasive linkage between SES and health is only partially accounted for by known mediators of the association, such as access to health care, diet, and exercise. A collection of suspected but "hidden" mediators of the SES–health association has become apparent in the findings of recent studies. It is now clear, for example, that exposures to chronic and acutely stressful events are disproportionately arrayed along a gradient of social class. Grzywacz, Almeida, Neupert, and Ettner (2004) found, in an analysis of data from a National Study of Daily Experiences, that lower SES was associated with higher severity levels of both subjectively and objectively ascertained daily life stressors. Lupien and colleagues have also shown, in a program of research on the social class differences in stress hormone production, that lower SES is associated with higher levels of salivary cortisol secretion, beginning as early as 6 years of age and intensifying over the course of middle childhood (Lupien, King, Meaney, & McEwen, 2000). The greater basal activation of the hypothalamic-pituitary-adrenocortical (HPA) axis in lower SES children appears unrelated to baseline cognitive processes (Lupien, King, Meaney, & McEwen, 2001), but is linked in some manner to how low versus high SES children process positive and negative attributes. Children from low SES families, when presented with hypothetically anomalous pairings of adjectives and animals (e.g., an intelligent giraffe, a stupid lion), for example, more often endorsed the impossibility of such creatures, suggesting a systematic difference in conceptualization of the possible among low SES children. Given the known effects of glucocorticoids on cognition and memory (Sapolsky, 1996), such SES differences in cognitive processes and appraisals may be attributable in part to differential activation of adrenocortical circuitry.

Primate Hierarchies and Subjective Social Position

Recent findings also suggest that linkages between SES and health may involve not only the objective, material aspects of social class membership, but one's subjective, self-appraised position in a hierarchy of ordered social relationships. As reviewed by Sapolsky (2005), nonhuman primate species form stable, often linearly transitive social dominance hierarchies that serve to order social relationships, promote cooperation among troop members, and minimize the occurrence of aggression and violence. Contrary to prevalent impressions, monkeys occupying subordinate social positions are not always the most stressed, and there are both between-species and between-troop differences: in the physiologic "costs" of dominant and subordinate positions, in the despotic versus egalitarian character of a troop's culture, and in the predisposition of the group to peaceable versus violent solutions to conflict and competition (Abbott et al., 2003; Boehm, 1999; Sapolsky, 2004; Sapolsky & Share, 2004).

Nonetheless, primate troops all form dominance hierarchies, even in captivity, and hierarchical positions are demonstrably related to health and risk factor susceptibility. Subordinate positions in monkeys are associated with upregulated adrenocortical activation and impaired immune competence (Gust et al., 1991; Sapolsky, 1989). Monkeys fed atherogenic diets show greater development of atherosclerotic disease in subordinate individuals, except under conditions of social instability, in which dominant animals sustain the higher rates of coronary disease (Kaplan, Manuck, Clarkson, Lusso, & Taub, 1982). Even within experimental paradigms, subordinate social status among cynomolgus monkeys is associated with greater susceptibility to respiratory pathogens (Cohen et al., 1997). If disease risk is ordered by social position in primates with equal access to material resources, these observations suggest that something about social subordination per se may alter susceptibility to the agents of disease. Furthermore, if primate hierarchies are meaningfully analogous to the socioeconomic stratifications of human societies, findings on dominance and health raise an altogether different account for the health effects of SES. It suggests that the health correlates of one's socioeconomic position may be traceable, at least in part, to experiences of subordination, rather than of material deprivation.

Such a hypothesis derives additional support from recent research on the influences of subjectively, rather than objectively, determined social position, on the effects of income inequality rather than absolute income, and on the health and physiological correlates of social position in class-rooms of preschool children. Several recent reports by Adler and her col-leagues indicate that an individual's subjective appraisal of position within relevant social groups may be as potent a predictor—or an even a more potent predictor—of health status than SES itself. A study by Goodman et al. (2003), for example, found that self-rated, subjective social status among adolescents was associated with obesity independent of SES derived from parent education and household income. Ostrove, Adler, Kuppermann, and Washington (2000) showed, in a large, multiethnic sample of U.S. women, that self-perceived social ordering was significantly related to health status and accounted for a substantial portion of the association between objec-tive SES and health. In yet another study, Adler, Epel, Castellazzo, and Icko-vics (2000), using the same self-reported social status assessment, found that self-evaluations of social standing contributed to both psychological and physical health, independent of the specific material resources linked to SES.

A growing literature on the health effects of income inequality similarly raises the possibility that processes of social comparison figure prominently in the SES–health association. Research by Wilkinson (1996), Kawachi and Kennedy (2002), and others contends that income inequality erodes social bonds and causes chronic stress, leading to impairments in adaptation and in health. Lynch, Smith, Kaplan, and House (2000), on the other hand, argue that SES–health associations are due principally to fewer material and economic resources among the poor, resulting in diminished capaci-ties for avoiding health risks and preventing illness. Although this large and sometimes contentious body of work is beyond the scope of this chapter, sev-eral reviewers have concluded that the debate between psychosocial (social capitalist) and neomaterialist accounts of SES effects is not yet finished or resolved (Macinko, Shi, Starfield, & Wulu, 2003; Shortt, 2004). Readers of this literature may logically query why *both* social capitalist and neomaterial-ist explanations of the SES–health gradient could not contribute to a more definitive accounting of SES effects than either position on its own.

Child Hierarchies

Finally, an often-unrecognized dimension of social development in young children is their formation of dominance hierarchies that define and con-strain many aspects of dyadic and group behavior. Resembling the domi-nance structures of nonhuman primate troops (Bernstein, 1976), human children as young as 2 to 3 years of age form social hierarchies within weeks of their assembly into social groups, in settings such as preschool or kin-dergarten (Strayer & Trudel, 1984; Vaughn & Waters, 1978). Hierarchical organization within such groups is marked by a broad array of dominance and subordination behaviors, ranging from verbal and physical competition for scarce resources (e.g., a valued toy or a teacher's attention) and personal imitation to acts of leadership or interpersonal violence. Preschool social hierarchies become increasingly stable as children develop, and in older children, such structures appear less dependent on agonistic or competitive behaviors, and are more reflective of peer friendships and affiliative interactions (Strayer, 1989).

New evidence for the social partitioning of health and health risk factors among dominant and subordinate human children is derived from studies in progress in the Boyce-Alkon laboratory at the Institute of Human Development and School of Public Health, University of California, Berkeley. In a cross-sectional pilot study examining social position, stress reactivity, and health problems in preschool age children, Boyce and colleagues (Boyce, 2004; Goldstein, Bensadoun, Trancik, Adler, & Boyce, 1999) found that children occupying higher social positions in their preschool groups showed lower heart rate reactivity, lower baseline salivary cortisol concentrations, lower parasympathetic and sympathetic reactivity, and fewer parent-reported chronic medical conditions (see Figure 3.1) Notably, these results parallel the previously cited finding of Lupien, King, Meaney, and McEwen (2000) that lower SES children have higher salivary cortisol levels and a second report by Steptoe et al. (2002) demonstrating poorer cardiovascular recovery from stressors among lower grade British civil servants. Together, the findings suggest that one's ordinal position within proximal social groups may itself be associated with health risk factors and illness, in ways that are comparable to the health correlates of dominance in nonhuman primates and to the effects of SES on health in human adults. The influence of SES on health may be both analogous and partially attributable to the biologically mediated effects of low position within the "pecking orders" of childhood social groups.

Adult Health Effects of Childhood Adversities

Socially partitioned differences in children's stressful experience and in the activation of neurobiological pathways may affect not only concurrent, child health, but health in adulthood as well, decades forward in time. Based on research exploring the "fetal programming" of postnatal differences in stress reactivity and behavior (e.g., Owen, Andrews, & Matthews, 2005), a variety of investigators have assembled evidence that SES-related experiences of disadvantage and adversity in early life bear longitudinal associations with health, illness, and mortality in adult life. Of particular heuristic value are the theoretical frameworks for a life-course approach to chronic disease epidemiology developed by Kuh and Ben-Shlomo (2004) and for the

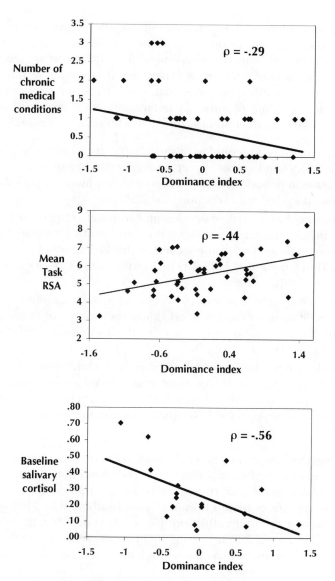

Figure 3.1   Health and stress reactivity by dominance status in preschool children (Boyce, 2004).

delineation of latent, pathway, and cumulative effects proposed by Keating and Hertzman, (1999). In the latter frame of reference, linkages between early socioeconomic environments and adult health status are observed to occur independent of intervening experience (latent effects), through the setting of early health trajectories (pathway effects), or according to the intensity and duration of unfavorable environmental exposures (cumulative effects). Among the findings consistent with such frameworks are:

- Data from the Dunedin Study indicating that children who grew up in low SES families had poorer cardiovascular health, a threefold increase in periodontal disease, and a higher incidence of substance abuse at age 26 years (Poulton et al., 2002).
- Evidence that the risk of developing a major affective disorder requiring hospitalization in adulthood was significantly increased among fetuses exposed during the second or third trimester of pregnancy to the Dutch famine of 1944–1945 (Brown, van Os, Driessens, Hoek, & Susser, 2000).
- The strong, graded relation found in the Adverse Childhood Experiences Study between childhood exposures to abuse or household dysfunction and multiple risk factors for the leading causes of death in adults (Anda et al., 1999; Dube et al., 2003; Felitti et al., 1998).
- The long term, beneficial effects of an early childhood intervention in Chicago and Ypsilanti on educational, health, and forensic outcomes in early adulthood (Berrueta-Clement, Schweinhart, Barnett, Epstein, & Weikart, 1984; Reynolds, Temple, Robertson, & Mann, 2001).

Taken together, these and other findings converge on a conclusion that experiences of adversity and protection in early development are keenly relevant to health over the life course and that childhood stressors are capable of setting trajectories toward lives of relative health and well being or lives of chronic and persistent affliction. Especially vulnerable, given this patterning of risk, are children growing up in impoverished or blighted social conditions, within lower SES families, neighborhoods or communities.

Variability in the SES–Health Relation

Because of the potency and consistency of the SES–health gradient, in both child and adult populations, the extensive variability in this association goes often unrecognized or ignored. Figure 3.2 shows scatter plots of reading scores, for example, among Canadian and U.S. children of different SES (Willms, 2004). Although the graded, monotonic relation of SES and reading level is apparent in both groups, it is also evident that there is strik-

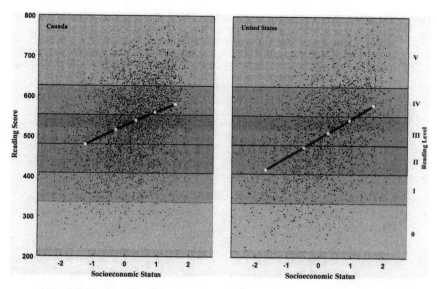

Figure 3.2.   Literacy achievement by socioeconomic status in Canadian and U.S. children (Willms, 2004).

ing variability in the associations. There are children of high SES families who have quite low reading scores, and conversely, there are low SES children who achieve atypically high scores. The R^2s for Canada and the U.S. data are .11 and .21, respectively, indicating that on average 15% of the variance in reading scores is attributable to socioeconomic variation. SES associations with other health and educational outcomes show equivalent and sometimes greater scatter in the distributions of individual data points. Why, if SES is so strong a correlate of health and educational outcomes, is there such extensive variability in its capacity to accurately predict outcomes of interest? With its known relations to medical care access, diet, exercise, life stressors, neighborhood violence, and stress biology, why does SES capture so small a portion of the variability in outcomes? The answer may lie in the striking differences found in children's physiological reactivity to stressors—differences in reactivity that appear early in life, become increasingly stable over the course of development, and appear to interact with environmental stressors in the prediction of maladaptive outcomes.

NEUROBIOLOGY OF THE HUMAN STRESS RESPONSE

Environmental events signaling threats to survival or well-being produce a set of complex, highly orchestrated responses within the neural circuitry of the brain and peripheral neuroendocrine pathways regulating metabolic, immunologic, and other physiological functions. This elaborate and tightly integrated repertoire of responses results in a shift to a state of biological and behavioral preparedness, involving increases in heart rate and blood pressure, metabolic mobilization of nutrients, preferential redirection of energy resources and blood to the brain, and the induction of vigilance and fear. The neural basis for the organism's stress response comprises two anatomically distinct but functionally integrated circuits: the corticotropin releasing hormone (CRH) system and the locus coeruleus-norepinephrine (LC-NE) system (Chrousos, 1998; McEwen, 1998; Meaney, 2001). Co-activation of the these two systems, along with their linkages to emotion regulatory brain regions such as the amygdala, the anterior cingulate, and the prefrontal cortex, produce the coordinated biobehavioral changes associated with the stress response in mammalian species.

The CRH system comprises two distinguishable subsystems, one centered in the paraventricular nucleus (PVN) of the hypothalamus and involved in the homeostatic regulation of the hypothalamic-pituitary-adrenocortical (HPA) axis, and the other involved in the circuitry of the amygdala and its connections. Within the former subsystem, CRH is released into the portal blood supply of the pituitary in a circadian fashion by neurons in the PVN and serves as the primary trigger for production of pro-opiomelanocortin (POMC) polypeptide by the anterior pituitary. In the second subsystem, CRH cell bodies are more widely represented in areas outside the hypothalamus, including the amygdala, the substantia innominata, the bed nucleus of the stria terminalis, and in the prefrontal, insular, and cingulate regions of the cortex (Gold & Chrousos, 2002; Owens & Nemeroff, 1991). Two or more types of CRH receptors have been found: CRH1 receptors in the anterior pituitary and other brain regions, which are involved in generating fear-related behavior; and CRH2 receptors that seem to play a counterregulatory role in anxiety. POMC is cleaved into its component proteins, corticotropin (ACTH) and ß-endorphin (Smith et al., 1998), and ACTH is transported in plasma to the adrenal cortex, triggering secretion of cortisol, the principal human glucocorticoid regulating blood pressure, glucose metabolism, and immune competence. Glucocorticoids also inhibit those neuroendocrine axes promoting growth and reproduction (Gold, Goodwin, & Chrousos, 1988).

The actions of cortisol within target cells are mediated through direct effects on gene transcription and inhibition of other, proregulatory transcription factors (van der Saag, Caldenhoven, & van de Stolpe, 1996). Whereas such effects acutely facilitate essential biological responses to stress and threat, chronic glucocorticoid secretion is associated with pathogenic processes and disease states, including major depression, insulin resistance and diabetes, hypertension and atherosclerosis, bone loss, and disorders related to diminished immune functions (Gold & Chrousos, 1999; McEwen, 1998). The hippocampus, a brain region closely involved in memory and learning, is particularly susceptible to the degenerative effects of glucocorticoids (Bremner & Vermetten, 2001; Sapolsky, 1996). Circulating cortisol therefore adaptively regulates the activation level of the HPA axis through a process of feedback inhibition at the hypothalamus, the pituitary, and centers outside the hypothalamus, such as the hippocampus and prefrontal cortex (Dallman et al., 1987).

The LC-NE system comprises the noradrenergic cells of the brainstem and their projections to the amygdala, hippocampus, mesolimbic dopamine system, and the prefrontal cortex (Aston-Jones, Rajkowski, Kubiak, Valentino, & Shipley, 1996). LC activation of hypothalamic centers also contributes to activation and regulation of the autonomic nervous system (ANS), initiating the so-called "fight or flight" responses to challenge. The ANS, comprising sympathetic, parasympathetic, and enteric branches, modulates physiologic arousal and recovery in the periphery and produces the familiar biological signs of stressful encounters, including heart rate and respiratory rate acceleration, sweat production, dry mouth, and, if sufficiently severe, loss of urinary or fecal continence. These biological responses are mediated both by direct autonomic innervation of target organs and by secretion of catecholamines by the adrenal medulla. Immune regulatory effects of the catecholamines, as well as those of CRH and the glucocorticoids, appear due to differential effects on T-helper-1/T-helper-2 cells and type 1/type 2 cytokine production (Habib, Gold, & Chrousos, 2001). Through such direct effects on immune cells, experiences of severe or prolonged stress may influence susceptibility to a variety of infectious, autoimmune/inflammatory, or neoplastic diseases (Elenkov & Chrousos, 1999).

Although anatomically distinct, the functioning of the CRH and LC-NE systems is highly integrated and cross-regulatory. CRH-expressing neurons in the amygdala, for example, project directly to the LC, escalating the firing rate of LC neurons, enhancing NE release, and producing many of the fear-related behaviors associated with stressful experience (Meaney, 2001; Valentino, Curtis, Page, Pavcovich, & Florin-Lechner, 1998). These CRH-mediated pathways from the amygdala to the LC may also underlie many of the symptoms of anxiety disorders, such as acoustic startle responses, vigilance, symptoms of avoidance, and recurrent emotional memories. Reciprocally, activation of NE secreting neurons in the LC has been shown to increase CRH production in the PVN (Habib, Gold, & Chrousos, 2001). This cross-regulatory process is only one of several ways in which the LC-NE and CRH are functionally interactive (Gold & Chrousos, 2002; Viau, 2002) and together constitute a primary integrative pathway by which psychologically and emotionally relevant environmental signals result in the behavioral, autonomic, and immunologic manifestations of human pathology

(Cacioppo et al., 1998; Heilig, Koob, Ekman, & Britton, 1994; McEwen & Stellar, 1993). Dysregulated activation of these systems has been implicated, as well, in the genesis of the major neuropsychiatric disorders (Bloom & Kupfer, 1995), and the experimental administration of the systems' neurohormonal products produces many of the physiological and behavioral symptoms that characterize affective and anxiety disorders (Dunn & Berridge, 1990; Heilig, Koob, Ekman, & Britton, 1994).

These homeostatic systems protecting survival and stability under conditions of stress appear early in phylogeny, showing both genetic expression and comparable biological functions in multiple animal species from invertebrates to primates. The CRH and LC-NE systems have a complex, highly interactive repertoire of central and peripheral stress responses, which together mobilize neurobiological and behavioral resources in defense of the organism's integrity and well being. Although these neurobiological responses are protective and essential in acutely stressful conditions, they can become themselves pathogenic when persistently activated under circumstances of chronic or overwhelming stress and adversity.

Individual Differences in Stress Reactivity

Over the past 15 years, Dr. Abbey Alkon, the MacArthur Research Network on Psychopathology and Development, multiple students, postdoctoral fellows, and I have explored normative variability in the reactivity of these stress-responsive neural systems among children from infancy to roughly 8 years of age. These studies initially relied on integrated measures of autonomic reactivity—such as heart rate and blood pressure—to standardized stressors comprising social, cognitive, physical, and emotional challenges. Measures were subsequently expanded to include differentiated scoring of sympathetic activation (pre-ejection period using impedance cardiography) and parasympathetic withdrawal (the magnitude of respiratory sinus arrhythmia or the high frequency, respiratory band of heart rate variability), as well as adrenocortical activation indexed with assays of salivary cortisol. Much attention was dedicated to establishing the ecological validity of the standardized laboratory challenges, the test–retest reliability of the reactivity measures, and their empirical validity in studies of physical and mental health in early and middle childhood (Alkon et al., 2003; Boyce et al., 2001). These measures of reactivity have now been employed in multiple epidemiologic studies of children (and one of semifree-ranging rhesus macaques) comprising observational cohort, quasiexperimental, and experimental designs. It is the consistency and reliability of these studies' findings that form the empirical foundation for the first of the three claims: that the character of the identified biology–context interactions demands a reconceptualization of stress reactivity as a biological sensitivity to social context.

CLAIM 1: STRESS REACTIVITY AS
BIOLOGICAL SENSITIVITY TO CONTEXT

The assumption that exaggerated stress reactivity is univalently associated with stress-related morbidities has been questioned in a number of studies revealing that high reactivity phenotypes under specific environmental conditions may be associated with protective rather than harmful effects and generate normative or improved health outcomes. Such bivalent effects of stress reactivity on human and primate morbidities have thematically characterized a series of studies in our laboratory. Examining cardiovascular and immunologic reactivity in two cohorts of 3–5 year old children, for example, significant interactions (Figure 3.3A) were detected with environmental stressors in the prediction of respiratory illness incidence over the ensuing several month periods (Boyce et al., 1995). Specifically, the noted interactions suggested bidirectional effects of reactivity on illness incidence: Highly reactive children in high stress families or child-care centers sustained significantly higher rates of respiratory illness than their low reactive peers, but equally reactive children in low stress settings were the healthiest of all children in the samples. By contrast, among low reactivity children, respiratory illness incidence was largely unrelated to environmental stress levels, showing approximately the same, midlevel illness rates in both low and high stress conditions. Similarly significant interactions were found for injury incidence (Boyce, 1996).

Although prospective in design, both of these studies were observational in nature and lacked experimental data on the incidence of illnesses or injuries among the same group of highly reactive children in both low and high stress conditions. In a subsequent study of semifree-ranging rhesus macaques, however, such quasiexperimental conditions were satisfied (Boyce, O'Neill-Wagner, Price, Haines, & Suomi, 1998). The troop of macaques, which had been previously assessed for their degree of biobehavioral reactivity to novel or challenging stimuli, lived in a 6-acre wooded habitat in rural Maryland, on the grounds of the National Institutes of Health Primate Center. In 1993, the troop experienced a 6-month period of protective confinement to a small, 1,000-square-foot building during a construction project on the habitat grounds. The confinement proved highly stressful, however, and the incidence of violent injuries increased fivefold during the confinement period. Blinded ascertainment of medically attended injury rates from veterinary records produced evidence for a significant interaction between reactivity status and confinement stress, which is plotted in Figure 3.3B. As with the prior studies of children, low reactivity animals showed little effect of the confinement, whereas those with high reactivity showed dramatically higher rates of violent injuries

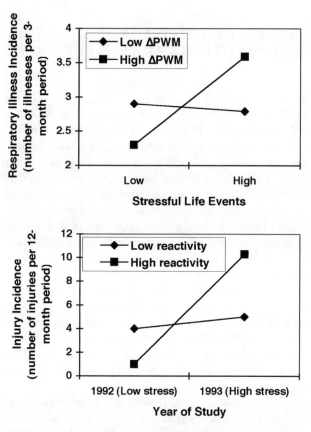

Figure 3.3.   Interactions among laboratory-based stress reactivity
and environmental stressors in predicting of health outcomes.
A: Immune reactivity (changes in pokeweed mitogen response)
× family stressful events and respiratory illness incidence in kin-
dergartners ($N = 99$). B: Biobehavioral reactivity × confinement
stress and injury incidence in a troop of semi-free ranging rhesus
monkeys ($N = 36$).

in the high stress situation but lower rates in the preceding, low stress
condition.

These findings documenting reactivity × context interactions in the
prediction of biomedical outcomes have been supplemented by recent
observations from the same group of investigators and several others on
associations among stressors, reactivity, and psychological symptoms in children and young adults. There is reason to believe that the influence of
biological reactivity on mental health outcomes may be even more profound than those observed for biomedical disorders. Worthman, Angold,

and Costello (1998) found associations in Appalachian children between high adrenocortical reactivity and future diagnoses of anxiety disorders and between low reactivity and diagnoses of conduct disorder. In other work examining cross-sectional data from the Wisconsin Study of Families and Work, main effects of autonomic reactivity on risk for both internalizing and externalizing spectrum psychopathology in middle childhood have been reported (Boyce et al., 2001). A third paper, by Gannon, Banks, Shelton, and Luchetta (1989), found that college students with laboratory evidence of exaggerated autonomic reactivity showed higher rates of physical symptoms and depression under stressful circumstances, but lower than average rates under low or minimally stressful conditions. Finally, a recent randomized experimental study in our laboratory by Quas, Bauer, and Boyce (2004) again showed an interaction effect between autonomic reactivity and social context, with highly reactive children showing significantly better memory for a previous, standardized stressful event in a supportive social environment and poorer memory under conditions of low support, relative to a low reactivity comparison group. Although not all research examining reactivity × context interactions have replicated these findings (see, e.g., Musante et al., 2000), a sufficiently substantial number of studies have produced homologous results to suggest a robust phenomenon worthy of further and more explicit analysis.

Biological Sensitivity to Context:
The Dandelion and the Orchid

The cited evidence for bivalent, context-dependent health effects of highly reactive phenotypes suggests that reactivity may reflect not simply overarousal of neurobiological pathways, but rather sensitivity to both harmful and protective contextual effects. Highly reactive children appear to experience either the best or the worst of psychiatric and biomedical outcomes, within the populations from which they are drawn. Under conditions of adversity, such children sustain higher rates of disease, disorder, and injuries than their more normatively reactive peers from the same environments. On the other hand, equally reactive children in low stress, protective social environments experience substantially lower rates of health problems than their low reactive peers. These results suggest that the highly reactive biological profiles found in this subset of children reveal a unique sensitivity or "permeability" to the influence of environmental conditions (Boyce et al., 1995).

A Swedish idiomatic expression, *maskrosbarn* or "dandelion child," refers to the capacity of some children—not unlike those with low reactivity phenotypes—to survive and even thrive in whatever circumstances they encounter, in much the same way that dandelions prosper, irrespective of soil, sun, drought, or rain. Observations of such children have generated an extensive developmental literature on the phenomenon of resilience, the capacity for positive adaptation despite experiences of significant adversity (Luthar, Doernberger, & Zigler, 1993; Masten, 2001). A contrasting Swedish neologism, *orkidebarn* or "orchid child," might better describe the context-sensitive individual, whose survival and flourishing is intimately tied, like that of the orchid, to the nurturant or neglectful character of the ambient environment. In conditions of neglect, the orchid promptly declines, whereas in conditions of support and nurture, it is a flower of unusual delicacy and beauty.

An important caveat is that variation in children's phenotypic sensitivity to social context would likely only come into play within settings that approximate species-typical parenting environments. In the most extreme cases, where parenting is absent or pernicious, no degree of context "insensitivity" would be adequate to protect a child from the privations of inattention or abuse. When outright survival is at stake, adaptive differences in a child's permeability to parental influence become irrelevant. At the other extreme, one could imagine parenting environments so extraordinarily enriched with emotional, cognitive, and material provision that differences the developmental and health outcomes of dandelion and orchid children would become vanishingly, perhaps imperceptibly small. When all needs are lavishly met for each child, the advantages of a biological "openness" to social context recede. It is thus likely that phenotypic variation in context sensitivity operates as a true determinant of adaptive health endpoints only within the relatively normative range of early social contexts, in which the vast majority of children are raised. *All* children are vulnerable in settings of parental neglect or deprivation, but very few are at risk in environments of emotional and material abundance.

To summarize, epidemiologic studies examining environmental stressors and stress reactivity in children, young adults and nonhuman primates have yielded notably consistent findings in several different laboratories. Specifically, such studies have often identified small subgroups of highly reactive individuals—usually 15% to 20% of the study sample—whose health outcomes appear tightly bound to the stressful or protective nature of their most proximal social environments. Highly reactive children sustain unusually poor outcomes in conditions of chronic or recurrent adversity, such as those that often characterize low SES families and neighborhoods. Equally reactive children in conditions of support and predictability, by contrast, seem to experience unusually salubrious outcomes, as if more susceptible than their peers to the beneficence and protection such conditions provide. These results call into question the conventional view of stress reactivity as a univalently risk-engendering characteristic and suggest instead that reactivity may be a marker for a heightened sensitivity to the character of the social world. The results also suggest that highly sensitive children growing up in lower versus higher SES settings could be expected to evince a "hypertypicality" in the health effects of their SES- partitioned stressors and supports. That is, reactive children in highly stressful, low SES settings may show even more deleterious effects on health, whereas highly reactive children in highly supportive, high SES settings may show even greater health protection, compared to their less reactive peers. Individual differences in children's sensitivity to contextual circumstances might thus offer an account for the noted variability in SES–health relations.

CLAIM 2: THE ONTOGENY OF CONTEXT SENSITIVITY

As summarized by Boyce, Ellis, and Essex in two articles in *Development and Psychopathology* (Boyce & Ellis, 2005; Ellis, Essex, & Boyce, 2005), biological sensitivity to context may not only moderate associations between social context and health, but may be itself a product of early social contextual influences. Within rodent and primate models of stress reactivity developed by Meaney (Liu et al., 1997; Meaney, 2001), Suomi (Byrne & Suomi, 2002; Champoux, Higley, & Suomi, 1997; Linnoila et al., 1994; Suomi, 1987), and their colleagues, there is evidence that individual differences are determined by strain-related genetic variations, by aspects of early maternal–infant experience, and by interactions among gene expression and experiential factors. On one hand, clear biobehavioral differences exist between strains of mice and rats on dimensions such as behavioral and adrenocortical reactivity to stressors. BALBc mice, for example, are inherently more fearful and show more vigorous glucocorticoid responses to stressors than do C57 mice (Zaharia, Kulczycki, Shanks, Meaney, & Anisman, 1996), and comparable differences exist between Fisher 344 and Long-Evans rats (Dhabhar, McEwen, & Spencer, 1993). Heritable, genetic factors similarly influence the neurobiological systems that underpin temperamental differences in behavior in species and subspecies of nonhuman primates. One study comparing neurobiological differences between Indian-origin and Chinese-hybrid rhesus monkeys found significantly lower CSF 5-hydroxyindoleacetic acid levels (5-HIAA, a metabolite of serotonin) in Chinese-hybrid monkeys beginning at 6 months of age, suggesting "strain" differences in the magnitude of central serotonergic activity (Champoux, Higley, & Suomi, 1997). Another study by Lyons, Yang, Sawyer-Glover, Moseley, and Schatzberg (2001) showed that hippocampal atrophy, which has been associated with environmental stress-related increases in cortisol secretion, is partially heritable, raising questions regarding an attribution of hippocampal volume variation to purely experiential factors. Such biobehavioral differences are likely due, at least in part, to heritable variation in the alleles that regulate stress responsive biological systems in these animals.

On the other hand, a variety of investigators have also shown that perturbations in early experience resulting from parent–infant behavior can have important regulatory effects on the calibration of biological systems, including the CRH system and HPA axis (Hofer, 1994; Lubach, Coe, & Ershler, 1995; Meaney, 2001; Plotsky & Meaney, 1993; Sanchez, Ladd, & Plotsky, 2001). An experimental procedure known as *handling*, in which rodent pups are separated from their mothers for 3–15 minutes each day over the first several weeks of life, results in permanent down-regulatory changes in the CRH system at the level of the PVN and central nucleus of the amygdala and, as a consequence, produces a decreased exposure to the adrenocortical and autonomic effects of stressful events. Such downregulatory effects have been shown to result from increased glucocorticoid receptor expression following changes in mothering behavior—that is, the intensity of licking and grooming and other characteristic maternal behaviors—upon the pups' return to the nest. Furthermore, handling can override the genetic propensities shared with a fearful, highly reactive mother by inducing maternal behaviors that produce long term underarousal in the infants' adrenocortical and autonomic response systems (Champagne & Meaney, 2001). Studies of nonhuman primates have also revealed a capacity for early, stress-engendering disruptions of social experience to produce long-term changes in neurobiological reactivity (Harlow, Harlow, & Suomi, 1971; Sanchez, Ladd, & Plotsky, 2001). Maternal separations produce predictable changes in peripheral and central neural circuitry, including alterations in functional immune competence (Lubach, Coe, & Ershler, 1995), up-regulation of autonomic responses to physical stressors (Martin, Sackett, Gunderson, & Goodlin-Jones, 1988), increased CRH expression in CSF (Coplan et al., 1996), and dysregulatory changes in HPA axis reactivity (Shannon, Champoux, & Suomi, 1998). Sapolsky's work (Sapolsky, 1990; Sapolsky & Share, 1994) among wild olive baboons has also revealed associations between dominance status and adrenocortical activation, suggesting that experiences related to social adeptness and dominance tended to lower cortisol levels in individuals occupying higher status positions.

Finally, the work of Szyf, Meaney, and colleagues (Meaney & Szyf, 2005; Weaver, Cervoni, et al., 2004) has explored the convergence of these genetic and contextual effects on biological sensitivity to context by studying how aspects of social experience can epigenetically regulate the expression of genes that guide development of stress responsive neural circuitry. Utilizing a handling paradigm in litters of rat pups, the investigators found distinctive and reversible patterns of DNA methylation among pups of high versus low licking and grooming mothers, which in turn led to differential expression of the glucocorticoid receptor gene and alterations in HPA sensitivity to environmental stressors. Hypomethylation of gene regulatory regions correlates with active chromatin structure and with the intensity of transcriptional activity, making methylation patterns a stable signature of the epigenomic status of a regulatory sequence (Weaver, Diorio, Seckl, Szyf, & Meaney, 2004). An individual's level of biological sensitivity to context thus seems to be a conjoint product of heritable genetic variation, differences in early social experience, and the epigenomic influence of such experience on the transcriptional expression of key, regulatory genes.

CONFLICTING EVIDENCE IN HUMAN STUDIES

A picture that is both less elegantly rendered and inherently more complex emerges from a review of the *human* literature on the ontogeny of context sensitivity or stress reactivity. In parallel to genetic evidence from nonhuman primates, studies of children and their parents affirm a moderate heritability of reactivity phenotypes (Bartels, de Geus, Kirschbaum, Sluyter, & Boomsma, 2003; Busjahn, Faulhaber, Viken, Rose, & Luft, 1996; Cheng, Carmelli, Hunt, & Williams, 1997; Matthews et al., 1988; Turner & Hewitt, 1992). A parental history of hypertension has been shown predictive of autonomically mediated blood pressure reactivity in children (e.g., Lemne, 1998), and elevated cortisol levels have been identified in the nondepressed, first-degree relatives of patients with major depression, suggesting that hypercortisolism might be appropriately viewed as a trait measure of a heritable diathesis to affective disorders (Holsboer, Lauer, Schreiber, & Krieg, 1995). Also paralleling the animal literature, various research programs have produced findings supporting experiential, contextual contributions to the emergence of stress reactivity. Studies in human children suggest, for example, that disruptions in early attachment relationships are associated with up-regulatory changes in stress-responsive systems (Essex, Klein, Cho, & Kalin, 2002; Hertsgaard, Gunnar, Erickson, & Nachmias, 1995; Meyer, Chrousos, & Gold, 2001; Nachmias, Gunnar, Mangelsdorf, Parritz, & Buss, 1996; Willemsen-Swinkels, Bakermans-Kranenburg, Buitelaar, van IJzendoorn, & van Engeland, 2000). Studies by Heim, Newport, et al. (2000) and Yehuda (2002; Yehuda, Halligan, & Bierer, 2001; Yehuda, Halligan, & Grossman, 2001) also document the psychobiological sequelae of early abusive experiences, in the form of increases in both basal and reactive ACTH and cortisol expression.

However, another collection of findings summarized by Gunnar and Vazquez (2001) and Heim, Ehlert, and Hellhammer (2000) challenges those studies with evidence of paradoxical *suppression* of HPA activation under conditions of stress. Such "hypocortisolism"—that is, lower basal cortisol levels, less HPA reactivity, or a flattening of the circadian cortisol cycle among higher risk samples—has been noted by multiple investigators in a variety of research settings. Yehuda et al. (2001) reported, for example, that among adult children of Holocaust survivors, those with a self-reported history of childhood trauma showed diminished, rather than elevated, 24-hour urinary cortisol levels, relative to a comparison group with no history of trauma. Carlson and Earls (1997) found low morning cortisol levels and an absence of the normal circadian decline in cortisol among children living in Romanian orphanages. Infants with colic (White, Gunnar, Larson, Donzella, & Barr, 2000), children with psychosocial dwarfism (Vazquez, Watson, & Lopez, 2000), and children living near the epicenter of a major earthquake (Goenjian et al., 1996) have all shown lower morning cortisol levels and a flattening of the normal circadian cycle, relative to control children without such conditions or experiences. Children characterized as shy or introverted similarly showed diminished cortisol reactivity to normative stressors such as the beginning of a new school year (Davis, Donzella, Krueger, & Gunnar, 1999; de Haan, Gunnar, Tout, Hart, & Stansbury, 1998). These findings with regard to the HPA system are notably similar to those of two other studies in which stressful life events were found inversely related to cardiovascular (rather than adrenocortical) reactivity in children or youth (Chesterman, Boyce, & Winkleby, 1989; Musante et al., 2000). That is, children reporting a higher number or severity of stressful life events showed diminished cardiovascular responses to challenge, relative to peers reporting fewer stressful events. In an interesting parallel to such observations in children, Heim, Ehlert, and Hellhammer (2000) reviewed evidence for associations between hypocortisolism and stress-related disorders in adults and similarly concluded that low cortisol patterns are sometimes associated with experiences of stress or adversity or with stress-related disorders.

In response to these paradoxical findings of both increased and decreased stress circuit activation under conditions of adversity in early life, Boyce and colleagues (Boyce & Ellis, 2005; Ellis, Essex, & Boyce, 2005) have presented an evolutionary-developmental theory positing that natural selection has favored developmental mechanisms (i.e., conditional adaptations) that function to adjust levels of biological sensitivity to context to match familial and ecological conditions encountered. Just as the timing of girls' sexual development may be sensitive to paternal investment (Ellis, 2004), individual differences in context sensitivity may track specific features of early childhood environments. Specifically, humans may have evolved developmental mechanisms that detect and internally encode information about levels of supportiveness versus stressfulness in such environments, as a basis for calibrating the activation thresholds and response parameters within stress reactivity systems to match those environments.

Based on the claim that individual differences in stress reactivity represent variation in susceptibility to both positive and negative features of

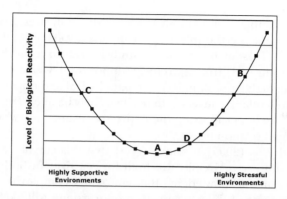

Figure 3.4. Hypothesized curvilinear relation of biologic reactivity to early stress and adversity.

the social environment, the presented theory postulates a U-shaped, curvilinear relationship between levels of supportiveness versus stressfulness in early childhood environments and the development of biological sensitivity to context (see Figure 3.4; Boyce & Ellis, 2005; Ellis, Essex, & Boyce, 2005). The right side of Figure 3.4 depicts expected reactivity levels for individuals who experience very high levels of stress in early childhood. Consistent with the experimental animal studies and epidemiologic human research summarized here, these individuals are hypothesized to develop heightened reactivity profiles as a means of assuring survival and reproductive fitness in a demonstrably hostile and threatening environment. The left side of Figure 3.4 shows predicted reactivity levels for individuals whose early childhoods are characterized by intensive, stable care giving and family support. These individuals are also hypothesized to develop exaggerated reactivity profiles, which function in this context to garner the health and survival benefits of highly supportive rearing environments. An elevated biological sensitivity to context is thus viewed as increasing adaptive competence in highly *stressful* environments by augmenting vigilance to threats and dangers and in highly *protective* environments by increasing susceptibility to social resources and ambient support.

Finally, the middle of Figure 3.4 reflects the anticipated, relatively muted reactivity profiles of individuals whose early childhood experiences are characterized by moderate levels of ongoing stress and threat. These individuals, occupying the broad, normative range of species-typical contextual stressors, are hypothesized to develop comparatively low reactivity profiles as a way of gating or filtering highly prevalent, moderate level stressors. Notably, comparisons of subjects at points A and B in Figure 3.4 (i.e., a sample with relatively high levels of family stress) would result in a conclusion that early adversity is associated with greater stress reactivity. Comparisons at points C and D (i.e., a sample with relatively low levels of family stress), on the other hand, would generate the inference that early adversity produces diminished reactivity. Inasmuch as no single study is likely to cover the full range of early environments (from extremely supportive, low stress to extremely unsupportive, high stress families), the paradoxical and opposing findings of past research relating adversity to reactivity may be due to the limitations of any single study in capturing the entire spectrum along which the proposed U-shaped relation holds.

Boyce and Ellis (2005) further suggest that this curvilinear, quadratic association with early adversity will hold for reactivity in both the LC-NE and CRH systems, acknowledging that far greater complexity in the interplay and balancing of the two stress response systems will likely surface as these relations are explored. Ellis et al. (2005) further present provisional evidence from two studies commensurate with the hypothesized U-shaped association. A theory based on current knowledge of the genetic and experiential antecedents of high reactivity/context sensitive phenotypes, along with provisional evidence in support of that theory, thus suggests that biological sensitivity to context not only moderates known associations between adverse environments and health outcomes in children and experimental animals, but is itself the adaptive product of variation in environmental adversity.

CLAIM 3: CONTEXT SENSITIVITY IN THE SOCIAL PARTITIONING OF DISEASE

Finally, the third claim—for which the smallest body of evidence can currently be assembled—suggests that the known, substantive variability in the SES–health association may be partially accountable to phenotypic variation in biological sensitivity to context among individuals in different social class groups. A small group of studies in adult samples has explored the relations among SES, reactivity, and health. Lynch, Everson, Kaplan, Salonen, and Salonen (1998) examined cardiovascular reactivity and SES as predictors of intima-media thickening in the arteries of Finnish men in the Kuopio Ischemic Heart Disease Risk Factor Study, finding that participants with heightened cardiovascular reactivity born into poor families had the highest rate of atherosclerotic progression. Merritt, Bennett, Williams, Sollers, and Thayer (2004) similarly found that healthy African American men with profiles of high "John Henryism" (high-effort coping with psychosocial demands) and low educational attainment had higher heart rate and blood pressure reactivity. Carroll, Ring, Hunt, Ford, and Macintyre (2003) prospectively studied nearly 1,000 participants in the West of Scotland Twenty-07 Study and reported that cardiovascular reactivity was predictive of future hypertension, with the magnitude of the prediction varying by SES. Steptoe, Willemsen, Kunz-Ebrecht, and Owen (2003), Sloan et al. (2005), and Kapuku, Treiber, and Davis (2002) all similarly found that low SES was associated with various aspects and measures of resting or reactive cardiovascular risk. Interestingly, a paper by Suchday, Krantz, and Gottdiener (2005) reported a result opposite to those of the preceding studies: that is, high SES patients with known histories of coronary artery disease displayed higher blood pressure responses to mental stress in the laboratory than did their low SES counterparts. Moving beyond cardiovascular measures of reactivity, a study by Owen, Poulton, Hay, Mohamed-Ali, and Steptoe (2003) revealed higher C-reactive protein concentrations (a measure of inflammation) and higher T-lymphocyte and natural killer cell counts among lower SES volunteers from the Whitehall II cohort. Finally, Manuck, Flory, Ferrell, and Muldoon (2004) found that allelic variation in the serotonin transporter gene promoter region moderated the association between low SES and serotonergic responsivity, as measured by prolactin responses to the serotonin releasing agent, fenfluramine.

An even smaller number of studies of SES, reactivity, and health have been conducted with child or adolescent participants. In two papers on cognitive appraisal biases in low versus high SES teenagers, Chen, Matthews, and colleagues (Chen, Langer, Raphaelson, & Matthews, 2004; Chen & Matthews, 2001) found that threat interpretations of ambiguous scenarios partially mediated the relation between low SES and cardiovascular reactivity. The Treiber research group has reported that low SES boys with anxious-disruptive behavioral disorders exhibited greater blood pressure reactivity, but that upper SES youth evinced greater heart rate reactivity to social stressors (Barnes et al., 2000; Dobkin, Treiber, & Tremblay, 2000; Dobkin, Tremblay, & Treiber, 1998). Taken together, these pieces of emerging evidence on the associations among SES, biological sensitivity to context, and health suggest that: (a) lower SES populations more frequently develop exaggerated, hyperdynamic autonomic or adrenocortical responses to standardized laboratory challenges; (b) such SES-related reactivity is also linked to other risk factors, such as declines in immune competence or the appearance of inflammatory markers, and to incident disease; and (c) such associations are not uniform in character or direction, an observation reminiscent of the previously detailed bidirectional relation between environmental stress and reactivity. What remains to be elucidated is whether the overall variability in SES–health relations is attributable in part to the variability in biological sensitivity to context that emerges and consolidates in the early years of life. Confirmation of this hypothesis would move the field dramatically toward a more explicit accounting of how resilience and vulnerability modify the developmental consequences of lower SES environments.

ETHICAL IMPLICATIONS OF VARIABILITY
IN CONTEXT SENSITIVITY

A final issue of concern is the set of ethical dilemmas raised by the observed variation in context sensitivity among communities of children. How does the discovery of highly sensitive, reactive children change the practical or moral arguments for ensuring protected, nurturing childhood environments? Among the implications of such questions are issues regarding the interventions that would logically follow from that knowledge. On one hand, one might argue that the exaggerated sensitivity of certain individuals to ambient environmental adversities should mandate a population-wide reduction in stress exposure and the provision of enhancements to general societal supports. The progressive, federally defined decreases in acceptable environmental lead exposures and blood lead levels in children, for example, were due in part to the discovery of a subset of children with genetically derived, exceptional sensitivities to lead effects on heme biosynthesis pathways (Wetmur, Lehnert, & Desnick, 1991). It was thus the elucidation of a vulnerable subpopulation that prompted a population-wide mandate for decreased exposure to a physical toxin. The same could plausibly be true for social environmental protections.

On the other hand, the identification of genetically vulnerable individuals offers the opportunity to construct surveillance processes and interventions that are specifically targeted to individuals at greatest biological risk for a given category of disease (Khoury, Burke, & Thomson, 2000). Within the field of developmental psychopathology, for example, knowledge of the gene polymorphisms associated with risk for anxiety and affective disorders could potentially lead to school-based interventions capable of preventing children from entering trajectories toward such disorders. In another example, Omenn (2000) pointed out that individuals with a genetic trait that decreases the catabolism of nicotine were less likely to be tobacco dependent, suggesting the possibility of preventive interventions targeting the metabolically at-risk individuals. It is important to note that, as argued by Turkheimer (1998), the establishment of genetic contributions to disease etiology does not necessitate genetic or even biological interventions. In Suomi's studies, cited earlier, the provision of expert, highly nurturing foster care for vulnerable young monkeys created dramatically beneficial effects, even though the means of identifying such monkeys involved sophisticated biobehavioral assays of stress responses. Although adjustments in the environmental component of biology–context interactions may be currently more technically feasible and acceptable, the most recent work of Sapolsky and colleagues (Kaufer et al., 2004) serves as a harbinger of genetic interventions that could plausibly alter even the most fundamental, molecular aspects of human emotional and behavioral regulation. Whatever the future of gene therapies, the potential for psychosocial and societal intercessions into human adversities could be served in important ways by the study of biological sensitivity to context.

A second point is that, however powerful and persuasive the economic arguments may be favoring societal investments in children (see Heckman & Lochner, 2000, for a compelling example of this argument), there are even deeper ethical rationales. Societal utility (in terms of population health or economic prosperity) is clearly one basis for improving children's circumstances, but identifying more fundamental ethical grounds and elevating the argument beyond the strictly utilitarian are essential complements. In Rawls' (1971) formulation of "natural justice," the core argument is that choices of fair social arrangements are inextricably influenced by one's perceptions of how these arrangements affect one's own personal circumstances. "Haves" and "have-nots," for example, view greater income equity differently. A thought experiment, the "veil of ignorance," imagines what social arrangements individuals would choose if they were unable to know the positions they would hold in the resulting society. This line of reasoning has particular force with respect to children, who have little opportunity to influence societal choices, and most would presumably choose for children to have high quality physical and social environments and equitable access to developmental opportunities. What matters here is the degree to which unchosen circumstances or misfortunes interfere with the child's baseline level of opportunity.

Even the equality of opportunity rationale promulgated by Rawls (1971) is eclipsed by a stronger ethical obligation to cease the societal harm done to vulnerable children. Halpern, Keating, and Boyce (Boyce & Keating, 2004; Halpern, Jutte, Gaydos, & Boyce, 2006) move beyond both economic/utilitarian and distributive justice arguments on behalf of children, to a set of more primary moral obligations. First, if current societal structures—such as schools, neighborhoods, and municipalities—play a causal role in harming vulnerable, lower SES children, increasing their risks of mental and physical illness, society must have the strongest kind of ethical imperative, that is, the obligation to change institutions to desist from harm. Second, the quality of life during childhood is itself a core issue, independent of life course consequences. Because of their relative powerlessness within both societies and families, children are in a vulnerable position in regard to the meeting of basic needs. Asserting that they have rights to nurturance, as the relevant international conventions do, is an attempt to raise the profile of such expectations. Third, the moral obligation to children is especially compelling, given the steadily accumulating evidence that early interventions can dramatically change developmental trajectories and life circumstances. The Perry Preschool project (Schweinhart,

Barnes, & Weikart, 1993), the Carolina Abecedarian Project (Campbell & Ramey, 1994), the Child Development Project (Battistich, Schaps, Watson, & Solomon, 1996), and the Ottawa Project (Offord & Jones, 1983) are all examples of controlled experiments providing early developmental interventions and demonstrating important, long-term effects on salient outcomes, including educational attainments, delinquency and arrest rates, teenage pregnancy risks, and antisocial behavior.

I have become convinced that the protection of children is the key that could potentially unlock one of our world's most tenacious and contentious problems: that is, the systematic maldistribution of opportunity and misfortune. As the science of developmental psychopathology deepens and expands, it is my hope that we might, as a nation and people, sustain a change of heart about the value of children and the centrality of their well-being in determining the health and strength of our society's future. There is arguably no calling more compelling and no imperative more urgent than the protection of children's health and the preservation of their opportunities for rich, rewarding and uncommon lives.

ACKNOWLEDGMENTS

Research reported here was supported by the supported by grants from the MacArthur Foundation Research Network on Psychopathology and Development, the National Institute of Mental Health (R01-MH062320 and R01-MH44340), and the Division of Intramural Research of the National Institute of Child Health and Human Development.

REFERENCES

Abbott, D. H., Keverne, E. B., Bercovitch, F. B., Shively, C. A., Mendoza, S. P., Saltzman, W., et al. (2003). Are subordinates always stressed? A comparative analysis of rank differences in cortisol levels among primates. *Hormones and Behavior, 43*(1), 67–82.

Adler, N. E., Boyce, W. T., Chesney, M. A., Cohen, S., Folkman, S., Kahn, R. L., et al. (1994). Socioeconomic status and health: The challenge of the gradient. *American Psychologist, 49*(1), 15–24.

Adler, N. E., Boyce, W. T., Chesney, M. A., Folkman, S., & Syme, S. L. (1993). Socioeconomic inequalities in health: No easy solution. *Journal of the American Medical Association, 269*(24), 3140–3145.

Adler, N. E., Epel, E. S., Castellazzo, G., & Ickovics, J. R. (2000). Relationship of subjective and objective social status with psychological and physiological functioning: Preliminary data in healthy, White women. *Health Psychology, 19*(6), 586–592.

Alkon, A., Goldstein, L. H., Smider, N., Essex, M., Kupfer, D., & Boyce, W. T. (2003). Developmental and contextual influences on autonomic reactivity in young children. *Developmental Psychobiology, 42*(1), 64–78.

Anda, R. F., Croft, J. B., Felitti, V. J., Nordenberg, D., Giles, W. H., Williamson, D. F., et al.

(1999). Adverse childhood experiences and smoking during adolescence and adulthood. *Journal of the American Medical Association, 282*(17), 1652–1658.

Aston-Jones, G., Rajkowski, J., Kubiak, P., Valentino, R. J., & Shipley, M. T. (1996). Role of the locus coeruleus in emotional activation. *Progress in Brain Research, 107,* 379–402.

Bardone, A. M., Moffitt, T. E., Caspi, A., Dickson, N., Stanton, W. R., & Silva, P. A. (1998) Adult physical health outcomes of adolescent girls with conduct disorder, depression, and anxiety. *Journal of the American Academy of Child and Adolescent Psychiatry, 37*(6), 594–601.

Barnes, V. A., Treiber, F. A., Musante, L., Turner, J. R., Davis, H., & Strong, W. B. (2000). Ethnicity and socioeconomic status: impact on cardiovascular activity at rest and during stress in youth with a family history of hypertension. *Ethnicity and Disease, 10*(1), 4–16.

Bartels, M., de Geus, E. J., Kirschbaum, C., Sluyter, F., & Boomsma, D. I. (2003). Heritability of daytime cortisol levels in children. *Behavioral Genetics, 33*(4), 421–433.

Battistich, V., Schaps, E., Watson, M., & Solomon, D. (1996). Prevention effects of the Child Development Project: Early findings from an ongoing multisite demonstration trial. *Journal of Adolescent Research, 11*(1), 12–35.

Bellamy, C., & UNICEF. (2005). *The state of the world's children 2005: Childhood under threat.* New York: UNICEF.

Bernstein, I. S. (1976). Dominance, aggression and reproduction in primate societies. *Journal of Theoretical Biology, 60,* 459–472.

Berrueta-Clement, J. R., Schweinhart, L. J., Barnett, W. S., Epstein, A. S., & Weikart, D. P. (1984). *Changed lives: The effects of the Perry Preschool Program on youths through age 19.* Ypsilanti, MI: High Scope Press.

Bhutta, Z. A. (2004). Beyond Bellagio: Addressing the challenge of sustainable child health in developing countries. *Archives of Diseases of Childhood, 89,* 483–487.

Black, R. E., Morris, S. S., & Bryce, J. (2003). Where and why are 10 million children dying every year? *Lancet, 361*(9376), 2226–2234.

Bloom, F. E., & Kupfer, D. J. (1995). *Psychopharmacology* (4th ed.). New York: Raven Press.

Boehm, C. (1999). *Hierarchy in the forest: The evolution of egalitarian behavior.* Cambridge, MA: Harvard University Press.

Boyce, W. T. (1992). The vulnerable child: New evidence, new approaches. *Advances in Pediatrics, 39,* 1–33.

Boyce, W. T. (1996). Biobehavioral reactivity and injuries in children and adolescents. In M. H. Bornstein & J. Genevro (Eds.), *Child development and behavioral pediatrics: Toward understanding children and health* (pp. 35–58). Mahwah, NJ: Lawrence Erlbaum Associates.

Boyce, W. T. (2004). Social stratification, health and violence in the very young. *Annals of the New York Academy of Sciences, 1036,* 47–68.

Boyce, W. T. (2006). Biology and context: Symphonic causation and the origins of childhood psychopathology. In D. Cicchetti & D. J. Cohen (Eds.), *Developmental psychopathology: Developmental neuroscience* (Vol. II, pp. 797–817). Hoboken, NJ: John Wiley & Sons.

Boyce, W. T., Chesney, M., Alkon-Leonard, A., Tschann, J., Adams, S., Chesterman, B., et al. (1995). Psychobiologic reactivity to stress and childhood respiratory illnesses: Results of two prospective studies. *Psychosomatic Medicine, 57,* 411–422.

Boyce, W. T., & Ellis, B. J. (2005). Biological sensitivity to context: I. An evolutionary-developmental theory of the origins and functions of stress reactivity. *Development & Psychopathology, 17*(2), 271–301.

Boyce, W. T., & Keating , D. P. (2004). Should we intervene to improve childhood circumstances? In D. Kuh & Y. Ben-Shlomo (Eds.), *A life course approach to Chronic disease epidemiology* (2nd ed., pp. 415–445). Oxford: Oxford University Press.

Boyce, W. T., O'Neill-Wagner, P., Price, C. S., Haines, M., & Suomi, S. J. (1998). Crowding stress and violent injuries among behaviorally inhibited rhesus macaques. *Health Psychology, 17*(3), 285–289.

Boyce, W. T., Quas, J., Alkon, A., Smider, N., Essex, M., & Kupfer, D. J. (2001). Autonomic reactivity and psychopathology in middle childhood. *British Journal of Psychiatry, 179,* 144–150.

Bremner, J. D., & Vermetten, E. (2001). Stress and development: Behavioral and biological consequences. *Development & Psychopathology, 13,* 473–489.

Brown, A. S., van Os, J., Driessens, C., Hoek, H. W., & Susser, E. S. (2000). Further evidence of relation between prenatal famine and major affective disorder. *American Journal of Psychiatry, 157*(2), 190–195.

Busjahn, A., Faulhaber, H. D., Viken, R. J., Rose, R. J., & Luft, F. C. (1996). Genetic influences on blood pressure with the cold-pressor test: A twin study. *Journal of Hypertension, 14*(10), 1195–1199.

Byrne, G., & Suomi, S. J. (2002). Cortisol reactivity and its relation to homecage behavior and personality ratings in tufted capuchin (Cebus apella) juveniles from birth to six years of age. *Psychoneuroendocrinology, 27*(1–2), 139–154.

Cacioppo, J. T., Berntson, G. G., Malarkey, W. B., Kiecolt-Glaser, J. K., Sheridan, J. F., Poehlmann, K. M., et al. (1998). Autonomic, neuroendocrine, and immune responses to psychological stress: The reactivity hypothesis. *Annals of the New York Academy of Sciences, 840,* 664–673.

Campbell, F., & Ramey, C. (1994). Effects of early intervention on intellectual and academic achievement: A follow-up study of children from low-income families. *Child Development, 65,* 684–698.

Carlson, M., & Earls, F. (1997). Psychological and neuroendocrinological sequelae of early social deprivation in institutionalized children in Romania. *Annals of the New York Academy of Sciences, 807,* 419–428.

Carroll, D., Ring, C., Hunt, K., Ford, G., & Macintyre, S. (2003). Blood pressure reactions to stress and the prediction of future blood pressure: Effects of sex, age, and socioeconomic position. *Psychosomatic Medicine, 65*(6), 1058–1064.

Caspi, A., McClay, J., Moffitt, T. E., Mill, J., Martin, J., Craig, I. W., et al. (2002). Role of genotype in the cycle of violence in maltreated children. *Science, 297*(5582), 851–854.

Caspi, A., Sugden, K., Moffitt, T. E., Taylor, A., Craig, I. W., Harrington, H., et al. (2003). Influence of life stress on depression: moderation by a polymorphism in the 5-HTT gene. *Science, 301*(5631), 386–389.

Champagne, F., & Meaney, M. J. (2001). Like mother, like daughter: Evidence for non-genomic transmission of parental behavior and stress responsivity. *Progress in Brain Research, 133,* 287–302.

Champoux, M., Higley, J. D., & Suomi, S. J. (1997). Behavioral and physiological characteristics of Indian and Chinese-Indian hybrid rhesus macaque infants. *Developmental Psychobiology, 31*(1), 49–63.

Chen, E., Langer, D. A., Raphaelson, Y. E., & Matthews, K. A. (2004). Socioeconomic status and health in adolescents: the role of stress interpretations. *Child Development, 75*(4), 1039–1052.

Chen, E., & Matthews, K. A. (2001). Cognitive appraisal biases: An approach to understanding the relation between socioeconomic status and cardiovascular reactivity in children. *Annals of Behavioral Medicine, 23*(2), 101–111.

Chen, E., Matthews, K. A., & Boyce, W. T. (2002). Socioeconomic differences in children's health: How and why do these relationships change with age? *Psychological Bulletin, 128*(2), 295–329.

Cheng, L. S., Carmelli, D., Hunt, S. C., & Williams, R. R. (1997). Segregation analysis of cardiovascular reactivity to laboratory stressors. *Genetic Epidemiology, 14*(1), 35–49.

Chesterman, E., Boyce, W. T., & Winkleby, M. A. (1989). *Psychosocial predictors of maternal and infant health: A "sense of permanence" as a mediating variable (Abstract).* Paper presented at the Society of Behavioral Medicine Annual Meeting, San Francisco.

Chrousos, G. P. (1998). Stressors, stress, and neuroendocrine integration of the adaptive response. The 1997 Hans Selye Memorial Lecture. *Annals of the New York Academy of Sciences, 851*(1 Spec No), 311–335.

Cohen, P., Pine, D. S., Must, A., Kasen, S., & Brook, J. (1998). Prospective associations between somatic illness and mental illness from childhood to adulthood. *American Journal of Epidemiology, 147*(3), 232–239.

Cohen, S., Line, S., Manuck, S. B., Rabin, B. S., Heise, E. R., & Kaplan, J. R. (1997). Chronic social stress, social status, and susceptibility to upper respiratory infections in nonhuman primates [see comments]. *Psychosomatic Medicine, 59*(3), 213–221.

Columbia Accident Investigation Board. (2003). *Report of the Columbia Accident Investigation Board.* Washington, DC: National Aeronautics and Space Administration.

Coplan, J. D., Andrews, M. W., Rosenblum, L. A., Owens, M. J., Friedman, S., Gorman, J. M., et al. (1996). Persistent elevations of cerebrospinal fluid concentrations of corticotropin-releasing factor in adult nonhuman primates exposed to early-life stressors: Implications for the pathophysiology of mood and anxiety disorders. *Proceedings of the National Academy of Sciences, 93*(4), 1619–1623.

Dallman, M. F., Akana, S. F., Cascio, C. S., Darlington, D. N., Jacobson, L., & Levin, N. (1987). Regulation of ACTH secretion: Variations on a theme of B. *Recent Progress in Hormone Research, 43*, 113–173.

Davis, E., Donzella, B., Krueger, W. K., & Gunnar, M. R. (1999). The start of a new school year: Individual differences in salivary cortisol response in relation to child temperament. *Developmental Psychobiology, 35*, 188–196.

de Haan, M., Gunnar, M. R., Tout, K., Hart, J., & Stansbury, K. (1998). Familiar and novel contexts yield different associations between cortisol and behavior among 2-year-olds. *Developmental Psychobiology, 31*, 93–101.

Dhabhar, F. S., McEwen, B. S., & Spencer, R. L. (1993). Stress response, adrenal steroid receptor levels and corticosteroid-binding globulin levels—a comparison between Sprague-Dawley, Fischer 344 and Lewis rats. *Brain Research, 616*(1–2), 89–98.

Dingle, J. H., Badger, G. F., & Jordan, W. S. (1964). *Illness in the home: A study of 25,000 illnesses in a group of Cleveland families.* Cleveland: Press of Western Reserve University.

Dobkin, P. L., Treiber, F. A., & Tremblay, R. E. (2000). Cardiovascular reactivity in adolescent boys of low socioeconomic status previously characterized as anxious, disruptive, anxious-disruptive or normal during childhood. *Psychotherapy & Psychosomatics, 69*(1), 50–56.

Dobkin, P. L., Tremblay, R. E., & Treiber, F. A. (1998). Cardiovascular reactivity and adolescent boys' physical health. *Pediatrics, 101*(3), E11.

Dube, S. R., Felitti, V. J., Dong, M., Chapman, D. P., Giles, W. H., & Anda, R. F. (2003). Childhood abuse, neglect, and household dysfunction and the risk of illicit drug use: The adverse childhood experiences study. *Pediatrics, 111*(3), 564–572.

Dunn, A. J., & Berridge, C. W. (1990). Physiological and behavioral responses to corticotropin-releasing factor administration: Is CRF a mediator of anxiety or stress responses? *Brain Research Reviews, 15*(2), 71–100.

Elenkov, I. J., & Chrousos, G. P. (1999). Stress hormones, Th1/Th2 patterns, pro/anti-inflammatory cytokines and susceptibility to disease. *Trends in Endocrinology and Metabolism, 10*, 359–368.

Ellis, B. J. (2004). Timing of pubertal maturation in girls: An integrated life history approach. *Psychological Bulletin, 130*(6), 920–958.

Ellis, B. J., Essex, M. J., & Boyce, W. T. (2005). Biological sensitivity to context: II. Empirical explorations of an evolutionary-developmental hypothesis. *Development & Psychopathology, 17*(2), 303–328.

Essex, M. J., Klein, M. H., Cho, E., & Kalin, N. H. (2002). Maternal stress beginning in infancy may sensitize children to later stress exposure: Effects on cortisol and behavior. *Biological Psychiatry, 52,* 776–784.

Felitti, V. J., Anda, R. F., Nordenberg, D., Williamson, D. F., Spitz, A. M., Edwards, V., et al. (1998). Relationship of childhood abuse and household dysfunction to many of the leading causes of death in adults. The Adverse Childhood Experiences (ACE) Study. *American Journal of Preventive Medicine, 14*(4), 245–258.

Fombonne, E., Simmons, H., Ford, T., Meltzer, H., & Goodman, R. (2001). Prevalence of pervasive developmental disorders in the British nationwide survey of child mental health. *Journal of the American Academy of Child and Adolescent Psychiatry, 40*(7), 820–827.

Gannon, L., Banks, J., Shelton, D., & Luchetta, T. (1989). The mediating effects of psychophysiological reactivity and recovery on the relationship between environmental stress and illness. *Journal of Psychosomatic Research, 33*(2), 167–175.

Goenjian, A. K., Yehuda, R., Pynoos, R. S., Steinberg, A. M., Tashjian, M., Yang, R. K., et al. (1996). Basal cortisol, dexamethasone suppression of cortisol, and MHPG in adolescents after the 1988 earthquake in Armenia. *American Journal of Psychiatry, 153,* 929–934.

Gold, P. W., & Chrousos, G. P. (1999). The endocrinology of melancholic and atypical depression: Relation to neurocircuitry and somatic consequences. *Proceedings of the Association of American Physicians, 111*(1), 22–34.

Gold, P. W., & Chrousos, G. P. (2002). Organization of the stress system and its dysregulation in melancholic and atypical depression: High vs low CRH/NE states. *Molecular Psychiatry, 7*(3), 254–275.

Gold, P. W., Goodwin, F. K., & Chrousos, G. P. (1988). Clinical and biochemical manifestations of depression. Relation to the neurobiology of stress (1). *New England Journal of Medicine, 319*(6), 348–353.

Goldstein, L., Bensadoun, J., Trancik, A., Adler, N., & Boyce, W. T. (1999). *Differences in physical and mental health indices among preschoolers' social status groups.* Paper presented at the biannual meeting of the Society for Research in Child Development, Albuquerque, NM.

Goodman, E., Adler, N. E., Daniels, S. R., Morrison, J. A., Slap, G. B., & Dolan, L. M. (2003). Impact of objective and subjective social status on obesity in a biracial cohort of adolescents. *Obesity Research, 11*(8), 1018–1026.

Grzywacz, J. G., Almeida, D. M., Neupert, S. D., & Ettner, S. L. (2004). Socioeconomic status and health: A micro-level analysis of exposure and vulnerability to daily stressors. *Journal of Health and Social Behavior, 45*(1), 1–16.

Gunnar, M. R., & Vazquez, D. M. (2001). Low cortisol and a flattening of expected daytime rhythm: potential indices of risk in human development. *Development & Psychopathology, 13*(3), 515–538.

Gust, D. A., Gordon, T. P., Wilson, M. E., Ahmed-Ansari, A., Brodie, A. R., & McClure, H. M. (1991). Formation of a new social group of unfamiliar female rhesus monkeys affects the immune and pituitary adrenocortical systems. *Brain, Behavior & Immunity, 5*(3), 296–307.

Haan, M. N., Kaplan, G. A., & Syme, S. L. (1989). Socioeconomic status and health: Old observations and new thoughts. In J. P. Bunker, D. S. Gomby, & B. H. Kehrer (Eds.), *Pathways to health: The role of social factors* (pp. 76–135). Menlo Park, CA: Henry J. Kaiser Family Foundation.

Habib, K. E., Gold, P. W., & Chrousos, G. P. (2001). Neuroendocrinology of stress. *Neuroendocrinology, 30*(3), 695–728.

Halpern, J., Jutte, D., Gaydos, M., & Boyce, W. T. (2006). *Early social dominance and mental health: Ethical obligations to the very young.* Manuscript submitted for publication.

Harlow, H. F., Harlow, M. K., & Suomi, S. J. (1971). From thought to therapy: Lessons from a primate laboratory. *American Scientist, 59*(5), 538–549.

Heckman, J. J., & Lochner, L. (2000). Rethinking myths about education and training: Understanding the sources of skill formation in a modern economy. In S. Danzinger & J. Waldfogel (Eds.), *Securing the future: Investing in children from birth to college* (pp. 47–83). New York: Russell Sage Foundation.

Heilig, M., Koob, G. F., Ekman, R., & Britton, K. T. (1994). Corticotropin-releasing factor and neuropeptide Y: Role in emotional integration. *Trends in Neuroscience, 17*(2), 80–85.

Heim, C., Ehlert, U., & Hellhammer, D. H. (2000). The potential role of hypocortisolism in the pathophysiology of stress-related bodily disorders. *Psychoneuroendocrinology, 25*(1), 1–35.

Heim, C., Newport, D. J., Heit, S., Graham, Y. P., Wilcox, M., Bonsall, R., et al. (2000). Pituitary-adrenal and autonomic responses to stress in women after sexual and physical abuse in childhood. *Journal of the American Medical Association, 284*(5), 592–597.

Hertsgaard, L., Gunnar, M. R., Erickson, M. F., & Nachmias, M. (1995). Adrenocortical responses to the strange situation in infants with disorganized/disoriented attachment relationships. *Child Development, 66*(4), 1100–1106.

Hofer, M. A. (1994). Early relationships as regulators of infant physiology and behavior. *Acta Pediatrica Supplements, 397*, 9–18.

Holsboer, F., Lauer, C. J., Schreiber, W., & Krieg, J. C. (1995). Altered hypothalamic-pituitary-adrenocortical regulation in healthy subjects at high familial risk for affective disorders. *Neuroendocrinology, 62*(4), 340–347.

Kaplan, J. R., Manuck, S. B., Clarkson, T. B., Lusso, F. M., & Taub, D. M. (1982). Social status, environment, and atherosclerosis in cynomolgus monkeys. *Arteriosclerosis, 2*, 359–368.

Kapuku, G. L., Treiber, F. A., & Davis, H. C. (2002). Relationships among socioeconomic status, stress induced changes in cortisol, and blood pressure in African American males. *Annals of Behavioral Medicine, 24*(4), 320–325.

Kaufer, D., Ogle, W. O., Pincus, Z. S., Clark, K. L., Nicholas, A. C., Dinkel, K. M., et al. (2004). Restructuring the neuronal stress response with anti-glucocorticoid gene delivery. *Nature Neuroscience, 7*(9), 947–953.

Kawachi, I., & Kennedy, B. P. (2002). *The health of nations: Why inequality is harmful to your health.* New York: The New Press.

Keating, D. P., & Hertzman, C. (1999). *Developmental health and the wealth of nations: Social, biological, and educational dynamics.* New York: The Guilford Press.

Khoury, M. J., Burke, W., & Thomson, E. J. (Eds.). (2000). *Genetics and public health in the 21st century: Using genetic information to improve health and prevent disease* (Vol. 40). Oxford: Oxford University Press.

Krieger, N. (2001). Theories for social epidemiology in the 21st century: An ecosocial perspective. *International Journal of Epidemiology, 30*, 668–677.

Kuh, D., & Ben-Shlomo, Y. (2004). *A life course approach to chronic disease epidemiology* (2nd ed.). Oxford: Oxford University Press.

Lemne, C. E. (1998). Increased blood pressure reactivity in children of borderline hypertensive fathers. *Journal of Hypertension, 16*(9), 1243–1248.

Linnoila, M., Virkkunen, M., George, T., Eckardt, M., Higley, J. D., Nielsen, D., et al. (1994). Serotonin, violent behavior and alcohol. *EXS, 71*, 155–163.

Liu, D., Diorio, J., Tannenbaum, B., Caldji, C., Francis, D., Freedman, A., et al. (1997). Maternal care, hippocampal glucocorticoid receptors, and hypothalamic-pituitary-adrenal responses to stress. *Science, 277*, 1659–1662.

Lubach, G. R., Coe, C. L., & Ershler, W. B. (1995). Effects of early rearing environment on immune responses of infant rhesus monkeys. *Brain, Behavior & Immunity, 9*(1), 31–46.

Lupien, S. J., King, S., Meaney, M. J., & McEwen, B. S. (2000). Child's stress hormone levels correlate with mother's socioeconomic status and depressive state. *Biological Psychiatry, 48*(10), 976–980.

Lupien, S. J., King, S., Meaney, M. J., & McEwen, B. S. (2001). Can poverty get under your skin? Basal cortisol levels and cognitive function in children from low and high socioeconomic status. *Development & Psychopathology, 13*, 653–676.

Luthar, S. S., Doernberger, C. H., & Zigler, E. (1993). Resilience is not a unidimensional construct: Insights from a prospective study of inner-city adolescents. *Developmental Psychopathology, 5,* 703–717.

Lynch, J. W., Everson, S. A., Kaplan, G. A., Salonen, R., & Salonen, J. T. (1998). Does low socioeconomic status potentiate the effects of heightened cardiovascular responses to stress on the progression of carotid atherosclerosis? *American Journal of Public Health, 88*(3), 389–394.

Lynch, J. W., Smith, G. D., Kaplan, G. A., & House, J. S. (2000). Income inequality and mortality: Importance to health of individual income, psychosocial environment, or material conditions. *British Medical Journal, 320*(7243), 1200–1204.

Lyons, D. M., Yang, C., Sawyer-Glover, A. M., Moseley, M. E., & Schatzberg, A. F. (2001). Early life stress and inherited variation in monkey hippocampal volumes. *Archives of General Psychiatry, 58*(12), 1145–1151.

Macinko, J. A., Shi, L., Starfield, B., & Wulu, J. T., Jr. (2003). Income inequality and health: A critical review of the literature. *Medical Care Research Review, 60*(4), 407–452.

Manuck, S. B., Flory, J. D., Ferrell, R. E., & Muldoon, M. F. (2004). Socio-economic status covaries with central nervous system serotonergic responsivity as a function of allelic variation in the serotonin transporter gene-linked polymorphic region. *Psychoneuroendocrinology, 29*(5), 651–668.

Marmot, M. G., Bosma, H., Hemingway, H., Brunner, E., & Stansfeld, S. (1997). Contribution of job control and other risk factors to social variations in coronary heart disease incidence [see comments]. *Lancet, 350*(9073), 235–239.

Martin, R. E., Sackett, G. P., Gunderson, V. M., & Goodlin-Jones, B. L. (1988). Auditory evoked heart rate responses in pigtailed macaques (Macaca nemestrina) raised in isolation. *Developmental Psychobiology, 21*(3), 251–260.

Masten, A. S. (2001). Ordinary magic: Resilience processes in development. *American Psychologist, 56*(3), 227–238.

Matthews, K. A., Manuck, S. B., Stoney, C. M., Rakaczky, C. J., McCann, B. S., Saab, P. G., et al. (1988). Familial aggregation of blood pressure and heart rate responses during behavioral stress. *Psychosomatic Medicine, 50*(4), 341–352.

McEwen, B. S. (1998). Protective and damaging effects of stress mediators. *New England Journal of Medicine, 338*(3), 171–179.

McEwen, B. S., & Stellar, E. (1993). Stress and the individual. Mechanisms leading to disease. *Archives of Internal Medicine, 153*(18), 2093–2101.

Meaney, M. J. (2001). Maternal care, gene expression, and the transmission of individual differences in stress reactivity across generations. *Annual Review of Neuroscience, 24,* 1161–1192.

Meaney, M. J., & Szyf, M. (2005). Maternal care as a model for experience-dependent chromatin plasticity? *Trends in Neurosciences, 28*(9), 456–463.

Merritt, M. M., Bennett, G. G., Williams, R. B., Sollers, J. J., 3rd, & Thayer, J. F. (2004). Low educational attainment, John Henryism, and cardiovascular reactivity to and recovery from personally relevant stress. *Psychosomatic Medicine, 66*(1), 49–55.

Meyer, S. E., Chrousos, G. P., & Gold, P. W. (2001). Major depression and the stress system: A life span perspective. *Development & Psychopathology, 13*(3), 565–580.

Musante, L., Treiber, F. A., Kapuku, G., Moore, D., Davis, H., & Strong, W. B. (2000). The effects of life events on cardiovascular reactivity to behavioral stressors as a function of socioeconomic status, ethnicity, and sex. *Psychosomatic Medicine, 62*(6), 760–767.

Nachmias, M., Gunnar, M. R., Mangelsdorf, S., Parritz, R. H., & Buss, K. (1996). Behavioral inhibition and stress reactivity: The moderating role of attachment security. *Child Development, 67*(2), 508–522.

Offord, D., & Jones, M. B. (1983). *Skill development: A community intervention program for the prevention of antisocial behaviour.* New York: Raven Press.

Omenn, G. S. (2000). Genetics and public health: Historical perspectives and current challenges and opportunities. In M. J. Khoury, W. Burke, & E. J. Thomson (Eds.), *Genetics and public health in the 21st century: Using genetic information to improve health and prevent disease* (Vol. 40, pp. 25–44). Oxford: Oxford University Press.

Ostrove, J. M., Adler, N. E., Kuppermann, M., & Washington, A. E. (2000). Objective and subjective assessments of socioeconomic status and their relationship to self-rated health in an ethnically diverse sample of pregnant women. *Health Psychology, 19*(6), 613–618.

Owen, D., Andrews, M. H., & Matthews, S. G. (2005). Maternal adversity, glucocorticoids and programming of neuroendocrine function and behaviour. *Neuroscience and Biobehavioral Review, 29*(2), 209–226.

Owen, N., Poulton, T., Hay, F. C., Mohamed-Ali, V., & Steptoe, A. (2003). Socioeconomic status, C-reactive protein, immune factors, and responses to acute mental stress. *Brain, Behavior & Immunity, 17*(4), 286–295.

Owens, M. J., & Nemeroff, C. B. (1991). Physiology and pharmacology of corticotropin-releasing factor. *Pharmacology Review, 43*(4), 425–473.

Plotsky, P. M., & Meaney, M. J. (1993). Early, postnatal experience alters hypothalamic corticotropin-releasing factor (CRF) mRNA, median eminence CRF content and stress-induced release in adult rats. *Brain Research & Molecular Brain Reviews, 18*(3), 195–200.

Poulton, R., Caspi, A., Milne, B. J., Thomson, W. M., Taylor, A., Sears, M. R., et al. (2002). Association between children's experience of socioeconomic disadvantage and adult health: A life-course study. *Lancet, 360,* 1640–1645.

Quas, J. A., Bauer, A., & Boyce, W. T. (2004). Physiological reactivity, social support, and memory in early childhood. *Child Development, 75*(3), 797–814.

Ramphal, S. (1999). Commentary: Debt has a child's face. *The progress of nations* (pp. 27–33). New York: UNICEF.

Rawls, J. (1971). *A theory of justice.* Cambridge, MA: Belknap/Harvard University Press.

Reynolds, A. J., Temple, J. A., Robertson, D. L., & Mann, E. A. (2001). Long-term effects of an early childhood intervention on educational achievement and juvenile arrest: A 15-year follow-up of low-income children in public schools. *Journal of the American Medical Association, 285*(18), 2339–2346.

Rutter, M. (2002). Nature, nurture, and development: From evangelism through science toward policy and practice. *Child Development, 73*(1), 1–21.

Rutter, M. (2005). Environmentally mediated risks for psychopathology: Research strategies and findings. *Journal of the American Academy of Child and Adolescent Psychiatry, 44*(1), 3–18.

Rutter, M., & Sroufe, L. A. (2000). Developmental psychopathology: Concepts and challenges. *Development & Psychopathology, 12*(3), 265–296.

Sanchez, M. M., Ladd, C. O., & Plotsky, P. M. (2001). Early adverse experience as a developmental risk factor for later psychopathology: Evidence from rodent and primate models. *Development & Psychopathology, 13*(3), 419–449.

Sapolsky, R. M. (1989). Hypercortisolism among socially subordinate wild baboons originates at the CNS level. *Archives of General Psychiatry, 46,* 1047–1051.

Sapolsky, R. M. (1990). Adrenocortical function, social rank, and personality among wild baboons. *Biological Psychiatry, 28,* 862–885.

Sapolsky, R. M. (1996). Why stress is bad for your brain. *Science, 273,* 749–750.

Sapolsky, R. M. (2004). Social status and health in humans and other animals. *Annual Review of Anthropology, 33,* 393–418.

Sapolsky, R. M. (2005). The influence of social hierarchy on primate health. *Science, 308*(5722), 648–652.

Sapolsky, R. M., & Share, L. J. (1994). Rank-related differences in cardiovascular function among wild baboons: Role of sensitivity to glucocorticoids. *American Journal of Primatology, 32,* 261–275.

Sapolsky, R. M., & Share, L. J. (2004). A pacific culture among wild baboons: its emergence and transmission. *Public Library of Science Biology, 2*(4), E106.

Schweinhart, L., Barnes, H., & Weikart, D. (1993). *Significant Benefits: The High/Scope Perry Preschool Study Through Age 27* (No. 10). Ypsilanti, MI: High/Scope Press.

Shannon, C., Champoux, M., & Suomi, S. J. (1998). Rearing condition and plasma cortisol in rhesus monkey infants. *American Journaj of Primatology, 46*(4), 311–321.

Shortt, S. E. (2004). Making sense of social capital, health and policy. *Health Policy, 70*(1), 11–22.

Sin, D. D., Svenson, L. W., Cowie, R. L., & Man, S. F. (2003). Can universal access to health care eliminate health inequities between children of poor and nonpoor families?: A case study of childhood asthma in Alberta. *Chest, 124*(1), 51–56.

Sloan, R. P., Huang, M. H., Sidney, S., Liu, K., Williams, O. D., & Seeman, T. (2005). Socioeconomic status and health: Is parasympathetic nervous system activity an intervening mechanism? *International Journal of Epidemiology, 34*(2), 309–315.

Smedley, B. D., & Syme, S. L. (2000). *Promoting health: Intervention strategies from social and behavioral research.* Washington, DC: Institute of Medicine, National Academy Press.

Smith, G. W., Aubry, J. M., Dellu, F., Contarino, A., Bilezikjian, L. M., Gold, L. H., et al. (1998). Corticotropin releasing factor receptor 1-deficient mice display decreased anxiety, impaired stress response, and aberrant neuroendocrine development. *Neuron, 20*(6), 1093–1102.

Spady, D. W., Schopflocher, D. P., Svenson, L. W., & Thompson, A. H. (2005). Medical and psychiatric comorbidity and health care use among children 6 to 17 years old. *Archives of Pediatrics and Adolescent Medicine, 159*(3), 231–237.

Starfield, B. (1991). Childhood morbidity: Comparisons, clusters, and trends. *Pediatrics, 88*(3), 519–526.

Starfield, B., Hankin, J., Steinwachs, D., Horn, S., Benson, P., Katz, H., et al. (1985). Utilization and morbidity: Random or tandem? *Pediatrics, 75*(2), 241–247.

Starfield, B., Katz, H., Gabriel, A., Livingston, G., Benson, P., Hankin, J., et al. (1984). Morbidity in childhood: A longitudinal view. *New England Journal of Medicine, 310*, 824–829.

Steptoe, A., Feldman, P. J., Kunz, S., Owen, N., Willemsen, G., & Marmot, M. (2002). Stress responsivity and socioeconomic status: A mechanism for increased cardiovascular disease risk? *European Heart Journal, 23*, 1757–1763.

Steptoe, A., Willemsen, G., Kunz-Ebrecht, S. R., & Owen, N. (2003). Socioeconomic status and hemodynamic recovery from mental stress. *Psychophysiology, 40*(2), 184–191.

Strayer, F. F. (1989). Co-adaptation within the early peer group: A psychobiological study of social competence. In B. H. Schneider (Ed.), *Social competence in developmental perspective* (pp. 145–172): Kluwer Academic.

Strayer, F. F., & Trudel, M. (1984). Developmental changes in the nature and function of social dominance among young children. *Ethology and Sociobiology, 5*, 279–295.

Suchday, S., Krantz, D. S., & Gottdiener, J. S. (2005). Relationship of socioeconomic markers to daily life ischemia and blood pressure reactivity in coronary artery disease patients. *Annals of Behavioral Medicine, 30*(1), 74–84.

Suomi, S. J. (1987). Genetic and maternal contributions to individual differences in Rhesus monkey biobehavioral development. In N. Krasnagor (Ed.), *Psychobiological aspects of behavioral development* (pp. 397–419). New York: Academic Press.

Syme, S. L. (1998). Social and economic disparities in health: Thoughts about intervention. *Milbank Quarterly, 76*(3), 493–505, 306–497.

Syme, S. L. (2005). Historical perspective: The social determinants of disease —some roots of the movement. *Epidemiologic Perspectives & Innovations, 2*(1), 2.

Turkheimer, E. (1998). Heritability and biological explanation. *Psychological Review, 105*(4), 782–791.

Turner, J. R., & Hewitt, J. K. (1992). Twin studies of cardiovascular response to psychological challenge: A review and suggested future directions. *Annals of Behavioral Medicine, 14*(1), 12–20.

Valentino, R. J., Curtis, A. L., Page, M. E., Pavcovich, L. A., & Florin-Lechner, S. M. (1998). Activation of the locus ceruleus brain noradrenergic system during stress: Circuitry, consequences, and regulation. *Advances in Pharmacology, 42*, 781–784.

van der Saag, P. T., Caldenhoven, E., & van de Stolpe, A. (1996). Molecular mechanisms of steroid action: A novel type of cross-talk between glucocorticoids and NF-kappa B transcription factors. *European Respiratory Journal, Supplement 22*, 146s-153s.

Vaughn, B., & Waters, E. (1978). Social organization among preschooler peers: Dominance, attention and sociometric correlates. In D. R. Omark, F. F. Strayer & D. Freedman (Eds.), *Dominance relations: An ethological view of human conflict and social interaction* (pp. 359–380). New York: Garland STPM Press.

Vazquez, D. M., Watson, S. J., & Lopez, J. F. (2000, July). *Failure to terminate stress responses in children with psychosocial dwarfism: A mechanism for growth failure.* Paper presented at the International Conference of Infant Studies, Brighton, England.

Verhulst, F. C., & Van der Ende, J. (1995). The eight-year stability of problem behavior in an epidemiologic sample. *Pediatric Research, 38*(4), 612–617.

Viau, V. (2002). Functional cross-talk between the hypothalamic-pituitary-gonadal and -adrenal axes. *Journal of Neuroendocrinology, 14*(6), 506–513.

Weaver, I. C., Cervoni, N., Champagne, F. A., D'Alessio, A. C., Sharma, S., Seckl, J. R., et al. (2004). Epigenetic programming by maternal behavior. *Nature Neuroscience, 7*(8), 847–854.

Weaver, I. C., Diorio, J., Seckl, J. R., Szyf, M., & Meaney, M. J. (2004). Early environmental regulation of hippocampal glucocorticoid receptor gene expression: Characterization of intracellular mediators and potential genomic target sites. *Annals of the New York Academy of Sciences, 1024*, 182–212.

Wells, K. B., Golding, J. M., & Burnam, M. A. (1988). Psychiatric disorder in a sample of the general population with and without chronic medical conditions. *American Journal of Psychiatry, 145*(8), 976–981.

Wetmur, J. G., Lehnert, G., & Desnick, R. J. (1991). The delta-aminolevulinate dehydratase polymorphism: Higher blood lead levels in lead workers and environmentally exposed children with the 1–2 and 2–2 isozymes. *Environmental Research, 56*(2), 109–119.

White, B. P., Gunnar, M. R., Larson, M. C., Donzella, B., & Barr, R. G. (2000). Behavioral and physiological responsivity and patterns of sleep and daily salivary cortisol in infants with and without colic. *Child Development, 71*, 862–877.

White, K. L., Williams, T. F., & Greenberg, B. G. (1961). The ecology of medical care. *New England Journal of Medicine, 265*, 885–892.

Wilkinson, R. G. (1996). *Unhealthy societies: The afflictions of inequality.* London: Routledge.

Willemsen-Swinkels, S. H., Bakermans-Kranenburg, M. J., Buitelaar, J. K., van IJzendoorn, M. H., & van Engeland, H. (2000). Insecure and disorganised attachment in children with a pervasive developmental disorder: Relationship with social interaction and heart rate. *Journal of Child Psychology & Psychiatry, 41*(6), 759–767.

Willms, J. D. (2004). *Reading achievement in Canada and the United States: Findings from the OECD Programme for International Student Assessment.* Gatineau, Quebec, Canada: Human Resources Skills and Development Canada.

Worthman, C. M., Angold, A., & Costello, E. J. (1998, February 26–28). *Stress, reactivity and psychiatric risk in adolescents.* Paper presented at the biennial meeting of the Society for Research on Adolescence, San Diego, CA.

Yehuda, R. (2002). Post-traumatic stress disorder. *New England Journal of Medicine, 346*(2), 108–114.

Yehuda, R., Halligan, S. L., & Bierer, L. M. (2001). Relationship of parental trauma exposure and PTSD to PTSD, depressive and anxiety disorders in offspring. *Journal of Psychiatric Research, 35*(5), 261–270.

Yehuda, R., Halligan, S. L., & Grossman, R. (2001). Childhood trauma and risk for PTSD: Relationship to intergenerational effects of trauma, parental PTSD, and cortisol excretion. *Development & Psychopathology, 13,* 733–753.

Zaharia, M. D., Kulczycki, J., Shanks, N., Meaney, M. J., & Anisman, H. (1996). The effects of early postnatal stimulation on Morris water-maze acquisition in adult mice: Genetic and maternal factors. *Psychopharmacology (Berl), 128*(3), 227–239.

Zahn-Waxler, C., Klimes-Dougan, B., & Slattery, M. J. (2000). Internalizing problems of childhood and adolescence: Prospects, pitfalls, and progress in understanding the development of anxiety and depression. *Development & Psychopathology, 12*(3), 443–466.

Chapter 4

Understanding Developmental Processes of Resilience and Psychopathology: Implications for Policy and Practice

Byron Egeland
University of Minnesota

Much has changed in the study of psychopathology since the publication in 1984 of the special issue of *Child Development* devoted to the new field of developmental psychopathology. One of the major changes was the shift from a linear approach, where it was believed that a variable leads directly to an outcome or that variables contributing to an outcome make independent contributions to such outcomes. Perhaps the best example is the nature–nurture debate, where each side erroneously assumed that genes and environment made separate and independent contributions to the phenotypic outcomes of development (Gottlieb & Tucker-Halpern, 2002). As a result of recent research findings showing that social context is a powerful determinant of phenotypic expression (e.g., Caspi et al., 2002), this dualistic conception of causality is being replaced by an interactive or coactive view of causality.

The thesis of this symposium, as well as a basic premise of the field of developmental psychopathology, is that the processes and mechanisms underlying human development and behavior are not explainable by a linear model within a biological or social approach. Rather, a

83

multilevel integrative analysis is required (Cacioppo, Berntson, Sheridan, & McClintock, 2000). This does not mean that all research examining the developmental precursors and pathways leading to psychopathology must include both the broad domains of biology and the social world. Certainly, within each of these domains, there are many levels of analysis that require an examination of interactive and co-active effects.

My goal in this chapter is to review selected findings on resilience and psychopathology from the Minnesota Longitudinal Study of Parents and Children (MLSPC), a 30-year longitudinal study of high-risk families, and discuss the implications of these findings for clinical practice and policy. Our focus has been on developmental outcomes, the family, the broader context in which development occurs, and the dynamic interaction or transaction of the child and environment. Specifically, we were interested in tracing patterns of developmental adaptation at each developmental period. At the time we began our study, the mapping of the genome did not exist, and the measures of brain development and other biological functions underlying behavior were crude or nonexistent. Moreover, our interest in developmental adaptation did not necessitate the inclusion of biological assessments to trace patterns of continuity/discontinuity across the life span.

The initial aim of MLSPC was to use a prospective approach to study the antecedents of good and poor parenting and parent–child relationships, with a particular emphasis on identifying the antecedents and consequences of child maltreatment in high-risk families with young children. Even though we remain interested in the causes and consequences of maltreatment, the emphasis of our work has expanded to include the identification of the developmental pathways and processes that lead to child maladaptation, behavior problems, and psychopathology, as well as to competent functioning and resilience. Before reviewing our findings and their implications for practice and policy, I briefly describe the historical context at the time we designed the study.

INTEGRATING CLASSICAL RISK RESEARCH WITH A DEVELOPMENTAL PERSPECTIVE

We were greatly influenced in the design of our longitudinal study by the risk research approach that became popular in the 1960s and 1970s. During this period, a number of studies were initiated that followed samples of children who were at risk for psychiatric disorders, particularly schizophrenia. Because of problems inherent in the study of individuals after they were diagnosed with schizophrenia, Mednick and McNeil (1968) proposed following prospectively a sample of children of parents diagnosed with schizophrenia in an effort to understand the etiology of the disorder.

The goal of these studies was to establish a link between the risk factor and schizophrenia or a "marker of schizophrenia," which consisted of schizotype characteristics that were assumed to be related to the adult disorder. The expectations for this early risk research were high, and a number of characteristics were found to be associated with these markers and a number of differences were found between children who were high versus low risk for schizophrenia (Watt, Anthony, Wynne, & Rolf, 1984). Overall, however, the findings were disappointing and did not provide much information about the etiology of schizophrenia.

There are a number of reasons why these early risk studies provided little information about the etiology of schizophrenia. During this time, a developmental perspective was not integrated into mainstream clinical psychology or psychiatry. With a few exceptions, most investigators viewed child and adolescent psychopathology as a downward extension of adult psychopathology. Even though these early studies of children at risk for schizophrenia were longitudinal, they lacked a developmental perspective.

The early longitudinal studies were only interested in homotypic continuity of symptoms or schizotypal characteristics across time. This search for symptom continuity was based on the assumption that child psychopathology was a downward extension of adult psychopathology. Without a developmental perspective, the early risk researchers did not recognize that, generally, continuity lies at the level of function and meaning, and that the patterns of behavior and adaptation leading to psychopathology are likely to differ in each developmental period.

Norman Garmezy, one of the leaders of the Risk Research Consortium (a group of 14 risk research projects studying the etiology of schizophrenia), and Thomas Achenbach, his PhD student here in Minnesota, were two individuals who brought a developmental framework to risk research and the field of child psychopathology. Garmezy's leadership in the field of risk research, along with his developmental perspective, provided much of the impetus for the new field of developmental psychopathology.

Another explanation for the disappointing findings of the early risk research is that they were based on a linear model. It was assumed that a single risk factor or the concurrence of a combination of risk factors could be identified that was directly related to the occurrence of the disorder. One of the first studies to consider the interactive effects of risk was the Rochester Longitudinal Study. Several years prior to our study, Sameroff and his colleagues enrolled a sample of children of parents who had a variety of psychiatric diagnoses and found that parents' mental illness was related to child outcomes. However, a better predictor of poor child outcomes was low socioeconomic status (Sameroff, Seifer, Baldwin, & Baldwin, 1993). Their findings highlighted the environment as being as important as the child's biological heritage. More importantly, they found the interactive effects of the child's environment and biological heritage were the best predictor of the functioning of high-risk children born of parents with schizophrenia and other disorders.

Realizing the shortcomings of a linear model for interpreting findings from the early risk studies of children born to mothers diagnosed with schizophrenia, Gottesman and Shields (1972) proposed a model where schizophrenia was believed to occur as a result of a combined biological vulnerability and environmental adversity. Gottesman, a behavior geneticist and colleague of Norman Garmezy, argued that the individual was born with an inherited diathesis, but would not become schizophrenic unless the stress was above a certain threshold. In this model, the biological vulnerability and environmental factors are seen as independent, and the inherited diathesis is seen as fixed. Only the variability in the environment resulted in the expression of the illness. Even though Gottesman's interactionist model represented a major advance for the field, the emphasis was on separating influences into discrete categories rather than recognizing their interdependence.

In the summer of 1973, Arnold Sameroff, who was a visiting professor at ICD, provided me with a preprint copy of a chapter that strongly influenced the design of the MLSPC. Sameroff and Chandler (1975) added a dynamic component to the interactional model. In this classic chapter, they proposed the transactional model, which emphasized the interdependence of the individual and environment in the form of a complex interplay between the two. The child influences the environment, the environment influences the child, and each is changed in a dynamic fashion as they interact across time. Child outcomes are not due to biology or environment, but to a complex interplay between the two. Sameroff & Chandler's view of the interdependence of the individual and his or her social world and their transaction across time provided a model for our original grant proposal to study the antecedents of child maltreatment.

POSITIVE FUNCTIONING OF CHILDREN AT RISK

One of the findings that most surprised the early risk researchers was the unexpected "health" of children at risk due to parental mental illness. These findings led Garmezy and others to focus on positive adaptation, as well as psychopathology, in a high-risk sample. In 1977, Garmezy initiated Project Competence, a longitudinal study of elementary- age school children designed to identify processes leading to competence as well as maladaptation (Garmezy, Masten, & Tellegen, 1984).

Researchers attempting to understand positive outcomes among high-risk children had a difficult time explaining or conceptualizing this phenomenon. The term *invulnerable* was first applied to the subgroup of well-functioning children of mentally ill parents. However, invulnerability implied that the child possessed an inherent characteristic that made him or her immune to the negative effects of risk and adversity. Anthony (1974) used the analogy of three dolls made of glass, plastic, and steel who are exposed to the same risk, a blow of the hammer. The first doll breaks, the second shows a dent and thus is scarred for life, and the third is unfazed by the blow. He goes on to say that the "outcomes would be different if their environments were to buffer the blows" (Anthony, 1987). The implication is that the child may be predisposed to either break or withstand the blow and that only the environment can moderate the effects of adversity.

Despite the popular appeal that some individuals possess a certain characteristic that makes them immune to risk and adversity, researchers quickly recognized that the concept of invulnerability is unrealistic. Over time, invulnerability gave way to the less provocative term "resilience." Even though resilience implies an acquired and dynamic ability to cope, it, like invulnerability, has been viewed by many as an inherent characteristic possessed by some individuals that makes them able to cope with adversity. This view of resilience fails to accurately describe or account for positive functioning in the face of adversity. One reason is that positive functioning of children experiencing adversity varies across domains, situations, and ages, suggesting that resilience is a dynamic, state-like quality of the system, rather than a trait-like feature of the individual. Clearly, this phenomenon, like child psychopathology, must be viewed within a developmental framework.

DESIGN OF THE MINNESOTA LONGITUDINAL STUDY OF PARENTS AND CHILDREN

Using a risk research strategy to study the antecedents and consequences of early maltreatment, we enrolled a sample of first-time pregnant women who were patients at the Minneapolis Public Health Clinic. The risk factor was poverty, which also included a number of co-occurring risk factors, such as mother's age at the time of the birth of her first child (mean 20.5; range 12–34 years), marital status (62% single parents), and educational level (41% did not complete high school). In selecting the constructs and variables that would predict the range of parenting and parent–child relationship outcomes, we were influenced by the findings from the Rochester Longitudinal Study that showed social context was a more powerful risk factor than any of the parental illness measures, and that the dynamic transaction of the child and social context were of critical importance for understanding developmental outcome. I was also influenced by attachment theory.

Bowlby (1969/1982) argued that children develop within a network of influences operating on many levels: genetic, biological, psychological, and social. It was also about this time that Bronfenbrenner (1977) proposed his ecological model. He described a range of environmental influences such as community, cultural, and economic, which have indirect effects on parenting practices and the child, to parenting practices that have direct effects on the child. To account for the range of parenting and child outcomes, we selected concepts and variables from different ecological levels including: child temperament and characteristics assessed at birth, 3, and 6 months; parents' personality, beliefs, attitudes, and expectations regarding their child and their relationship with their child; observations of parent–child interaction; process and dynamics within the family; and life circumstances (e.g. social support and stressful live events). Based on these concepts, detailed and comprehensive assessments at frequent time periods (e.g., 8 times during the first year, not counting nurses' daily ratings of infant temperament while the baby was in the newborn nursery), using multiple informants in multiple settings including our own preschool where children were observed every day, were used to assess the range of developmental adaptation and factors influencing these outcomes.

The MLSPC reflects an innovative integration of two perspectives. In a broad sense, our perspective was a risk research approach involving a study of the child and different levels of his or her environment and social context. With the introduction of Alan Sroufe as a co-Principal Investigator in 1978, a strong developmental perspective informed our study of high-risk children. It was about this time that Alan and Everett Waters wrote their seminal *Child Development* article on the organizational model of development (Sroufe, 1990; Sroufe & Waters, 1977). The organizational model provided the developmental framework for our study of competence and psychopathology. Although the field of developmental psychopathology does not subscribe to a particular theory, the organizational model of development has become the dominant model for understanding normal and atypical development across the lifespan (Cicchetti, 1993; Cicchetti & Cohen, 1995; Sroufe and Rutter, 1984).

According to the organizational perspective, development is a hierarchical integrative process that occurs within and across biological, social, emotional, cognitive, representational, and linguistic systems. At each period of development, a qualitative reorganization occurs whereby the individual moves from a state of diffuse organization to greater integration. Through this series of qualitative reorganizations, prior experience and adaptation are not lost, but instead are incorporated into new patterns of adaptation (Sroufe & Waters, 1977; Werner, 1957). At each developmental period, adaptation or competence refers to the individual's ability to use internal and external resources to successfully negotiate developmentally salient issues. For example, successful adaptation or competence in infancy would include a secure parent–infant attachment relationship, whereas maladaptation would include an anxious pattern of attachment. A child's pattern of adaptation at one developmental period is probabilistically, not deterministically, related to later levels of functioning. Because development is cumulative, competence at one point in time is likely to be related to competence in the next developmental period. Conversely, maladaptation at a particular developmental period (e.g., insecure attachment) increases the likelihood of maladaptation at the next developmental period, and the longer the individual is on the deviant pathway, the greater the likelihood of psychopathology (Egeland & Carlson, 2003). This perspective has informed our understanding of pathways toward competence and psychopathology in the context of prior adversity.

RESILIENCE AS PROCESS

Influenced by this organizational perspective, we have come to conceptualize resilience as a developmental process, contrary to the earlier views, already described, that represented resilience as a static trait of the individual. In our view, resilience "refers to an ongoing process of garnering resources that enable the individual to negotiate current issues adaptively and provides a foundation for dealing with subsequent challenges as well as for recovering from reversals of fortune" (Yates, Egeland, & Sroufe, 2003). Thus, children with a history of early competence are better able to take advantage of the resources available to them in the face of adversity. Whereas competence (and maladaptation) refers to the quality of functioning at a particular developmental period, resilience (and psychopathology) refers to a developmental process over time.

Within this view, an early history of positive developmental adaptation engenders resilience. However, with the notable exceptions of the Kaui Longitudinal Study (Werner & Smith, 1992) and Murphy and Moriarty's 1976 study of vulnerability and coping, much of the research on resilience has focused on middle childhood and adolescence. Consequently, the role of an early history of developmental competence is absent from most discussions of protective factors and resilience. Our body of data highlights the need to consider early development in any discussion of resilience. Our findings have repeatedly demonstrated the importance of an early history of positive developmental adaptation as a powerful source of enduring influence on a child's subsequent developmental adaptation, even in the face of adversity (Egeland, Carlson, & Sroufe, 1993; Yates et al., 2003). We have found that a developmental history of consistent and supportive care fosters early competence, which in turn plays a crucial role in later adaptation, even in the face of adversity. A competent child, when faced with adversity, is better able to use both internal and external resources to cope and achieve positive adaptation compared to a child with an early history of maladaptation.

Specific findings highlight the importance of early competence in the development of resilience and provide support for the conceptualization of resilience as a process. For example, from our disadvantaged sample, we selected a subsample of families who had experienced a substantial number of stressful life events during the preschool years (Pianta, Egeland, & Sroufe, 1990). Using cluster analysis, a group of resilient children was identified based on academic achievement, social acceptance, emotional health, and low behavior problem scores. This group was compared to another group of children who were functioning in the average to poor range on these measures in Grades 1 to 3. Compared to the average/poor functioning group, the resilient children were found to have higher scores on language skills, quality and organization of the home environment (HOME scales), and, for girls, maternal characteristics (e.g., ego strength). Child IQ (WPPSI) was not found to be a protective factor for boys or girls. The most important predictor among this high-stressed subsample of children who were functioning competently in middle childhood was an early history of positive developmental adaptation (Egeland & Kreutzer, 1991). A history of positive developmental adaptation consisted of a secure mother–infant attachment relationship, flexibility and creativity in approach to a frustrating problem situation at 24 and 42 months, and effective, persistent, and enthusiastic problem solving by the mother–child dyad at 24 and 42 months. This history of developmental competence over the first 42 months was more than a protective factor—it played a key role in the process of resilience.

What are the mechanisms by which an early history of positive adaptation engenders resilience? First, an early history of developmental competence is relevant to the acquisition of coping capacities and enables the child to draw on both internal and external resources (Egeland et al., 1993; Yates et al., 2003). Of the many internal and external resources that have been identified as protective factors, the most widely identified and perhaps the most significant is an alternative supportive caregiver. In our own work, we have found that an alternative caregiver, long-term psychotherapy, or a supportive spouse were protective factors for individuals who were maltreated but broke the cycle of abuse in the next generation (Egeland, Bosquet, & Levy-Chung, 2002). High-risk adolescents who graduated from high school despite expectations that they would drop out due to low grades and poor school performance reported that the number one reason they did graduate was because a particular teacher took an interest in them and provided support (Englund, Luckner, Whaley, & Egeland, 2004). Appleyard,

Egeland, van Dulmen, and Sroufe (2005) found that good quality social support moderated the effects of high family stressful life events, whereas disruptive social support exacerbated the negative effects of stress.

It is not surprising that good quality alternative social support is a major protective factor against the negative consequences of various forms of adversity. Most children who experience adversity at some point are exposed to a caring adult, teacher, coach, relative, minister, or neighbor. However, many children for whom supportive adults are available have not achieved a level of social competence whereby they can use this resource to achieve a positive developmental adaptation in the face of adversity. A protective mentoring relationship with an older individual is helpful only for children who have the capacity to effectively engage their social environment (Yates et al., 2003). To engage the social environment, the child must be able to trust others and have the competence to interact in a productive recipro-cal fashion.

A history of competence provides the foundation that enables the child to take advantage of available social support. Children who cope in the face of adversity are likely to have a history of a secure attachment in infancy and, enabled by the development of behavioral and emotional self-regu-lation, a capacity to function in an autonomous fashion in toddlerhood (Egeland & Kreutzer, 1991). These competencies develop within a warm, sensitive, emotionally responsive interaction between infant and primary caregiver. Through repeated positive interactions, the infant develops expectations that his or her needs will be met and a confidence in the avail-ability of the caregiver as a source of comfort in times of distress. According to Bowlby (1969/1982) and other attachment theorists, through these early experiences, children develop a cognitive model that influences the qual-ity of later interactions with others. The securely attached child internalizes a representation (i.e., an inner working model) of relationships as caring and trustworthy and of the self as worthy of love. As these children grow up, they expect to be accepted by their peers, and they feel confident in seek-ing assistance from others, such as teachers, when needed. Conversely, the infant whose caregiver is unavailable, inconsistent, or rejecting will develop a belief that others cannot be trusted and that the self is unworthy of love. Children who have negative expectations about self and the availability of others are less likely to take advantage of internal and external resources, especially social support, in times of distress. According to Bowlby, inner working models continue to affect how people feel about themselves and relate to others throughout their lifespan. These deep assumptions about self and others affect perceptions and expectations that ultimately influ-ence behavior. Therefore, a child's early history affects his or her ability to take advantage of the social support in the environment through its impact on inner working models.

An early history of competence not only plays a key role in the process of resilience and later positive adaptation, but also has special significance for self-righting of deflection from developmental adaptation. We hypothesized that securely attached infants who later show maladaptive functioning would rebound quickly should life circumstances improve. Attachment theory suggests that, despite change in developmental adaptation, early experience remains influential in later functioning. To test this hypothesis, we compared two groups of children in elementary school on teacher judgments of peer competence and emotional health (Sroufe, Egeland & Kreutzer, 1990). Children in both groups had been functioning (equivalently) poorly on three assessments across the 3½- to 4½-year period. One group, however, had shown consistently positive adaptation during the infant and toddler periods, including secure attachment, whereas the other group had functioned poorly throughout their early years. Compared to children with poor early adaptation, children showing positive adaptation in the infant/toddler period showed greater rebound in the elementary school years, despite poor functioning in the intervening preschool period. Results from regression analyses indicated that early adaptation added unique variance in predicting adaptation in middle childhood, even after more recent assessments of adaptation were included. Thus, there was a lasting impact of early history, even in the context of current or intermediate developmental adaptation. A similar study in adolescence showed that level of functioning in adolescence depended on both early and later developmental adaptation. A positive early foundation appeared to be a protective factor for some children, allowing them to rebound from a difficult middle childhood (Sroufe, Carlson, Levy, & Egeland, 1999).

In summary, our results demonstrate that resilience as a process begins early and continues throughout development. Competence in early development appears to be a particularly salient contributor to resilience processes throughout childhood and adolescence. Competence at one developmental period promotes competence at later developmental periods. Furthermore, early competence predicts a more adaptive response to later adversity (i.e., resilience) and a return to adaptation after a period of maladaptation (i.e., recovery). A history of competence seems to allow individuals to take advantage of resources in their environment through its influence on inner working models. These findings have clear implications for intervention, which is discussed later.

Even though we have argued for the importance of the role of an early history of competence in the process of resilience, we do not rule out the importance of other systems that allow an individual to take advantage of various resources in coping with adversity. As Masten and Coatsworth (1998) point out, there are "powerful adaptive systems" that foster and protect the development of competence in optimal as well as adverse environments. Future resilience research needs to examine the role of various adaptive systems in coping with adversity across the life span.

ANTECEDENTS AND PATHWAYS TO ANXIETY DISORDER

Two papers have emerged from MLSPC that have focused on the etiology and pathways leading to anxiety disorder in childhood and adolescence. In our first paper, we examined the roles of maternal anxiety, child temperament, and quality of attachment during infancy in predicting lifetime rates of anxiety disorders at 17.5 years (Warren, Huston, Egeland, & Sroufe, 1997). Remarkably, despite the 16-year gap between assessment of predictor and outcome variables, we found significant associations between several of the infant risk measures and anxiety disorders. Specifically, infant temperament variables that reflected low thresholds of arousability and decreased ability to modulate arousal were associated with increased risk for anxiety disorders. Also, having an anxious/resistant attachment relationship at 12 months was associated with a two-fold increase in risk of developing one or more anxiety disorders. Furthermore, when temperament and attachment variables were considered simultaneously in regression analyses, anxious/resistant attachment, but not temperament, remained a significant predictor of anxiety disorders, highlighting the potentially critical role of the parent–child relationship in the etiology of anxiety disorders.

In a second paper, we examined a comprehensive model of the etiology and maintenance of anxiety symptoms across development within a developmental psychopathology framework (Bosquet & Egeland, in press). Using path analyses, findings revealed several potential factors that may mediate associations between infant temperament (nonoptimal summary score from the Neonatal Behavioral Assessment Scale) and anxious attachment and anxiety risk. Notably, neonatal temperament and an insecure attachment history in infancy made independent contributions to the prediction of emotion regulation difficulties in preschool, and emotion regulation difficulties in preschool predicted anxiety symptoms in childhood. Furthermore, anxiety symptoms show moderate stability throughout childhood and adolescence, suggesting that children who experienced anxiety difficulties early in development were at risk for remaining anxious. Insecure attachment in infancy also predicted later developmental incompetence in middle childhood, which was associated with increased anxiety symptoms during preadolescence. Insecure attachment also predicted insecure peer representations in preadolescence, and these representations of relationship predicted anxiety symptoms in adolescence. Finally, although developmental incompetence predicted various negative outcomes, including depressive and externalizing symptoms, the overall model tested was specific in predicting anxiety symptoms and not psychopathology in general. Specifically, the model accounted for 20% of the variance in predicting anxiety disorders, and the same model only accounted for 7% and 7% of the variance in predicting depressive and externalizing symptoms respectively.

EXTERNALIZING BEHAVIOR PROBLEMS

Our studies of pathways toward externalizing behavior problems further demonstrate the salience of early relational experiences for later adjustment. Our results suggest that an early history of anxious attachment, particularly anxious-avoidant ("A") attachment, is a major factor placing a young child on a pathway to disruptive and oppositional behavior in preschool. During the preschool period, observers rated a subsample of children with anxious attachment histories as more dependent on their teachers, less socially skilled, and less agentic (i.e., confident, assertive) than children with secure attachment histories. Furthermore, teachers rated anxious-avoidant children as more impulsive and as having more total behavior problems than children in either the secure or anxious-resistant group, suggesting more and varied behavior problems in the avoidant group. In a second set of analyses, we found significant differences in attachment histories between a group of children with acting out/inattentive behavior problems and a comparison group of competent preschoolers. Of the 14 children classified as anxiously attached at both 12 and 18 months, only two were in the well-functioning group in preschool. In contrast, 15 of the 21 stable secure children were in the competent preschool group (Erickson, Sroufe, & Egeland, 1985).

Although results supported continuity between attachment quality and preschool behavior, there were exceptions to predicted outcomes. Examination of these exceptions demonstrated developmental coherence, although the results of these analyses must be considered tentative due to the small sample. We found that change from anxious attachment in infancy to competent functioning in preschool was related to quality of caregiving at 42 months. Mothers of children without behavior problems in preschool were observed to be respectful of children's autonomy, allowing the child to explore and attempt tasks without intrusion. These mothers were warm and supportive, structuring tasks carefully, providing well-timed cues to help the child, and setting firm, consistent limits without being hostile. Moreover, home environments provided the stimulation necessary to foster healthy development through appropriate play materials and active parental involvement. The occurrence of stressful life events was unrelated to deflections in developmental pathways from infancy to preschool. Children who demonstrated a change from a secure attachment in infancy to behavior problems in preschool experienced less effective caregiving in the intervening period. Based on laboratory observations, mothers of these children were found to be less supportive of their children's efforts to solve problems at 24 months, and less effective in structuring tasks and setting consistent expectations at 42 months. Home observations at 30 months found these children lacking in age-appropriate play material and mother–child interaction in the home, compared with preschool children without behavior problems (Erickson et al., 1985).

Consistent with the developmental pathway model, longitudinal data demonstrated that adaptation and maladaptation in early development were increasingly related to functioning in middle childhood and adolescence, and change was lawful. Of the preschool acting-out group, 81% showed significant behavior problems in 2 of the first 3 years of elementary school as rated by teachers, compared to 27% of the competent children in preschool (Egeland, Kalkoske, Gottesman, & Erickson, 1990). Deflections in expected pathways (decline as well as improvement) in individual functioning between preschool and elementary school were related to change in maternal stressful life events, overall maternal functioning (e.g., decrease or increase in depression), family relationship status, and organization in the home. Specifically, decline in functioning was related to high scores on family stressful life events and maternal depression, and low scores on the stimulation, quality, and organization of the home environment. Those who showed improved functioning were found to have higher scores on measures of the home environment and lower scores on measures of maternal depression. These findings demonstrate that when caregiving and contextual factors remain stable, children tend to develop along a pathway established by early experience. When the caregiving and contextual factors change, there are likely to be associated changes in the developmental trajectory (Egeland et al., 1990).

A study of the relations between behavior problems in middle childhood and psychopathology in adolescence demonstrated the pathogenic effect of a cumulative history of maladaptation (Egeland, Pianta, & Ogawa, 1996). Looking prospectively, we found that 33% of children with no identified behavior problems in early elementary school met criteria for a clinical diagnosis as assessed by the Kiddie Schedule of Affective Disorders and Schizophrenia interview (K-SADS-MCP; Ambrosini, Metz, & Prabucki, 1989) at age 17½ years. In contrast, 71% of children above the clinical cutoff on behavior problems in early elementary school met criteria for conduct disorder at 17½ years. Looking retrospectively, we found that 88% of the individuals diagnosed with conduct disorder in adolescence had an early history of behavior problems. These findings support the notion that conduct disorder, like anxiety disorders, is a developmental construction and that one's early developmental history is of special significance.

Further support for the importance of early history is reflected in the findings from the study of early-onset life course persistors versus adolescent-onset antisocial behavior (Aguilar, Sroufe, Egeland, & Carlson, 2000). Based on parent, child, and teacher reports on the Child Behavior Checklist, the following groups were formed: never antisocial (NA), cases classified as "not antisocial early" and "not antisocial in adolescence"; adolescent-onset (AO), cases classified as "not antisocial early" and "antisocial in adolescence"; and early-onset life course persistent (EOP), cases classified as "antisocial early" and "antisocial in adolescence." Analyses indicated significant differences between the groups on measures of psychosocial but not temperament or neuropsychological factors. Overall, the results supported the presence of childhood-onset life course persisting and adolescence-onset antisocial behavior groups. These two groups differed on indices of socioemotional history within the first 3 years. Compared with the AO and NA groups, the EOP adolescents experienced significantly more early risk factors (single parenthood, mother's reported depression and overall life stress from the child's birth to 48 months, observed maternal sensitivity to infant signals at 3 and 6 months, attachment quality, indices of maltreatment, and mother's support and involvement with the child at 24 and 42 months). In addition, individuals in the EOP group were more likely to have been avoidantly attached at 12 and 18 months compared to the never antisocial group. The effects of these risk factors appeared to be cumulative in the development of antisocial behavior.

In our sample, we have repeatedly found a strong link between child abuse and neglect and later externalizing behavior problems (Egeland, Sroufe, & Erickson, 1983). To better understand this link, we have examined the developmental process by which children who were maltreated at an early age enter a pathway of externalizing behavior that ultimately leads to delinquency and antisocial behavior in adolescence (Egeland, Yates, Appleyard, & van Dulmen, 2002). Using structural equation modeling, we investigated the link between maltreatment in the early years and externalizing problems in middle childhood. Two developmental process variables—emotional and behavioral dysregulation and alienation from the primary caregiver—in the preschool period, both of which were based on observations of parents and children, were used to account for the link between early child maltreatment and externalizing in middle childhood. The observational variables used to form the dysregulation latent construct were a low score on ego control (i.e., the child lacked ability to deal with frustration) and high scores on intensity of help seeking and negative affect. The observational scales making up the alienation construct were a high rating on avoidance of mother, compliance with mother, and negativity toward mother. Our results indicated that alienation and, to a much lesser extent, dysregulation, helped explain the relation between early maltreatment and later antisocial behavior. The model including the developmental process variables was a better representation of the data than the model considering only the direct effect between early maltreatment and later antisocial behavior. Physical abuse in early childhood led to alienation in preschool, which then predicted early onset externalizing problems in the elementary school years, ultimately resulting in antisocial behavior in adolescence. These results suggest that alienation is a probable consequence of early maltreatment that contributes to the process leading to early onset externalizing trajectory.

In summary, our findings indicate moderate to high stability in externalizing symptoms from preschool to elementary school to adolescence. A history of anxious-avoidant attachment may be an important risk factor for early and persistent externalizing problems. Even though an insecure attachment history in infancy may initiate a deviant pathway ultimately leading to conduct disorder, supportive caregiving in the toddler and preschool period may lead to a deflection toward a more competent developmental pathway. Conversely, insensitive, unresponsive, and/or harsh caregiving has a cumulative impact on children's risk for developing persistent externalizing symptoms. Child abuse may be a particularly potent risk factor for externalizing symptoms through its impact on children's feelings of alienation.

DISSOCIATION

Our interest in dissociation began early when we observed that many of our mothers who were abused as children displayed dissociative symptoms such as disturbances of memory and identity (Egeland, Jacobvitz, & Sroufe, 1988). These mothers appeared to have erratic access to autobiographical memory, and to "split off" thoughts and emotions that normally would be integrated. Dissociation can be thought of as a structural separation of mental processes (thoughts, perceptions, emotions, and memory) that are ordinarily integrated (Spiegel & Cardeña, 1991). Dissociation is a coping mechanism in the face of severe trauma. By interfering with the normal storage, retrieval, and integration of thoughts, feelings, and memories, dissociation protects the individual by decreasing the hyperarousal and intense emotion and dysregulation associated with severe trauma (Putnam, 2000). This process manifests along a continuum of severity producing a range of clinical symptoms and, in extreme cases, gives rise to a set of psychiatric syndromes known as dissociative disorders.

Based on our interest in understanding the mechanisms involved in the transmission of maltreatment across generations, we tested the hypothesis that mothers who repeated the cycle appeared to dissociate. We compared mothers who were abused as children and who maltreated their own children to mothers who broke the cycle of abuse (Egeland & Sussman-Stillman, 1996). Thirty percent of mothers broke the cycle of abuse and 40% repeated the cycle (the remainder provided borderline care). We found that mothers who broke the cycle scored lower on the Dissociative Experience Scale (DES) than mothers who repeated the cycle. We concluded that, although dissociation during a traumatic event may serve a protective function by psychologically removing the individual from overwhelming trauma, over time dissociation becomes maladaptive. By dissociating, individuals compartmentalize their experiences, separating feelings from thoughts and actions. As a consequence, mothers who dissociated during their own childhood abuse and subsequently failed to integrate their experiences may be at greater risk for abusing their own children without empathy or feelings of pain. Our data also indicated that mothers who were low on dissociation scores despite an abuse history frequently reported positive psychotherapy experiences as a child or adolescent (Egeland & Sussman-Stillman, 1996). It appeared that mothers who received long-term intensive psychotherapy were able to integrate the abusive experience and understand how it affected their development of self and how they related to their own children. We hypothesized that mothers who dissociated repeated the cycle because they were less sensitive to the child's needs, lacked empathy, and did not connect the pain they experienced as a child with the pain they inflicted on their child.

Our observation that not all mothers who were abused dissociated the abusive experience led us to study the "etiology" of dissociative symptoms in the broader sample. In our first study, we examined the continuity of dissociative symptoms from infancy through young adulthood, the effects of trauma occurring at different ages, and the interactive effects of trauma and a disorganized pattern of attachment (Ogawa, Sroufe, Weinfield, Carlson, & Egeland, 1997). In our analyses, we were guided by several models, including Liotti's (1992) theory linking disorganized attachment, later trauma, and dissociation in adulthood, and Waller, Putnam, and Carlson's (1996) proposition that psychopathological dissociation is deviant and distinct from normal dissociative processes. We found moderate relations between trauma and concurrent dissociative symptoms from toddlerhood to elementary school. However, we also noted a shift in associations between trauma and dissociation in adolescence and young adulthood that indicated the importance of early trauma compared to later trauma in the development of dissociative behaviors. One explanation for the long term consequences of early trauma is that early trauma occurs during a critical developmental period when children are generally more dissociative and thus more likely to cope with trauma through dissociative defenses. Cole, Alexander, and Anderson (1996) argue that dissociation during the preschool period is a normative phenomenon. They provide evidence indicating that dissociative pathology in adulthood is most likely to occur when severe trauma, especially sexual abuse, occurs between the ages of 3 and 5. Dissociation at that age is one means for regulating emotions. Preschool children tend to see the world as "black or white." They use pretend play, imaginary playmates, and fantasy, which allow the preschoolers to isolate and tolerate confusing and complex aspects of their emotional world. As new cognitive skills emerge, preschoolers are able to coordinate and integrate multiple diverse aspects of an individual. Until this occurs, the young child simply ignores one part of an experience in order to deal with another.

The combination of a disorganized pattern of attachment in infancy and an early history of trauma emerged as strong predictors of dissociative symptoms in adolescence and young adulthood. A disorganized attachment history has been found to be a major risk factor for a variety of disorders (Carlson, 1998) and, in the case of dissociation, a disorganized attachment appears to make the individual more vulnerable to the negative effects of stress and trauma. Conversely, we found that a strong sense of self in early childhood (42- to 54-months) served as a protective factor against the development of later dissociative symptoms in the face of early trauma. The findings also supported the idea of a distinct group with pathological levels of dissociation, suggesting that pathological dissociation is not simply the high end of a continuum, but rather a separate group that represents an extreme deviation from normal development.

Before discussing the findings from the third study, which involved a more detailed examination of the relation between a disorganized pattern of attachment and dissociation (Carlson, 1998), I briefly describe attachment disorganization. Over the course of the first year, the majority of infants develop an attachment relationship with their primary caregiver. Based on a history of interaction with the primary caregiver, infants form a secure or anxious pattern of attachment. These attachment patterns represent an organized dyadic strategy for regulation of arousal when distressed and provide a secure base for exploration (Ainsworth, Blehar, Waters, & Wall, 1978; Sroufe, 1996). For some infants, however, no organized attachment pattern evolves from the infant–caregiver relationship (Carlson, 1998). In cases where the primary caregiver is frightening or frightened or where the caregiver is maltreating the child, the child may not develop an organized attachment pattern (Main & Hesse, 1990). If the infant is frightened by the caregiver, this places the infant in a paradox. The infant can neither approach the caregiver for comfort, nor flee. Such infants appear disorganized and disoriented, responding to distress in inconsistent ways (e.g., appearing to approach and avoid the caregiver at the same time).

In our third study, attachment disorganization in infancy was found to significantly predict behavior problems in preschool, elementary school, and high school, and psychopathology assessed by the K-SADS Diagnostic Interview at age 17½. Attachment disorganization, but not other forms of insecure attachment, appeared to have particular long-term implications for the development of dissociative symptoms in childhood and adolescence. Using regression analyses and structural equation modeling, we found disorganized attachment increased a child's risk for developing dissociative symptoms even with middle childhood behavior problems taken into account.

Results from these studies point to several key conclusions regarding development, developmental psychopathology, and intervention. First, dissociative symptoms have different meanings at different developmental stages, being more normative in early childhood and more indicative of pathology in later development. Second, the findings again implicate the importance of early experiences in both risk and resilience. In this case, although trauma at all ages was associated with dissociative symptomatology, the findings were particularly strong for early trauma and a history of disorganized attachment in infancy. The reasons for this association between early experiences and later dissociative pathology may be varied, ranging from the impact of early trauma and caregiving experiences on the brain and the development of self-regulatory abilities and sense of self, the increased risk for later developmental maladaptation following earlier maladaptation, and the fact that children exposed to trauma early in development are more likely to experience more severe and chronic trauma. Just as early trauma was a potent risk factor, a strong sense of self early in development was an important protective factor. Finally, the findings suggest that dissociation may be a mediator of the intergenerational transmission of child abuse and amenable to psychotherapeutic intervention.

IMPLICATIONS OF THE MLSPC FINDINGS FOR POLICY AND PRACTICE

For nearly 30 years, the MLSPC has examined the antecedents and pathways leading to positive as well as negative developmental outcomes resulting from risk and adversity. We have conducted this research within a broad developmental framework and across multiple levels of psychosocial analysis. Throughout our work, as highlighted in the findings presented in this chapter, we find that early experience plays a special role in developmental processes leading to psychopathology as well as to competence and resilience, and that early experience continues to have an effect for self-righting of deflection from developmental adaptation.

ENHANCING THE QUALITY OF THE
PARENT–CHILD RELATIONSHIP

Our studies of the development of anxiety disorders are just one example of how research conducted within a framework that integrates classical risk and developmental perspectives can inform our approach to intervention. We observed moderate stability of anxiety symptoms across development, suggesting that once children develop symptoms, they are likely to persist in the absence of effective intervention. Our data suggest that promoting emotion regulation abilities from an early age may significantly reduce children's risk for developing anxiety difficulties. Although characteristics of the child, such as temperament, may influence the child's emotion regulation abilities, our findings suggest that the quality of the parent–child relationship has a substantial influence. Evidence from multiple studies, including our own, suggest that programs that promote the development of secure attachment relationships may foster competent emotion regulation abilities, and consequently reduce risk for anxiety disorders as well as other disorders marked by emotion regulation difficulties (Egeland & Bosquet, 2002).

Repeatedly, our findings suggest that secure attachment relationships not only promote emotion regulation, but also support developmental competence and secure internal representations of self and self-in-relation-to-others, both of which appear to moderate pathways toward positive adaptation. Our results consistently demonstrate that early developmental competence operates as a powerful protective factor across childhood and adolescence. The implications of this research are clear—we must design programs and policies that promote positive developmental outcomes in the infancy and toddler periods, particularly programs that focus on enhancing the quality of parenting and the parent–child relationship.

This recommendation is certainly not new to those of us interested in preventing behavior problems, school failure, and psychopathology. There are many major local, state, and national programs designed to enhance positive development in the early years. These programs are highly varied in terms of goals, underlying assumptions and principles, recipients of program services (e.g., child, parent, or family), method of service delivery (e.g., home-based vs. center-based), and quantity and timing of services, as well as characteristics and training of interveners (Berlin, O'Neal, & Brooks-Gunn, 1998). Evaluative data on these early prevention/intervention programs are similarly varied, although long-term follow-up of both center-based (e.g., High/Scope) and home visitation indicate long-term benefits, including substantial financial benefits in the form of reduced economic burden on these families (Reynolds & Temple, in press).

POSITIVE REPRESENTATION
AND INTERNAL WORKING MODELS (IWM)

Even though most educators and mental health specialists would agree that early intervention is crucial for preventing later problems, they do not agree on the specific focus or goals. Our findings suggest that prevention programs for young children and their families should be designed to promote positive representational models by focusing on the relationship between parents and infant. We have concluded that both resilience and psychopathology derive from developmental processes that involve multiple levels, including internal processes such as representations of the self, of others, and of the self-with-others, which are formed in the early years. In addition, representations appear to be one of the mechanisms that account for continuity of both positive adaptation and maladaptation across developmental periods (Carlson, Sroufe, & Egeland, 2004).

The child whose past experience has resulted in a belief that others can be counted on for support is more likely to solicit and use available support for dealing with adversity, compared to a child who expects to be rebuffed by his social world. Similarly, the young child whose primary caregiver is emotionally unavailable or responds in an inconsistent, rejecting, or harsh fashion will expect others to be unavailable, rejecting, or hostile and view the self as unworthy of the love of others. Repeated patterns of interaction between infant and caregiver lay the foundation for mental representations, or inner working models, of the self and of relationships that guide contemporaneous and future behavior (Bowlby, 1969/1982).

According to a recent review (Berlin, 2005), there are 14 investigators who have used attachment theory and research as a framework for designing early preventative/intervention programs, and who have attempted to evaluate their program. In 1995, van Ijzendoorn and his colleagues did a review and meta-analysis of 12 attachment interventions and concluded that there were two types of programs: those designed to help parents become more sensitive to infant cues, and those designed to change parents' representation of how they were cared for by their own parents. It should be noted that, in another meta-analysis, these investigators found stronger relation between parents' IWM and their child's attachment classification than between parent behavior and their child's attachment classification (de Wolff & van Ijzendoorn, 1997). Parents' behavior does not serve as the linking mechanism or moderator between parent IWM and the child attachment classification (van Ijzendoorn, 1995). This suggests that efforts to modify parents' behavior will likely fail to the extent that the core representations that guide the behavior remain untouched by interventions. Thus, future treatment efforts must extend beyond the level of manifest behavior to tap core developmental processes and constructs that underlie observed patterns of continuity and intergenerational transmission.

Programs designed to change parents' representational model can be traced to the work of Fraiberg (1980) and the infant-parent psychotherapy (IPP) movement. Her eloquent description of "ghosts in the nursery" has provided a set of psychodynamic principles along with insight-oriented psychotherapy to help parents understand how their childhood experiences influence the care they provide their child. Fraiberg's IPP approach to change parents' representational models has abandoned the more traditional psychoanalytic principles in favor of Bowlby's (1980) attachment theory of IWM and research findings based on that theory.

Based on the findings from the MLSPC and using some of the principles from IPP, we developed STEEP (Steps Toward Effective Enjoyable Parenting), a comprehensive preventative program for high-risk, first-time mothers and their infants (Egeland & Erickson, 2004). This broad attachment-based program began during pregnancy with home visits that were flexible, allowing the facilitator to meet the mother where she was, to address needs as identified and defined by the mother, and to move as slowly as necessary in developing a trusting relationship. After delivery, the mother was invited to join a group of seven to nine other mothers with newborns. The group was led by the same facilitator who recruited the mother and made the home visits. For the next year (it is now a 2-year program), mother and infant met with the facilitator at least once a week, alternating between home visits and group. The goals of STEEP included: promote healthy realistic attitudes, beliefs, and expectations about pregnancy, childbirth, and childrearing and the parent–child relationship; foster greater understanding of child development and form realistic expectations for child behavior; promote a sensitive, predictable response to the baby's cues and signals; enhance parents' ability to see things from the child's point of view; facilitate the creation of a home environment that is safe, predictable, and conducive to optimal development; help parents identify and strengthen support networks for themselves and their child; and build and support life management skills and effective use of resources (Egeland & Erickson, 2004). One of the procedures used to help mothers achieve these goals involved assisting the mother to examine her feelings and experiences of her own childhood and to move toward a healthy resolution of early relationship issues in a way that freed her to respond in the most flexible, appropriate, and nurturing way to her own child. With a grant from NIMH to implement and evaluate, we found that the program had a positive impact on a number of outcome measures, including maternal sensitivity, although no differences were found between treatment and control group on the percentage of securely attached infants at 13 or 19 months. Although we did not have the resources to assess change at the level of mothers' representations, new tools such as the Adult Attachment Interview and its clinical applications provide powerful techniques for assessing parental attachment representations over time.

Lieberman, Weston, and Pawl (1991) used the IPP approach to promote a secure attachment among a group of children identified as anxiously attached at approximately 12 months, and found after 1 year that the intervention group was rated higher on goal-corrected partnership behavior, and lower on child avoidance and child anger toward the mother compared to the control group. The findings were encouraging. However, there were no differences between treatment and control on attachment classification at 12 months and there was no assessment of the parents' IWM. We are not aware of any attachment intervention that was designed to change parents' IWM that actually assessed IWM using the Adult Attachment Interview or any other accepted measure of representation (Egeland, Weinfield, Bosquet, & Cheng, 2000). Slade (2005) used Fonagy & colleagues' (2002) construct of reflective functions to design an attachment intervention to enhance mothers' capacity to "keep the baby in mind, to make sense of baby's internal states, emotions, thoughts, and intentions as well as her own." As an outcome measure, they used The Parent Development Interview (Slade, Aber, Berger, Bresgi, & Kaplan, 2003) to assess reflective functioning, which is similar to the Adult Attachment Interview. According to the investigators, the preliminary findings from a randomized clinical trial are encouraging (Slade, Sadler, & Mayes, 2005).

The goal of the attachment-based interventions is to promote a secure parent–infant attachment relationship that results in the child developing a representational model of parents being emotionally available and responsive, and of self as being worthy of parents' love. In our work, we find such secure representations to be a powerful antecedent of social competence (Sroufe, Egeland, & Carlson, 1999). As noted, the evaluation of the existing attachment-based interventions is quite encouraging, although most have not shown significantly more securely attached infants in the intervention group compared to the control group. There are many reasons these interventions have not had a positive effect on attachment classifications, one of which is that the programs have attempted to change parents' behavior, particularly maternal sensitivity, and have not focused on parents' representational models (Egeland et al., 2000). With less high-risk populations, the most effective attachment intervention appears to be a strategy that focuses on maternal sensitivity. We have argued that, for more high-risk multiproblem families where parents are more likely to have a negative representation of their caregiver and, consequently, a more negative representation of self, attachment-based interventions may need to focus more on the parents' IWM. Data indicate (Sroufe, Carlson, et al., 1999) that intervening at the level of behavior is tantamount to a "Band-Aid" solution, failing to address the underlying process that shapes the behavior.

To be sure, working individually with parents to help them resolve their own developmental histories is critical, but this kind of work must be complemented by a more systems-level approach at the level of the parent–child relationship and the family system (Egeland et al., 2000). The most effective time to intervene for the purpose of promoting a secure attachment and hence a positive IWM of self and self-in-relation-to-others is during the time the model is being formed, which is thought to be the infancy and toddler period. In a recent study with older children, Toth, Maughan, Manly, Spagnola, and Cicchetti (2002) conducted a randomized trial preventative intervention with a sample of maltreated children and their parents. A measure of the child's internal representation of self and self-in-relation-to-others was used to evaluate the efficacy of two interventions: a modified infant–parent psychotherapy approach designed to promote a positive representational model, and a psychoeducational program for addressing parenting skills and adaptive competence in children. In addition, there was a control group of maltreated children who did not receive either of the interventions. Children in the Preschool Parent Psychotherapy group exhibited a significant decrease in maladaptive maternal representation, negative self representation, and a significant increase in positive expectation of mother–child relationship over time, compared to the alternative intervention and control groups. There was no assessment of mother's IWM.

Toth and colleagues (2002) found that, at least through the preschool years, the internalized mother–child relationship continued to evolve and remained open to reorganization. This raises questions: At what age do representational models become more stable and less amenable to change? Is there a sensitive period as assumed and, if so, does it extend beyond preschool? Bowlby (1969/1982, 1980) suggested that attachment representations should become increasingly resistant to change as long as the caregiving environment remains basically stable. This was not, however, intended to be a deterministic view of development. Bowlby described the internal working model as dynamic, suggesting that it should change in response to a substantially changed caregiving environment in order to remain an adaptive system. It should not respond to minor perturbations in the attachment relationship, but considerable shifts in the relationship should spur corresponding changes in the internal working model. Unfortunately, there is very little empirical data to support or refute Bowlby's theoretical assertion.

Using a variety of different measures, we found continuity in relationship and self-representation across four age periods from early childhood to adolescence (Carlson et al., 2004). The behavioral measure of mother–infant attachment relationship, the Strange Situation, was related to representation in early childhood, which supported Bowlby's hypothesis that representations of self and self-in-relation-to-others are drawn from patterns of early attachment experience and continue to guide the individual, particularly with regard to relationships.

In low-risk samples, the stability between attachment assessed in infancy and attachment representation assessed in adulthood is quite good (Waters, Merrick, Treboux, Crowell, & Albersheim, 2000). In our high-risk sample, we did not find significant stability between attachment patterns in infancy and attachment representation assessed at age 19. Overall, there was substantial shifting toward insecurity in late adolescence, particularly toward the dismissing classification. In a poverty environment that poses many challenges to optimal functioning, it appears that, within the attachment relationship, security may be difficult to maintain (Weinfield, Whaley, & Egeland, 2004). Significant correlates of attachment continuity and discontinuity were evident across a variety of age periods and across child and maternal characteristics as well as the overall caregiving environment. Findings with regard to temperament indicate that infants who would subsequently shift from early security to later insecurity were identified by their mothers as requiring more stimulation to respond, having shorter attention spans, and squirming and kicking more during caregiving activities than infants who remained secure at both time points. High maternal life stress differentiated the transition away from the security group, with the transition group mothers reporting high levels of life stress at a greater proportion of assessments. Elements of the family home environment emerged as markers of change from insecurity to later security. Families where attachment insecurity was stable, as compared to the transition-away-from-insecurity group, had lower quality physical environments available to the child. The transition-away-from-insecurity group may have been better able to provide some of the basic trappings of a safe, organized, stimulating environment. It is also possible, however, that the difference in physical environment may have reflected a different commitment in the two groups to the needs of the child; the transition-away-from-insecurity group may have been demonstrating a greater sensitivity to the child's need for a safe yet stimulating environment. Observations in a series of semistructured tasks for parent and child at age 13 indicated that the ability of the family to work toward a common goal while fostering individual growth was significantly lower in the transition-away-from-security group than in the stable secure group. This may be a marker of change in family interaction in the transition group as they foster autonomous thinking and security less effectively.

Results from the study of continuity and change in organized attachment security indicate the existence of coherent discontinuity across the age period from infancy to adolescence. The lawful changes in attachment security across this time period were related to child characteristics and experience, maternal experience, quality of home environment, and quality of parent–child interaction. These findings do not diminish the importance of infancy and toddlerhood as a sensitive period for intervention. However, based on these findings, the window of opportunity for effecting change in attachment representation seems to exist across the entire age range from infancy to adolescence. Even though these findings have important theoretical and practical implications, there are many unanswered questions about the nature and process of change in organized attachment security.

As viewed from an organizational model of development, interventions resulting in a secure parent–infant attachment relationship and positive internal representation provide the foundation for later positive developmental adaptation. As development is cumulative, competence at one age increases the likelihood of functioning in a competent fashion at the next developmental period. Competence at each period of development decreases the probability of psychopathology at subsequent developmental periods, and competence increases the likelihood that the child who faces trauma and adversity can take advantage of available resources in order to cope. As part of the developmental process leading to resilience and positive adaptation, an early history of competence in the form of a secure parent–infant attachment relationship has special significance for subsequent developmental outcomes. Similarly, the longer the child is on a developmental pathway of competence, the greater the likelihood that the child will remain on this pathway (Cicchetti, Toth, & Rogosch, 2000; Egeland & Carlson, 2003). Although an early history of competence is important, competence at later ages has also been found to decrease the likelihood of psychopathology. Certainly, prevention programs exist that are designed to promote competence. However, most efforts to prevent mental illness focus on eliminating risk and treating maladaptation rather than focusing on promoting competence not just in infancy but across ages. As a result of the study of resilience, there has been an increasing interest in promoting competence through positive models of prevention and intervention (Yates & Masten, 2004). Most efforts to prevent mental illness, however, continue to focus on eliminating risk and treating the problems rather than focusing on promoting competence. The reason is that most prevention and intervention efforts derive from the "disease" model, which focuses on the individual's problems and weaknesses rather than strengths.

The findings from our study of developmental trajectories from infancy to adulthood show that lawful change occurs as a result of major changes in the individual's environment. These change agents exist across different ecological levels and systems such as the individual, family, and school. It is also the case that continuity of competence is sustained across developmental periods where the environment is supportive and stable (Sroufe, Carlson, Collins, & Egeland, 2005). Unfortunately, in a poverty environment where support and resources are lacking and risk and adversity outweigh protective and promotive factors, maladaptation is likely to be sustained across development. It was encouraging to find, however, that positive circumstances, particularly significant relationships, lead to positive change in developmental trajectory, which has implications for promoting and sustaining competence. In the next section, I briefly discuss some strategies for promoting competence and wellness.

RELATIONSHIPS AND PROMOTING COMPETENCE

Relationships play a key role in our view of resilience (Yates et al., 2003). Relationships are a major resource used by individuals in coping with adversity, and an early secure attachment relationship is part of the process that enables the child to use available resources, particularly alternative sources of support. The variable most often associated with change in developmental trajectory is relationships, particularly family relationships. For example, we found a 40-point decline in Bayley Scores of Infant Development for a group of children whose parents were emotionally unresponsive (Egeland & Sroufe, 1981). In another study, increases in IQ scores in preschool were related to good quality parent–child relationships observed in a series of semistructured tasks (Pianta & Egeland, 1994). Good quality relationships were associated with breaking the cycle of abuse across generations (Egeland et al., 2002) and deflections from behavior problems in preschool to functioning in the normal range in the early school years (Egeland et al., 1990). A major focus of programs to promote competence, as well as interventions to treat deficits, must be on improving the child's relational environment. For the young child, the relational environment primarily involves the family, but as the child gets older the environment expands to include a range of significant others from the various contexts that make up the child's social world.

There have been a variety of school-based programs that have been successful in promoting competence. One area, however, that has received little attention is the relationship between the teacher and the child. A national survey of adolescents revealed that the single most common factor associated with healthy outcomes across all domains of functioning was that youth reported having a relationship with an adult that they experienced as supportive to them, which in most instances was a teacher. It is important for the teacher to understand that she and the children in her class each bring a representational model that plays an important role in terms of what behaviors and cues the teacher attends to, how they are interpreted, and what to expect of others. These expectations guide their interactions and affect the quality of the relationship between teacher and child (Pianta, 1999). For example, if a child is constantly seeking the attention of a teacher, the teacher may interpret this child as being very needy and demanding. Another teacher may interpret this child's behavior as a child who is vulnerable and in need of support. Programs like Pianta's, that help teachers understand that they and their children have representational models of self and relationships that influence how they interact with their students, have tremendous promise as an effective intervention to promote competence.

One final note—our families moved frequently and, as a consequence, changed school districts, which made it difficult for the child to establish a relationship with a teacher. A change in school policy that allows for continuity of school placement would be beneficial to the child, along with a change in the organization of elementary schools allowing a child to have more contact with the same teacher. Much could be done with the school environment that would facilitate a better relationship between child and teacher.

COMPREHENSIVE AND FLEXIBLE INTERVENTIONS

In the design of our longitudinal study, we selected poverty as our risk factor because it is considered a pervasive stressor affecting many aspects of individual and family functions (Brooks-Gunn & Duncan, 1997). We have seen negative effects in a variety of areas of child functioning, including intellectual attainment and school performance as well as an increased likelihood of social, emotional, and behavioral problems (Sroufe et al., 2005). Family functioning is also negatively impacted by poverty. We have found high rates of child maltreatment and other parenting problems, substance abuse, psychopathology, particularly depression, and chaotic home environment. In the broader context, poverty is very often associated with violent neighborhoods, poor and crowded living conditions, poor quality schools, and a greater likelihood of associating with deviant peers. In this section, the recommendation for flexible and comprehensive programs applies primarily to high-risk families, particularly poverty families with young children who are participating in parenting programs. For these families, it is imperative to match the individual's needs and circumstances to the intervention delivery regardless of the goals of the intervention. Interventions, particularly those focused on parenting and the parent–child relationship, must involve a set of goals and principles that are implemented in a flexible fashion, rather than an approach consisting of teaching a specific "parenting curriculum."

From our intense involvement with the STEEP families, we learned that parents living in poverty were often dealing with multiple challenges and barriers that needed to be addressed before they could devote themselves to improving their relationship with their child. For those parents who are particularly young, their own developmental needs as adolescents may compete with the needs of their infants, and for those young women who bear emotional scars from their own troubled childhoods, there may be residual issues of mistrust or even psychopathology that hinder parenting intervention efforts. We found the STEEP mothers higher on 9 of 13 clinical scales from the MMPI compared to a subsample of pregnant women with low educational levels from the larger normative sample. The high scores on these scales revealed considerable personality dysfunction, deviant social beliefs, antisocial behavior, depression, anxiety, and feeling alienated from society (Egeland, Erickson, Butcher, & Ben-Porath, 1991). Psychiatric problems, along with the stress and lack of resources associated with poverty, are just a few of the characteristics that must be addressed when intervening with poverty families.

Preventative intervention programs dealing with high-risk families similar to those in STEEP must identify and deal with the unique needs and circumstances of each family. Unless these needs are addressed, the intervention is doomed to failure. In addition, such programs must be comprehensive, which means that medical, mental health, social, and drug and alcohol rehabilitation services be available. Inasmuch as most intervenors do not have the background and training to deal with such problems as drugs or mental illness, it is essential that parenting programs for high-risk parents have appropriate services readily available.

FOCUS ON MULTIPLE SETTINGS

A corollary to the recommendation to develop comprehensive preventative/intervention programs and policy is to focus on the context and settings that are salient for developmental adaptation at a particular age. We have been guided in our work by the transactional model of development, which says that child functioning at each period of development results from the child's transaction with his or her environment. This model requires attention to the multiple ecological levels with which the child transacts. Competence as well as maladaptation cannot be understood by simply examining the individual's transactions in a single context or system. For young children, the setting of most influence is the family and, as the child develops, the contexts expand to include peers, neighborhood, schools, and communities (Carlson & Sroufe, 1995). We have found that children at most risk for poor outcomes are those with problems in multiple settings (Sroufe et al., 2005). Masten and Wright (1998) noted that cumulative models of risk support interventions that reduce risk and promote successful adaptation in multiple contexts. Promoting competence across different settings that are salient at a particular age (e.g. family, school, and peers) is more likely to be successful than a focus on one particular setting. For example, a review of school-based violence prevention programs indicated that the most successful programs were those that included different systems and levels of the child's social world, particularly family and peers. Understanding the process and pathways leading to adaptive and maladaptive developmental outcomes is highly complex and requires a level of analyses approach. Similarly, effective interventions must target multiple levels of ecological influence that are salient at a particular age.

CONCLUSION

In designing the MLSPC, we learned from the first-generation risk research that the search for understanding the causes of psychopathology requires a developmental framework. Contrary to the belief of many first-generation risk researchers, child and adolescent psychopathology is not a downward extension of adult psychopathology. Similarly, developmental continuity does not mean homotypic continuity of symptoms and behavior, but rather lies at the level of function and meaning. Congruent with organizational perspective on development, we find that behaviors leading to psychopathology (and competence) differ at each developmental period, yet what we observe in childhood is developmentally linked to later outcomes through successive patterns of organization and adaptation. Finally, the antecedents and pathways leading to psychopathology are complex and cannot be explained by a single risk factor, or the concurrence of a combination of risk factors, directly related in a linear fashion to the occurrence of a disorder.

Over the past 30 years, the field has moved away from the linear approach to the study of adaptation toward more complex models that incorporate a dynamic, transactive, systems approach to understanding psychopathology. Sameroff, Seifer, and Bartko's (1997) transactional view of the interdependence of the individual and his environment and their dynamic transaction across time, and Gottlieb and Tucker-Halpern's (2002) view of the co-action across all levels of analysis provide a framework for understanding the complexities of the etiologies and pathways leading to psychopathology (and competence). Many interventions that are designed to prevent and treat behavior problems and psychopathology continue to be based on a linear approach rather than a dynamic process model. Unfortunately, we need not look any further than some of the attachment interventions to see programs based on a linear model (cf. Egeland et al., 2000). For some parents, "teaching" them to be more sensitive results in a secure attachment, but for high-risk families, a more comprehensive approach is needed—one that deals specifically with the unique needs and strengths of the family. This will require comprehensive policies and programs designed to incorporate a level of analysis approach that considers the transactive effects of the different levels of analysis in designing interventions.

Although the findings for the MLSPC suggest many avenues and approaches to intervening and preventing behavior problems and psychopathology, I chose in this chapter to focus on the parent–child relationship with the aims of assisting parents in becoming more skilled in their behavioral interactions with their child and promoting a more positive inner representation of self and others. Our findings suggest that a positive change in child functioning may be brought about by favorable environmental circumstances, particularly in the form of supportive relationships. We identified several factors that directly and indirectly affected the quality of the parent–child relationship and ultimately the child's functioning, including parental mental health, familial life stress, social connection and support, and the quality of romantic relationships with partners. Factors such as family stress, substance abuse, and maternal depression are barriers to successful intervention (Egeland et al., 2000). As we learned from STEEP, promoting parent well-being as well as empowering and providing skills for reducing and coping with stress are important goals of intervention because they improve the parent–child relationship and ultimately child functioning. In order to change the behaviors necessary for successful parent–child interaction and the individual's representational models that influence these behaviors, it is essential to consider the family's strengths and weaknesses, the family system, and the broader context in which the family functions.

Even though the focus of the implications for practice has been on the parent–child relationship in the early years, we find at later ages that good quality relationships and emotional support continue to be related to positive developmental adaptation. For example, we found that a good quality intimate relationship predicted positive deflections in functioning across adolescence to early adulthood for a group of adolescents diagnosed with conduct disorder. It was the quality of this intimate relationship that predicted desistance of antisocial behavior, not the status of involved or not involved in an intimate relationship (Roisman, Aguilar, & Egeland, 2004). Many such examples exist for implementing relationship-based interventions for promoting competence and preventing psychopathology across the life span. We have learned over the 30 years of our longitudinal study that we need multiple levels of analysis to fully understand development. So, too, we have come to recognize the need for multiple levels of intervention to effect positive change in the lives of children and their families. As our study continues, we are now exploring the transitions to adulthood and parenthood in the original cohort of children. The MLSPC is in a unique position to clarify the processes underlying positive change in developmental trajectories over time and over generations.

REFERENCES

Aguilar, B., Sroufe, L. A., Egeland, B., & Carlson, E. (2000). Distinguishing the early-onset/persistent and adolescence-onset antisocial behavior types: From birth to 16 years. *Development and Psychopathology, 12,* 109–132.

Ainsworth, M. D. S., Blehar, M. C., Waters, E., & Wall, S. (1978). *Patterns of attachment: A psychological study of the Strange Situation.* Hillsdale, NJ: Lawrence Erlbaum Associates.

Ambrosini, P. J., Metz, C., & Prabucki, K., (1989). Videotape reliability of the third revised edition of the K-SADS. *Journal of American Academic Child and Adolescent Psychology.* 28, 723–728.

Anthony, E. J. (1974). The syndrome of the psychologically invulnerable child. In E. J. Anthony & C. Koupernik (Eds.), *The child in his family: Children at psychiatric risk* (pp. 3–10). New York: Wiley.

Anthony, E. J. (1987). Risk, vulnerability, and resilience: An overview. In E. J. Anthony & B. Cohler (Eds.), *The invulnerable hild* (pp. 3–48). New York: Guilford Press.

Appleyard, K., Egeland, B., van Dulmen, M. H. M., & Sroufe, L. A. (2005). When more is not better: The role of cumulative risk in child behavior outcomes. *Journal of Child Psychology and Psychiatry, 46*(3), 235–245.

Berlin, L. J. (2005). Interventions to enhance early attachments: The state of the field today. In L. J. Berlin, Y. Ziv, L. Amaya-Jackson, & M. T. Greenberg (Eds.), *Enhancing early attachments: Theory, research, intervention, and policy* (pp. 3–33). New York: Guilford Press.

Berlin, L. J., O'Neal, C. R., & Brooks-Gunn, J. (1998). What makes early intervention programs work?: The program, its participants, and their interaction. *Zero to Three, 18,* 4–15.

Bosquet, M., & Egeland, B. (in press). The development and maintenance of anxiety symptoms from infancy through adolescence in a longitudinal sample. *Development and Psychopathology.*

Bowlby, J. (1980). *Attachment and loss: Vol. 3. Loss.* New York: Basic Books.

Bowlby, J. (1982). *Attachment and loss: Vol. 1. Attachment.* New York: Basic Books. (Original work published 1969)

Bronfenbrenner, U. (1977). Toward an experimental ecology of human development. *American Psychologist, 32,* 513–530.

Brooks-Gunn, J. & Duncan, G. J. (1997). The effects of poverty on children. *The Future of Children, 7*(2), 55–71.

Cacioppo, J. T., Berntson, G. G., Sheridan, J. F., & McClintock, M. K. (2000). Multi-level integrative analyses of human behavior: The complementing nature of social and biological approaches. *Psychological Bulletin, 126,* 829–843.

Carlson, E. A. (1998). A prospective longitudinal study of attachment disorganization/disorientation. *Child Development, 69,* 1107–1129.

Carlson, E. A., & Sroufe, L. A. (1995). The contribution of attachment theory and research to developmental psychopathology. In D. Cicchetti & D. Cohen (Eds.), *Developmental processes and psychopathology: Vol. 1, Theoretical perspectives and methodological approaches* (pp. 581–617). New York: Cambridge University Press.

Carlson, E. A., Sroufe, L. A., & Egeland, B. (2004). The construction of experience: A longitudinal study of representation and behavior. *Child Development, 75*(1), 66–83.

Caspi, A., McClay, J., Moffitt, T. E., Mill, J., Martin, J., Craig, I. W., et al.(2002). Role of genotype in the cycle of violence in maltreated children. *Science, 297,* 851–854.

Cicchetti, D. (1993). Developmental psychopathology: Reactions, reflections, and projections. *Developmental Review, 13,* 471–502.

Cicchetti, D., & Cohen, D. (1995). Perspectives on developmental psychopathology. In D. Cicchetti & D. Cohen (Eds.), *Developmental psychopathology, Vol. 1: Theory and methods* (pp. 3–17). New York: Wiley.

Cicchetti, D., Toth, S. L., & Rogosch, F. A. (2000). The development of psychological wellness in maltreated children. In D. Cicchetti, J. Rappaport, I. Sandler, & R. P. Weissberg (Eds.), *The promotion of wellness in children and adolescents* (pp. 394–426). Washington, DC: Child Welfare League of America Press.

Cole, P. M., Alexander, P. C., & Anderson, C. L. (1996). Dissociation in typical and atypical development: Examples from father–daughter incest survivors. In L. K. Michelson & W. J. Ray (Eds.), *Handbook of dissociation: Theoretical, empirical, and clinical perspectives* (pp. 69–89). Plenum.

de Wolff, M. S., & van Ijzendoorn, M. H. (1997). Sensitivity and attachment: A meta-analysis on parental antecedents of infant attachment. *Child Development, 68,* 571–591.

Egeland, B., & Bosquet, M. (2002). Emotion regulation in early childhood: The role of attachment-oriented interventions. In B. S. Zuckerman, A. F. Lieberman, & N. A. Fox (Eds.), *Emotional regulation and developmental health: Infancy and early childhood.* (pp. 101–124). Skillman, NJ: Johnson & Johnson Pediatric Institute.

Egeland, B., Bosquet, M., & Levy-Chung, A. K. (2002). Continuities and discontinuities in the intergenerational transmission of child maltreatment: Implications for breaking the cycle of abuse. In K. Browne, H. Hanks, P. Stratton, & C. Hamilton (Eds.), *The prediction and prevention of child abuse: A handbook* (pp. 217–232). New York: John Wiley & Sons.

Egeland, B., & Carlson, E. (2003). Attachment and psychopathology. In L. Atkinson (Ed.), *Clinical applications of attachment* (pp. 27–48). Mahwah, NJ: Lawrence Erlbaum Associates.

Egeland, B., Carlson, E., & Sroufe, L. A. (1993). Resilience as process. *Development and Psychopathology, 5*(4), 517–528.

Egeland, B. & Erickson, M. (2004). Lessons from STEEP: Linking theory, research and practice on the well-being of infants and parents. In A. Sameroff, S. McDonough, & K. Rosenblum (Eds.), *Treating parent–infant relationship problems* (pp. 213–242). New York, NY: Guildford.

Egeland, B., Erickson, M. F., Butcher, J. N., & Ben-Porath, Y. S. (1991). MMPI-2: Profiles of women at risk for child abuse. *Journal of Personality Assessment, 57*(2), 254–263.

Egeland, B., Jacobvitz, D., & Sroufe, L. A. (1988). Breaking the cycle of abuse. *Child Development, 59*(4), 1080–1088.

Egeland, B., Kalkoske, M., Gottesman, N., & Erickson, M. F. (1990). Preschool behavior problems: Stability and factors accounting for change. *Journal of Child Psychology and Psychiatry, 31*(6), 891–910.

Egeland, B., & Kreutzer, T. (1991). A longitudinal study of the effects of maternal stress and protective factors on the development of high risk children. In A. L. Green, E. M. Cummings, & K. H. Karraker (Eds.), *Life-span developmental psychology: Perspectives on stress and coping* (pp. 61–84). Hillsdale, NJ: Lawrence Erlbaum Associates.

Egeland, B., Pianta, R., & Ogawa, J. (1996). Early behavior problems: Pathways to mental disorders in adolescence. *Development and Psychopathology, 8,* 735–749.

Egeland, B., & Sroufe, L. A. (1981). Developmental sequelae of maltreatment in infancy. In R. Rizley & D. Cicchetti (Eds.), *New directions for child development: Developmental perspectives in child maltreatment* (pp. 77–92) San Francisco, CA: Jossey-Bass.

Egeland, B., Sroufe, L. A., & Erickson, M. F. (1983). Developmental consequences of different patterns of maltreatment. *Child Abuse and Neglect, 7,* 459–469.

Egeland, B. & Sussman-Stillman, A. (1996). Dissociation and abuse across generations. *Child Abuse and Neglect, The International Journal, 20*(11), 1123–1132.

Egeland, B., Weinfield, N. S., Bosquet, M., & Cheng, V. K. (2000). Remembering, repeating and working through: Lessons from attachment-based interventions. In J. D. Osofsky & H. E. Fitzgerald (Eds.), Infant Mental Health in Groups at High Risk. *WAIMH Handbook of Infant Mental Health* (Vol. 4; pp. 35–89). New York: John Wiley & Sons.

Egeland, B., Yates, T., Appleyard, K., & van Dulmen, M. (2002). The long-term consequences of maltreatment in the early years: A developmental pathway model to antisocial behavior. *Children's Services, 5*(4), 249–260.

Englund, M. M., Luckner, A. E., Whaley, G. J. L., & Egeland, B. (2004). Children's achievement in early elementary school: Longitudinal effects of parental involvement, expectations, and quality of assistance. *Journal of Educational Psychology, 96*(4), 723–730.

Erickson, M. F., Sroufe, L. A., & Egeland, B. (1985). The relationship between quality of attachment and behavior problems in preschool in a high risk sample. *Child Development Monographs, 50*(1–2), 147–166.

Fonagy, P., Target, M., Gergely, G., & Jurist, E. L. (2002). *Affect regulation, mentalization, and the development of self.* New York: Other Press.

Fraiberg, S. (Ed.). (1980). *Clinical studies in infant mental health.* New York: Basic Books.

Garmezy, N., Masten, A. S., & Tellegen, A. (1984). The study of stress and competence in children: A building block for developmental psychopathology. *Child Development, 55,* 97–111.

Gottesman, I., & Shields, J. (1972). *Schizophrenia and genetics: A twin study vantage point.* New York: Academic Press.

Gottlieb, G., & Tucker-Halpern, C. (2002). A relational view of causality in normal and abnormal development. *Development and Psychopathology, 14*(3), 421–435.

Lieberman, A. F., Weston, D. R., & Pawl, J. H. (1991). Preventive intervention and outcome with anxiously attached dyads. *Child Development, 62,* 199–209.

Liotti, G. (1992). Disorganized/disoriented attachment in the etiology of the dissociative disorders. *Dissociation, 4,* 196–204.

Main, M., & Hesse, E. (1990). Parents' unresolved traumatic experiences are related to infant disorganized attachment status: Is frightened or frightening parental behavior the linking mechanism? In M. Greenberg, D. Cicchetti, & E. M. Cummings (Eds.), *Attachment in the preschool years* (pp. 161–182). Chicago, IL: University of Chicago Press.

Masten, A. S., & Coatsworth, J. D. (1998). The development of competence in favorable and unfavorable environments. *American Psychologist, 53*(2), 205–220.

Masten, A. S., & Wright, M. O. (1998). Cumulative risk and protection models of child maltreatment. *Journal of Aggression, Maltreatment, and Trauma, 2*(1), 7–30.

Mednick, S. A., & McNeil, T. F. (1968). Current methodology in research on the etiology of schizophrenia: Serious difficulties which suggest the use of the high-risk group method. *Psychological Bulletin, 70,* 681–693.

Murphy, L. B., & Moriarty, A. E. (1976). *Vulnerability, coping, & growth from infancy to adolescence.* New Haven: Yale University Press.

Ogawa, J., Sroufe, L.A., Weinfield, N.S., Carlson, E., & Egeland, B. (1997). Development and the fragmented self: A longitudinal study of dissociative symptomatology in a non-clinical sample. *Development and Psychopathology, 4,* 855–879.

Pianta, R. C. (1999). *Enhancing relationships between children and teachers.* Washington, DC: American Psychological Association.

Pianta, R., & Egeland, B. (1994). The relation between depressive symptoms and stressful life events in a sample of disadvantaged mothers. *Journal of Consulting and Clinical Psychology, 62,* 1091–1095.

Pianta, R., Egeland, B., & Sroufe, L. A. (1990). Maternal stress and children's development: Prediction of school outcomes and identification of protective factors. In J. E. Rolf, A. Masten, D. Cicchetti, K. Nuechterlein, & S. Weintraub (Eds.), *Risk and protective factors in the development of psychopathology* (pp. 215–235). Cambridge, MA: Cambridge University Press.

Putnam, F. W. (2000). Dissociative disorders. In A. J. Sameroff & M. Lewis (Eds.), *Handbook of developmental psychopathology* (2nd ed., pp. 739–754). Dordrecht, Netherlands: Kluwer Academic.

Reynolds, A. J., & Temple, J. A. (in press). Economic returns of investments in preschool. In E. Zigler, W. Gilliam, & S. Jones (Eds.), *A vision for universal prekindergarten*. New York: Cambridge University Press.

Roisman, G. I., Aguilar, B., & Egeland, B. (2004). Antisocial behavior in the transition to adulthood: The independent and interactive roles of developmental history and concurrent experiences. *Development and Psychopathology, 16.* 857–871.

Sameroff, A. J., & Chandler, M. J. (1975). Reproductive risk and the continuum of caretaking casualty. In F. D. Horowitz, M. Hetherington, S. Scarr-Salapatek, & G. Siegel (Eds.), *Review of child development research* (Vol. 4, pp. 187–243). Chicago: Chicago University Press.

Sameroff, A. J., Seifer, R., Baldwin, A. L., & Baldwin, C. A. (1993). Stability of intelligence from preschool to adolescence: The influence of social and family risk factors. *Child Development, 64,* 80–97.

Sameroff, A. J., Seifer, R., & Bartko, W. T. (1997). Environmental perspectives on adaptation during childhood and adolescence. In S. S. Luthar, J. A. Barack, D. Cicchetti, & J. Weisz (Eds.), *Developmental psychopathology: Perspectives on adjustment, risk, and disorder* (pp. 507–526). Cambridge, UK: Cambridge University Press.

Slade, A. (2005). Parental reflective functioning: An introduction. *Attachment and Human Development, 7,* 269–281.

Slade, A., Aber, J. L., Berger, B., Bresgi, L., & Kaplan, M. (2003). *The parent development interview.* New York: City University of New York.

Slade, A., Sadler, L. S., & Mayes, L. (2005). Minding the baby: Enhancing parental reflective functioning in a nursing/mental health home visiting program. In L. J. Berlin, Y. Ziv, L. A. Jackson, & M. T. Greenberg (Eds.), *Enhancing early attachments: Theory, research, intervention and policy* (pp. 152–177). New York: Guilford Press.

Spiegel, D., & Cardeña, E. (1991). Disintegrated experience: The dissociative disorders revisited. *Journal of Abnormal Psychology, 100*(3), 366–378.

Sroufe, L. A. (1990). An organizational perspective on the self. In D. Cicchetti & M. Beeghly (Eds.), *The self in transition: Infancy to childhood* (pp. 281–307). Chicago: University of Chicago Press.

Sroufe, L. A. (1996). *Emotional development: The organization of emotional life in the early years.* New York, NY: Cambridge University Press.

Sroufe, L. A., Carlson, E. A., Collins, W. A., & Egeland, B. (2005). *The development of the person: The Minnesota study of risk and adaptation from birth to adulthood.* New York: Guilford Press.

Sroufe, L. A., Carlson, E. A., Levy, A. K., & Egeland, B. (1999). Implications of attachment theory for developmental psychopathology. *Development and Psychopathology, 11,* 1–13.

Sroufe, L. A., Egeland, B., & Carlson, E. (1999). One social world: The integrated development of parent–child and peer relationships. In W. A. Collins & B. Laursen (Eds.), *Relationships as developmental context: The 30th Minnesota symposium on child psychology* (pp. 241–262). Hillsdale, NJ: Lawrence Erlbaum Associates.

Sroufe, L. A., Egeland, B., & Kreutzer, T. (1990). The fate of early experience following developmental change: Longitudinal approaches to individual adaptation in childhood. *Child Development, 61,* 1363–1373.

Sroufe, L. A., & Rutter, M. (1984). The domain of developmental psychopathology. *Child Development, 55,* 17–29.

Sroufe, L. A., & Waters, E. (1977). Attachment as an organizational construct. *Child Development, 48.* 1184–1199.

Toth, S. L., Maughan, A., Manly, J. T., Spagnola, M., & Cicchetti, D. (2002). The relative efficacy of two interventions in altering maltreated preschool children's representational models: Implications for attachment theory. *Development and Psychopathology, 14.* 877–908.

van Ijzendoorn, M.H. (1995). Adult attachment representations. *Psychological Bulletin, 117,* 387–403

Waller, N. G., Putnam, F. W., & Carlson, E. B. (1996). Types of dissociation and dissociative types: A taxometric analysis of dissociative experiences. *Psychological Methods, 1,* 300–321.

Warren, S. L., Huston, L., Egeland, B., & Sroufe, L. A. (1997). Child and adolescent anxiety disorders and early attachment. *Journal of the American Academy of Child and Adolescent Psychiatry, 36,* 637–644.

Waters, E., Merrick, S., Treboux, D., Crowell, J., & Albersheim, L. (2000). Attachment security in infancy and early adulthood: A twenty-year longitudinal study. *Child Development, 71*(3), 684–689.

Watt, N. F., Anthony, E. J., Wynne, L. C., & Rolf, J. E. (Eds.). (1984). *Children at risk for schizophrenia: A longitudinal perspective.* Cambridge University Press.

Weinfield, N. S., Whaley, G. J. L, & Egeland, B. (2004). Continuity, discontinuity, and coherence in attachment from infancy to late adolescence: Sequelae of organization and disorganization. *Journal of Attachment and Human Development, 6(1), 73–97.*

Werner, E. E., & Smith, R. S. (1992). *Overcoming the odds.* New York: Cornell University Press.

Werner, H. (1957). The concept of development from a comparative and organismic point of view. In D. B. Harris (Ed.), *The concept of development* (pp. 125–148). Minneapolis: University of Minnesota Press.

Yates, T. M., Egeland, B., & Sroufe, L. A. (2003). Rethinking resilience: A developmental process perspective. In S. S. Luthar (Ed.), *Resilience and vulnerabilities: Adaptation in the context of childhood adversities* (pp.243–266). New York: Cambridge University Press.

Yates, T. M., & Masten, A. S. (2004). Fostering the future: Resilience theory and the practice of positive psychology. In P. A. Linley & S. Joseph (Eds.), *Positive psychology in practice* (pp. 521–539). Hoboken, NJ: John Wiley and Sons.

Chapter 5

The Interior Life of the Family: Looking From the Inside Out and the Outside In

Barbara H. Fiese
Mary Spagnola
Syracuse University

In the opening lines of their seminal book, *Inside the Family,* Kantor and Lehr (1975) remark, "We shall understand families when we understand how they manage the commonplace, that is, how they conduct themselves and interact in the familiar everyday surroundings of their own households" (p. ix). They go on to state, "It seems to us that if a theory or model of family behavior is to be viable, it must be applicable to 'healthy' or 'normal' family processes as well as to pathological ones" (p. ix). These words should resonate with developmental psychopathologists who take as a basic principle the consideration of normal and abnormal together (Rutter & Sroufe, 2000). In this chapter, we consider how family management of the commonplace contributes to health as well as to psychopathology. In order to understand these contributions, one must not only "get inside" family life, attending to its subtle nuances and individualized meaning, but also take a look as outsiders at how behavior and emotions are regulated in the family context.

Although developmental psychologists have long agreed that families are important in the socialization of children, as a separate and identifiable level of analysis family influences have been derived from smaller units such as parent–child dyads (Parke, 2004). The family as a distinct level of analysis includes the ways in which membership shifts across the life course and in historical time (Teachman, Tedrow, & Crowder, 2000), the emotional climate of the group (Epstein, Ryan, Bishop, Miller, & Keitner, 2003), and the transmission of traditions and beliefs across generations (Reiss, 1981). These family-level dynamics provide a context for child development such that mental health is supported through stable membership, positive emotional responsiveness, and traditions and beliefs that enrich daily life. In contrast, when the family as a group experiences multiple disruptions through instability in membership, negative emotional climate, or impoverishment of traditions, then children's well-being can be compromised.

The child is not a passive player in this important group. Children play an active role in shaping how the family carries out it daily routines, creates beliefs about relationships, and engages with the social world (Sameroff & Fiese, 2000). Thus, when one considers the family as a level of analysis, there is a focus on how the individual contributes to the functioning of the group as well as how the group affects the well-being of the individual.

Although it is beyond the scope of this chapter to cover all the possible ways that the family as a unit of analysis may be conceptualized and studied, we offer the following framework. First, we consider the family as a level of analysis and relevant domains of inquiry. Whereas there is long tradition in studying parenting in developmental psychopathology, a consideration of the family as a unit of analysis calls for additional areas to be examined, such as how the family goes about managing daily life and creating beliefs about close relationships. Second, we illustrate how narratives are used by individuals to interpret family-level events and how families create routines and rituals to support development. We consider the normative and developmental features of these family-level processes. Third, we consider childhood chronic illness as a family-level stressor that has applicability to developmental psychopathology as a risk condition. Fourth, we speculate on possible family-level mechanisms of effect. We conclude with future directions and challenges for the field of developmental psychopathology in tackling multilevel analyses that incorporate family systems perspectives.

FAMILY-LEVEL VERSUS LEVELS OF THE FAMILY

From the outset, one must recognize that studying families is a messy endeavor. Not only are families changing structures that make it difficult to define what constitutes a family (Teachman et al., 2000), methods of studying whole family process have not kept pace with developmental theory. Many family researchers take as their theoretical starting point the principles of general systems theory. Families are considered whole systems made up of smaller subsystems that operate under the principles of hierarchical

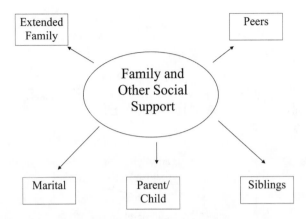

Figure 5.1. Subsystems of the family (Cummings, 1999).

order, well-defined boundaries, and maintaining balance through homeo-stasis (Sameroff, 1995). Although there has been some success in identify-ing how smaller subsystems affect each other, the broader principles are elusive to direct confirmation or disconfirmation. For example, it is fairly well established that the marital subsystem affects parenting and that when marital distress is combined with maladaptive parenting, then children are at increased risk for psychopathology (Cummings, Davies, & Campbell, 2000). Several models have been proposed that include multiple subsys-tems that, when taken together, account for individual differences in child outcome. One such model proposed by Cummings (1999) suggests that the family is composed of marital, parent–child, siblings, peers, and extended family subsystems (see Figure 5.1). Although a fruitful approach in its own right, an examination of subsystems is not necessarily the same as studying the family as a whole system. That is, the whole family is more than the sum of its parts. Looking inside the family, one must turn attention to what fami-lies do as a group including assigning roles, setting rules, establishing rou-tines, creating traditions, and telling stories about family experiences (see Figure 5.2).

Families are organic wholes whose composition shifts with birth, death, marriage, divorce, and remarriage. As a stabilizing force, families create rules for behavior and make clear what is acceptable to be a member of the group. As a holding place, families provide comfort and nurturance and a secure base from which to develop individual autonomy, and they serve as a model for connectedness among multiple individuals. A resolvable tension in the study of families is how to integrate the strivings and perceptions of the individual into the communal boundaries of the group. To gain access to the family-level as a whole, it is important to ask, "What is it that families do as a group and how do they collectively support individual development?"

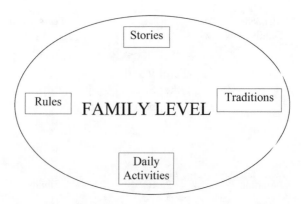

Figure 5.2.   Family-level processes.

To address this question, researchers not only observe families in their natural environments doing what families do, but also consider how families think about and represent these collective activities. Two aspects of family life may be particularly suited to address these questions: family narratives and routines. Narratives created about family events reflect how the individual interprets family-level behaviors. The practice of family routines and rituals sets the stage for sustaining interaction patterns and supports individual development. Prior to examining the developmental and protective aspects of family narratives and routines, we examine the theoretical distinctions between how individuals create representations of group activities and how group practices may affect the individual.

Family Representations and Practices

Although the stories that families tell about their experiences and the direct observation of family routine practices may provide access to the whole family, these activities in and of themselves do not suggest how levels of family process affect development. In order to address levels of family process, two general organizing principles are crucial: practices and representations. Reiss (1989) proposed that families maintain stability and continuity through their practices and representations. Family practices are directly observable, repeated over time, and are responsive to changes in the family life cycle. Family representations, on the other hand, are assessed indirectly through the interpretive process of the family and may guide as well as reinforce behavior patterns. Family representations and practices likely transact over time, with directly observable behavior affecting beliefs and beliefs guiding behavior (Sameroff & Fiese, 1992).

The representing family reflects beliefs about the manageability of relationships and the social world. When asked to recount familial experiences, individuals present images that vary in their relative coherence and depictions of the trustworthiness of relationships. For some individuals, family experiences are fraught with misunderstandings and repeated disappointments. For these individuals, there is a sense of unpredictability in relationships and reduced opportunities to create coherent images of family life. For other individuals, however, repeated interactions with family members are seen as sources of reward and personal experiences are integrated into a coherent whole. For developmental psychopathologists, representations of experiences with multiple family members provide access to the individual's working model of the family that may influence mental health and relationship functioning. Oftentimes, these images are created within the context of repetitive interactions that occur on a regular basis as the family carries out the routines of daily life. Family routines are, in part, one aspect of the practicing family.

Family practices can be observed by outsiders and are reportable by individual members of the family. Families create rhythms that regulate behavior and emotion, and provide predictability within group activities. For some families, there are clearly assigned roles, deliberate planning around daily and special events, and clear expectations for attendance. For other families, daily life is marked by shifting roles and unpredictable movement in and out of the group, and a sense of chaos predominates. Children raised in more chaotic environments are more susceptible to developing mental health problems and thus sustained chaos in and of itself may be a risk factor (Evans & English, 2002).

Family representations and practices are evaluated through different levels of assessment. Family representations are highly symbolic and intertwined with how families create meaning and define themselves as a group. In order to access the representing family, it is necessary to use indirect means that rely on the family's interpretation of events. Representations provide the insiders' account of family life. Family practices, in contrast, are directly observable and can be detected by outsiders. Family narratives and routines are two domains of family life that incorporate both representing and practicing elements (see Table 5.1).

TABLE 5.1
Examples of Representations and Practices Across Domains

Family Process Domains	Family Representations	Family Practices
Narratives	Coherence	Lessons Learned
	Relationships Beliefs	Mores
Routines	Symbolic Meaning	Role Assignment
	Ritual Affect	Deliberate Planning

DOMAINS OF FAMILY-LEVEL PROCESS

Narratives of Family Life

Storytelling as an Act.   As an act, families use stories to impart values and mores for conduct (Pratt & Fiese, 2004). The narrative environment of childraising is rich in accounts of personal experiences. Miller (Miller & Moore, 1989) found that parents in South Baltimore spoke about personal events eight times per hour, on average. Although all of these accounts may not be classified as narratives about family relationships, the ubiquitous nature of talk about daily activities and personal events suggests that the storied nature of relationships is accessible to children. In terms of the act of storytelling, researchers have considered how couples and families interact with each other while constructing a story about family events such as dinnertime (Fiese & Marjinsky, 1999). The interaction style evident in coconstructing the narrative was found to be consistent with interaction styles of the family as a whole when directly observed during a mealtime. The repetitive practice of engaging children in narratives about personal experiences provides a context in which rules of conduct are directly expressed, and directly observed interaction patterns reinforce these rules. Although storytelling may be situated in the practicing family, there are clear representational aspects to the tales that are told.

Relationship Beliefs and Narrative Coherence.   Family narratives also afford the opportunity to consider how relationships are represented and the beliefs that individuals hold about whole family process. Central to the study of narratives is the relative coherence of the tale. Typically considered on the level of the individual, coherence reflects the degree to which the individual has been able to integrate the different aspects of an experience and resolve incongruities (Fiese & Spagnola, 2005; Main & Goldwyn, 1984; McAdams, 1993; Pratt & Fiese, 2004). Coherence can be detected through an analysis of how the parts of the story are put together and the degree to which family relationships are depicted as rewarding and reliable. As we discuss later in this chapter, narratives about family experiences reflect the degree to which relationships cohere into a supportive whole or are seen as detached and disengaged. The types of narratives we examine are typically drawn from the family's experiences of collective gatherings such as mealtime and how they have faced challenges that affect the whole group such as dealing with chronic illness. We situate these narratives within the framework of daily activities and also consider how the coherence of the narrative affects overall family functioning. We also consider how the family conducts itself as a group and how beliefs about these practices are related to well-being. Before examining how representations and practices support development, we define more clearly what we mean by family routines and rituals.

Family Routines and Rituals

The majority of researchers active in the study of family routines and rituals agree that operationally defining routines and rituals is a challenge, at best (Boyce, Jensen, James, & Peacock, 1983; Fiese, 2006; van der Hart, 1983; Wolin & Bennett, 1984). There are several sources to this challenge. First, it is likely that every family and every family member has his or her own definition of what constitutes a routine or ritual. Indeed, it is this personalized and individualized aspect of family organization that may provide special meaning to group activities and gatherings. Second, rituals are highly symbolic in nature. They are dense with physical, patterned, and affective symbols. Family rituals involve not only the directly observable practices but also the personal, subjective, and interior held meanings associated with the routine events. Rather than consider these two dimensions as incompatible with each other, it is possible to distinguish between the routines of daily living and rituals in family life.

Definitions. Routines and rituals can be contrasted along the dimensions of communication, commitment, and continuity (Fiese et al., 2002). Routines typically involve instrumental communication such that information is conveyed that this is "what needs to be done." The language of routines is direct, implies action, and often includes designation of roles. Once the act is completed, there is little afterthought and there is an uninterrupted flow to daily life. Routines are repeated over time, with little alteration, and can be directly observed by outsiders.

Rituals, on the other hand, involve symbolic communication and signify "this is who we are as a group." The language of rituals is multilayered such that what may appear to the outsider as a mundane phrase may be dense with meaning for family members. There is an affective commitment to rituals that provides a feeling of belongingness and felt rightness to the activity. Oftentimes, the elements of a ritual are played over in memory before and after the event.

As one steps inside the family, it is apparent that what occurs in relatively mundane settings, such as mealtime, holds meaning and defines relationships within the context of whole family functioning. In a family mealtime study, 50 families with children between 5 and 7 years of age were videotaped during a meal conducted in their home (Fiese & Marjinsky, 1999). The researchers were not present for the taping and, on return, the family was interviewed about what was typical or atypical in that particular meal.

One family was observed having a rather lengthy discussion about peanut butter and jelly sandwiches. The discussion revolved around who liked jelly on the sandwich and who did not. Midway through the home visit conducted by the researcher, the father stopped the videotape and remarked that they have this conversation several times a week. The father explained that he and his older daughter preferred jelly on their sandwiches, whereas his younger daughter and wife did not. The father and daughter were considered the jokesters in the family, and mother and younger daughter were more task-oriented and could be relied on to get things done in the family. Furthermore, the daughters had created a system for categorizing their friends and neighbors as to whether they were a "jellied" person or not. What appeared to be a tedious mealtime conversation to the outsider held meaning for its members and defined not only personality characteristics but also reflected alliances within the family.

The astute reader will note that knowledge of the special significance of the event came not through direct observation but through careful analysis of how family members interpret their collective gathering. Let us next examine how family-level processes support development under relatively low risk conditions.

DEVELOPMENTAL FEATURES OF FAMILY REPRESENTATIONS AND PRACTICES

Family Narratives and Normative Development

The Act of Storytelling. Family narratives can be examined for how they are used in practice as well as the implicit meaning of such tales. There is some data to suggest that telling stories about family experiences increases in frequency as children develop from infancy, preschool, and into adolescence (Fiese, Hooker, Kotary, Schwagler, & Rimmer, 1995; Pratt, Norris, Arnold, & Filyer, 1999). The content of these stories is often used to impart family values and teach lessons such as what it means to work and strive for success (Fiese & Bickham, 2004), how to handle moral dilemmas (Pratt, Arnold, & Hilbers, 1998), or how to address personal transgressions (Fung, Miller, & Lin, 2004). The practice of storytelling to address personal transgressions may be an essential aspect of narrative conjunctions during normative development. When caregivers address a child's transgression through the use of narrative, they not only reinforce what is expected behavior but may also engage in active problem solving that can be applied to future dilemmas (Fung et al., 2004; Arnold, Pratt, & Hicks, 2004; Thorne, McLean, & Dasbach, 2004).

There is also evidence that family storytelling practices and coconstructive features in dyadic storytelling are associated with children's mental health (Fivush, Bohanke, Robertson, & Duke, 2004; Oppenheim, Nir, Warren, & Emde, 1997). Children's narratives have been examined in relation to family process variables such as parental discipline style (Solomonica-Levi, Yirmiya, Erel, & Samet, 2001), response to emotional distress (Warren, Oppenheim, & Emde, 1996) and prosocial behavior (Oppenheim, Nir et al., 1997). Representations of family problem solving and climate emerge such that representations or working models of how an individual should function within a relationship are created. This representation then guides the child's behavior, which may be expressed with competence or disorder.

Relationship Beliefs and Coherence. Two aspects of family narratives have been found to be associated with family functioning and child outcome: how relationships are depicted in the narrative, and the relative coherence of the narrative. When family members are called on to talk about their daily lives and how they face challenges together, a central feature of these accounts is the degree to which relationships are seen as manageable, understandable, and rewarding. When family members understand each other and can be called on in times of need, then there is a greater likelihood that the family will cohere as a group. Reiss (1981) identified this as a family-level process whereby families create belief systems, or paradigms, that dictate how individuals interact with each other and how the family goes about problem solving. One can tap into this process by asking families to talk about experiences that they had growing up as well as how they have faced particularly challenging times.

In a study of 50 families who had at least one child between 5 and 7 years of age, parents were asked to first tell a story to their child about a dinnertime when they were growing up and then to tell a story about a current dinnertime (Fiese & Marjinsky, 1999). The narratives were coded for relative coherence and for the trustworthiness of relationships. Although a significant correlation was found between narrative depictions of family of origin relationships and marital satisfaction, the ways in which relationships were depicted in the current family were most closely aligned with directly observed family interaction patterns and child behavior problems (Table 5.2). In cases where mothers and fathers described their family mealtimes as moments when others could be relied on, relationships were predictable and a source of satisfaction; there was more positive affect expressed at the dinner table and parents were less likely to report that their children had problematic behaviors. The following examples contrast these two images of family gatherings:

TABLE 5.2

Correlations Among Family Narrative Codes
and Measures of Family and Child Behavior

	Narrative Codes					
	Narrative Coherence		Relationship Expectations			
			Current Family		Family of Origin	
	Husband	Wife	Husband	Wife	Husband	Wife
Marital Satisfaction						
Husband	.13	.24	.34*	.16	.44**	.29
Wife	.04	.29	.17	.01	.33*	.42***
Family Dinnertime Affect						
Positive Affect	.14	.14	.61***	.57***	.30	.35*
Negative Affect	-.02	-.19	-.67***	-.53***	-.36*	-.16
Child Behavior Checklist						
Internalizing	-.11	-.26	-.42***	-.32*	.04	-.04
Externalizing	-.01	-.21	-.53***	-.40**	-.19	-.28
Total	.01	-.31*	-.50***	-.36**	-.10	-.16

Note: Data are from "Dinnertime stories connecting family practices with relationship beliefs and child adjustment" in *Monographs of the Society for Research in Child Development, 64*(2), by B. H. Fiese et al. (Eds.), 1999, Malden, MA: Blackwell.
*$p < .05$. **$p < .01$, ***$p < .0001$.

> I think dinnertime is an important time. When I was growing up you were expected to be there during dinner. It wasn't just a time for getting food. It was a time to socialize and be together and it was thought of and it is I feel it's very important for a family to eat together. I also think with little ones it's a time to try and attempt to teach you know good manners and ways of behaving and you know stuff like that. It's an ongoing lesson.

In this example, dinnertime is an opportunity to be together and also impart lessons. This depiction is in contrast to the following example:

> On the bad nights I hate dinnertime. I hate mealtime because it is confusing and you know especially if there is a meeting someone's got to go to or I have to go out to the grocery store then it is a time where we just feed them to get it over with.

In sum, when parents depict relationships as rewarding, manageable, and worthy of trust, they are more likely to engage in supportive interactions and their children are less likely to evidence problematic behaviors. Other researchers report that children's representations of family dynamics in response to story-stem prompts are associated with markers of child mental health including externalizing behavior (Oppenheim, Emde, & Warren, 1997), social competence (McHale, Neugebauer, Radin Asch, & Schwartz, 1999), and anxiety (Warren, Emde, & Sroufe, 2000). These personal narratives reflect, in part, how individuals make sense of group interactions and their role in contributing to family-level processes. Many of these representations are grounded in repetitive practices that occur as part of the family's daily routines and preparation for special events. We now turn to the study of family routines and rituals and their role in supporting healthy development.

Evolving Nature of Routines and Rituals

A defining characteristic of families is their changing nature and composition. The organization of family life is altered with the addition and loss of each member. The transition to parenthood is a period of particular vulnerability as new routines must be established and preexisting relationships maintained. The shifting nature of routines and rituals was examined in a study of 115 families whose oldest child was either an infant or of preschool age (Fiese, Hooker, Kotary, & Schwagler, 1993). The researchers reasoned that there would be more routinization in families whose oldest child was of preschool age than in households where parenting was directed toward the care of an infant. Overall, the preschool family group reported more regular practices associated with dinnertime, weekends, and annual celebrations than the infant family group. Furthermore, the symbolic meaning associated with family rituals was greater in the preschool family group. The authors speculated that when parents are engaged in the intense day-to-day demands of caring for an infant, there is little time left for organized collective activities. Once children are of preschool age, however, they can be more active contributors to organized events such as mealtime, birthday celebrations, and weekend outings to the zoo. With more active participation and repetition of activities, there is greater opportunity to create feelings of belonging and to attach symbolic significance to shared gatherings.

The continuity of routine practices throughout the early school years may aid in organizing family life such that children are better equipped to succeed in school and develop social competence. In a study of 70 families contacted first when one of their children was 4 years old and again when he or she was 9 years old, relative stability in family routines was found over the 5-year period, with modest increases in weekend activities (Fiese, 2000). Children's academic achievement at age 9 was related to routinization in the family when he or she was 4 years of age, controlling for current family routines. However, not all families maintained relative organization and

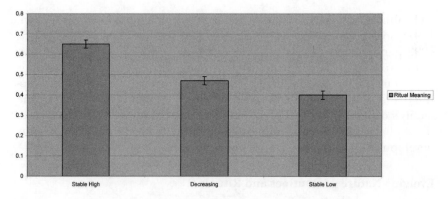

Figure 5.3.   Child social competence across ritual change.

meaning over the 5-year period. Groups were identified that maintained, decreased, or increased in the amount of affective meaning and importance ascribed to their rituals during this transition period. Children raised in households where rituals were maintained and held symbolic meaning throughout the period scored highest on measures of academic achievement, and children perceived themselves as more socially competent as measured by the Harter Perceived Competence Scale (Harter, 1982; see Figure 5.3).

The relevance of family routines and rituals extends into adolescence. Even though adolescents spend relatively less time at home, they continue to be influenced by family practices (Crouter, Head, McHale, & Tucker, 2004). In particular, adolescents who report more affective meaning in their family rituals have a stronger sense of self, feel that they belong to a group and are worthy of love, and are less likely to exhibit problematic drinking during the transition to college (Fiese, 1992, 1993). These findings are consistent with epidemiological reports whereby adolescents who regularly eat dinner with their families are less likely to smoke cigarettes or marijuana, drink alcohol, are less susceptible to depression, and are more likely to get better grades (Eisenberg, Olson, Neumark-Sztainer, Story, & Bearinger, 2004).

To summarize, the regular practice of routines during early development and into adolescence provides an organizational template for interacting within the group. When there is a certain degree of regularity to these collective activities, then children perform better in school and feel a sense of competence. Beyond the regularity of routines is the meaning and affective connections made during regular gatherings. When family practices hold symbolic meaning, then children feel a stronger sense of self and belonging that, in turn, may protect them from engaging in risky behaviors.

INTERSECTIONS OF INDIVIDUAL
AND FAMILY-LEVEL PROCESS

When one considers the evolution of family routines and the creation of family narratives during normative development, the dynamic influences of family and individual on each other becomes more evident and one can glimpse how the individual child is embedded in family-level processes and how family-level processes are affected by individual strivings. A closer examination of the pattern of relations found in the questionnaire studies on family routines points to the integrative function of such practices. In the study of couples with infants or preschool age children, it was found that feelings associated with the cohesiveness of the marital relationship was most strongly related to family ritual meaning (Fiese et al., 1993). In a similar vein, in the study of adolescents, it was the dimensions of identity integration and lovability that were most strongly related to adolescent and parent report of ritual meaning (Fiese, 1992). Identity integration was defined as an inner sense of cohesion, and lovability refers to the extent to which the individual feels that he or she is worthy of love and can trust others. Taken together, these findings suggest that experiences within the group come to define characteristics of the individual. The representations of these practices add to the individual's sense of belonging to a group and provide a context in which the process of finding predictability in relationships and resolving inconsistent experiences can cohere into a unified whole. Whereas the study of family rituals reveals how reportable practices may contribute to connectedness within the family, the pattern of findings also suggest that integrating different relationship experiences is an important process for individual adaptation. The study of family stories and narrative coherence provides another way to access this aspect of family-level processes.

In the study of family narratives, when individuals depict whole family gatherings as rewarding experiences, then directly observed interactions were more cohesive and positive. In the case of normative development, we suspect that this is part of a transactional process. When mealtime interactions are characterized by responsiveness, positive affect, and effective problem solving, then the stories created about such events draw on the experienced practice and are incorporated into representations characterized by trustworthiness, reliability, and satisfaction. Returning to the dinner table, time after time, presents further opportunities for families to reinforce these beliefs as well as to create new stories that conform to the family's belief system.

Thus far, we have provided descriptive information about family level processes that may affect development. Consistent with principles of developmental psychopathology, we must also consider how whole family processes may protect children from high-risk conditions or may exacerbate the effects of risk. An examination of risk conditions also allows for speculations about the mechanisms of effects of family-level processes.

CHILDHOOD CHRONIC ILLNESS
AS A FAMILY-LEVEL STRESSOR

We have begun to apply our system of accessing family representations and practices to the study of families who have a child with a chronic illness. We opted to focus on this risk condition for several reasons. First, the management of a chronic illness presents a family-level challenge in organizing daily life to support the health and well-being of the child (Fisher & Weihs, 2000). Second, beliefs about the impact of the illness on family life are potentially related to the ability to effectively manage the illness and support the individual child. Third, children with chronic illness are at increased risk to develop mental health problems (Pless & Nolan, 1989). However, not all children with a chronic illness develop such problems, and thus these conditions provide an excellent opportunity to identify family-level factors that promote health and reduce risk.

Pediatric Asthma as a Risk Condition

Asthma is the most common chronic illness of childhood and the prevalence, severity, and mortality related to this illness is on the rise. Complications arising from managing childhood asthma have serious consequences for children, including repeated hospitalizations, poor school attendance, and death. In the United States, more than 11 million people reported having an asthma attack in the year 2000, and more than 5% of all children younger than 18 reported having asthma attacks (McCormick, Kass, Elizhauser, Thompson, & Simpson, 2000).

Although inconclusive, there is evidence to suggest that children with difficult-to-manage chronic illnesses are at greater risk for anxiety-related disorders than their healthy peers (e.g.,Cadman, Boyle, Szatmari, & Offord, 1987; Lavigne & Faier-Routman, 1992; Pless & Nolan, 1989). Children with asthma have been found to have significantly more internalizing symptoms than controls (Hamlett, Pellegrini, & Katz, 1992), with the presence of depression raising the risk of mortality (Strunk, 1987).

The risks associated with chronic medical illness appear to be mediated, in part, by medical adherence and family health and moderated by illness severity and family stress. Nonadherence to treatment protocols is high in pediatric populations, reaching levels upwards of 50% of children prescribed daily medical regimens (Bender & Klinnert, 1998; Gibson, Ferguson, Aitchison, & Paton, 1995). In the case of childhood asthma, poor adherence is associated with increased morbidity and risk of asthma-related death. Family dysfunction as evidenced by delaying treatment, high levels of criticism, and family conflict have been found to be related to nonadherence to medical regimens (Christiannse, Lavigne, & Lerner, 1989).

Current practice guidelines for the treatment of asthma emphasize the importance of daily and regular monitoring of asthma symptoms and detailed action plans in the event of an attack (National Institutes of Health, 1997). Many of the recommendations are framed as part of the family's daily or weekly routines, such as vacuuming the house once or twice weekly, monthly cleaning of duct systems, and monitoring peak flows on wakening. In this regard, patterns of medical adherence may be directly tied to family routines and indirectly associated with child mental health.

DISEASE MANAGEMENT ROUTINES AND CHILD MENTAL AND PHYSICAL HEALTH

Following our earlier work on family routines and rituals, we developed a questionnaire to evaluate the degree to which routines associated with disease management would be related to child health and well-being. One hundred thirty-three families with a child with asthma were drawn from two study sites (Fiese, Wamboldt, & Anbar, 2005). The families were relatively diverse across ethnic background (65% White, 20% African American, 8% Latino, 3% Asian, 1% Native American, 2% unspecified) and socioeconomic status (Mean Hollingshead score = 39.31; SD = 15.99). Parents completed the Family Ritual Questionnaire and an 8-item scale that specifically addressed disease management routines. A factor analysis of the responses revealed two reliable dimensions that accounted for 48% of the variance. We labeled the first factor Medication Routines, as most of the items pertained to when medications were taken and prescriptions filled. We labeled the second factor Routine Burden, as many of the items pertained to whether asthma care was viewed as a chore. In our first round of analyses, we were interested in three primary outcomes: medical adherence, caregiver quality of life, and child quality of life. Medical adherence was determined through electronic monitoring of inhaler use and parent report. Quality of life was determined through caregiver and child responses to asthma quality of life questionnaires (Juniper et al., 1996; Juniper, Guyatt, Ferrie, & Griffith, 1993). Quality of life measures may be of particular interest to developmental psychopathologists because they are closely associated with measures of depression and anxiety (Annett, Bender, Lapidus, DuHamel, & Lincoln, 2001). They have the advantage over other measures of depression and anxiety as they are more closely linked with the child's current health conditions and allow for an examination of health symptoms and emotions separately. Typically, quality of life measures include assessment of health symptoms, how much the illness has affected daily activities, and how much the illness contributes to worry and emotional functioning.

In terms of medical adherence, we found that the regularity of medication routines was associated with medical adherence but not quality of life. Routine burden, on the other hand, was related to quality of life but not medication use (see Table 5.3). This pattern of results is consistent with our earlier work in distinguishing between the observable reportable aspects of routines and the emotional investment in carrying out these routines on a regular basis. For families faced with the challenge of managing medical regimens, predictability and order are related to the daily practice of taking medications. In those cases where these daily activities are seen as a burden, there is an emotional cost to both parent and child. In cases where the family perceives daily care as a drain on personal resources, children worry

TABLE 5.3
Correlations[a] Between Asthma Routine Questionnaire
and Health Care Utilization, Adherence, and Quality of Life

| | Asthma Routines Questionnaire | |
	Medication Routines	Routine Burden
Physician Visits	.30***	.17*
Medication Adherence		
DOSER	.29**	.00
24-hour recall	.32***	.02
Adherence to Clinical Trials		
# controller puffs missed in last 7 days	-.35***	-.07
# controller puffs used in past 2 months	.20**	.11
# times used rescue inhaler in last 7 days	.00	.18*
Most number of rescue puffs at a time	-.20*	.10
Caregiver Quality of Life		
Activity	.01	-.28***
Emotion	.04	-.28***
Total	.03	-.29***
Pediatric Quality of Life		
Symptoms	-.01	-.21**
Activities	.03	-.15*
Emotions	-.04	-.32***
Total	-.01	-.25***

Note: From "Family asthma management routines: Connections to medical adherence and quality of life," by B. H. Fiese, F. S. Wamboldt, & R. D. Anbar, 2005, *Journal of Pediatrics, 146,* p. 174. Copyright 2005 by Elsevier. Reprinted with permission.

[a]Kendall's Tau.

*$p < .05$; **$p < .01$; ***$p < .001$.

more about their asthma symptoms, report that they have difficulty breathing, and that their daily activities are often interrupted by health symptoms. For caregivers, when routines are seen as burden they also report that their child's health prevents them from engaging in desired activities and that there is a personal cost to their emotional life. When there was less of an emotional investment in daily routines, there was more of an emotional drain on caregivers and children. We suspect that the interplay between daily routines and quality of life is part of a transactional process. Children who report more health symptoms may present more demands on their caregivers. The caregivers may feel ill equipped to meet the emotional and health needs of their child and develop feelings of incompetence and being overwhelmed. Daily routines may then become disrupted and regular activities outside disease management are replaced with attention to the child's symptoms with relatively little relief. We gain further insight into this process when we step back inside the family and consider how its members manage day-to-day affairs and the overall impact of the illness on the family as a whole.

Narrative Representations of the Impact of Illness on Family Life. In collaboration with Frederick Wamboldt at National Jewish Medical Research Center in Denver, Colorado, we have been evaluating family interviews through the use of the Asthma Impact Interview (Wamboldt & O'Connor, 1997). We have examined these interviews in terms of how they reflect beliefs about family relationships as well as their overall coherence (Fiese & Sameroff, 1999). Our primary outcomes of interest have been medical adherence, family functioning, and family strain. For the purposes of this chapter, we also include preliminary results in relation to child quality of life.

The Asthma Impact Interview is conducted in such a way as to have the family discuss how the child's illness has affected family life, the family as a whole, parents as individuals, and the child personally. Parents are asked to talk about their child's condition as they would over a cup of coffee with a friend, not the story that they tell their pediatrician. Most families resonate with the request and understand that we are trying to get inside the daily life of the family and understand the challenges they face on a daily basis. In one round of analyses of the narratives, we identified three management strategies adopted by families: reactive, coordinated care, and family partnerships. The *reactive group* is best characterized as using emergency measures rather than preventative actions to manage their child's asthma. Prominent in many of these interviews were escalating levels of negative affect, anxiety, and worry that prompted action. The *coordinated care group* is characterized by identifying one person in the family who is responsible for management, and the strategies typically follow the doctor's orders. The *family partnership group* was characterized by a team-based approach to management, and multiple members of the family pitch in to help. We found that the reactive group had the lowest rate of medical adherence overall and were most likely to use the emergency room for care 1 year following the interview (Fiese & Wamboldt, 2003b). Furthermore, the reactive group reported very little planning around family routines, whereas the family partnership group reported significantly more routine planning than either of the other groups.

We also examined a subset of 62 interviews for narrative coherence and beliefs about family relationships and their relation to family functioning (Fiese & Wamboldt, 2003a). We found that the beliefs associated with the trustworthiness of relationships were related to the overall impact of the illness on the family life. Narrative coherence, on the other hand, was not related to disease specific impact but was associated with family problem solving, communication, affective responsiveness, and overall general functioning (Table 5.4). We speculate that narrative coherence evolves over time much in the same way that communication patterns and problem solving evolves for the family. Beliefs about relationships, however, may be more susceptible to current strains associated with a specific condition such as the effects of a chronic illness on family resources.

In a follow-up analysis, we considered how narrative coherence may be related to the child's quality of life. We reason that if the caregiver is unable to create a coherent story of the child's illness, then the child may be receiv-

TABLE 5.4
Comparison of Narrative Dimensions with Family-Based Measures

	Narrative Coherence[a]	Relationship Expectations
Family Assessment Device[b]		
Problem Solving	-.25*	-.25*
Communication	-.27*	-.22
Roles	-.18	-.13
Affective Responsiveness	-.33**	-.06
Affective Involvement	-.09	-.17
Behavior Control	-.10	-.23
General Functioning	-.25*	-.31**
Impact on the Family		
Financial	.05	-.22
General Impact	-.05	-.28*
Social Relationships	.03	-.24
Coping	-.09	-.27*
Total Impact	.00	-.25*

Note: From "Coherent accounts of coping with a chronic illness: Convergences and divergences in family measurement using a narrative analysis," by B. H. Fiese and F. S. Wambolt, 2003, *Family Process, 42,* pp. 3–45. Copyright 2003 by Blackwell Publishing. Reprinted by permission.
[a]Partialled for effect of mother education. [b]Higher FAD scores reflect poorer family functioning.
*$p < .05$; **$p < .01$

ing the message that their illness is a source of strain and one that can not be easily managed. On the other hand, when parents are able to create a coherent synthesis of their child's condition, they send the message that the disease is manageable and does not need to overwhelm daily activities. We found that the overall coherence evidenced in the Asthma Impact Interview was associated with the child's report of asthma effects on daily activities ($r(62) = .30, p < .05$), how much their condition affected their emotions ($r(62) = .28, p < .05$), and their overall quality of life ($r(62) = .28, p < .05$). This pattern of relations should be taken cautiously as the overall strength of the relationship is relatively weak. However, they do suggest that when caregivers experience a difficult time creating a coherent account of their child's condition, then their child feels more emotionally vulnerable and is more likely to avoid desired activities due to their symptoms. Interestingly, this pattern of findings held when considering severity of asthma symptoms. Thus, we do not believe that coherence is necessarily directly affected by severity of the illness.

The Intersection of Daily Practices and Family Representations

Although our research with families with a child with chronic illness is in its formative stage, we begin to see how family-level processes may influence family and child adaptation under a risk condition. When daily life is relatively well organized, families engage in patterned interactions that support their child's health and well-being. It is easier to remember to take your medication when day and night are structured in a predictable manner. When daily routines become a burden, then caregivers are more likely to experience the demands of daily life as an emotional drain with few reliable resources. The emotional drain then becomes part of the family's representation of how the illness has affected family life. Response to care is compromised, and children and parents experience a poorer quality of life overall. The link we found between deliberate planning of family routines and management styles depicted in the narrative suggests one mechanism of effect. When demands for care disrupt the normal flow of family life and caregivers feel burdened by added demands of disease management, there is less attention to planning (which could relieve the burden) and prevention. Take, for example, a narrative presented by a caregiver that was categorized in the reactive management group.

> Well, we more or less suspected that she had asthma for a while. And I guess you know I noticed more that she complained about feeling tight in her chest or whatever, and she was doing some wheezing. But I come from a family where my mother was a hypochondriac and I know from my own experience, kids do tend to when they don't want to go to school or something, they make up things about why they don't want to go so I just choose to ignore a lot of

it. One night she was upset about something I think we had an argument or something and she was crying it was late at night it was about 10 o'clock at night and I was very angry with her and she was complaining about this tightness in her chest and she needed to get to the doctor and of course I just thought it was a way to get my attention and I was ignoring her but she kept insisting so as angry as I was I loaded her in the middle of the night we went to the emergency room.

In this example, action is taken only after the child's symptoms became so severe that it was necessary to seek emergency care. We note in several of these narratives that the family's response to the child's symptoms is often accompanied with strong emotions, some of which seem to escalate to the point of being out of control. Feelings of burden may lead to increased negative affect and few avenues of containing or regulating affect. Repetitive interactions in routine settings accompanied by escalating and dysregulated affect then may affect the child's representation of relationships and mental health. Let us now step back inside the life of the family through the eyes of children.

Children's Narratives of Whole Family Process.   Thus far, we have primarily considered caregiver's perceptions and depictions of whole family process and their relation to child and family functioning. There is growing evidence in the field of developmental psychopathology that children's perceptions of relationships serve as important mediators of stress and adaptation (Grych, Wachsmuth-Schlaefer, & Klockow, 2002). Drawing on the work of attachment researchers and others (Bretherton, Prentiss, & Ridgeway, 1990; Emde, 2003; McHale et al., 1999), we have found storytelling to be a reliable means to gain access into the child's representation of relationships. Consistent with our focus on whole family process, we have developed a set of story stems that pertain to family mealtimes, bedtime, special celebrations, and vacations. For the purposes of this chapter, we describe our findings with dinnertime stories told by children with asthma. Children are presented with a picture of a relatively clean and well-organized kitchen. Scaled to picture size, children are also presented with a table, chairs, a plastic pizza, and doll figures. The child is instructed to "tell a story about this family at dinner." At the end of the meal, the child is told that one of the children in the family has an asthma attack and asked "What happens next?" At the end of the story, the child is presented with picture of a disheveled kitchen (e.g., trash on the floor, dead plants in the window, dishes overturned) and asked to tell a similar set of stories.

Overall, we find that children describe family relationships in the disheveled kitchen as less rewarding, less involved, and more likely to include negative affect (Figure 5.4). On one hand, this may be a stereotyped response and reflect exposure to televised images of disorganized families. Certainly,

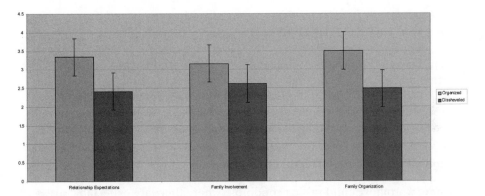

Figure 5.4. Children's representations of family life under two story stem conditions.

we cannot rule this out. Yet, on the other hand, how children characterize disorganized family life reveals pertinent elements of disruption and potential effects on child functioning. Take, for example, one child's response to the organized and disheveled kitchen scenes.

> Organized Kitchen Scene: First of all, the brother sits there, the sister sits there, and the mother sits there and the father sits there. And, they make sure the kids have washed their hands. And then they all sit down and wait for everybody to get to the table and they jus sort of start eating and talking about their day.
>
> Disheveled Kitchen Scene: Well this family nobody cares if they wash their hands or not, they just start scarfing down dinner. The brother's talking about how he wants this video game and the sister's talking about how she wants these dolls, and the father's talking about how many times other states have lost the Superbowl, and the mother is talking about how many dishes are in the sink and complaining and they're all talking at the same time so it doesn't make any sense.

In the first scenario, family relationships are ordered, predictable, and, even though mundane, convey a sense that others care ("they make sure the kids have washed their hands"). In the second scenario, there is little emotional investment, and interactions are dysregulated to the point that "it doesn't make any sense." When we examined the relation between the child's depiction of relationships in the stories and parent report of family functioning and child behavior problems, we found several significant relations. Under the disheveled kitchen condition when children depicted relationships more negatively, parents reported more difficulties in assigning family roles ($r(49) = -.38$, $p < .01$), parents were less affectively responsive ($r(49) = -.34$, $p < .01$), and family functioning in general was worse overall ($r(49) = -.28$, $p < .05$).

FAMILY-LEVEL MECHANISMS

In this concluding section, we consider different family-level mechanisms of influence on individual development and also address limitations and suggestions for future research. Returning to our two domains of family-level processes (representations and practices) makes it possible to contrast normative development with maladaptive functioning under risky conditions.

Family Practices and Effectual Competence

Under normative child-raising conditions where there are expectable stressors and adequate resources, the predictable practice of family routines is related to expressions of parental (Sprunger, Boyce, & Gaines, 1985), academic (Fiese, 2000), and social (Fiese et al., 2002) competence. The predictability of routines may also serve as a protective factor for competence. Brody and Flor (1997) demonstrated that routines are closely associated with academic and social competence for African American children raised with few economic resources. When family life is relatively predictable and there is an order to the day, then there is a greater likelihood that individuals will feel competent and well-equipped to meet daily challenges. Learning to care for an infant while juggling career demands, setting aside a time and a place to do homework, and getting home in time for dinner after sports practice are examples of how daily practices within the family are folded into the stream of everyday life. When the family is stressed by demands they are ill-equipped to face, ineffectual strategies (e.g., panic, emergency responding) are employed and there is little regularity or predictability to daily life. Disruptions in routines have the potential to compromise individual health; something as straightforward and scheduled as taking medications twice a day may become an insurmountable task. Although every family experiences stress and daily hassles, resilient families are able to get back on track as evidenced in their organized daily practices.

Family narratives that include the practice of imparting lessons learned and addressing personal transgressions offer an opportunity for behavioral guidance. A story told about how a parent effectively dealt with a personal experience such as a disagreement with a teacher, rejection by a peer, or conflict with a sibling offers the opportunity to problem solve and provide effective solutions for future challenges. These are opportunities to learn from the past prompted by experiences in the present. When the family is faced with challenges that appear new at every turn, there is less opportunity to learn from the past. The narratives of daily life are then framed as responses to emergencies with little emphasis on deliberate planning. At the extreme, stories are never told and heritages are lost across gen-

erations. In some of the examples highlighted in this chapter, stressful situations were associated with family narratives that tend to be disjointed,
difficult to follow, and rarely reassuring directions for future behavior.

The synthesized image of the practicing family under normative conditions is one with regular and predictable routines, effortful planning to
meet new challenges, and capitalizing on past experiences to impart values and lessons to the next generation. Under stressful conditions that
lead to compromised functioning, the practicing family has few behavioral
guides, rarely learns from past mistakes, and sees little rationale for planning ahead. The consequences of disrupted daily practices are feelings of
incompetence and ineffectual group guidance.

Family Representations and Connectedness

The normative evolution of family rituals over time aids in creating a sense
of belonging to the group. Repetitive interactions experienced at the dinner
table, eager anticipations of shared family times, and serving witness at celebrations such as weddings or bar mitzvahs cement feelings of being part of
something larger than oneself. The symbolic representation of these gatherings adds to the individual's sense of self as a member of a valued group.
The individual then creates representations that include support, trust, and
reassurance that the group will survive. When rituals are disrupted due to
a chronic stressor, then there is an emotional cost and drain to the individual. Rather than looking forward to family gatherings or events, exchanges
are a chore and burden. Attending to the needs of others predominates
images of the represented family in such a way that the group is envisioned
as disjointed, interactions strained, and there is little reassurance that the
group as a whole will be stable over time.

When the individual considers his or her place in the represented family, under normative conditions there is the opportunity to integrate different experiences into a coherent whole. The cohesiveness of the group
becomes associated with the relative coherent identity of the individual
such that relationships are considered understandable, sources of support,
and expected to remain so over time. Under maladaptive conditions, the
represented family is one of disjuncture and disengagement. Relationships
do not make sense as they are not predictable, they are rarely sources of
support, and others must be called in from outside the family to maintain
balance. Often times the represented family under maladaptive conditions
is marked by escalating negative affect and expectations for harm. Relationships are overwhelming and attempts at resolving inconsistencies in experience are marked by disappointments. Representations of unrewarding
family relationships are likely to be woven into transactions that distance
individuals from the group over time.

Family-Level Monitoring Processes

We speculate that there are at least two family-level monitoring processes that serve to regulate behavior and emotion in the family and thereby contribute to adaptive or maladaptive outcomes in children. The first type is behavioral monitoring. When gathered together on a regular basis, family members have the opportunity to monitor others' behavior. This can include attention to when everyone is expected to be home, who has good manners at the dinner table, and whether a prescribed medication was taken. We know that monitoring the physical whereabouts of children under high-risk conditions has been identified as a protective factor for a variety of outcomes including behavior problems, drug and alcohol abuse and delinquency, and early pregnancy (e.g., Dishion & McMahon, 1998; Pettit, Laird, Dodge, Bates, & Criss, 2001; Waizenhofer, Buchanan, & Jackson-Newsom, 2004). Under less extreme circumstances, the practice of family routines may affect child outcome by regulating behavior on a regular basis through monitoring activities.

A second process may be affective monitoring. We found worse outcomes in children when family representations serve to escalate negative affect. We see this in stories that children tell about family gatherings and in narratives that parents provide of challenging conditions. Other narrative researchers have also commented on this pattern of escalation (e. g., Oppenheim, Nir, Warren, & Emde, 1997). What it portends on the level of the family is attention to how families, as a group, monitor and respond to affect. Under promotive conditions, family members can freely express their emotions, but the intensity is often regulated by normative expectations for a particular family. Families may differ in their "set point" of negative affect expression. For some families, a slightly raised voice is seen as cause for comment; for others, free flowing exchanges at a heightened pitch are seen as the norm. It is unlikely that there is a uniform set point that pertains to all families. However, every family regulates emotions and monitors expressions by individuals. When affect monitoring breaks down, there is a cost to the individual and the family as a whole. For the individual, unpredictable and inconsistent responsiveness to emotions may be associated with poor affect regulation. For the family as a whole, poor affect monitoring contributes to chaotic interactions and an inability to carry out plans.

Limitations and Future Directions

There are clear limitations to the research we have conducted thus far. Our sample sizes are relatively small and our data analytic strategies have relied primarily on patterned relations. There is a need to apply some of these methods and concepts to larger and more diverse samples and to incorporate more sophisticated analytic strategies. In our ongoing studies, we have recruited more ethnically and economically diverse families and are following some of them longitudinally. These efforts will allow us to chart whether changes in routines are preceded or followed by family-level stressors, as well as whether stability in practices and representations are related to child mental health.

We have suggested that family representations and practices transact over time and we have yet to directly test this model. We have been encouraged by the recent report of the Minnesota longitudinal study that representations of relationships and social development operate in a reciprocal manner from infancy to adolescence (Carlson, Sroufe, & Egeland, 2004). We agree with these scholars that proposing a particular model of the specific relations between representations and behavior detracts from the organizational principles of development. We aim to follow this lead by examining regulatory functions at the family level that may lead to a greater appreciation of the transactions between family practices and representations.

Another limitation of our work to date has been the failure to test alternative models. We recognize that there are several alternative explanations to our findings. Although, for example, we have mentioned behavior and affect monitoring as two potential processes, we also recognize that variables more traditionally associated with developmental psychopathology such as parental warmth, attachment patterns, and conflict resolution may afford a more parsimonious explanation than our model. In addition, future efforts must also consider the ways in which parental psychopathology may derail whole family process.

Our journey inside the life of the family has led us to consider some key elements of whole family process. We do not in any way propose that family routines, rituals, and narratives about family events are necessarily distinct from more traditional variables such as warmth, cohesiveness, and conflict. Rather, these aspects appear to be embedded in routines, rituals, and narratives. What we do propose, however, is that routines and rituals make sense to families and give them a common language to communicate with researchers. Whereas it may be difficult for family members to comment and discuss such constructs as "hierarchical order" and "boundaries," they appear to have an intuitive sense of their family's identity when framed as part of their daily activities. In this regard, the study of daily activities in the family context opens a window on the multilevel and dynamic, transactional processes in the family. Close study of these processes has the potential to take us inside what is a very personal, unique, and potentially compelling aspect of development.

The family as a level of analysis and influence on children's well-being calls for a keen appreciation for the complexities as well as the subtleties family life. As a unit of analysis, it is not sufficient to merely identify who belongs to the group (although this can be a challenging endeavor given the shifting nature of who may be in or out of a family at any given point in time). One must also consider the extent to which the individual is engaged with the group. It is for this reason that such concepts as cohesiveness, belongingness, and coherence are pivotal in the study of family-level processes. These are not easy concepts to measure, but they reflect family-level organizational principles. Some of these characteristics have been noted in studies of dyadic relationships. For example, coherence is important in understanding how attachment relationships are represented and guide behavior (Main, Kaplan, & Cassidy, 1985). When considering family-level analysis, however, coherence refers not only to the synthesis of experiences within a relationship between two people, but also to how relationships among several people are regulated and cohere, or remain whole, over time (Fiese & Spagnola, 2005). These representations are grounded in repetitive exchanges, sometimes fleeting, and sometimes in mundane activities such as mealtimes or bedtime stories. These exchanges involve multiple members of the family, extend across generations, and are dense in symbolic meaning. It is for this reason that it is important to consider not only how individuals interact with each other in gathered settings such as mealtimes, but also how individuals represent these collective events.

The integration of family practices and representations calls for a synthesis of two research traditions in developmental psychopathology. The direct observation of dyads has a long and fruitful history. Typically, the coding of dyadic exchanges involves a focus on reciprocity, careful attention to initiation and maintenance of targeted behaviors, and how particular tasks or problems are solved. Family-level interactions share the same characteristics, but an added dimension is how the group as a whole maintains balance and integrity in face of disruptions. For example, the McMaster Mealtime Interaction Coding System (Dickstein, Hayden, Schiller, Seifer, & San Antonio, 1994) includes a Task Accomplishment scale not unlike dyadic measures used in clean-up tasks. The distinguishing feature in the family-level measure is the attention to how the group, as a whole, reacts to interruptions or challenges to having the meal run smoothly. The aim of directly observing behavior has often been tied to assumptions that if one were to alter behavior of a given family member, then there would be an alteration in the child's development or mental health. For example, changing patterns of parent attention and behavior control should reduce coercive cycles and child disruptive behaviors (Patterson, DeGarmo, & Forgatch, 2004). The focus on family representations, in contrast, draws from another tradition also well known to developmental psychopathology, that of psychodynamic theory and attachment theory. From this vantage point, how individuals represent relationships is proposed to guide behavior with the assumption that a change in representations would ultimately affect a change in mental health status (Fonagy, 2000). The family-level model being proposed here would integrate these two traditions. Although not without precedence (Reiss, 1989), this synthesis calls for theoretical and method-ological advances that have yet to be realized. The challenge will be to find theoretically driven methods of analysis that capitalize on these two tradi-tions. For example, one could ask how it is that the repetitive daily interac-tions at the dinner table come to form a mental representation associated with feelings of belonging to the group. This type of question demands longitudinal studies, is potentially amenable to experimental manipulation and clinical interventions, and will require innovative strategies that likely integrate qualitative and quantitative research methods.

The integration of family-level practices and representations may be framed as a multilevel transactional process whereby how the group inter-acts together comes to form the individual's representation of collective experiences, which, in turn, guides behavior. The transactional model has been an extremely useful heuristic in developmental psychopathology. The challenge for the future will be to integrate multiple methods that allow for testable multilevel analyses of the reciprocal influences of family represen-tations and practices.

In addition to addressing the complexities and subtleties of family life, it is crucial that developmental psychopathology be prepared for the chang-ing composition of families. Immigration, divorce, remarriage, and same-sex couples add another level of consideration in terms of what it means to study families. As family practices are often grounded in experiences from the past, how cultural heritages are blended in newly formed unions will become increasingly important as children are more likely to be raised by parents of distinct ethnic heritages in the foreseeable future (Parke, 2004). This presents an opportunity to consider how ethnic and socioeco-nomic contexts transact to either protect or place children at risk for devel-opmental problems. As developmental transition points are often times when daily family practices are reorganized to meet the needs of the child, how these practices are negotiated between parents of different cultural heritages may not only provide useful insights for variations in practices, but also be instructive about the process of acculturation and its affect on child development. An insider's view of family dynamics may be particu-larly revealing as observers from different ethnic heritages have been found to interpret family-level interactions in different ways (Gonzales, Cauce, & Mason, 1996).

The future brings many challenges for families as well as family research-ers in developmental psychopathology. Further refinement in methods of observation and narrative analysis appear warranted. Broadening studies to include more ethnically diverse and immigrant families is essential to better understand variations that occur during developmental transitions as well as transitions to new environments. The time appears ripe for more clinical interventions to test causal pathways (Cowan & Cowan, 2002). A cautionary note is in order, however. Many of the family-level dynamics discussed in this chapter, although amenable to change, are not likely to be effective in clinical trials that rely on a one-size-fits-all approach. Because of the variability in practices and interpretive quality to family life, more tailored approaches are indicated (Fiese & Wamboldt, 2001). Perhaps the greatest challenge will be to families themselves; increasing rates of poverty, suboptimal health for many family members, and parental job instability place children at great developmental risk. With steadfast attention to policies that allow families to celebrate their practices in meaningful ways, perhaps children's well-being can be better protected.

ACKNOWLEDGMENTS

Preparation of this paper was supported, in part, by a grant from the National Institute of Mental Health (R01 MH051771) to the first author and an Administration for Children and Families Head Start Graduate Student Research Scholar grant to the second author.

REFERENCES

Annett, R. D., Bender, B. G., Lapidus, J., DuHamel, T. R., & Lincoln, A. (2001). Predicting children's quality of life in an asthma clinical trial: What do children's reports tell us? *Journal of Pediatrics, 139*, 854–861.

Arnold, M. L., Pratt, M. W., & Hicks, C. (2004). Adolescent's representations of parents' voices in family stories: Value lessons, personal adjustment, and identity development. In M. W. Pratt & B. H. Fiese (Eds.), *Family stories and the life course* (pp. 163–186). Mahwah, NJ: Lawrence Erlbaum Associates.

Bender, B. G., & Klinnert, M. D. (1998). Psychological correlates of asthma severity and treatment outcome in children. In H. Kotses & A. Harver (Eds.), *Self-management of asthma* (pp. 63–88). New York: Marcel Dekker.

Boyce, W. T., Jensen, E. W., James, S. A., & Peacock, J. L. (1983). The Family Routines Inventory: Theoretical origins. *Social Science and Medicine, 17*, 193–200.

Bretherton, I., Prentiss, C., & Ridgeway, D. (1990). Family relationships as represented in a story-completion task at thirty-seven and fifty-four months of age. *New Directions for Child Development, 48*, 85–105.

Brody, G. H., & Flor, D. L. (1997). Maternal psychological functioning, family processes, and child adjustment in rural, single-parent, African American families. *Developmental Psychology, 33*, 1000–1011.

Cadman, D., Boyle, M., Szatmari, P., & Offord, D. (1987). Chronic illness, disability, and mental social well-being: Findings of the Ontario Child Health study. *Pediatrics, 10*, 75–80.

Carlson, E. A., Sroufe, L. A., & Egeland, B. (2004). The construction of experience: A longitudinal study of representation and behavior. *Child Development, 75*, 66–83.

Christiannse, M. E., Lavigne, J. C., & Lerner, C. V. (1989). Psychosocial aspects of compliance in children and adolescents with asthma. *Developmental and Behavioral Pediatrics, 10,* 75–80.

Cowan, P. A., & Cowan, C. P. (2002). Interventions as tests of family systems theories: Marital family relationships in children's developmental psychopathology. *Development and Psychopathology, 14,* 731–759.

Crouter, A. C., Head, M. R., McHale, S. M., & Tucker, C. J. (2004). Family time and the psychosocial adjustment of adolescent siblings and their parents. *Journal of Marriage and Family, 66,* 147–162.

Cummings, E. M. (1999). Some considerations on integrating psychology and health from a lifespan perspective. In T. L. Whitman, T. V. Merluzzi, & R. D. White (Eds.), *Life-span perspectives on health and illness* (pp. 277–294). Mahwah, NJ: Lawrence Erlbaum Associates.

Cummings, E. M., Davies, P. T., & Campbell, S. B. (2000). *Developmental psychopathology and family process.* New York: Guilford.

Dishion, T. J., & McMahon, R. J. (1998). Parental monitoring and the prevention of child and adolescent problem behavior: A conceptual and empirical formulation. *Clinical Child and Family Psychology Review, 1,* 61–75.

Eisenberg, M. E., Olson, R. E., Neumark-Sztainer, D., Story, M., & Bearinger, L. H. (2004). Correlations between family meals and psychosocial well-being among adolescents. *Archives Pediatric and Adolescent Medicine, 158,* 792–796.

Emde, R. N. (2003). Early narratives: A window to the child's inner world. In R. N. Emde, D. P. Wolf, & D. Oppenheim (Eds.), *Revealing the inner worlds of young children* (pp. 3–26). Oxford: Oxford University Press.

Epstein, N. B., Ryan, C. E., Bishop, D. S., Miller, I. W., & Keitner, G. I. (2003). The McMaster Model: A view of healthy family functioning. In F. Walsh (Ed.), *Normal family processes* (3rd ed., pp. 581–607). New York: Guilford.

Evans, G., & English, K. (2002). The environment of poverty: Multiple stressor exposure, psychophysiological stress, and socioemotional adjustment. *Child Development, 73,* 1238–1248.

Fiese, B. H. (1992). Dimensions of family rituals across two generations: Relation to adolescent identity. *Family Process, 31,* 151–162.

Fiese, B. H. (1993). Family rituals in alcoholic and nonalcoholic households: Relation to adolescent health symptomatology and problematic drinking. *Family Relations, 42,* 187–192.

Fiese, B. H. (2000). Family matters: A systems view of family effects on children's cognitive health. In R. J. Sternberg & E. L. Grigorenko (Eds.), *Environmental effects on cognitive abilities* (pp. 39–57). Mahwah, NJ: Lawrence Erlbaum Associates.

Fiese, B. H. (2006). *Family routines and rituals.* New Haven, CT: Yale University Press.

Fiese, B. H., & Bickham, N. L. (2004). Pincurling grandpa's hair in the comfy chair: Parents' stories of growing up and potential links to socialization in the preschool years. In M. W. Pratt & B. H. Fiese (Eds.), *Family stories across time and generations* (pp. 259–277). Mahwah, NJ: Lawrence Erlbaum Associates.

Fiese, B. H., Hooker, K. A., Kotary, L., & Schwagler, J. (1993). Family rituals in the early stages of parenthood. *Journal of Marriage and the Family, 57,* 633–642.

Fiese, B. H., Hooker, K. A., Kotary, L., Schwagler, J., & Rimmer, M. (1995). Family stories in the early stages of parenthood. *Journal of Marriage and the Family, 57,* 763–770.

Fiese, B. H., & Marjinsky, K. A. T. (1999). Dinnertime stories: Connecting relationship beliefs and child behavior. In B. H. Fiese et al. (Eds.), *The stories that families tell: Narrative coherence, narrative interaction, and relationship beliefs. Monographs of the Society for Research in Child Development, 64*(2), Serial No. 257 (pp. 52–68). Malden, MA: Blackwell.

Fiese, B. H., & Sameroff, A. J. (1999). The family narrative consortium: A multidimensional approach to narratives. In B. H. Fiese et al. (Eds.), *The stories that families tell: Narrative coherence, narrative interaction, and relationship beliefs. Monographs of the Society for Research in Child Development.* (Vol. 64(2), Serial no. 257, pp. 1–36). Malden, MA: Blackwell.

Fiese, B. H., & Spagnola, M. (2005). Narratives in and about family relationships: An examination of coding schemes and guide for family researchers. *Journal of Family Psychology, 19,* 51–61.

Fiese, B. H., Tomcho, T., Douglas, M., Josephs, K., Poltrock, S., & Baker, T. (2002). Fifty years of research on naturally occurring rituals: Cause for celebration? *Journal of Family Psychology, 16,* 381–390.

Fiese, B. H., & Wamboldt, F. S. (2001). Family routines, rituals, and asthma management: A proposal for family based strategies to increase treatment adherence. *Families, Systems, and Health, 18,* 405–418.

Fiese, B. H., & Wamboldt, F. S. (2003a). Coherent accounts of coping with a chronic illness: Convergences and divergences in family measurement using a narrative analysis. *Family Process, 42,* 3–15.

Fiese, B. H., & Wamboldt, F. S. (2003b). Tales of pediatric asthma management: Family based strategies related to medical adherence and health care utilization. *Journal of Pediatrics, 143,* 457–462.

Fiese, B. H., Wamboldt, F. S., & Anbar, R. D. (2005). Family asthma management routines: Connections to medical adherence and quality of life. *Journal of Pediatrics, 146,* 171–176.

Fisher, L., & Weihs, K. L. (2000). Can addressing family relationships improve outcomes in chronic disease? *The Journal of Family Practice, 49,* 561–566.

Fivush, R., Bohanke, J., Robertson, R., & Duke, M. (2004). Family narratives and the development of children's emotional well-being. In M. W. Pratt & B. H. Fiese (Eds.), *Family narratives across time and generations* (pp. 55–76). Mahwah, NJ: Lawrence Erlbaum Associates.

Fonagy, P. (2000). Attachment and borderline personality disorder. *Journal of the American Psychoanalytic Association, 48,* 1129–1146.

Fung, H., Miller, P. J., & Lin, L. (2004). Listening is active: Lessons from the narrative practices of Taiwanese families. In M. W. Pratt & B. H. Fiese (Eds.), *Family stories and the life course: Across time and generations.* (pp. 303–326). Mahwah, NJ: Lawrence Erlbaum Associates.

Gibson, N. A., Ferguson, A. E., Aitchison, T. C., & Paton, J. Y. (1995). Compliance with inhaled asthma medication in preschool children. *Thorax, 50,* 127–1279.

Gonzales, N. A., Cauce, A. M., & Mason, C. A. (1996). Interobserver agreement in the assessment of parental behavior and parent–adolescent conflict: African American mothers, daughters, and independent observers. *Child Development, 67*(1483–1498).

Grych, J. H., Wachsmuth-Schlaefer, T., & Klockow, L. L. (2002). Interparental aggression and young children's representations of family relationships. *Journal of Family Psychology, 16,* 259–272.

Hamlett, K. W., Pellegrini, D. S., & Katz, K. S. (1992). Childhood chronic illness as a family stressor. *Journal of Pediatric Psychology, 17,* 33–47.

Harter, S. (1982). The perceived competence scale for children. *Child Development, 53,* 87–97.

Juniper, E. F., Guyatt, G. H., Feeny, D. H., Ferrie, P. J., Griffith, L. E., & Townsend, M. (1996). Measuring quality of life in the parents of children with asthma. *Quality of Life Research, 5,* 27–34.

Juniper, E. F., Guyatt, G. H., Ferrie, P. J., Griffith, L. E. (1993). Measuring quality of life in asthma. *American Review of Respiratory Distress, 147,* 832–838.

Kantor, D., & Lehr, W. (1975). *Inside the family.* San Francisco: CA: Jossey-Bass.

Lavigne, J., & Faier-Routman, J. (1992). Psychological adjustment to pediatric physical disorders: A meta-analytic review. *Journal of Pediatric Psychology, 17,* 133–157.

Main, M., & Goldwyn, R. (1984). Predicting rejection of their infant from mother's representation of her own experience: Implications for the abused and abusing intergenerational cycle. *Child Abuse and Neglect, 8,* 203–217.

Main, M., Kaplan, N., & Cassidy, J. (1985). Security in infancy, childhood, and adulthood: A move to the level of representation. In I. Bretherton & E. Waters (Eds.), *Growing points in attachment theory and research. Monographs for the Society for Research in Child Development* (Vol. 50, pp. 66–104).

McAdams, D. P. (1993). *The stories we live by: Personal myths and the making of the self.* New York: William Morrow.

McCormick, M. C., Kass, B., Elizhauser, A., Thompson, J., & Simpson, L. (2000). Annual review of child health care access and utilization. *Pediatrics, 105*(1), 219–230.

McHale, J. P., Neugebauer, A., Radin Asch, A., & Schwartz, A. (1999). Preschooler's characterizations of multiple family relationships during family doll play. *Journal of Clinical Child Psychology, 28,* 256–268.

Miller, P., & Moore, B. B. (1989). Narrative conjunctions of caregiver and child: A comparative perspective on socialization through stories. *Ethos, 17,* 428–449.

National Institutes of Health. (1997). *Guidelines for the diagnosis and management of asthma* (No. NIH Publication No. 97–4051). Washington, DC: Author.

Oppenheim, D., Emde, R., & Warren, S. (1997). Children's narrative representations of mothers: Their development and associations with child and mother adaptation. *Child Development, 68,* 127–138.

Oppenheim, D., Nir, A., Warren, S., & Emde, R. N. (1997). Emotion regulation in mother–child narrative co-construction: Associations with children's narratives and adaptation. *Developmental Psychology, 33,* 284–294.

Parke, R. D. (2004). Development in the family. *Annual Review of Psychology, 55,* 365–399.

Patterson, G. R., DeGarmo, D. S., & Forgatch, M. S. (2004). Systematic changes in families following prevention trials. *Journal of Abnormal Child Psychology, 32,* 621–633.

Pettit, G. S., Laird, R. D., Dodge, K. A., Bates, J. E., & Criss, M. M. (2001). Antecedents and behavior-problem outcomes of parental monitoring and psychological control in early adolescence. *Child Development, 72,* 583–598.

Pless, I., & Nolan, T. (1989). Risks for maladjustment associated with chronic illness in childhood. In D. Shaffer, I. Philips, & N. B. Enzer (Eds.), *Prevention of mental disorders, alcohol, and other drug use in children and adolescents* (pp. 191–224). Rockville, MD: Office of Substance Abuse Prevention.

Pratt, M. W., Arnold, M. L., & Hilbers, S. M. (1998). A narrative approach to the study of moral orientation in the family: Tales of kindness and care. In E. E. Aspaas Skoe & A. L. Von der Lippe (Eds.), *Personality development in adolescence: A cross-national and life span perspective* (pp. 61–78). London: Routledge.

Pratt, M. W., & Fiese, B. H. (2004). Families, stories and the life course: An ecological context. In M. W. Pratt & B. H. Fiese (Eds.), *Family stories across time and generations.* Mahwah, NJ: Lawrence Erlbaum Associates.

Pratt, M. W., Norris, J., Arnold, M. L., & Filyer, R. (1999). Generativity and moral development as predictors of value socialization narratives for young persons across the adult lifespan: From lessons learned to stories shared. *Psychology and Aging, 14,* 414–426.

Reiss, D. (1981). *The family's construction of reality.* Cambridge, MA: Harvard University Press.

Reiss, D. (1989). The practicing and representing family. In A. J. Sameroff & R. Emde (Eds.), *Relationship disturbances in early childhood* (pp. 191–220). New York: Basic Books.

Rutter, M., & Sroufe, L. A. (2000). Developmental psychopathology: Concepts and challenges. *Development and Psychopathology, 12,* 265–296.

Sameroff, A. J. (1995). General systems theories and developmental psychopathology. In D. Cicchetti & D. Cohen (Eds.), *Handbook of developmental psychopathology* (Vol. 1, pp. 659–695). New York: Wiley.

Sameroff, A. J., & Fiese, B. H. (1992). Family representations of development. In I. Sigel, A. V. McGillicuddy-DeLisi, & J. J. Goodnow (Eds.), *Parent belief systems: The psychological consequences for children*. Hillsdale, NJ: Lawrence Erlbaum Associates.

Sameroff, A. J., & Fiese, B. H. (2000). Transactional regulation: The developmental ecology of early intervention. In S. J. Meisels & J. P. Shonkoff (Eds.), *Early intervention: A handbook of theory, practice, and analysis* (pp. 3–19). New York: Cambridge University Press.

Solomonica-Levi, D., Yirmiya, N., Erel, O., & Samet, I. (2001). The associations among observed maternal behavior, children's narrative representations of mothers, and children's behavior problems. *Journal of Social and Personal Relationships, 18,* 673–689.

Sprunger, L. W., Boyce, W. T., & Gaines, J. A. (1985). Family–infant congruence: Routines and rhythmicity in family adaptations to a young infant. *Child Development, 56,* 564–572.

Strunk, R. C. (1987). Deaths from asthma in childhood: Patterns before and after professional intervention. *Pediatric Asthma, Allergy, & Immunology, 1,* 5–13.

Teachman, J. D., Tedrow, L. M., & Crowder, K. D. (2000). The changing demography of America's families. *Journal of Marriage and the Family, 62,* 1234–1246.

Thorne, A., McClean, K. C., & Dasbach, A. (2004). When parents' stories go to pot: Telling personal transgressions to teenage kids. In M. W. Pratt & B. H. Fiese (Eds.), *Family stories and the lifecourse: Across time and generations* (pp. 187–209). Mahwah, NJ: Lawrence Erlbaum Associates.

van der Hart, O. (1983). *Rituals in psychotherapy: Transitions and continuity*. New York: Irvington.

Waizenhofer, R.N., Buchanan, C.M., & Jackson-Newsom, J. (2004). Mothers' and fathers' knowledge of adolescents' daily activities: Its sources and its links with adolescent adjustment. *Journal of Family Psychology, 18,* 348–360.

Wamboldt, F. S., & O'Connor, S. (1997). *Asthma Impact Interview*. Denver, CO: National Jewish Medical Research Center.

Warren, S., Emde, R., & Sroufe, L. A. (2000). Internal representations: Predicting anxiety from children's play narratives. *Journal of the American Academy of Child and Adolescent Psychiatry, 39,* 100–107.

Warren, S., Oppenheim, D., & Emde, R. (1996). Can emotions and themes in children's play predict behavior problems? *Journal of the American Academy of Child and Adolescent Psychiatry, 35*(10), 1331–1337.

Wolin, S. J., & Bennett, L. A. (1984). Family rituals. *Family Process, 23,* 401–420.

Chapter 6

Peer Dynamics in the Development and Change of Child and Adolescent Problem Behavior

Thomas J. Dishion
Timothy F. Piehler
Child and Family Center, University of Oregon

INTRODUCTION

A compelling feature of child and adolescent problem behavior is that it is often performed in reaction to or in the company of peers. Early studies of delinquent behavior indicated that the peer dynamic underlying delinquent behavior was so ubiquitous that it was not worth further study in understanding the etiology of delinquent behavior (Healy, 1927). Indeed, that has been the key issue in the study of child and adolescent problem behavior across disciplines: Are peer dynamics an epiphenomenon of the problem or are they etiologically relevant?

In this chapter, the role of peers in the development of child and adolescent problem behavior is explored at three levels. First, the macrodynamics of social networks are considered with respect to the emergence of deviant peer cliques in some school settings. Second, it is proposed that deviant peer cliques form the social field within which friendships emerge

151

and develop. The microsocial dynamics of child and adolescent friendships potentially amplify deviant behavior and provide a social context for the long-term maintenance of deviant lifestyles. The third level of analysis is the intrapersonal factors that enable the child to regulate exposure to deviant peer cliques and friendships and that protect the child from the social influence processes of friendships.

These three levels of analysis reflect the emphasis of an ecological framework (Bronfenbrenner, 1989) on the simultaneous consideration of the embedded systems of development, from the macro environment level such as the school, the interpersonal environment such as friendships, and the intrapersonal characteristics such as self-regulation. In addition to considering the three levels, it is appropriate to delineate how the three levels interrelate to one another, for example, to consider how families and peers may jointly define contexts that have dramatic effects on child and adolescent social and emotional development. Finally, the concept of development is critical for an understanding of peer relation dynamics underlying problem behavior. As children develop over time, each successive stage sets the foundation for future development. Critical self-regulatory skills may emerge in early to middle childhood but carry forward in setting the stage for pathogenic peer environments as well as the mode of responding to such environments.

The three levels just described are discussed in this chapter in the form of the following hypotheses:

1. The deviant confluence hypothesis: Peer network dynamics in elementary and middle school lead to the clustering of children with high levels of problem behavior. In particular, the exclusion or rejection of children from conventional peer networks leads to the development of a behavioral repertoire that attracts other rejected children to form deviant peer cliques.

2. The deviancy training hypothesis: Deviant peer cliques form a social context in which friendships are selected and developed that promote, influence, and socialize new forms of problem behavior. This influence dynamic is referred to as "microsocial" and can be readily identified and measured in videotaped friendship interactions.

3. Self-regulation hypothesis: Individual differences in adolescent intrapersonal self-regulation moderate vulnerability to deviant peer influences in general and in deviancy training dynamics in friendships in particular.

In the sections that follow, the rationale for proposing these three hypotheses is developed. In addition, data are presented examining the empirical support.

PEER NETWORK DYNAMICS

Sociometry

In the 1930s, psychologists began systematically looking at the network dynamics of children's peer relationships in the classroom (Moreno, 1933). Of particular interest for many years was the extent to which children were liked or accepted in the public school environment. Indeed, it was found that children with poor peer relations tended to have myriad difficulties, including long-term adjustment problems (Rolf, Masten, Cicchetti, Nuechterlein, & Weintraub, 1990).

A critical juncture in the study of children's peer relations was the measurement and conceptualization that peer rejection was a separate indicator from peer liking (Peery, 1979). The original strategy for quantifying rejection and acceptance was to compare the algebraic sum of the two indices to the total number of nominations received. The former was referred to as *social preference* and the latter as *social impact*. Coie, Dodge, and Coppotelli (1982) formulated a series of groups that was to affect two decades of research on peer relations: rejected, neglected, controversial, average, and popular.

Of particular interest to social developmental researchers was the link between aggression and peer rejection. Classic studies by Coie and Kupersmidt (1983) and Dodge (1983) revealed that in contrived playgroups, aggression was the primary precipitant of peer rejection. In the studies by Dodge, it was estimated that within 3 hours, the aggressive child became the rejected child in novel play groups of school-age children.

This work stimulated hundreds of carefully conducted studies on the antecedents and sequelae of peer rejection in middle childhood and early adolescence. Indeed, it was clear that rejected children were not a homogeneous group (French, 1988). However, it was suspected that peer rejection set the stage for subsequent peer relationship and social developmental difficulties. Although peer rejection was correlated with several adolescent outcomes, it became challenging to identify the unique contribution of peer rejection to outcomes such as truancy, delinquency, and maladjustment (Asher & Parker, 1987). It was not until recently that longitudinal research established the link between peer rejection in school-age children and young adult outcomes such as chronic antisocial behavior (Nelson & Dishion, 2004). If rejection predicts adult maladaptation, the next question is, "What is the mechanism?" Patterson and Dishion (1985) proposed that social skill deficits in combination with poor parent monitoring predicted adolescent delinquency. Despite the use of structural equation modeling, the link between social skill deficits and delinquency was not fully articulated. Later, it was proposed that such skill deficits related to the child's rejection by the conventional peer group, which then promoted clustering of children into deviant peer groups. This hypothesis was tested in a longitudinal analysis linking school-age rejection to early adolescent involvement with deviant peers. It was found that peer rejection (i.e., social preference) uniquely predicted involvement with deviant peers at age 11 to 12, once controlling for academic skills deficits, earlier antisocial behaviors, and parenting practices (Dishion, Patterson, Stoolmiller, & Skinner, 1991). This finding was later referred to as the *deviant peer confluence hypothesis* (Dishion, Patterson, & Griesler, 1994).

The measurement of the formation of deviant peer cliques turns out to be complicated. It is not as simple as to merely ask children whether their friends engaged in deviant behavior. The most obvious problem is mono method bias (Cook & Campbell, 1979). However, careful sociological investigators had long established more appropriate and thorough measures of adolescent peer cliques. For example, the work by Kandel (1978, 1986) revealed that over the course of the year, the friendship cliques that survived became more similar on attitudes of deviance. This is the first work that revealed the salience of deviant attitudes in forming adolescent peer groups. The process was referred to as *homophily* and was found to be critical for both formation and maintenance of adolescent peer cliques. A methodological detail worth noting was that friendship cliques were defined on mutual nominations. The use of nominations to define a clique seems quite obvious; however, developmental researchers tended to neglect the concept of cliques in their own work. A notable exception is the work by Cairns (1983) and colleagues examining a child's view of the social network environment.

Over the past 10 years, however, developmental researchers have relied on the concept of reciprocal liking nominations in the analysis of friendships. Significant work by Vitaro, Gendreau, Tremblay, and Oligny (1998) revealed the power of examining the characteristics of reciprocal friendships and their influence on the development of antisocial behavior. In this longitudinal research, it was found that reciprocal friends with moderate levels of antisocial behavior were the most likely to increase their problem behavior in the follow-up assessments. Youth with high levels of problem behavior and those with low levels of problem behavior did not appear to change as dramatically as did those in the moderate range.

There are several methodological challenges in defining meaningful peer cliques from peer nomination data used in sociometrics. Figure 6.1 provides an overview of a possible pattern of nominations that would not capture a clique if one were to rely solely on reciprocal nominations. In examining Figure 6.1, the arrows refer to in and out nominations. For example, an arrow from Fred to George reveals that Fred selected George

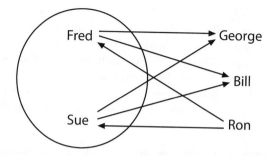

Figure 6.1 Fred and Sue have the same pattern of relationships.

as a friend in a nomination procedure. For George, this is an "in" nomination and Fred an "out" nomination. Note that Fred and Sue in the Figure 6.1 diagram have an identical pattern of in and out nomination. However, if we were to use reciprocal linkages as the criteria for defining a clique, then Fred and Sue would not be listed in the same peer group. However, it is clear from perusing Figure 6.1 that Sue and Fred walk in very similar social worlds.

The second methodological problem in defining peer cliques from nomination data is that missing data problems create artificial nonlinks among individuals. This could explain, for example, the lack of connection between Fred and Sue in Figure 6.1. The use of a single nomination in many ways undermines the strength of the peer nomination procedure. When an individual datum is used to indicate a reciprocal linkage, then the overall measurement strategy becomes less reliable. However, one strength of the peer nomination method is that attributes of individuals are based on aggregate perceptions of an entire social group.

An alternative approach is to cluster analyze the in and out nominations to define groups of individuals with similar patterns. These groups could be thought of as cliques in that they walk in very similar social worlds with respect to who they like and by whom they are liked. This measure was used in recent work by Dishion, Light, Yasui, and Stormshak (2004).

Empirical Support

To examine the deviant peer confluence hypothesis, it is necessary to link peer rejection, peer liking, and the formation of deviant peer cliques to growth and problem behavior at a critical juncture in social development. Dishion, Light, et al. (2004) focused on the deviant peer confluence hypothesis using a sample of 1,200 middle school students participating in the Next Generation Project funded by the National Institute of Drug Abuse.

These youth were representative of the sixth grade population of students enrolled in all eight public middle schools within a suburban community context. Eighty percent of the middle school students agreed to participate in the Next Generation Project in the sixth grade. If they agreed to participate, they were assessed in the sixth, seventh, and eighth grades using peer sociometrics and self-reported surveys. Eighty percent of the sample was retained through the eighth grade. Using these data the following constructs were formed:

1. The Problem Behavior Construct. Student self-reports on the surveys included several items on their antisocial behavior (lying, stealing, and aggression) and substance use (e.g., tobacco, alcohol, and marijuana use). A construct score for problem behavior was formed by aggregating the students' self-reported antisocial behavior and substance use.

2. Peer Rejection. The number of nominations received on the peer nomination item, "student whom I dislike" divided by the total number of nominees was used as an index of peer rejection.

3. Peer Liking. This score was based on the number of nominations received for the item "students I like as friends" divided by the number of nominees in each school.

4. Deviant Peer Cliques. An empirical strategy was used to form the deviant peer cliques. Cluster analysis was used to form groups of students with similar in and out nominations as previously described. Once the groups were formed, the students' self-reports of their own behavior defined the deviancy level of each clique.

The central hypothesis was that peer rejection leads to alternative strategies for forming friendship groups, especially in the school context. The macrolevel dynamic is referred to as "social augmentation." Through careful analysis, different scoring procedures were devised to define social augmentation. Empirically, it was found that a multiplicative term (rejection × liking) was most predictive of movement into a deviant peer group. In statistical terms, an interaction between rejection and liking would be reflected in such a multiplicative term.

Figures 6.2a and 6.2b show the distribution of social augmentation and deviant peer confluence across the eight schools participating in this study. Note that simple inspection of these variables reveals normal distributions. In addition, schools vary rather dramatically with respect to social augmentation in Years 1 and 2 of the study and deviant peer confluence by Year 3 of the study. Inspection of Figure 6.2 suggests that School Number 5 is certainly the most problematic with respect to this macrolevel peer dynamic.

The next step in the testing of the deviant peer confluence hypothesis is to link individual differences in social augmentation with growth in

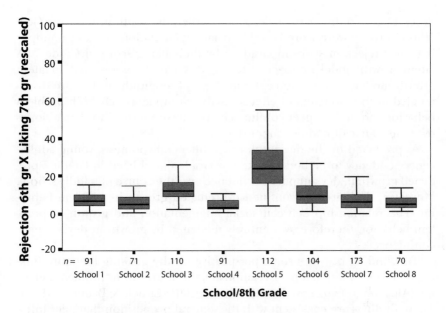

Figure 6.2a   Social Augmentation as a function of school.

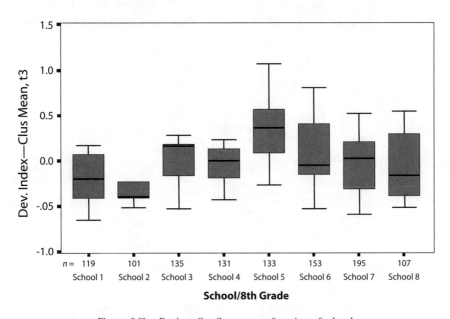

Figure 6.2b   Deviant Confluence as a function of school.

deviant peer confluence. As described earlier, the youth in the Next Generation Project were scored on the social augmentation index by multiplying their rejection score in Grade 6 by their liking score in Grade 7. A latent growth model approach to testing this hypothesis was used. In latent growth modeling, the intercept and slope of longitudinal data are disentangled in the modeling of effects. As shown in Figure 6.3, both problem behavior and deviant peer confluence produced statistically reliable slopes over the course of middle school (Grades 6, 7, and 8).

As predicted by the deviant peer confluence hypothesis, young adolescents' tendency to be both disliked in Grade 6 and liked in Grade 7 predicted growth in deviant peer confluence over the course of middle school. Moreover, deviant peer confluence predicted growth in problem behavior. The relationship between social augmentation and growth in problem behavior, therefore, was entirely mediated by growth in deviant peer confluence.

This finding provides some perspective on the growing literature linking children's marginal peer relationships with growth in problem behavior (Alexander, Piazza, Mekos, & Valente, 2001; Ennett & Bauman, 1994). These findings are consistent with the general proposition that peer influences emerge as leading predictors of problem behavior in early adolescence (Chassin, Presson, Sherman, Montello, & McGrew, 1986; Oetting & Beauvais, 1987). Although considerable evidence supports problem behav-

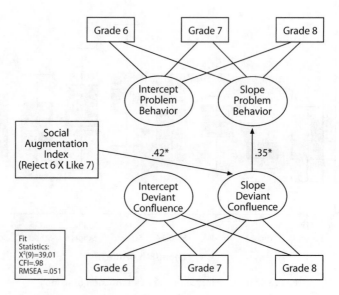

Figure 6.3   A latent growth model of deviant confluence and problem behavior (Dishion, Light, et al., 2004.)

ior emerging from the formation of deviant peer groups, the study of the dynamics within the constituent friendships is a relatively recent development in the research.

MICROSOCIAL DYNAMICS OF FRIENDSHIPS

Overview

A critical idea in social and emotional developmental research is that friendships provide a unique niche within which emerge critical attributes that promote or detract from social adaptation (Piaget, 1954; Sullivan, 1953). There has been important work that contributes to our understanding of the cognitive and social underpinnings of friendship in childhood and adolescence (e.g., Berndt, 1989). Although considerable progress has been made in studying normative friendship development, the most startling evidence for friendship's impact on social and emotional development comes from studying the dark side. In his presidential address, Hartup (1996) discussed the evidence linking the influence of adolescent friendships on problem behavior. Anecdotal and empirical evidence together suggest that many serious crimes are in fact a direct result of the company children keep. Each child is spurred on by the friendship, culminating in acts that neither would dream of doing on their own. From a developmental psychopathology perspective, however, it is important to try to link dynamics within friendships to individual differences in forms of psychopathology as well as normative development. Panella and Henggeler (1986) were the first to study friendship interactions as they relate to individual differences in child and adolescent psychopathology. In these interaction assessments, in general these researchers found a link between global ratings of social competence and adolescents being diagnosed with conduct disorder. On a microsocial level, well-adjusted youth made fewer interruptions, whereas conduct disordered youth made more. This finding was reminiscent of those reported by Austin and Draper (1984) regarding the construct of "bossiness." Children that were disliked and aggressive were more likely to be bossy with their friends when compared with normative controls.

Inspired by this research, the friendships of the Oregon Youth Study boys (Capaldi & Patterson, 1987; Patterson, Reid, & Dishion, 1992) were studied repeatedly over the course of adolescence. These 205 European American males were videotaped with their identified best friend at ages 13 to 14 over a 25- to 30-minute period. These interactions were coded twice by two separate teams of observers.

The first code captured the interpersonal dynamics of the friendships following the observation strategy used for family interaction (Dishion et al., 1983). In this study, the interpersonal process was described by four summary scores: positive engagement, converse, negative engagement, and directives. Examining the rates of these behaviors among the boys interacting with their friends, it was found that there were very few distinctions in the observed interpersonal dynamics of boys identified as antisocial compared with those identified as normative. Reminiscent of the Austin and Draper (1984) finding, boys identified as antisocial used a higher level of directives within their friendships compared with that of normal boys. Moreover, sequential analyses revealed very few differences except for reciprocal negative engagement. Antisocial boys were more likely to reciprocate a negative behavior given that one member of the dyad was negative.

Most important theoretically were the variables in which there were no differences found. For example, much of the literature on antisocial children has emphasized that they lack social skills. It was assumed that positive behavior would reflect social skills within the friendship dyads. However, there were no differences found between antisocial and normal youth on the use of positive interpersonal behaviors.

Perhaps the most significant finding was that the antisocial youth tended to select friends from the neighborhood setting, whereas normal boys selected friends from the school environment and organized peer activities. In addition, the antisocial boys' friendships were shorter in duration compared with those of the normal controls. These findings are summarized by Dishion, Andrews, and Crosby (1995).

In the coding system that was used to study the interpersonal dynamics, it was found that approximately 75% of the interactive behavior in adolescent friendships was coded as simply converse (i.e., talk). However, perusal of the videotapes revealed that there were striking differences in the content of what the boys were talking about. In particular, it appeared that many of the boys focused almost exclusively on topics that would be considered "deviant," whereas others seemed to have a wider range of conversation topics. It was also clear that coding the content of a conversation was quite complex. The meaning of a locution varies dramatically by the pragmatics of the statement. For example, "We don't like drugs" means one thing when accompanied with a wink and a smile and another when said seriously. To develop a coding system that was reliable, we simplified the coding of content into two topics, deviant talk and normative talk. In addition, we were interested in the responses to these topics. The code "laugh" was used to capture positive responses to a given topic. The code "pause" was used to capture hesitance or interpersonal distance in response to a given topic.

Once the data were coded, it became quite clear that the rate and duration of deviant talk was an efficient way to discriminate normal from problem youth. However, in many ways, the argument was circular. It is not surprising that youth engaged in high levels of problem behavior talk about such behavior with their friends. Therefore, it was important empirically to demonstrate that the dynamic in the friendships (a) was elicited by responses within the dyad, and (b) predicted future behavior over and above past behavior.

Sequential analyses were used to link reactions to deviant topics that might encourage the emergence of those topics later. As hypothesized, a contingent laughter to deviant talk was more characteristic of dyads in which both youth had been arrested by age 14. In such dyads, laughter led to deviant talk, and conversely, deviant talk led to more laughter. In contrast, in dyads in which neither boy had been arrested by age 14, laughter was not contingent on deviant talk but rather on normative talk. From a reinforcement perspective, the differential pausitive responses to "operants" such as deviant and normative talk fit well within a matching law framework (McDowell, 1988). From a matching law perspective, it is not the absolute level of reinforcement for behavior that determines choices to increase that behavior; it is the relative rate of reinforcement. Thus, laughter in response to deviant talk needs to be compared to laughter in response to normative talk. When the relative rate of reinforcement for deviant talk is higher than that of normative talk, it is expected that deviant talk will dominate in the relationship. Indeed, the matching law applied quite well to the dyadic data in the adolescent friendships (Dishion, Spracklen, Andrews, & Patterson, 1996). That is, the level of deviant talk matched the relative rate of reinforcement for such behaviors in these friendships.

This process was referred to as *deviancy training*. The deviancy training process had been found to predict future levels of drug use, delinquency, and violent behavior even when controlling for past behavior (Dishion, Capaldi, Spracklen, & Li, 1995; Dishion, Eddy, Haas, Li, & Spracklen, 1997; Dishion et al., 1996). Therefore, the evidence that a friendship interactive mechanism was influential in the emergence of early adolescent male problem behavior was supported in the Oregon Youth Study boys.

In addition to the passive longitudinal Oregon Youth Study, about 2 years later the Adolescent Transitions Program pilot study was conducted. This study involved the random assignment of high-risk young adolescents to one of four conditions:

1. Parent-only family management training.
2. A peer group self-regulation intervention.
3. Parent group and peer group interventions (1 and 2 combined).
4. Self-directed change condition using materials only.

In addition, a quasiexperimental control group was added when the randomized study was completed in which the group was selected using the same strategy as in the previous study but not randomized, simply followed.

The results of this study revealed that random assignment to the peer group intervention resulted in improved family interactions on one hand, but increases in problem behavior on the other hand (Dishion & Andrews, 1995). In a careful analysis of the group dynamics associated with growth in problem behavior, indeed, it was found that deviancy training within the contrived intervention groups was predictive of iatrogenic growth in problem behavior (Dishion, Burraston, & Poulin, 2001).

In many ways the tendency to search out peers and develop friendships that are imbedded in deviant behavior could be thought of as a *strange attractor dynamic*. Within a dynamic systems framework, strange attractors are nonlinear tendencies to engage in a specific behavior that involves two components. One is a tendency to switch and engage in deviant talk when discussing normative topics, and the other is the inability to move out of a deviant topic once it has been established. Granic and Dishion (2003) tested this idea in a subsample of the Adolescent Transitions adolescents that included both males and females. Granic and Dishion (2003) used duration as an indicator of an attractor for deviant talk. Duration of deviant talk was calculated for each dyad over the course of the 30-minute videotaped interaction. It was hypothesized that dyads that tended to increase their deviant talk bouts over the course of the 30-minute interaction could be thought of as being in an attractor for deviance. Slope scores were computed for each dyad, and those were related to the individual's behavior 2 to 3 years following the videotaped observation. Indeed, a tendency to be attracted to deviant talk with respect to longer durations was associated with individual differences in growth and problem behavior as defined by authority conflict (e.g. arrest, school suspensions, school expulsions, drug abuse, and treatment for drug abuse dependence).

Empirical Support

Until recently, the interpersonal dynamics and the deviant nature of the dyads had not been connected. The hypothesis that deviance organizes the interpersonal dynamics of some friendships requires that those two dimensions be coded separately and independently. More recently we examined the interpersonal dynamics of adolescent friendships in juxtaposition to the deviance of the friendship to understand long-term patterns of problem behavior development (Dishion, Nelson, Winter, & Bullock, 2004).

In this effort, the concept of entropy became a useful, quantitative index for capturing interpersonal organization. Entropy is a concept that most recently has been used in information theory to explain the level of organization within a communication (Attneave, 1959). When the various states of one communication predict the same set of states in the follow-up communication, the system could be considered as low entropy. Basically, low

$$Hc = \Sigma \ P_{ij} \ \ln \frac{1}{P_{ij}}$$

Figure 6.4.   The computation of entropy:
an index of mirosocial organization (Attneave, 1959).

measures of entropy suggest that a high level of information is conferred
between communication one and two. The formula for entropy is summarized in Figure 6.4.

A related development in the study of interpersonal dynamics is the formulation of a state–space grid (Lewis, 2000). A state–space grid provides a
visual organization of a two-dimensional communication such as the one
just described. If one examines a state–space grid, it is possible to visually
track the course of the interaction between two individuals over an observation period. For example, Figure 6.5 shows the four interpersonal behaviors
provided in the original coding of the Oregon Youth Study boys: negative,
directive, converse, and positive (Dishion, Andrews, & Crosby, 1995). The
dyad with low entropy is primarily concentrated in the converse section
of the state–space grid. Thus, it is quite likely that if one of these youth
engages in converse, the following will do the same. Note that the dyad also
tends to return to converse when they are in other parts of the state–space
grid. In contrast, in the high entropy dyad, the interactions between two
youth are virtually all over the map. In this way, entropy can be considered
as an appropriate index for describing the interpersonal organization of a
friendship interaction.

In the longitudinal analysis, we were first interested in whether the
dynamic organization of the dyad discriminated between early onset problem youth and well-adapted youth in the Oregon Youth Study. Thirty-nine
boys were defined as early onset antisocial on the basis of having been
arrested at least once by age 14 and having a total of three juvenile offenses
by the time they were 18. In contrast, well-adapted boys ($n = 33$) had never
been arrested by age 24 and were consistently low in antisocial behavior.

Most interesting is the characteristics of the boys' friendships at age 14,
16, and 18. These are summarized in Table 6.1. As can be seen for well-
adjusted boys, the duration of their friendships tended to increase with age.
This outcome would be expected if well-adjusted friendships tended to be
more successful and longer lasting. However, unexpected was the finding
that the time spent together in well-adjusted dyads tended to decrease as
the boys got older. At age 14, boys spent an average of 14 hours per week
with their best friend. However, by age 18 boys spent about 10 hours per

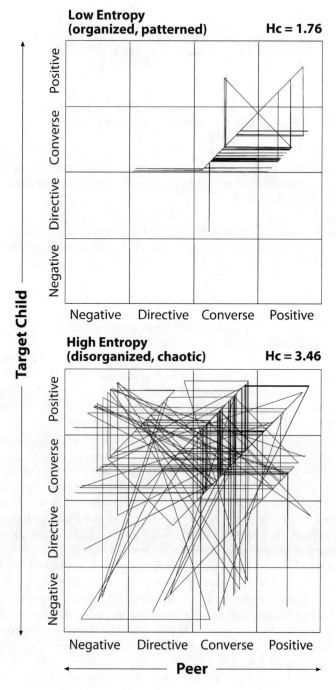

Figure 6.5. Peer process state-space grids.

TABLE 6.1

Means of Friendship Characteristics for Well-Adjusted and Antisocial Boys

	Age 14		Age 16		Age 18	
	Mean	SD	Mean	SD	Mean	SD
Well-adjusted	(n = 32)		(n = 32)		(n = 29)	
Friendship duration (months)	50.00	42.87	59.03*	46.24	77.24†	47.63
Time spent together (hours/week)	14.34†	18.47	12.87†	18.37	10.76**	8.08
Antisocial	(n = 35)		(n = 32)		(n = 35)	
Friendship duration (months)	50.43	51.98	36.65*	31.26	53.37†	50.51

Note. Levels of significance are based on univariate ANOVAs comparing groups at each time point.

†$p < .10$. *$p < .05$. **$p < .01$.

week with their best friend. In contrast, at age 14, early-starting antisocial boys spent 22 hours per week with their best friend and by age 18 spent nearly 34 hours per week in the company of their friend.

The videotapes of the boys with their friends were also coded at ages 14, 16, and 18. The entropy of the friendship interactions is summarized in Figure 6.6; the box plots are a visual technique for examining the normality of the distribution as well as the spread of the distribution. Two developmental patterns are worth noting. First, entropy decreases from early to late

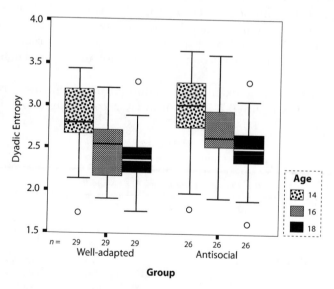

Figure 6.6 Entropy in friendship interaction through adolescence.

adolescence in both the well-adapted and the antisocial dyads. This suggests that the interpersonal dynamics of the friendships become more organized from early to late adolescence. That is, they become more predictable and less chaotic. In addition, it was found that entropy indeed discriminated well-adapted from antisocial dyads. Specifically, it was found that the antisocial dyads had less entropy than did the well-adapted dyads. In other words, the interactions of antisocial boys were generally more complex and chaotic than those of well-adapted boys. Finally, it is worth noting that the entropy score provides a normal distribution parameter for describing the overall organization of the friendship interactions. This addresses a rather significant problem in the analysis of social interaction dynamics in that sequential analyses can be highly influenced by base rates and the marginal distributions of the behaviors of interest (Bakeman & Gottman, 1986).

The second question of interest was the extent to which entropy predicted long term social developmental outcomes in addition to the deviant content of the friendship interaction. Each of the videotapes was coded for deviancy training, including the duration of deviant talk, and coder impressions of the dyads' endorsement of antisocial behavior and substance use. In addition, at age 24, parent, youth, and youth reports of criminal and delinquent behavior were assessed. Table 6.2 summarizes the results of the prediction analyses using entropy and deviant peer process as predictors. Inspection of Table 6.2 reveals the results of the hierarchical regression model. In Step 1, the entropy at age 14 and the deviant peer process were entered into the equation. As can be seen, only deviant peer process predicted antisocial behavior at age 24. In Step 2, deviant peer process, entropy, and the interaction between the two were entered into the regression equation. In this analysis, entropy, deviant peer process, and the interactive term all reliably accounted for variation in antisocial behavior at age 24.

The next step was to examine the nature of the interactive term. This is summarized in Figure 6.7. The dyads were separated into low and high

TABLE 6.2
Prediction of Antisocial Behavior at 24 Years of Age

Model	Rsq. Change	F Change	Stand. Beta	T test
Step 1	.07	6.97, $p < .001$		
w5 peer Hc			.06	.84, $p =$ ns
w5 DPP			.24	3.31, $p < .01$
Step 2	.03	6.41, $p < .05$		
w5 peer Hc			.62	2.67, $p < .01$
w5 DPP			1.84	2.90, $p < .01$
DPP × HC			-1.83	-2.53, $p < .05$

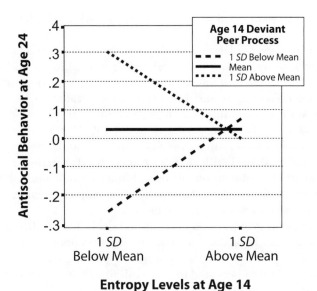

Figure 6.7. Deviant peer process by entropy interaction.

entropy. Low entropy dyads were those that were below a standard deviation below the mean. High entropy dyads were those that were one standard deviation above the mean. Inspection of Figure 6.7 reveals that dyads that were low in entropy and high in deviant content were those that were at the highest risk for antisocial behavior at age 24. In contrast, dyads that were both low in entropy and low in deviant content were those least likely to be antisocial at age 24. This finding suggests that dyads organized in deviance were very likely to persist in their antisocial behavior from adolescence to adulthood. Conversely, dyads organized in nondeviance were very unlikely to engage in antisocial behavior in adulthood. Thus, the hypothesis is supported that friendship interactions that are dynamically organized around deviant behavior are prognostic of the maintenance and persistence of antisocial behavior from adolescence to adulthood.

The organization of friendship dyadic interactions effectively discriminates between dyads with varying levels of problem behavior and is able to predict antisocial outcomes. However, the organizational skills assessed in entropy are focused on the specific ability of adolescents to maintain certain interpersonal behaviors throughout an interaction and not the more general ability to have a mutually engaged and reciprocal interaction. We were interested to see if the more general skill of having a responsive and reciprocal conversation with a friend would mirror entropy findings in predicting deviant content and problem behavior (Piehler & Dishion, 2006).

In order to assess adolescents' ability to successfully interact and engage with a friend, we employed the construct of mutuality. Dyadic mutuality has typically been operationalized through ratings of responsiveness, reciprocity, and cooperation and has been demonstrated to be correlated with positive developmental outcomes in children in parent–child dyads (Deater-Deckard & Petrill, 2004; Kochanska, 1997; Kochanska & Murray, 2000). We also included ratings of self-centeredness and other-mindedness, as well as conflict, shared understanding, and shared attitudes and values in our assessment of dyadic mutuality. In addition to dyadic mutuality, we also examined durations of deviant talk in the friendship interactions of adolescents with varying levels of antisocial behavior.

Three different groups of adolescents were selected on the basis of self-reported antisocial behavior over five yearly assessments. The first group was referred to as *early starters*. These youth had high levels of problem behavior at age 11 that persisted through middle adolescence and included antisocial behavior and substance use. The second group was referred to as *late starters*. These were youth who showed few signs of problem behavior in early adolescence but by middle adolescence had reported significant levels of substance use and problem behavior. Finally, a third group was formulated describing adolescents with no evidence of problem behavior from early adolescence through middle adolescence. This group was referred to as *successful*. There were 40 multiethnic adolescents in each group, both male and female. Each brought in a friend for a 40-minute videotaped conversation.

In examining differences in dyadic mutuality across the three groups, it was found that early starters demonstrated a deficit in mutuality in their interactions when compared with late-starting and successful adolescents. That is, early starters' interactions were less responsive and reciprocal with their friends. The deficit in mutuality seen in early starters is consistent with Moffitt's (1993) theories about the etiologies of the early- and late-starting pathways. She theorizes that early starters lack early positive socialization experiences from parents and later from peers. When compared with early-starting youth, late starters have relatively positive early socialization experiences and undergo a relatively normative assertion of autonomy in adolescence. It may be that early starters' lack of positive socialization is in part responsible for a deficit in the skills necessary for a mutual interaction. Late starters are also much less likely to engage in antisocial behavior into adulthood than early starters (Loeber, 1991). Thus, the skills associated with mutuality may be indicative of the persistence of antisocial behavior from adolescence into adulthood.

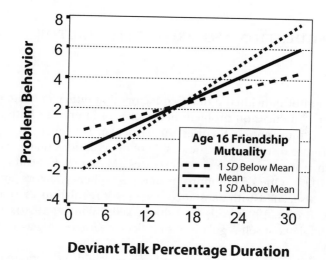

Figure 6.8   Deviant talk by mutuality in predicting problem behavior.

Deviant talk and dyadic mutuality each accounted for a significant amount of variance in self-reported antisocial behavior. In addition, the interaction between mutuality and deviant talk also accounted for a reliable amount of variance. Figure 6.8 illustrates this interaction. For those adolescents with low to moderate levels of deviant talk, higher levels of mutuality predicted lower levels of antisocial behavior. For adolescents who spent more time discussing nondeviant topics, those with higher levels of mutuality were more likely to engage in nondeviant behavior. For those adolescents with high levels of deviant talk, higher levels of mutuality predicted higher levels of antisocial behavior. These adolescents are skillfully and successfully engaging each other in topics of deviance, and are likely to engage in higher levels of antisocial behavior. Thus, higher levels of mutuality would appear to indicate a greater behavioral engagement in the topic discussed. This finding corresponds well with the entropy results, indicating that highly deviant youth who are also highly mutually engaged and organized in their social interactions relevant to deviant topics are demonstrating poorer outcomes than those youth with poor organization and less engagement in their interactions involving deviant topics. Seen within the ecological framework, mutuality represents an intrapersonal characteristic of adolescents, the ability to be responsive and reciprocal with a friend, functioning in interpersonal interactions to shape the level of engagement that adolescents will have in deviant content.

SELF-REGULATION AS A PROTECTIVE FACTOR

Overview

Investigation of individual difference factors that either mediate or moderate peer influences on problem behavior is of interest to both developmental and intervention theories. In particular, resilience, as a process, suggests future directions for the design of interventions that serve to protect youth from negative peer experiences (Masten & Coatsworth, 1995; Werner, 1995). One of the more promising resiliency factors, applied to problems associated with substance use, is self-regulation or self-control (Miller & Brown, 1991; Wills & Dishion, 2003; Windle, 1990). The construct of adolescent self-regulation is particularly interesting as an index of resiliency.

Two decades of programmatic research on child temperament consistently reveal attentive control and inhibitory control as central to adjustment in socialization (Kohnstamm, Bates, & Rothbart, 1989). The capacity for self-control of action and emotion falls under the rubric of executive attention (Rothbart, Ellis, & Posner, 2004). Recent neural imaging studies (e.g., Sowell & Jernigan, 1998) provide evidence of substantial adolescent and postadolescent brain development in frontal areas thought to serve executive functions such as attentive control. These executive functions are largely located in the prefrontal cortex and, more specifically, the anterior cingulate cortex (ACC; Frith & Frith, 2001).

Linking neural imaging studies to pragmatic measures that assess individual differences and attentive control has been a recent goal. Posner and colleagues developed a task under conditions of neural imaging that linked alerting, orienting, and executive attention to activity in the ACC (Fan, McCandliss, Sommer, Raz, & Posner, 2002). The basic strategy in the attention network task (i.e., ANT Task) is to use perceptual conflict (i.e., Stroop, 1935) to engage various aspects of attention. The variation in reaction time is considered to be a useful index of attentive regulation such as the ability to alert, orient to new stimuli, and to deal with distractive stimuli.

From a developmental perspective, it makes sense that the form of self-regulation would vary from early childhood through young adulthood. For example, in the work by Kochanska (1993; 2002; Kochanska, Murray, Jacques, Koenig, & Vandegeest, 1996), inhibitory control is a key component of self-regulation in early childhood. However, as children adapt in new contexts such as the public school setting, other facets of self-regulation are likely to become critical. For example, as demands increase for children to complete tasks with multiple steps such as chores or homework, it is critical that behavior activation becomes a key component of self-regulation. In adolescence, with the introduction of free time and autonomy, it becomes critical for young people to resist temptation and stay the course on long-term objectives related to academic achievement and/or skill development. Finally, in young adulthood, a key component of self-regulation is the selection and identification of social and economic contexts that fit well with one's social, motor, and intellectual abilities.

Although we often give attention to the developmental variation on constructs such as self-regulation, rarely is that variation systematically measured. Recent work in children's social and emotional development, however, suggests that self-regulation in children is integral to skill development and prosocial behavior (Eisenberg & Fabes, 1998; Eisenberg et al., 2003).

Wills and Dishion (2003) proposed that self-regulation would serve as a moderator variable in the etiology of problem behavior in adolescence and young adulthood. This hypothesis was recently tested in research by Vitale et al. (2005) in early to middle adolescence. These investigators found that young adolescents with inhibitory control abilities were much less influenced by deviant peers. That is, the link between friendship deviance and antisocial behavior was weak for those with higher levels of inhibition.

Empirical Support

In our recent research on understanding and preventing adolescent problem behavior, we assessed self-regulation among adolescents at ages 15 to 17 years. We used two strategies for the assessment of self-regulation. The first was the Rothbart measure of temperament extended into adolescence (Rothbart et al., 2004). This measure includes two scales assessing effortful attention control, otherwise referred to as *attention control*. In addition, we assessed the youths' ability to alert, orient, and to exercise executive control within the context of a computerized attention task referred to as the ANT. To consider the role of self-regulation in the development of problem behavior, we formulated three developmental groups on the basis of longitudinal data from six yearly assessments. Both male and female adolescents following early- ($n = 39$), late-starting ($n = 38$), and successful ($n = 37$) pathways were selected for the study.

The assessment of temperament included both youth and parent report. The effortful control factor includes the following subfactors: activation control, attention, and inhibitory control. The ANT assessment involves a flanker conflict paradigm that includes a central target arrow flanked on either side by arrows pointing in either the same (congruent) or the opposite (incongruent) direction of the target arrow. Incongruent trials generally produce longer reaction times than do congruent trials, as the presence of incongruent flanker arrows causes a degree of attention conflict. The

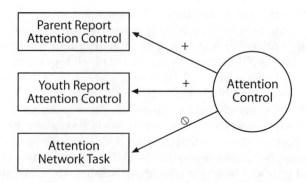

Figure 6.9   The self-regulation construct.

task allows calculation of individual difference scores in attention control. The score is computed by means of subtraction of congruent flanker trial reaction times from incongruent flanker reaction trials.

Figure 6.9 provides an overview of the self-regulation construct as assessed in the sample. Table 6.3 provides the data obtained on the entire sample of adolescents in the Project Alliance sample. In general, we found no covariation between the youths' performance on the ANT conflict task with either child or parent report of self-regulation. However, self-regulation was correlated moderately between parent and child reports ($r = .34$). Therefore, we included only parent and child reports to index self-regulation in our analyses of resilience.

Figure 6.10 provides an overview of the findings relating self-regulation by the timing or the development of antisocial behavior in the sample. As can be seen, there is an orderly progression from less self-regulation to more self-regulation when considering early starters, late starters, and successful students, respectively. Also of interest is the normality of the distribution across the two samples. The child report shows less variation than does the parent report; however, both show increasing self-regulation associated with the developmental onset of antisocial behavior and the probable prognosis (Moffitt, 1993; Patterson & Yoerger, 1993).

TABLE 6.3
Correlations Among Measures
of Attention Control in Middle Adolescence

	1	2	3
1. Child report	1.00		
2. Parent report	.34	1.0	
3. ANT conf. task	.08	.01	1.0

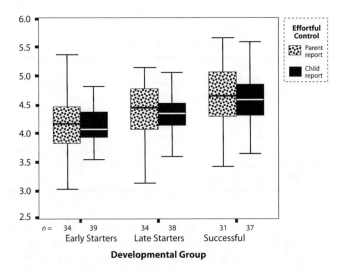

Figure 6.10.   Self-regulation by timing for the development of anti-social behavior.

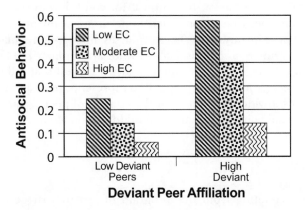

Figure 6.11   Self-regulation as an interpersonal moderator of peer influences.

The central idea is that if self-regulation is a protective factor, then youth that are highly self-regulated are likely to be less influenced by deviant peers. Figure 6.11 and Table 6.4 summarize our findings to these analyses. A general construct for the youths' antisocial behavior was formulated on self-reported delinquency and antisocial behavior and substance use. As revealed in a hierarchical linear regression, both self-regulation and deviant peer involvement significantly predicted antisocial behavior in middle adolescence. It is relevant that self-regulation added to the prediction

TABLE 6.4
Antisocial Behavior Predicted by Self-Regulation
and Deviant Peer Involvement

Model	Rsq. Change	F Change	Stand. Beta	T Test
Step 1	.43	144.0, $p < .001$		
SR			-.19	-4.8, $p < .01$
DP			.58	14.3, $p < .01$
Step 2	.46	20.7, $p < .001$		
SR			-.22	-5.6, $p < .001$
DP			.52	12.6, $p < .001$
SR × DP			-.18	-4.5, $p < .001$

accounting for 43% of the variation in antisocial behavior. In a second step, the interaction between self-regulation and deviant peer involvement was entered into the equation. Perusal of Table 6.4 reveals that a significant interaction was found between self-regulation and deviant peer involvement.

As revealed from Figure 6.11, there was a clear tendency for youth who were high in self-regulation to be less affected by the influence of deviant peers on antisocial behavior. In contrast, for youth low in self-regulation, the level of antisocial behavior varied quite dramatically as a function of their deviant peer involvement. These analyses linking self-regulation, deviant peer involvement, and antisocial behavior are summarized by Gardner and Dishion (2004). In general, these analyses suggest that self-regulation is, indeed, a very promising construct that represents, perhaps, a protective influence for individual resilience in the context of peer dynamics posing risk for antisocial behavior in early and middle adolescence.

SUMMARY

The findings resulting from this program of research suggest that peer influence can be seen as a series of multilevel social adaptations. Our work and that of many others have focused primarily on the period between early adolescence and late adolescence. For several reasons, this period may be particularly important when it comes to understanding peer influence. We have argued that peers serve a critical evolutionary function, especially for marginalized youth (Dishion, Nelson, et al., 2004; Dishion, Poulin, & Medici Skaggs, 2000). Marginalized youth tend to pull themselves from conventional contexts involving relationships with prosocial adults and peers and formulate novel, deviant social groups. It is ubiquitous across cultures that delinquent behaviors peak during adolescence, whereas other forms of problem behavior do so during young adulthood. This tendency for adolescent surge in illegal behavior has been referred to as the *age–crime curve* by Hirschi and Gottfredson (1983). It may be true that the size and amplitude of the curve can be modified, but it is unlikely that any society will not see a peak in problem behavior during this developmental period.

Problem behavior peaks because it is very much a team activity (Gold, 1970). As revealed in our analyses and that of others, there is a bidirectional link between involvement in deviant peer groups and problem behavior. That is, deviant peer groups lead to more problem behavior, and more problem behavior leads to an increased tendency to become involved with deviant peers (Dishion & Owen, 2002; Keenan, Loeber, Zhang, Stouthamer-Loeber, & van Kammen, 1995).

Identifying the multilevel nature of peer influence is an important advantage of the ecological perspective. It is clear that institutions such as public school systems, mental health programs, and even prevention programs can create contexts that either amplify the deviant peer group or minimize deviant peer clustering. Several investigators have found that creating peer contexts that serve as intervention targets can have iatrogenic effects on problem behavior (Gifford-Smith, Dodge, Dishion, & McCord, 2005). An interesting and important feature of the macro environment is that a combination of rejection and liking covaries with the formation of deviant peer cliques. This finding suggests that efforts to engineer peer environments that minimize acrimony and optimize cooperative and prosocial acceptance are likely to have significant effects on community-level antisocial behavior. It is odd that this has rarely been done except in school and community-wide efforts to reduce bullying (Olweus, 1993). One would hypothesize, based on these data, that school environments that have high levels of critical teasing and rejection are those most likely to produce groups of youth that define themselves in terms of deviant and antisocial behavior.

From an intervention standpoint, it is clear that peer influence serves as an important target for the prevention of conduct problems, violence, and drug abuse. The youth most at risk for these outcomes are those who are the most drawn to deviant peer groups. It is therefore important to promote a multilevel strategy. The first level is clearly to target school environments, beginning in elementary school, that promote peer acceptance, reduce peer rejection, and provide adult-supervised and organized activities influential in prosocial and healthy development. Such programs used to be standard fare for the public school environment and included organized sports and other recreational activities at no cost to all participating students. Unfortunately, programs such as these have been privatized so that only those who can afford organized activities can receive them. The impact of these policies on social and emotional development in general and in the formation of deviant peer groups in particular is a worthy topic for scientific and political inquiry.

Once peer groups are formed and friendships created on the basis of problem behavior and deviancy, it seems much more difficult to change these dynamics. In fact, in our review of the literature, it appeared that prevention programs that target high-risk youth and that deliver those interventions in peer groups are the most likely to have iatrogenic effects. It is at these beginning stages of the formation of a problem behavior trajectory that adult interventions that aggregate peers may do the most harm. At this stage, it is likely that family-centered interventions that provide adults with the tools to monitor and set limits on peer activities as well as support prosocial activities are those that are most likely to be effective. In our intervention work, we found that random assignment to a family intervention in early adolescence among high-risk youth increased parent monitoring, which in turn reduced problem behavior (Dishion, Nelson, & Kavanagh, 2003).

Another viable intervention target is the focus on self-regulation. Among motivated youth, improvements in self-regulatory skills can certainly reduce their vulnerability to deviant influences. Programmatic work by Lochman and colleagues reveal that cognitive behavioral interventions that focus on goal setting and self-control reduce aggressive behavior in schools (Lochman, 1992; Lochman, Barry, & Pardini, 2003; Lochman & Wells, 1996). Most of this work, however, focuses on aggression and self-regulation. Substance use and other forms of problem behavior, however, require a different type of self-regulation from that associated with aggression. Children who are emotionally reactive are more prone to anger and to respond aggressively. However, many events involve mutual activities within the context of a peer group. For example, in a careful analysis of initial smoking episodes, Friedman, Lichtenstein, and Biglan (1985) found that 80% involved two or more youth initiating smoking at the same time in unsupervised households after school. Thus, the other form of self-regulation involves monitoring goals relative to peer influences. To date, there have been no interventions that target this important motivational structure. However, it can be assumed that when problem behavior in adolescence results in negative life outcomes, the motivation structure changes; at these points, "treatment" can have a significant impact on self-regulatory skills.

Taken as a whole, comprehending the multiple levels of factors that contribute to the peer clustering and peer influence in adolescence suggests that an ecological perspective is critical for both understanding and preventing negative life outcomes for young adolescents. However, it is clear that a narrow focus on environmental influences is likely to miss an important feature of the individual. From all available evidence, it appears that biological factors such as genetic vulnerability demarcate those individuals who are in fact most sensitive to the environment, and therefore, possibly most responsive to preventive interventions.

REFERENCES

Alexander, C., Piazza, M., Mekos, D., & Valente, T. (2001). Peers, schools and adolescent cigarette smoking. *Journal of Adolescent Health, 29*, 22–30.

Asher, S. R., & Parker, J. G. (1987). Peer relations and later personal adjustment: Are low-accepted children at risk? *Psychological Bulletin, 102*, 357–389.

Attneave, F. (1959). *Applications of information theory to psychology: A summary of basic concepts, methods, and results.* New York: Holt Rinehart & Winston.

Austin, A. M. B., & Draper, D. C. (1984). Verbal interactions of popular and rejected children with their friends and non-friends. *Child Study Journal, 14*, 309–323.

Bakeman, R., & Gottman, J. M. (1986). *Observing interaction: An introduction to sequential analysis.* New York: Cambridge University Press.

Berndt, T. J. (1989). Friendships in childhood and adolescence. In W. Damon (Ed.), *Child development today and tomorrow* (pp. 332–349). San Francisco: Jossey-Bass.

Bronfenbrenner, U. (1989). Ecological systems theory. In R. Vasta (Ed.), *Annals of child development, Vol. 6. Six theories of child development: Revised formulations and current issues* (pp. 187–249). London: JAI.

Cairns, R. B. (1983). Sociometry, psychometry, and social structure: A commentary on six recent studies of popular, rejected, and neglected children. *Merrill-Palmer Quarterly, 29*(4), 429–437.

Capaldi, D., & Patterson, G. R. (1987). An approach to the problem of recruitment and retention rates for longitudinal research. *Behavioral Assessment, 9*, 169–177.

Chassin, L., Presson, C. C., Sherman, S. J., Montello, D., & McGrew, J. (1986). Changes in peer and parent influence during adolescence: Longitudinal versus cross-sectional perspectives on smoking initiation. *Developmental Psychology, 22*, 327–334.

Coie, J. D., Dodge, K. A., & Coppotelli, H. (1982). Dimensions and types of social status: A cross-age perspective. *Developmental Psychology, 18*, 557–570.

Coie, J. D., & Kupersmidt, J. B. (1983). A behavioral analysis of emerging social status in boys' groups. *Child Development, 54*, 1400–1416.

Cook, T. D., & Campbell, D. T. (1979). *Quasi-experimentation: Design and analysis issues.* Boston: Houghton Mifflin.

Deater-Deckard, K., & Petrill, S. A. (2004). Parent–child dyadic mutuality and child-behavior problems: An investigation of gene–environment processes. *Journal of Child Psychology and Psychiatry, 45*, 1171–1179.

Dishion, T. J., & Andrews, D. (1995). Preventing escalations in problem behaviors with high-risk young adolescents: Immediate and 1-year outcomes. *Journal of Consulting and Clinical Psychology, 63*, 538–548.

Dishion, T. J., Andrews, D. W., & Crosby, L. (1995). Antisocial boys and their friends in early adolescence: Relationship characteristics, quality, and interactional process. *Child Development, 66*, 139–151.

Dishion, T. J., Burraston, B., & Poulin, F. (2001). Peer group dynamics associated with iatrogenic effects in group interventions with high-risk young adolescents. In C. Erdley & D. W. Nangle (Eds.), *Damon's new directions in child development: The role of friendship in psychological adjustment* (pp. 79–92). San Francisco: Jossey-Bass.

Dishion, T. J., Capaldi, D., Spracklen, K. M., & Li, F. (1995). Peer ecology of male adolescent drug use. *Development and Psychopathology, 7*, 803–824.

Dishion, T. J., Eddy, J. M., Haas, E., Li, F., & Spracklen, K. (1997). Friendships and violent behavior during adolescence. *Social Development, 6*, 207–223.

Dishion, T. J., Gardner, K., Patterson, G. R., Reid, J. R., Spyrou, S., & Thibodeaux, S. (1983). *The Family Process Code: A multidimensional system for observing family interaction.* (Unpublished coding manual).

Dishion, T. J., Light, J. M., Yasui, M., & Stormshak, E. A. (2004, August). *A network analysis of the confluence hypothesis in early adolescence.* Paper presented at the biennial conference of the International Society for the Study of Behavior and Development, Ghent, Belgium.

Dishion, T. J., Nelson, S. E., & Kavanagh, K. (2003). The Family Check-Up for high-risk adolescents: Preventing early-onset substance use by parent monitoring. In J. E. Lochman & R. Salekin (Eds.), Behavior-oriented interventions for children with aggressive behavior and/or conduct problems [Special Issue]. *Behavior Therapy, 34,* 553–571.

Dishion, T. J., Nelson, S. E., Winter, C. E., & Bullock, B. M. (2004). Adolescent friendship as a dynamic system: Entropy and deviance in the etiology and course of male antisocial behavior. *Journal of Abnormal Child Psychology, 32,* 651–663.

Dishion, T. J., & Owen, L. D. (2002). A longitudinal analysis of friendships and substance use: Bidirectional influence from adolescence to adulthood. *Developmental Psychology, 28*(4), 480–491.

Dishion, T. J., Patterson, G. R., & Griesler, P. C. (1994). Peer adaptation in the development of antisocial behavior: A confluence model. In L. R. Huesmann (Ed.), *Aggressive behavior: Current perspectives* (pp. 61–95). New York: Plenum.

Dishion, T. J., Patterson, G. R., Stoolmiller, M., & Skinner, M. S. (1991). Family, school, and behavioral antecedents to early adolescent involvement with antisocial peers. *Developmental Psychology, 27,* 172–180.

Dishion, T. J., Poulin, F., & Medici Skaggs, N. (2000). The ecology of premature adolescent autonomy: Biological and social influences. In K. A. Kerns, S. M. Contreras, & A. M. Neal-Barnett (Eds.), *Explaining associations between family and peer relationships* (pp. 27–45). Westport, CT: Praeger.

Dishion, T. J., Spracklen, K. M., Andrews, D. W., & Patterson, G. R. (1996). Deviancy training in male adolescent friendships. *Behavior Therapy, 27,* 373–390.

Dodge, K. A. (1983). Behavioral antecedents: A peer social status. *Child Development, 54,* 1386–1399.

Eisenberg, N., & Fabes, R. A. (1998). Prosocial development. In W. Damon & N. Eisenberg (Eds.), *Handbook of child psychology: Social, emotional, and personality development* (pp. 701–779). New York: Wiley.

Eisenberg, N., Valiente, C., Morris, A. S., Fabes, R. A., Cumberland, A., Reiser, M., et al. (2003). Longitudinal relations among parental emotional expressivity, children's regulation, and quality of social emotional functioning. *Developmental Psychology, 39,* 3–19.

Ennett, S. T., & Bauman, K. E. (1994). The contribution of influence and selection to adolescent peer group homogeneity: The case of adolescent cigarette smoking. *Journal of Personality and Social Psychology, 67*(4), 653–663.

Fan, J., McCandliss, B. D., Sommer, T., Raz, A., & Posner, M. I. (2002). Testing the efficiency and independence of attentional networks. *Journal of Cognitive Neuroscience, 14,* 340–347.

French, D. C. (1988). Heterogeneity of peer-rejected boys: Aggressive and nonagressive subtypes. *Child Development, 59,* 882–886.

Friedman, L. S., Lichtenstein, E., & Biglan, A. (1985). Smoking onset among teens: An empirical analysis of initial situations. *Addictive Behaviors, 10,* 1–13.

Frith, U., & Frith, C. (2001). The biological basis of social interaction. *Current Directions in Psychological Science, 10,* 151–155.

Gardner, T., & Dishion, T. J. (2004). *Effortful control and the moderation of deviant peer influence in middle adolescence.* Manuscript submitted for publication.

Gifford-Smith, M., Dodge, K. E., Dishion, T. J., & McCord, J. (2005). Peer influence in children and adolescents: Crossing the bridge from developmental to intervention science. *Journal of Abnormal Child Psychology, 33,* 255–265.

Gold, M. (1970). *Delinquent behavior in an American city.* San Francisco: Brooks & Coleman.

Granic, I., & Dishion, T. J. (2003). Deviant talk in adolescent friendships: A step toward measuring a pathogenic attractor process. *Social Development, 12,* 314–334.

Hartup, W. W. (1996). The company they keep: Friendships and their developmental significance. *Child Development, 67,* 1–13.

Healy, W. (1927). *The individual delinquent: A textbook of diagnosis and prognosis for all concerned in understanding offenders.* Boston: Little Brown.

Hirschi, T., & Gottfredson, M. (1983). Age and the explanation of crime. *American Journal of Sociology, 89,* 552–583.

Kandel, D. B. (1978). Similarity in real-life adolescent friendship pairs. *Journal of Personality and Social Psychology, 36*(3), 306–312.

Kandel, D. B. (1986). Process of peer influence on adolescence. In R. K. Silbereisen (Ed.), *Development as action in context* (pp. 33–52). Berlin, Germany: Springer.

Keenan, K., Loeber, R., Zhang, Q., Stouthamer-Loeber, M., & van Kammen, W. B. (1995). The influence of deviant peers on the development of boys' disruptive and delinquent behavior: A temporal analysis. *Development and Psychopathology, 7*(4), 715–726.

Kochanska, G. (1993). Toward a synthesis of parental socialization and child temperament in early development of conscience. *Child Development, 64,* 325–347.

Kochanska, G. (1997). Mutually responsive orientation between mothers and their young children: Implications for early socialization. *Child Development, 68,* 94–112.

Kochanska, G. (2002). Committed compliance, moral self, and internalization: A mediational model. *Developmental Psychology, 38,* 339–351.

Kochanska, G., Murray, K., Jacques, T. Y., Koenig, A. L., & Vandegeest, K. A. (1996). Inhibitory control in young children and its role in emerging internalization. *Child Development, 67,* 490–507.

Kochanska, G., & Murray, K. T. (2000). Mother–child mutually responsive orientation and conscience development: From toddler to early school age. *Child Development, 71,* 417–431.

Kohnstamm, G. A., Bates, J. E., & Rothbart, M. K. (1989). *Temperament in childhood.* Oxford: John Wiley & Sons.

Lewis, M. D. (2000). The promise of dynamic systems approaches for an integrated account of human development. *Child Development, 71,* 36–43.

Lochman, J. E. (1992). Cognitive–behavioral intervention with aggressive boys: Three-year follow-up and preventive effects. *Journal of Consulting and Clinical Psychology, 60,* 426–432.

Lochman, J. E., Barry, T. D., & Pardini, D. A. (2003). Anger control training for aggressive youth. In A. E. Kazdin & J. R. Weisz (Eds.), *Evidence-based psychotherapies for children and adolescents* (pp. 263–281). New York: Guilford.

Lochman, J. E., & Wells, K. C. (1996). A social–cognitive intervention with aggressive children: Prevention effects and contextual implementation issues. In R. D. Peters & R. J. McMahon (Eds.), *Preventing childhood disorders, substance abuse, and delinquency* (pp. 111–143). Thousand Oaks, CA: Sage.

Loeber, R. (1991). Antisocial behavior: More enduring than changeable? *Journal of the American Academy of Child and Adolescent Psychiatry, 30,* 393–397.

Masten, A. S., & Coatsworth, J. D. (1995). Competence, resilience, and psychopathology. In D. Cicchetti & D. J. Cohen (Eds.), *Developmental psychopathology: Risk, disorder, and adaptation* (Vol. 2, pp. 715–752). New York: Wiley.

McDowell, J. J. (1988). Matching theory in natural human environments. *Behavior Analyst, 11,* 95–109.

Miller, W. R., & Brown, J. M. (1991). Self-regulation as a conceptual basis for the prevention and treatment of addictive behaviours. In N. Heather, W. R. Miller, & J. Greeley (Eds.), *Self-control and the addictive behaviours* (pp. 3–82). Sydney, Australia: McMillan.

Moffitt, T. E. (1993). Adolescence-limited and life course persistent antisocial behavior: Developmental taxonomy. *Psychological Review, 100,* 674–701.

Moreno, J. L. (1933). Psychological and social organization of groups in the community. *Proceedings & Addresses of the American Association on Mental Deficiency, 38,* 224–242.

Nelson, S. E., & Dishion, T. J. (2004). From boys to men: Predicting adult adaptation from middle childhood sociometric status. *Development and Psychopathology, 16*(2), 441–459.

Oetting, E. R., & Beauvais, F. (1987). Peer cluster theory, socialization characteristics, and adolescent drug use: A path analysis. *Journal of Consulting and Clinical Psychology, 34,* 205–213.

Olweus, D. (1993). *Bullying at school: What we know and what we can do.* Oxford, UK: Blackwell.

Panella, D., & Henggeler, S. W. (1986). Peer interactions of conduct-disordered, anxious-withdrawn, and well-adjusted black adolescents. *Journal of Abnormal Child Psychology, 14*(1), 1–11.

Patterson, G. R., & Dishion, T. J. (1985). Contributions of families and peers to delinquency. *Criminology, 23,* 63–79.

Patterson, G. R., Reid, J. B., & Dishion, T. J. (1992). *Antisocial boys.* Eugene, OR: Castalia.

Patterson, G. R., & Yoerger, K. (1993). Development models for delinquent behavior. In S. Hodgins (Ed.), *Mental disorder and crime* (pp. 140–172). Thousand Oaks, CA: Sage.

Peery, C. J. (1979). Popular, amiable, isolated, rejected: A reconceptualization of sociometric status in preschool children. *Child Development, 50,* 1231–1234.

Piaget, J. (1954). *The construction of reality in the child.* Oxford: Basic Books.

Piehler, T. F., & Dishion, T. J. (2006). *Interpersonal dynamics within adolescent friendship: Dyadic mutuality and deviant talk and the development of antisocial behavior.* Manuscript submitted for publication.

Rolf, J., Masten, A. S., Cicchetti, D., Nuechterlein, K. H., & Weintraub, S. (Eds.). (1990). *Risk and protective factors in the development of psychopathology.* Cambridge: Cambridge University Press.

Rothbart, M. K., Ellis, L. K., & Posner, M. I. (2004). Temperament and self-regulation. In R. F. Baumeister & K. D. Vohs (Eds.), *Handbook of self-regulation: Research, theory, and applications* (pp. 357–370). New York: Guilford Press.

Sowell, E. R., & Jernigan, T. L. (1998). Further MRI evidence of late brain maturation: Limbic volume increases and changing asymmetries during childhood and adolescence. *Developmental Neuropsychology, 14,* 599–617.

Stroop, J. R. (1935). Studies of interference in serial verbal reactions. *Journal of Experimental Psychology, 18*(6), 643–662.

Sullivan, H. S. (1953). *The interpersonal theory of psychiatry.* New York: Norton.

Vitale, J. E., Newman, J. P., Bates, J. E., Goodnight, J., Dodge, K. A., & Pettit, G. S. (2005). Deficient behavioral inhibition and anomalous selective attention in a community sample of adolescents with psychopathic traits and low-anxiety traits. *Journal of Abnormal Child Psychology, 33,* 461–470.

Vitaro, F., Gendreau, P. L., Tremblay, R. E., & Oligny, P. (1998). Reactive and proactive aggression differentially predict later conduct problems. *Journal of Child Psychology and Psychiatry, 39,* 377–385.

Werner, E. E. (1995). Resilience in development. *Current Directions in Psychological Science, 4,* 81–85.

Wills, T. A., & Dishion, T. J. (2003). Temperament and adolescent substance use: A transactional analysis of emerging self-control. In P. Frick & W. Silverman (Eds.), *Temperament and childhood psychopathology* [Special Issue]. *Journal of Clinical Child and Adolescent Psychology, 33,* 69–81.

Windle, M. (1990). A longitudinal study of antisocial behaviors in early adolescence as predictors of late adolescence substance use: Gender and ethnic group differences. *Journal of Abnormal Psychology, 99,* 86–91.

Depression in Youth:
A Developmental
Psychopathology Perspective

Judy Garber
Vanderbilt University

Depression is considered one of the most burdensome and disabling diseases in the world (Murray & Lopez, 1996). Approximately 25% of individuals will experience a clinically significant episode of depression in their lifetime, and many more will have subthreshold levels of symptoms. Social and occupational impairment as well as other psychopathology (e.g., substance use disorders, anxiety disorders) and suicidality often accompany mood disorders. Depression tends to recur, with over 75% of depressed individuals having more than one episode over the life course (Keller & Boland, 1998). Symptoms often begin during childhood or, more frequently, in adolescence (Kandel & Davies, 1986; Pine, Cohen, Gurley, Brook, & Ma, 1998). Early identification of the processes that underlie the development of depression should facilitate prevention and treatment.

Depression is a complex condition that lends itself well to study from a developmental psychopathology perspective. Indeed, Sroufe and Rutter discussed depression in their classic paper on developmental psychopathology in 1984, and again in their update in 2000. Issues central to the field of developmental psychopathology that are particularly relevant to the study of depression include (a) continuities and discontinuities, (b) multiple levels of analysis that integrate genetic, biological, psychological, and social-contextual causal mechanisms, and (c) risk and protective processes.

181

This chapter has two aims. First, the issue of the continuity and discontinuity of depression is discussed. At least two kinds of continuity are relevant: (a) continuity from normal sadness to depressive disorders, and (b) continuity between childhood and adult depression. Second, a multilevel framework for understanding the mechanisms underlying the development of depression is outlined, and evidence from the literature and my own work relevant to this perspective is presented. Finally, remaining gaps in our knowledge are highlighted and directions for future research are suggested.

CONTINUITIES AND DISCONTINUITIES

The study of the continuity in depression is important because it may provide valuable information about its origins and developmental course. Two broad continua of interest are from normal sadness to depressive disorders, and between child and adult depression. Several additional questions follow with regard to the second type of continuity including: Are the basic symptoms that define the disorder the same across development? Are the underlying causal processes the same in childhood- and adult-onset depressions? Is there within-individual continuity across time? Do the same processes account for initial onset and recurrence?

Continuity From Normal Sadness to Depressive Disorders

Depression can be defined as a symptom, a syndrome, or a nosologic disorder. The single symptom of sadness or depressed affect is a subjective state experienced by most individuals at various points in their lives, and by itself is not necessarily pathological. The syndrome of depression is comprised of more than an isolated dysphoric mood, and occurs in combination with other symptoms to form a symptom-complex or syndrome. When this clinical syndrome is characterized by a particular symptom picture with a specifiable course, outcome, etiology, and treatment response, then it is considered a distinct nosologic disorder. The symptoms that comprise the diagnosis of Major Depressive Disorder according to the current nomenclature (i.e., American Psychiatric Association, 1994) are listed in Table 7.1.

Thus, the phenomenon of depression spans normality to disorder in a dimensional way, although the more severe disorders that comprise bipolar affective psychoses are likely discontinuous with normal variations of mood (Perris, 1992; Ruscio & Ruscio, 2000). This is similar to IQ, which can function both as a continuous dimension from low levels associated with mental retardation to high levels associated with genius, as well as a discontinuous categorical disorder such as Down Syndrome, which has a distinct

TABLE 7.1

Symptoms of a Major Depressive Episode

- Depressed mood (in children and adolescents, mood can be irritable rather than sad).
- Anhedonia: decreased interest or pleasure in most activities
- Decrease or increase in appetite; weight loss or gain (not intentional). In children: a failure to make expected weight gains
- Sleep problems (insomnia or hypersomnia)
- Fatigue or loss of energy
- Psychomotor agitation or retardation
- Feelings of worthlessness or excessive guilt
- Difficulty concentrating or making decisions
- Recurrent thoughts of death, suicidal ideation or attempt

For a diagnosis, five or more of these symptoms have to have been present more days than not during the same time for at least 2 weeks. At least one symptom must be either (a) depressed mood or (b) anhedonia. Symptoms are a change from the person's typical functioning and cause impairment or significant distress.

Symptoms of Dysthymic Disorder

Depressed mood (or irritability in children and adolescents) plus two of the following symptoms are present more of the time than not for at least 2 years (at least 1 year in children and adolescents), and never without these symptoms for more than 2 months at a time. Symptoms cause impairment or significant distress.

- Decreased appetite or overeating
- Sleep problems (insomnia, hypersomnia)
- Fatigue; low energy
- Low self-esteem
- Trouble concentrating or making decisions
- Hopelessness

etiology from other, more continuous forms of mental retardation. Rutter, Harrington, Quinton, and Pickles (1994) noted a distinction between minor and major depressive disorders, thereby questioning the continuity between these conditions. They found that whereas adult minor depression was associated with prior conduct disturbance, this was not the case for major depression, which showed a high degree of consistency and specificity over time.

Rutter and Sroufe (2000) argued that the key issue regarding continuity from the typical to the atypical concerns the extent of continuity or discontinuity in the mechanisms that underlie the condition. Are the causes of transient sadness the same, just less intense, as the causes of major depressive disorder? Do the same mechanisms underlie depressive mood, syndrome, and disorders?

There are few universal predictors of what produces sad affect, although loss of a significant relationship probably comes close (Brown & Harris,

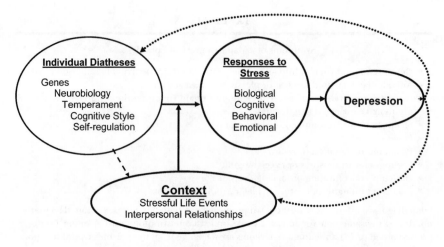

Figure 7.1   A multilevel biopsychosocial model of depression.

1978, 1989). Nevertheless, there is tremendous individual variability in the intensity, duration, covarying symptoms, and impairment associated with depressive mood after experiencing a loss or other stressors. These individual differences likely contribute to the progression from sadness to disorder in some people but not others.

Although most individuals with depressive diagnoses have dysphoric mood, only a subset of those who experience sadness go on to have a full mood disorder. Thus, if similar mechanisms cause depressive mood, syndrome, and disorder, other factors are needed to explain the progression from one to the other over time or differences in this progression among individuals, even if it is just a matter of degree. That is, why do some people react with greater distress to the same life event than do others? A multilevel framework, outlined in Figure 7.1 and discussed later, is proposed to explain such individual variability in responses to stress.

Continuity Between Childhood and Adult Depression

A second type of continuity concerns the link between childhood-onset and adult-onset depression. Are these the same disorders? Are the basic symptoms that define the depression fundamentally the same across development? This kind of continuity can take two forms: homotypic—the phenotypic expression is the same from childhood to adulthood (i.e., behavioral stability), and heterotypic—the underlying processes that produce symptoms are essentially the same over time even if the behavioral manifestations are different (Kagan & Moss, 1962). That is, there may be developmental differences in how symptoms are expressed but the symptoms do not differ when considered as higher level constructs.

An example of heterotypic continuity in depression is how the experience and expression of the symptom of anhedonia varies with development. In young children, anhedonia might be characterized by a lack of interest in playing with toys, in adolescents as a pervasive sense of boredom, and in adults, as a lack of interest in sex. Although on the surface it might appear that these reflect different symptoms, the core underlying constructs would be the same—a loss of interest in age-appropriate activities that are normally reinforcing. This issue of heterotypic continuity is not unique to depression. For instance, when defining aggression developmentally, biting and hair-pulling are considered expressions of aggression in toddlers, whereas verbal sarcasm or using weapons are more common forms of aggression in teens (Loeber & Hay, 1997).

According to developmental theorists (e.g., Avenevoli & Steinberg, 2001; Carlson & Garber, 1986; Cicchetti & Schneider-Rosen, 1984; Cicchetti & Toth, 1998), the manner in which depression is experienced and expressed depends, in part, on the individual's level of physiological, social, and cognitive development. The transition into adolescence, in particular, represents a critical juncture in which emergent biological changes, social competencies, and cognitive capacities influence the reorganization of behavior (Steinberg et al., 2006). Thus, a developmental perspective predicts that there probably would not be "homotypic" continuity (i.e., phenotypic or symptomatic consistency) across development. Rather, there is coherence in the organization of behaviors such that "Continuity lies not in isomorphic behaviors over time but in lawful relations to later behavior, however complex the link" (Sroufe & Rutter, 1984, p. 21). Cicchetti and Toth (1991) similarly stated that "Continuity is manifest in lawful relations, and not in isomorphic behavior" (p. 4), with the specific manifestations of some depressive symptoms expected to vary with development.

Even if there is discontinuity in the phenotypic expression of depressive symptoms but heterotypic continuity of the underlying constructs, there is another continuity question regarding whether the specific characteristics that comprise the syndrome of depression differ with development. Although certain "core symptoms" invariantly may be a part of depression at any age (Carlson & Kashani, 1988), other depressive symptoms may vary with developmental level. That is, different combinations of symptoms may characterize depression at different ages. This could result from limitations due to physiological maturation, cognitive capacity, or linguistic ability to develop, experience, and/or express certain depressive symptoms (Cicchetti & Schneider-Rosen, 1984).

For example, symptoms such as guilt and hopelessness may be particularly affected by cognitive development. Young children might have the prerequisites for the emergence of guilt, such as an awareness of standards regarding prohibited behavior and simple forms of perspective-taking (Kagan, 1982; Zahn-Waxler, Chapman, & Cummings, 1984), and might even experience some rudimentary forms of guilt (e.g., after a transgression for which they are punished), but they are less capable of experiencing depressive guilt, which involves more advanced beliefs about control and personal responsibility (Weiner & Graham, 1985). With the advent of abstract thinking, adolescents develop increasing concerns for social issues and moral principles (Keating, 2004; Piaget, 1971), which are ripe ground for the occurrence of depressive cognitions about moral inadequacy and guilt. Similarly, young children might not be capable of experiencing sustained hopelessness, given their level of cognitive development and their tendency to be present-oriented (Piaget, 1971; Singer & Revenson, 1996). The capacity to experience hopelessness increases with development, as adolescents become more concerned with and oriented toward the future (Greene, 1986; Nurmi, 1991).

Although not an explicit symptom of depression, attributions about the causes of events are related to the symptoms of guilt (i.e., self-blame) and hopelessness (i.e., expectations about the future), and its emergence also is affected by cognitive development. Children below about age 8 tend not to understand that internal causes of events are stable over time or across situations (Rholes & Ruble, 1984), and they believe that negative traits can change or even become positive over time (Freedman et al., 2000; Lockhart, Chang, & Story, 2002). Moreover, young children tend to confuse the concepts of ability and effort, which are both internal but differ on stability and globality (Nicholls, 1978, 1984, 1990). By about age 10, children begin to recognize the consistency of some traits (e.g., generosity, intelligence) across time and situations (Alvarez, Ruble, & Bolger, 2001; Rholes & Ruble, 1984). They adopt more of a fixed-entity concept of ability (Dweck & Leggett, 1988), which is believed to limit the effect of increased effort (Nicholls & Miller, 1984; Normandeau & Gobeil, 1998; Stipek & DeCotis, 1988). By about age 12, however, children comprehend that although a generally stable trait, ability also is malleable, such that persistent effort can improve certain abilities over time (Barenboim, 1981; Blumenfeld, Pintrich, & Hamilton, 1986). Thus, symptoms of guilt and hopelessness as well as the related construct of attributional style change with cognitive development, and therefore may not be part of the depressive syndrome at younger ages.

Despite cautions from developmental psychopathologists (e.g., Carlson & Garber, 1986; Cicchetti & Toth, 1991; Sroufe & Rutter, 1984) about possible discontinuity between children and adults in the symptoms that comprise the syndrome of depression, however, the general consensus among clinicians has been that the essential symptoms of depression are isomorphic across development (see, e.g., Carlson & Kashani, 1988; Ryan et al., 1987). Cicchetti and Toth (1998) noted, "Most often the criteria associated with adult depression have been applied to children, and developmental considerations that may affect the etiology, course, and outcome of depression in children and adolescents have been minimized or disregarded entirely" (p. 222).

Weiss and Garber (2003) conducted a meta-analysis to examine whether there are developmental differences in the phenomenology of depression, at both the individual symptom and syndrome levels. At the symptom level, 19 of the 29 depressive symptoms evaluated showed significant variability across studies, even after controlling for gender, sample type, and informant. For these 19 symptoms, there were developmental effects for which some as-yet-unknown, between-study factors influenced their magnitude. Moreover, of the 10 symptoms that did not show significant variability, six showed significant developmental effects. Five of the six symptoms (anhedonia, hopeless, hypersomnia, weight gain, social withdrawal) were higher among more developmentally advanced individuals. Thus, the available evidence was not sufficiently consistent across the 16 studies reviewed to reach a firm conclusion regarding continuity of the manifestation of depressive symptoms across development.

At the syndrome level, the results of five studies also were inconsistent, with two supporting developmental isomorphism, two supporting developmental differences, and one providing some support for each position. Thus, based on a review of the empirical data available at that point, Weiss and Garber (2003) suggested that it may be premature to conclude that depression is developmentally isomorphic, at either the symptom or syndrome level. This does not mean that clinicians cannot identify children who meet the adult diagnostic criteria for depression (e.g., Ryan et al., 1987). However, the presence of children fitting these adult criteria does not preclude the possibility that other symptoms, unique to children, are part of childhood depression, or that some of the adult symptoms are not part of the child syndrome.

Increases in the Prevalence of Depression From Childhood to Adolescence. Another important fact relevant to continuity is that depression becomes more prevalent during adolescence, particularly for girls. Several theorists have speculated about the causes of the increase in depression during adolescence (Angold & Rutter, 1992), and the gender difference (Cyranowski, Frank, Young, & Shear, 2000; Hankin & Abramson, 1999; Nolen-Hoeksema & Girgus, 1994), but this issue is far from resolved. The transition from childhood to adolescence is a particularly salient developmental period for the study of the continuity of depression given that many biological, social, psychological, and cognitive changes take place during this time

(Steinberg et al., 2006). Adolescence is marked by a rise in the occurrence of depressive mood, symptoms, and disorder. Point prevalence rates for sad mood range from 10% to 18% for preadolescent children (e.g., Kashani & Simonds, 1979) and from about 15% to 50% for adolescents (Petersen, Sarigiani, & Kennedy, 1991). In adolescents, the prevalence of sad mood is between 10% to 20% based on parents' report (Achenbach, 1991) and 20% to 40% by teens' self-report (e.g., Achenbach, 1991; Kandel & Davies, 1982), with the rates being generally higher for adolescent girls than boys (e.g., Petersen et al., 1991). The prevalence of irritable mood also is high during adolescence.

With regard to the syndrome of depression, prevalence rates have ranged from 5% (Achenbach, 1991) to over 20% (Albert & Beck, 1975; Roberts, Lewinsohn, & Seeley, 1991) depending on how the syndrome is defined and measured. Finally, prevalence rates for major depressive disorders among children (6 to 11 years old) range from 0.4% to 3%, and among adolescents range from 0.4% to 8.3%. (Birmaher, Ryan, Williamson, Brent, Kaufman, Dahl, et al., 1996; Fleming & Offord, 1990), with an average across 10 studies of 3.6% (Lewinsohn & Essau, 2002). Thus, depressive disorders are more common among adolescents compared to children.

Gender differences in the prevalence of depression emerge during adolescence (Ge, Lorenz, Conger, Elder, & Simons, 1994; Hankin et al., 1998; Nolen-Hoeksema & Girgus, 1994; Petersen et al., 1991; Zahn-Waxler, Race, & Duggal, 2005). The rates are nearly 2:1 among adult females compared to adult males in developing countries (Culbertson, 1997). This is true for clinical diagnoses of major depression and dysthymia, as well as subclinical levels of depressive symptoms (Nolen-Hoeksema & Girgus, 1994). This gender difference is not typically found before adolescence, however. Among preadolescents, either no gender differences in rates of depressive symptoms have been found (Angold & Rutter, 1992; Fleming, Offord, & Boyle, 1989; Petersen et al., 1991; Velez, Johnson, & Cohen, 1989), or boys have more depression than girls (e.g., Anderson, Williams, McGee, & Silva, 1987; Costello et al., 1988; Nolen-Hoeksema, Girgus, & Seligman, 1992). This gender ratio shifts during early to middle adolescence, with a small gender difference found for the ages of 13 and 15, a much greater increase in differences between males and females emerging from the ages of 15 and 18 (Hankin et al., 1998). Using multicohort longitudinal analyses, Ge et al. (1994) showed a trend toward an increase in depression among girls relative to boys around the ages of 13 to 14. Garber, Keiley, and Martin (2002) similarly found that among girls, depressive symptoms showed a significant pattern of growth over adolescence, whereas in boys it did not. Thus, there is discontinuity in the prevalence of depression from childhood to adolescence, with the rates rising in girls and remaining the same or even decreasing in boys. Identifying the mechanisms that account for this gender difference across the adolescent transition is critical for understanding the development of depressive disorders.

Within-Individual Continuity Across Time.   Within-individual continuity is whether an individual who is depressed at one point in time is depressed later in development. Research focusing on this type of continuity requires longitudinal designs that can explore depressive symptoms, syndrome, and/or disorders over time in the same people. Indeed, one of the strongest predictors of future depression is prior depression, which is one reason it often is difficult to explain much more of the variance in subsequent depression once prior depression is controlled.

In one of the few studies to examine the continuity of the symptom of depression, Holsen, Kraft, and Vitterso (2000) found that depressed mood was most stable among adolescents who had high initial levels. Moreover, whereas boys' depressed mood scores tended to remain relatively stable, girls' scores showed a curvilinear pattern with a peak during middle adolescence. Holsen et al. also showed that the stable, trait component of depressed mood increased with age, whereas the temporal, state component decreased with age. Few studies, however, have reported the within-individual stabilities of depressed mood or other individual symptoms (e.g., sleep disturbance, anhedonia) over time or across developmental transitions. This could be done, however, by investigators who have examined the syndrome or disorder, given that information about depressed mood and other symptoms should be available.

More studies (e.g., Cole, Martin, Powers, & Truglio, 1996; Finch, Saylor, Edwards, & McIntosh, 1987; Kandel & Davies, 1986; Nolen-Hoeksema et al., 1992) have examined the continuity of depressive syndrome as measured with questionnaires, and generally have found high stability over brief periods of time, and decreasing stability over time. For example, test–retest reliability of the Children's Depression Inventory (CDI) has been found to be about .60 at 6 months (Finch et al., 1987), .60, .58, and .56 across three different 1-year intervals, .39 over 2 years, and .16 over 3 years (Devine, Kempton, & Forehand, 1994). Similarly, the 1- and 2-year stabilities of the Center for Epidemiological Scale for Depression (CES-D) have been found to be .53 and .36 respectively (Garrison, Jackson, Marsteller, McKeown, & Addy, 1990). Using a nationally representative sample of American children first assessed at ages 4 to 16, the 3-year stability of parents' ratings of the anxious/depressed syndrome using the Child Behavior Checklist was .50 (McConaughy, Stanger, & Achenbach, 1992); stability of the anxious/depressed syndrome over 3 years ranged from small-to-moderate ($r = .24$) to large ($r = .60$), depending on the informant (i.e., parent, teacher, child) and gender (Achenbach, Howell, McConaughy, & Stanger, 1995). Thus, there is moderate stability across as much as 3 years in self- and

other-reported symptoms of depressive syndrome, although stability estimates tend to diminish as the time span between assessments increases
(Tram & Cole, 2004).

Using structural equation modeling, Cole and Martin (2005) conducted
latent trait–state analyses to examine the longitudinal structure of depressive
syndrome using the self- and parent-report version of the CDI in children
(Grades 4–6, N = 648) and adolescents (Grades 7–9, N = 1489). Whereas
children's self-reports reflected an autoregressive pattern, on which individual differences are less stable over time, more than a stable trait dimension,
parents' reports about their children's depressive symptoms reflected more
of a stable trait dimension, on which individual differences are stable over
time. Adolescents' and their parents' reports both reflected a stable trait
dimension of depressive symptoms more than an autoregressive dimension. Thus, the continuity of the syndrome of depression varies depending
on the age of the target and the type of informant.

At the level of depressive disorder, individuals with a prior history of a
depressive disorder are at significant risk for subsequent depressive episodes. The majority will experience another episode in their adult life (Kandel & Davies, 1986; Rao et al., 1995), and many cases of recurrent adult
depression had their initial onsets during adolescence (Pine et al., 1998).
Children with mood disorders have recurrent depressive episodes during
adolescence (Emslie et al., 1997; Kovacs, 1996; Kovacs et al., 1984a; Kovacs
et al., 1984b) and adulthood (Garber, Kriss, Koch, & Lindholm, 1988; Harrington, Fudge, Rutter, Pickles, & Hill, 1990; Weissman et al., 1999). Adolescents have recurrences later in adolescence (Lewinsohn et al., 1994;
McCauley et al., 1993) and into adulthood (Lewinsohn, Rohde, Klein, &
Seeley, 1999; Rao, Hammen, & Daley, 1999; Weissman et al., 1999). Recurrence rates among children and adolescents have ranged from 26% to 35%
in 1 year, 40 to 45% in 2 years (Asarnow et al., 1988; Kovacs et al., 1984b),
and from 45% to 72% over 3 to 7 years (Emslie et al., 1997; Harrington et
al., 1990; Kovacs et al., 1984b; Lewinsohn, Rohde, et al., 1999; McCauley
et al., 1993). Such recurrent episodes are associated with negative functional outcomes in school, work, and interpersonal relationships (Rao et
al., 1999), even after recovery (Puig-Antich et al., 1985; Rao et al, 1995).

Thus, depression is characterized by modest stability, although this varies for the symptom, syndrome, and disorder. Stability rates become higher
for disorder but lower for symptoms as the time interval between assessments increases (Avenevoli & Steinberg, 2001). Avenevoli and Steinberg
suggested that variability in stability rates is partially attributable to inconsistencies in the way in which stability has been measured over time at the
different levels of depression. For example, whereas the stability of depressive disorder typically is measured in terms of whether there has ever been
a recurrent episode of depression within a broad period of time (e.g., the

last 10 years), studies of the stability of depressive mood and syndrome typically have used a briefer and more recent interval (e.g., within 6 months). Therefore, it makes sense that recurrence of depressive disorder appears more stable than the symptom or syndrome.

Continuity in the Causes of Childhood- and Adult-Onset Depression. A critical developmental question is what accounts for the observed continuity and discontinuity of depression from childhood to adulthood. This issue is comprised of two questions. First, are the causes of childhood-onset depression the same as adult-onset mood disorders? Although childhood and adult depression have been found to have many of the same correlates, including dysregulation in neuroendocrine and neurochemical systems (Dahl & Ryan, 1996), stress (Compas, Grant, & Ey, 1994), negative cognitions (Garber & Hilsman, 1992), and dysfunctional interpersonal relationships (Gotlib & Hammen, 1992), several differences also have been found.

Genetic influences have been found to vary with age, although not consistently in the same direction. Whereas some studies (e.g., Eley, 1997; Gjone, Stevenson, Sundet, & Eilertsen, 1996; O'Connor, McGuire, Reiss, Hetherington, & Plomin, 1998b,; O'Connor, Neiderhiser, Reiss, Hetherington, & Plomin, 1998a) have reported a decrease in heritability with increasing age, several other studies have found the opposite (Eley & Stevenson, 1999; Rice et al., 2002; Scourfield et al., 2003; Silberg et al., 1999; Thapar & McGuffin, 1994). For example, using a sample of 395 twin pairs ages 8 to 16, Eley (1997) found that shared environment effects were greater in adolescents (.28) than children (.08), and heritability estimates of depressive symptoms were moderate in both groups; $h^2 = .34$ for children and $h^2 = .28$ for adolescents. In contrast, in a sample of 411 twin pairs ages 8 to 16, Thapar and McGuffin (1994) found a lower heritability estimate for self-reported depressive symptoms in children than in adolescents. Scourfield et al. (2003) more recently asserted that "The weight of evidence . . . supports the importance of early shared environmental influences on depressive symptom scores in younger children and adolescents, with these influences being replaced by new genetic and unique environmental influences as children grow older" (p. 975).

Developmental differences in heritability also have been found with regard to diagnosed depressive disorders, although again the findings are inconsistent. Early-onset mood disorders have been considered a more severe form of the disorder that are associated with increased familial loading of depression (e.g., Weissman, Warner, Wickramaratne, & Prusoff, 1988) and increased risk of relapse (Gonzales et al., 1985; Keller, Lavori, Lewis, & Klerman, 1983). In contrast, Harrington et al. (1990) reported that children with prepubertal onset of depression were at significantly lower risk of having major depression as adults than were postpubertal patients. Harrington et al. (1990) suggested that their findings could have been due to artifacts of their methodology such as poor measurement of prepubertal depression or the inaccurate documentation of the onset of puberty. In a subsequent study, Harrington et al. (1993) reported that compared to controls, both pre- and postpubertal onset major depressions had an increased familial loading for depressive disorders in first and second degree relatives. However, prepubertal onset MDD was significantly more likely to be associated with familial discord, criminality, and alcohol abuse than was postpubertal onset. Thus, family history may differ for pre- versus postpubertal onset MDD, particularly regarding comorbid disorders in relatives.

Differences between childhood- and adolescent-onset depressions also have been found with regard to psychosocial factors. Duggal, Carlson, Sroufe, and Egeland (2001) showed that depressive symptoms in childhood were predicted by an overall adverse family context characterized by maternal depressive symptoms, early care lacking in emotional supportiveness, abuse, and family stressors. In contrast, adolescent-onset depressive symptoms were more specifically associated with maternal depressive symptoms for females and nonsupportive early care for males.

Children and adolescents also differ with regard to the relations among negative cognitions, stress, and depressive symptoms (Abela, 2001; Conley, Haines, Hilt, & Metalsky, 2001; Nolen-Hoeksema et al., 1992; Turner & Cole, 1994). For example, Turner and Cole (1994) found an association between negative cognitions and depressive symptoms in children in Grades 4, 6, and 8, although support for the cognitive diathesis-stress model was only found for the eighth graders. Similarly, in a study of 280 third- and seventh-grade students over 6 weeks, Abela (2001) found a significant Grade × Attributional Style × Negative Life Events interaction, indicating support for the diathesis-stress hypothesis in seventh graders but not in third graders.

During adolescence, the relations among cognitions and depression tend to be relatively stable and become more similar to what is found in adults (Garber, Weiss, & Shanley, 1993). Thus, the etiological role of stress and negative cognitions may differ for children and adolescents. Overall, pre- and postpubertal onset mood disorders differ with regard to phenomenology, prevalence, sex distribution, outcome, and several potential etiological factors (e.g., heritability of self-reported depressive symptoms, family history of mood and other disorders, family dysfunction, and negative cognitions).

Continuity in the Causes of Onset and Recurrence.   Finally, one other kind of continuity concerns whether the factors associated with the onset of the first depressive episode are the same as those associated with its recurrence. Is there a distinction between the processes that initiate pathways and those that maintain or deflect individuals from these pathways? It is possible that whatever mechanisms were responsible for the early onset (e.g., genes, trauma) are the same as those that produce subsequent episodes. It also is possible, however, that in addition to the continuation of the effects of the original vulnerability factors, earlier depressive episodes produce changes in the person's biology, cognitions, and environment that further contribute to their increased likelihood of subsequent episodes.

A developmental perspective requires explaining how effects are carried forward and how they influence the way individuals respond in the future. How do prior episodes of depression change individuals to make them more or less vulnerable to future episodes? The "scarring" hypothesis suggests that earlier episodes of depression create a biological and/or psychological scar that sensitizes the individual to later exposures to even lower levels of the etiological agent(s). That is, having an episode of depression changes the individual in such a way as to make him or her more vulnerable to future episodes. Post (1992) proposed a "kindling hypothesis," in which the neurobiology of mood disorders changes as a function of the longitudinal course of the illness. Prior episodes of depression "leave behind neurobiological residues that make a patient more vulnerable to subsequent episodes" (Post, 1992, p. 1006).

Post (1992) further argued that the strength of the association between major life stress and episode onset declines from the first episode over successive recurrences, and stressful events may be particularly linked with childhood-onset depression. Although there is empirical support for Post's kindling hypothesis (e.g., Kendler, Thornton, & Gardner, 2000; Lewinsohn, Allen, Seeley, & Gotlib, 1999), recently the basic premise has been questioned (Monroe & Harkness, 2005). Monroe and Harkness proposed a Stress Sensitization model, suggesting that it takes less and more minor stress to precipitate a recurrent episode of depression than a first episode, but major life stressors still maintain their potency for precipitating recurrences.

Cognitive theories of depression (e.g., Abramson, Metalsky, & Alloy, 1989; Beck, 1976) now recognize that negative cognitions not only can contribute to the onset of mood disorders, but also that depression can alter the way individuals process information. Beck (1976) argued that after experiencing a depressive episode, individuals tend to adopt a more automatic negative way of interpreting events, which then makes them more vulnerable to subsequent episodes. Segal, Williams, Teasdale, and Gemar (1996) suggested that repeated stressors and depressive episodes contribute to progressive changes in information processing, which then reduces the threshold for triggering recurrence. Indeed, longitudinal studies with children have shown that prior depressive symptoms predict increases in negative cognitions (Cole, Martin, Peeke, Seroczynski, & Hoffman, 1998; Nolen-Hoeksema et al., 1992).

Interpersonal models of depression (e.g., Coyne, 1976; Hammen, 1991) have shown that depressed individuals tend to generate stressors, particularly within the social domain, that serve to increase their likelihood of interpersonal conflict and rejection, which in turn leads to further depression. Longitudinal designs are needed to examine the direction of these effects. Support for the reciprocal model has been found in a few studies of child and adolescent community samples (Cohen, Burt, & Bjorck, 1987; Cole, Nolen-Hoeksema, Girgus, & Paul, 2004; Kim, Conger, Elder, & Lorenz, 2003). Stress predicted increases in symptoms after controlling for prior symptom levels, and symptoms predicted increases in stress after controlling for prior stress.

Thus, it is important to examine the person effects on the environment as well as the environmental effects on the person (Bell & Chapman, 1986; Rutter, 2002). How does the person's behavior, which likely is in part genetically driven, shape and select experiences (Scarr & McCartney, 1983), and how do those effects contribute to developmental continuities and discontinuities over time? Various internal changes in the individual (e.g., brain structure, neuroendocrine functioning, affect regulation, cognitive processing, interpersonal interactions) can affect subsequent vulnerability. That is, there are dynamic changes in these biopsychosocial systems over time.

What can be concluded about the continuity and discontinuity of depression across development? First, the rates of depression increase from childhood to adolescence, particularly among females. Second, although there are many similarities in the symptoms that comprise the syndrome of depression at all ages, there also are noteworthy differences in the phenomenology and structure of depressive syndrome in children versus adults. Third, the course and outcome appear to be relatively similar across development, although earlier age of onset is associated with more severe and recurrent forms of depression and with increased risk of relapse. In general, some similar biological and psychosocial correlates have been found in depressed children and adults, although the links between these variables and the onset of depression in both children and adults needs to be studied further. Finally, over time, changes in the biopsychosocial systems produce mood disorders such that prior depression can alter these underlying processes and thereby increase the likelihood of recurrence.

A MULTILEVEL BIOPSYCHOSOCIAL MODEL OF DEPRESSION

The etiology of mood disorders requires a complex, multifactorial model (e.g., Akiskal & McKinney, 1975; Cicchetti & Toth, 1998; Kendler, Gardner, & Prescott, 2002), not unlike other common conditions such as heart disease and diabetes. No single risk factor accounts for all or even most of the variance. Rather, processes contributing to risk for depression span all levels of analysis including genetic, biological, psychological, interpersonal, and contextual. A comprehensive understanding of risk and protective processes requires an integration of multiple levels and methods of analysis of individual and contextual factors (Cicchetti & Dawson, 2002).

Depression is a heterogeneous condition characterized by both equifinality and multifinality (Cicchetti & Rogosch, 1996). Equifinality denotes that more than one causal pathway involving different combinations of factors can result in the same condition. Regarding depression, no necessary cause has yet been identified; rather, multiple risk factors and processes likely combine in various ways to produce depression. Multifinality indicates that some of the risk factors that produce one condition (i.e., depression) also may be part of the causal processes underlying other disorders. Many common risk factors (e.g., stress, neurobiological dysregulation, temperament, interpersonal problems) likely are part of the etiology of depression as well as other conditions, but the particular amalgamation of these factors with each other or with additional variables, as well as their dose and timing is what uniquely results in one condition rather than another.

A diathesis stress model often has been used to describe the etiology of depression (e.g., Abramson et al., 1989; Beck, 1976; Brown & Harris, 1978; Caspi et al., 2003; Monroe & Simons, 1991). According to this perspective, depression occurs in individuals with a preexisting vulnerability when exposed to stress. That is, individual biological and/or psychological predispositions combine with various contextual factors, particularly stressful life events and interpersonal difficulties, to produce depression.

Figure 7.1 shows a conceptual framework of the processes hypothesized to lead to depression. The relations among these variables are reciprocal and dynamic. That is, these multiple levels of analysis and multiple systems influence each other. According to this model, a combination of individual diatheses and contextual factors have direct, indirect (i.e., mediated), and interactive (i.e., moderated) effects on depression. The individual diatheses represent more distal and relatively stable (although potentially malleable) characteristics, which then influence how the person responds to specific situations and stressors. For example, when faced with stressful life events, individuals high on neuroticism tend to engage in maladaptive strategies such as emotional expression, escape avoidance, self-blame, confrontation, and less problem solving (Lee-Baggley, DeLongis, Voorhoeave, & Greenglass, 2004; Newth & DeLongis, 2004; O'Brien & DeLongis, 1996), which then can exacerbate the stressful situation with which they are trying to cope. In turn, such escalating stressful circumstances can alter biochemistry as well as self-schema and information processing, which can lead to further maladaptive behaviors, thereby generating more negative events, particularly within the social domain (Coyne, 1976; Hammen, 1991), and so on.

Thus, in classic Baron and Kenny (1986) terms, this is a mediated moderation model. Individual diatheses moderate the relation between stress and depression, and contribute to the manner in which the person responds to negative life events; such responses to stress then mediate the effect of the individual diatheses on subsequent depression. Simply stated, if an individual has particular biological and/or psychological "depressogenic" vulnerabilities, then encounters stressful life events and responds ineffectively such that the stressor is not adequately managed, then depression likely will result. Finally, once depression occurs, it then can feed back to the person's biology and cognitions as well as alter the context in such a way as to make it even more stressful, and the cycle continues. This "scarring" (Lewinsohn, Allen, et al., 1999) or "kindling" hypothesis (Post, 1992), which was described in the earlier section on within-person continuity across time, results in dynamic changes in these biopsychosocial systems over time.

Despite the call from developmental psychopathologists for comprehensive and integrated multilevel and multimethod analyses of the mediating and moderating relations between individual and contextual factors across development (Cicchetti & Toth, 1998), most studies have examined only components of this model, in part due to the complexity of these relations. In the remainder of this chapter, I highlight evidence from the literature and my own work that has addressed aspects of the model depicted in Figure 7.1. First, the Development of Depression Project (DDP) is described with regard to the participants, procedures, and measures. Then, findings from the literature and DDP relevant to components of the model are presented. Next, person–environment correlations highlighting relations among several components of the model are discussed. Finally, our attempts to test more integrated aspects of the model are reported. The concluding section notes limitations of the DDP as it provides directions for future research.

THE DEVELOPMENT OF DEPRESSION PROJECT

In the long tradition of developmental psychopathology research (e.g., Garmezy, 1977; Garmezy & Streitman, 1974; Sameroff, Seifer, & Zax, 1982), the Development of Depression Project (DDP) used a high-risk research design. Rutter and Sroufe (2000) have asserted that risk research is "paradigmatic of developmental psychopathology" and that "if risk processes are to be understood adequately, investigations need to include detailed longitudinal study of risk populations" (p. 266). DDP was a prospective study of psychosocial processes in children who had an increased probability of developing depression due to their mothers having had a history of a mood disorder. Although focusing on high-risk offspring limits our ability to generalize our findings to normative, community samples, it allowed us to identify a sample of children at increased risk for depression, but prior to their ever having had an episode.

The DDP was a longitudinal study of same-age participants across 6 years of adolescence. Most prior studies of offspring of depressed parents have included a large age range, often spanning 7 to 17 years old (e.g., Hammen, 1991; Weissman et al., 1987). One exception is the work of Radke-Yarrow (1998), who studied young children in a relatively narrow age range because she argued that doing so provides a more developmental orientation. We followed a same-age cohort of youth during the middle and high school years to track the development of depression. Multiple methods (e.g., questionnaires, interviews, observations), informants (child, mother, clinician) and variables were used to examine increases in depressive symptoms and the onset of depressive disorders. We primarily focused on psychosocial risk and protective factors, particularly negative cognitions and coping styles, and the contextual factors of stressful life events and interpersonal relationships, especially within the family. Nevertheless, we fully recognize the importance of genetics and biology in the etiology of mood disorders, and acknowledge that we did not conduct the study in a way that takes account of these important genetic and biological effects. As Rutter (2000) noted, however, genetic factors clearly play a part in the development of depression, but there also is "true environmentally mediated risk associated with negative life events and family negativity" (p. 139). The DDP was intended to contribute to our understanding of psychological and experiential aspects of the diathesis-stress model. We focused on these particular psychosocial aspects of development because they likely will be amenable to preventive and therapeutic interventions. "Understanding the more proximal mechanisms that might mediate the relation between genes and depression provides directions for interventions that can interrupt the indirect causal chain" (Silberg & Rutter, 2002, p. 26).

Method

Participants and Procedure.   Parents of 5th-grade children from metropolitan public schools were invited to participate in a study about parents and children. A brief health history questionnaire, comprised of 24 medical conditions (e.g., diabetes, heart disease, depression) and 34 medications (e.g., Prozac, Elavil, Valium), was sent with a letter describing the project to several thousand families. Of the 1,495 mothers who indicated an interest in participating, the 587 who had endorsed either a history of depression, use of antidepressants, or no history of psychopathology were interviewed further by telephone. The remaining families were excluded because the mother did not indicate depression or reported serious health problems (e.g., cancer, multiple sclerosis). Of the 587 mothers screened by telephone, 349 reported either a history of depression or no history of psychiatric problems. The 238 families not further screened were excluded because they did not indicate sufficient symptoms to meet criteria for a depressive disorder (38%), had other psychiatric disorders that did not also include a depressive disorder (19%), they or the target child had a serious medical condition (14%), were no longer interested (21%), the target child either was in the wrong grade or was in special education (6%), or the family had moved out of the area (2%). The Structured Clinical Interview for *DSM* diagnoses (SCID; Spitzer, Williams, Gibbon, & First, 1990), a widely used, semistructured clinical interview from which *DSM* diagnoses (American Psychiatric Association, 1994) can be made, then was conducted with the 349 mothers. Interrater reliability, calculated on a random subset of 20% of the SCID interviews, indicated 94% agreement (kappa = .88) for diagnoses of depressive disorders. The final sample of 240 families consisted of 185 mothers who had a history of a mood disorder during the target child's life (high risk group) and 55 mothers who were lifetime free of psychopathology (low risk group). Of the 185 mothers with depression histories, 38.4% had had two or more depressive episodes and 37.8% had been depressed for more than 2 years during the child's lifetime.

Children were first assessed when they were in 6th grade (Time 1). Follow-up interviews were conducted annually through their 12th-grade year. Different individuals, none of whom were aware of the mother's psychiatric history, interviewed the mother and child separately about the child, and administered a battery of questionnaires to them.

Participants were 240 mothers and their 6th-grade children (mean age = 11.86 years, *SD* = .57); 130 (54.2%) were female. The sample of adolescents was 82% White, 14.7% African American, and 3.3% other (Hispanic, Asian, Native American). Families were predominantly working class (e.g., nurses aide, sales clerk) to middle class (e.g., store manager, teacher), with the mean socioeconomic status (Hollingshead, 1975) of 41.84 (*SD* = 13.25).

This developmental period was selected for several reasons. First, this is the time when the rates of depression are known to increase (Hankin et al., 1998). Second, during these years, children are exposed to increased demands and new challenges such as the normative transitions of changing schools, and the biological, psychological, and social changes that accompany puberty (Graber, Brooks-Gunn, & Petersen, 1996; Steinberg et al, 2006). Thus, we expected to find greater variability on measures of stress throughout this time. Third, adolescents experience several salient developmental tasks during this time that could be affected by their relationship with their depressed mother, such as seeking autonomy and the emergence of romantic relationships. One disadvantage of starting at this age, however, is that some of the processes hypothesized to be related to the development of depression (e.g., parent–child relationship; negative cognitions, puberty), as well as some symptoms or disorders themselves, are likely to be well under way by this point for some children. Therefore, we also obtained a lifetime history of psychopathology so that we could differentiate onset of new disorders from recurrence.

Measures. Information across multiple domains was obtained using multiple methods and informants (see Table 7.2). Lifetime and current psychopathology were assessed with both self- and parent-report questionnaires, and clinical interviews. Mothers and adolescents were interviewed separately, and their responses were combined to create summary ratings.

TABLE 7.2
Methods and Measures Used in the Development of Depression Project

Domain	Method	Measures
Symptoms & Disorders	Self-report	CDI, YSR, PANAS
	Parent-report	P-CDI, CBCL
	Clinical Interview	K-SADS/LIFE, R-CDRS
Life Events	Self-report	LEQ
	Parent-report	FILE
	Interview	LEI-A
Family Environment	Self-report	FRI, CBQ, CRPBI, NRI
	Parent-report	FRI, CBQ, CRPBI
	Five-minute Speech Sample (T1 & T3)	Expressed Emotion: Criticism, Emotional Overinvolvement
	Mother-child interactions (observations) (T1)	Positive, Negative, Involvement
Cognitions	Self-report	Self-worth, CASQ, CHS, DEQ-A, RSQ

Note. T1 = Time 1; T3 = Time 3; PANAS = Positive and Negative Affectivity Scale (Watson et al., 1988); K-SADS = Schedule for Affective Disorders and Schizophrenia for school-aged children (Kaufman et al., 1997); LIFE = Longitudinal Interview Follow-up Evaluation (Keller et al., 1987); CDI = Children's Depression Inventory (Kovacs, 1985); P-CDI = Parent version of the CDI (Garber, 1984); R-CDRS = Revised Children's Depression Rating Scale (Poznanski et al., 1985); LEQ = Life Events Questionnaire (Johnson & McCutcheon, 1980); FILE = Family Inventory of Life Events (McCubbin & Patterson, 1987); LEI-A = Life Events Interview for Adolescents (Garber & Robinson, 1997a); FRI = Family Relations Inventory (Moos & Moos, 1981), CBQ = Conflict Behavior Questionnaire (Prinz, Foster, Kent, & O'Leary, 1979), CRPBI = Children's Report of Parent Behavior Inventory (Schludermann & Schludermann, 1970), NRI = Network of Relationships Inventory (Furman & Buhrmestor, 1985); CASQ = Children's Attributional Style Questionnaire (Seligman et al., 1984); CHS = Children's Hopelessness Scale (Kazdin, Rodgers, & Colbus, 1986); DEQ-A = Depressive Experiences Questionnaire for Adolescents (Blatt et al., 1992); RSQ = Response Styles Questionnaire (Nolen-Hoeksema & Morrow, 1991).

Life events were assessed annually about events that had occurred for the adolescent during the previous year using checklists and a Life Events Interview for Adolescents (LEIA; Garber & Robinson, 1997a), which was based on the Life Events and Difficulties Schedule (LEDS, Brown & Harris, 1978, 1989; Williamson et al., 1998), and the Life Stress Interview developed by Hammen, Adrian, Gordon, Jaenicke, and Hiroto (1987). The LEIA asked mothers and adolescents to describe the context of the event, what happened, who was involved, when it occurred, and what changed for the adolescent as a result of the event. Such semistructured interviews have been found to be better than checklists in overcoming problems of counting, recalling, and dating of events (Duggal et al., 2000).

Each event was rated for the degree of objective threat it had for the teen given the context on a seven-point scale from 1 (*none*) to 7 (*severe*). Raters were unaware of any information about the mothers' or adolescents' psychopathology. Interrater reliability of the objective stress ratings was obtained by having interviewers present the information about the events at the same time to two different groups who made independent ratings of the events. Based on 202 events, agreement among raters was 89.6%, with a kappa of .79. Interviews yielded a total event count and a total level of stress rating, which were highly correlated ($r = .92$). Thus, based on extensive interviewing about life events and symptoms, we were able to create a continuous record of their stress and psychopathology over the 6-year period.

The family environment also was assessed using multiple methods including questionnaires completed by mothers and teens, a five-minute speech sample (FMSS) of the mother describing her child, and observations of the mother and child in two laboratory interaction tasks. The FMSS was administered at Time 1 when the children were in sixth grade and again when the children were in eighth grade. An independent rater who was unaware of anything about the participants or study design coded the speech sample for "expressed emotion" (criticism, emotional overinvolvement).

Mother–child interactions were observed during two different 10-minute interaction tasks, which pulled for different kinds of parenting behaviors. One task involved resolving an area of conflict, and the other involved solving puzzles and teaching by the mother. For the conflict task, a global rating system was used that yielded three factors based on 16 behavioral and affective items: (a) negative and coercive behaviors and affect displayed by mothers toward their children; (b) how positive and comfortable mothers were with their children; and (c) how actively involved mothers were with their children during the task.

The other interaction involved a set of mazes and anagrams for the child to solve. These puzzles were designed to be easy initially and to become progressively more difficult. Mothers were instructed to "work with your child as you typically would work with him/her on a project or a school assignment." Different raters coded these interactions using a different macro as well as a micro coding system. A confirmatory factor analysis indicated a two-factor solution of negativity (criticism, issuing orders, trying to take control of the task away from the child, displaying negative affect) and positivity (smiling, laughing, using praise, a warm demeanor, consistent interest and involvement in the task, providing constructive assistance on the task). Finally, children's cognitions about their self-worth, attributions for events, hopelessness, self-criticism, and interpersonal dependency were assessed annually with self-report measures.

Individual Diatheses

A diathesis typically is defined as "a constitutional predisposition toward a particular state or condition" (Merriam-Webster, 2004). Here, however, the term *diathesis* is used more broadly to indicate a predisposition toward a particular condition (i.e., depression), but assumes nothing about its origin. Rather, the individual diatheses hypothesized to predispose persons to depression can be derived from genetic/biological factors and/or learned through experience. Moreover, these individual diatheses are not necessarily independent and can influence one another. They can have direct effects on the condition (i.e., depression) such that they increase the probability of developing the disorder, as well as indirect effects; for example, genes will be influential, in part, because "they affect either exposure, or sensitivity, to the environment rather than because they bring about the psychopathological phenotype directly" (Rutter & Silberg, 2002, p. 480). Thus, indirect genetic effects occur through gene–environment correlations and interactions with environmental risks (Silberg & Rutter, 2002). The individual diatheses outlined in the model include genes, neurobiology, temperament/personality, cognitions, and self-regulation.

Genes. Family, twin, and adoption studies have provided evidence of both genetic and environmental effects for unipolar depression (Plomin, 1990; Sullivan, Neale, & Kendler, 2000; Wallace, Schneider, & McGuffin, 2002). Estimates of heritability of depressive symptoms tend to be moderate, although these estimates vary as a function of informant, age, and severity of depressive symptoms (Eaves et al., 1997; Eley, Deater-Deckard, Fombonne, Fulker, & Plomin, 1998; Rende, Plomin, Reiss, & Hetherington, 1993; Thapar & McGuffin, 1994). Nonshared environmental effects also tend to be moderate (Eley et al., 1998). Twin studies indicate that for depressive symptom scores in general population samples of twins, the proportion of variance explained by additive genetic factors has been reported to be between 40% and 70% (Kendler, Neale, Kessler, Heath, & Eaves, 1993; McGuffin, Katz, Watkins, & Rutherford, 1996). In contrast, adoption studies have reported negligible genetic effects, small but significant shared environmental effects, and moderate nonshared environmental influences (Eley et al., 1998; van den Oord, Boomsma, & Verhulst, 1994).

Family studies indicate that having a depressed parent is one of the most powerful predictors of depression in children, which likely is due to both genetic and environmental influences (Beardslee, Versage, & Gladstone, 1998; Goodman & Gotlib, 1999). Compared to children of nondepressed parents, offspring of depressed parents are about three to four times more likely to develop a mood disorder (Lavoie & Hodgins, 1994; Weissman et al., 1987; Weissman, Warner, Wickramaratne, Moreau, & Olfson, 1997). They also are at increased risk of experiencing early-onset depressions (Weissman et al., 1987), with about a 40% chance of having a depressive episode before the age of 18 (Beardslee et al., 1998). In addition, high rates of depression have been found in first- and second-degree relatives of depressed children (e.g., Harrington et al., 1993; Kovacs, Devlin, Pollock, Richards, & Mukerji, 1997; Weissman, Warner, Wickramaratne, & Prusoff, 1988). Compared with families of normal controls, the first-degree relatives of depressed children have significantly higher rates of psychiatric disorder in general (53% versus 36%) and, more specifically, a higher incidence of MDD (25% versus 13%; Williamson et al., 1995).

Consistent with this literature, Hart, Chi, and Garber (2004) found that offspring of depressed mothers were significantly more likely to develop a major depressive episode (35.1%) compared to children of psychiatric well mothers (5.4%) during the early to middle adolescent years. In addition, having a grandparent (odds ratio = 1.50; $p < .05$) or a father (odds ratio = 2.26; $p < .05$) with a history of a mood disorder significantly increased the likelihood of the adolescent having any kind of depressive disorder (i.e., MDD, Dysthymia, Depression NOS, Adjustment disorder with depressed mood).

Within our high risk group only, we compared the family history of those adolescents who did versus did not develop an MDD and found that those adolescents who had had an MDD during the course of the study were more likely to have a grandparent with depression, particularly a maternal grandparent (see Figure 7.2), compared to those without an MDD. Such family studies, however, confound genetic effects with shared environmental effects (Rutter et al., 1990). Familial risk is likely a combination of genetic vulnerability as well as suboptimal rearing environments characterized by maladaptive parenting, marital dysfunction, and increased exposure to stressful life events. A central question is not so much whether depression is inherited or even what percent of the variance is accounted for by genes, but rather, *what* is inherited that places individuals at risk at different ages. That is, through what processes is risk transmitted? Genes can have both direct and indirect effects. Their consequences depend on their effects on

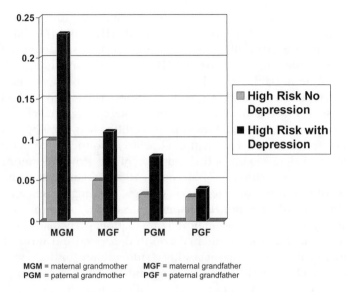

MGM = maternal grandmother   MGF = maternal grandfather
PGM = paternal grandmother   PGF = paternal grandfather

Figure 7.2 Percentage of high-risk adolescents with and without a major depressive episode whose grandparents had a history of depression.

the organism with regard to neurobiological functioning, personality, cognitive and affective processing, and self-regulation. These then can affect interpersonal interactions and stress generation. One pathway of genetic effects is through neurobiology.

Neurobiology. Depression is associated with multiple interacting disturbances in neurobiological regulation including neurochemical, neuroendocrine, and neurophysiological systems. It is beyond the scope of this chapter to review the vast amount of research concerning biological systems related to depression. Rather, just a few salient biological findings in youth are highlighted here. Psychobiological studies of depression in children generally have attempted to replicate results of studies with adults (Kaufman, Martin, King, & Charney, 2001). The biological systems related to emotional expression and regulation are especially likely to be important to the development of depression (Forbes & Dahl, 2005). In particular, stress-related neuroendocrinology (e.g., elevated stress hormones), autonomic activity (e.g., lower vagal tone), and cortical activation (e.g., relative right frontal EEG activation) have been related to mood disorders (Thase, Jindal, & Howland, 2002).

With the rapid growth of the fields of genetics, neurobiology, and affective neuroscience, it is becoming increasingly possible to study the biological mechanisms that underlie depressive disorders. Dysregulation of processes associated with responses to stress are presumed to be linked with abnormalities in the hypothalamic-pituitary-adrenal (HPA) axis (Plotsky, Owens, & Nemeroff, 1998), typically assessed through measures of abnormalities of corticotropic-releasing hormone (CRH) and the dexamethasone suppression test (Ryan & Dahl, 1993). Depressed children show both neuroendocrine and neurochemical dysregulation. Although basal cortisol levels do not consistently discriminate between depressed and normal children, the HPA axis response to stress does appear to differ between depressed and nondepressed children (Kaufman et al., 2001). Considerable neuroendocrinological evidence exists of dysregulation of the growth hormone (GH) system in depressed children (Dahl et al., 2000; Dinan, 1998), and hyposecretion of GH in response to pharmacologic challenge has been demonstrated in high risk children (Birmaher et al., 1999), suggesting a possible vulnerability marker. Neurochemical dysregulation, particularly in the serotonergic system, has been found in currently depressed and at-risk children (Birmaher et al., 1997), also suggesting a vulnerability for depression.

Depressed children show some sleep anomalies, such as prolonged sleep latencies, reduced REM latencies (especially in more severely depressed patients), increased REM density, and decreased sleep efficiency, although findings are inconsistent across studies, and several studies have failed to find differences between depressed and nondepressed children in EEG sleep patterns (Birmaher, Ryan, Williamson, Brent, & Kaufman, 1996; Dahl & Ryan, 1996). The absence of consistent patterns of sleep abnormalities in depressed youth compared to what has been found in adults has been attributed, in part, to the role of maturational changes, suggesting differences in the nature and function of sleep across development (Dahl & Ryan, 1996; Kaufman et al., 2001).

In addition, abnormal functioning of the prefrontal cortex-limbic-striatal regions in the brain, reduced prefrontal volume, and hippocampal abnormalities have been associated with adult depression (Davidson, Pizzagalli, Nitschke, & Putnam, 2002). Resting frontal brain asymmetry, that is, decreased activity of left relative to right hemisphere frontal brain regions, also has been linked with depression in adults and appears to persist into remission (Tomarken & Keener, 1998). Moreover, depressed patients who responded to SSRIs, particularly women, have been found to have significantly less relative right-sided activation compared to nonresponders (Bruder et al., 2001). Executive functions of the cortex, which include problem solving and the ability to concentrate, are clearly impaired and may be related to the findings of reduced activity in the prefrontal cortex (Howland & Thase, 1999; Thase & Howland, 1995).

Resting frontal brain asymmetry may indicate heightened vulnerability to depression. An assessment of at-risk populations who have not yet manifested depression represents a more direct test of whether left frontal hypoactivity indicates vulnerability than do studies of current or remitted depressed individuals. Studies of frontal brain asymmetry in children of depressed mothers have concentrated on infants and have found that they exhibit left frontal hypoactivity, which has been linked with decreased positive affect and increased negative affect during interactions (Dawson, Klinger, Panagiotides, Hill, & Spieker, 1992; Field, Fox, Pickens, & Nawrocki, 1995) compared to offspring of nondepressed mothers. Davidson and colleagues (2002) have proposed that decreased left frontal activation reflects an underactivation of the approach system and reduced positive emotionality.

Using a subset of our sample, Tomarken, Dichter, Garber, and Simien (2004) found that never-depressed adolescent offspring of depressed mothers (i.e., high risk) demonstrated the same pattern of relative left frontal hypoactivity that has been observed in currently depressed adults, adults with a history of depression, and high-risk infants. Across all three reference montages, there was greater relative left frontal activity in the low-risk group compared to the high-risk group. In addition, Risk (low vs. high risk) × Sex (male vs. female) analyses revealed more complex interactive relations, with sex indicating that high-risk females, but not high-risk males, demonstrated significantly greater left frontal hypoactivity when compared to their low-risk counterparts. This finding is intriguing and is consistent with other evidence of sex differences in depression that occur during early adolescence. If frontal brain asymmetry indicates differential risk for depression, it then should predict the onset of depression in interaction with other factors, particularly stressful events. Such prospective studies of neurobiological measures with high-risk samples need to be conducted.

Findings from other brain imaging studies have suggested that some individuals may have a biological predisposition to depression, characterized by relatively less left frontal lobe activation, and to have a heightened response to stressful events, resulting in depression (Reid, Duke, & Allen, 1998). In particular, Reid et al. suggested that significant differences in frontal activation between depressed and nondepressed individuals may be linked to individual differences in temperament and coping style. Thus, one mechanism through which neurobiology may impact psychopathology is temperament and personality.

Temperament/Personality. Several theorists have hypothesized a heritable, trait vulnerability factor common to most, if not all, emotional disorders. This trait has been given various labels including neuroticism (Eysenck, 1952), trait anxiety (Gray, 1982), behavioral inhibition (Kagan, Reznick, & Snidman, 1988), stress reactivity (Boyce, Barr, & Zeltzer, 1992), negative affectivity (Watson & Tellegen, 1985), and harm avoidance (Cloninger, 1987); although not exactly the same constructs, they overlap both conceptually and empirically. Each shares a trait disposition to experience negative affect. The term *neuroticism* often is used to refer to this trait, and is consistent with the emergence of the Big 5 as the dominant model of personality structure in children (e.g., Digman & Inouye, 1986; Digman & Shmelyov, 1996), adolescents (e.g., Digman, 1989; Graziano & Ward, 1992) and adults (e.g., Goldberg, 1992; McCrae & Costa, 1987).

Twin and adoption studies have shown that 40% to 60% of the variance in neuroticism can be attributed to genetic factors. Kendler, Pedersen, Neale, and Mathe (1995) suggested that part of the way genetic liability works is through increased sensitivity to environmental stressors. Boyce (chapter 3, this volume) has asserted that stress reactivity, or sensitivity to context is the product of heritable biological propensities as well as the influences of early social experience.

Neuroticism has been particularly linked with depression, and may be a marker of psychobiological sensitivity to stress. Prospective studies have shown that neuroticism predicts later negative affect and symptoms of emotional distress (Costa & McCrae, 1980; Larson, 1992; Levenson, Aldwin, Bosse, & Spiro, 1988), even after controlling for initial symptom levels (Gershuny & Sher, 1998; Jorm et al., 2000). Longitudinal studies have reported that neuroticism predicts both subsequent diagnoses and chronicity of major depression (Clark, Watson, & Mineka, 1994; Kendler et al., 2002; Kendler, Neale, Kessler, Heath, & Eaves, 1993; Roberts & Kendler, 1999). Particularly noteworthy is the work of Kendler and colleagues who found in a large adult female twin sample that neuroticism predicted the onset of MDD over a 1-year period (Kendler et al., 1993), and in a test of a multifactorial model of the development of depression showed that after stressful life events, neuroticism was the strongest predictor of the onset of major depression (Kendler et al., 2002).

Studies using measures of neurotic-like traits in children have found evidence of a link with vulnerability for depression. For example, elevated levels of behavioral inhibition have been observed in laboratory tasks with young offspring of depressed parents (Kochanska, 1991; Rosenbaum et al., 2000). Caspi, Moffit, Newman, and Silva (1996) reported that children who had been rated as inhibited, socially reticent, and easily upset at age 3 had elevated rates of depressive disorders at age 21. Similarly, van Os, Jones, Lewis, Wadsworth, and Murray (1997) found that physicians' ratings of behavioral apathy (lack of alertness) at ages 6, 7, and 11 predicted both adolescent mood disorders and chronic depression in middle adulthood. Finally, Gjerde (1995) found an interaction between temperament and gender such that females with higher levels of chronic depression during young adulthood had been described as shy and withdrawn at ages 3 to 4, whereas males with chronic depression had exhibited higher levels of under-controlled behaviors as young children. Thus, there is some evidence of an association between neurotic-like traits during childhood and subsequent depression, although it may depend on gender as well as how these traits are measured.

In our sample, we found that across adolescence, the high-risk youth reported significantly more negative affect than low-risk teens, and this was particularly true for high-risk girls (see Figure 7.3). Neuroticism also may be related to how individuals interpret negative events, as well as the likelihood of the occurrence of such events. Consistent with this view, we found significant correlations between negative affect (NA) and both depressive attributions and hopelessness across adolescence (see Figure 7.4). Thus,

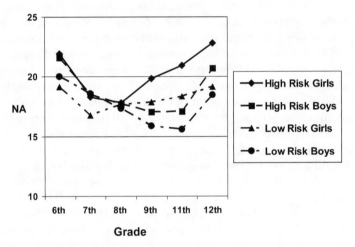

Figure 7.3   Negative affectivity (NA) for high- and low-risk girls and boys across adolescence.

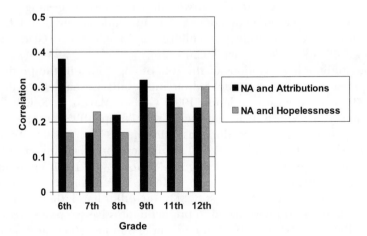

Figure 7.4   Correlations of negative affectivity (NA) with depressive attributions and hopelessness.

neuroticism may contribute to the likelihood that an individual will be pessimistic and interpret stressful life events negatively, or the same underlying genetic vulnerability and/or environmental adversity may contribute to both neuroticism and negative cognitions, which have been found to be associated with depression in youth.

Negative Cognitions. According to cognitive theories, depressed individuals have more negative beliefs about themselves, the world, and their future (Beck, 1967) and tend to make global, stable, and internal attributions for negative events (Abramson et al., 1989; Abramson, Seligman, & Teasdale, 1978). These negative cognitions are expected to be both concurrently associated with depression and to contribute to the onset and exacerbation of depressive symptoms. Cognitive theories of depression are inherently diathesis-stress models. When confronted with stressful life events, individuals who have such negative cognitive tendencies will appraise the stressors and their consequences negatively and hence will be more likely to become depressed than individuals who do not have such cognitive styles.

Several types of cognitions have been proposed to be related to depression, including low self-esteem, negative automatic thoughts, dysfunctional attitudes, and cognitive distortions (Beck, 1967), self-control (Rehm, 1977), control-related beliefs (Weisz & Stipek, 1982), self-efficacy (Bandura, 1977), depressive attributional style (Abramson et al., 1978), and hopelessness (Abramson et al., 1989). Cross-sectional studies with clinic and community samples of children consistently have shown a significant relation between negative cognitions, particularly low self-esteem and a pessimistic attributional style, and depression (Garber & Hilsman, 1992). Meta-analyses of studies reporting on attributional style and depression have demonstrated moderate to large effect sizes in cross-sectional studies, suggesting a strong concurrent association between negative attributional style and higher levels of depressive symptoms in children and adolescents (Gladstone & Kaslow, 1995; Joiner & Wagner, 1995).

Longitudinal investigations of the role of cognitions in the prediction of depression in youth have yielded varying results. Global self-worth (Allgood-Merton, Lewinson, & Hops, 1990; Garber, Martin, & Keiley, 2002; Hammen, 1988; Vitaro, Pelletier, Gagnon, & Baron, 1995) and perceived self-competence in specific domains (Hoffman, Cole, Martin, Tram, & Seroczynski, 2000; Vitaro et al., 1995) significantly predict child and adolescent depressive symptoms (e.g., Allgood-Merton et al., 1990; Vitaro et al., 1995) and diagnoses (Garber, Martin, & Keiley, 2002; Hammen, 1988), controlling for prior levels of depression. On the other hand, these same cognitive constructs also have failed to predict depressive symptoms (Dubois, Felner, Brand, & George, 1999; Robertson & Simons, 1989) and onset of new episodes (Goodyer, Herbert, Tamplin, & Altham, 2000). However, in one of these null studies (Robertson & Simons, 1989), participants were selected from a drug and alcohol treatment clinic, and the mean depression score, in this sample, was lower at the second assessment after treatment. Significant prospective relations also have been observed between attributional style and later depressive symptoms in children and young adolescents (e.g., Nolen-Hoeksema, Girgus, & Seligman, 1986, 1992; Panak & Garber, 1992; Seligman et al., 1984), although a few studies have failed to find this relation (Bennett & Bates, 1995; Hammen, Adrian, & Hiroto, 1988; Spence, Sheffield, & Donovan, 2002).

Evidence consistent with the cognitive diathesis-stress model of depression also has been found in children and adolescents (Abela, 2001; Dixon & Ahrens, 1992; Hankin, Abramson, & Siler, 2001; Hilsman & Garber, 1995; Joiner, 2000; Lewinsohn, Joiner, & Rohde, 2001; Nolen-Hoeksema et al., 1992; Panak & Garber, 1992; Robinson et al., 1995). In three different short-term longitudinal studies, we (Hilsman & Garber, 1995; Panak & Garber, 1992; Robinson, Garber, & Hilsman, 1995) have shown that among children who experienced high levels of a stressor (poor grades, peer rejection, and school transition), the relation between negative cognitions (e.g., about the self or causes of events) and depressive symptoms was stronger compared to those without such negative cognitions.

Are negative cognitions a precursor or simply a concomitant of depression? One approach to addressing this issue has been to examine whether individuals who are vulnerable to depression, but who have not yet had an episode, manifest negative cognitions. A few studies (Goodman, Adamson, Riniti, & Cole, 1994, Jaenicke et al., 1987) have found that offspring of depressed parents report lower self-esteem and more negative attributions than do low-risk offspring. Children's current levels of depressive symptoms were not controlled, however. Thus, differences between high- and low- risk children's cognitions could have been a function of their current depression level. We (Garber & Robinson, 1997b) found in our sample that the high-risk children, particularly those whose mothers had more chronic histories of depression, reported significantly more negative attributions, greater hopelessness, and lower perceived self-worth than did low-risk children, even when children's current levels of depression were controlled. Thus, the negative cognitions reported by high-risk children were not simply due to their current mood or scarring from a prior depressive episode. Rather, these cognitions might be state-independent markers of vulnerability among offspring of mothers with histories of mood disorders.

The finding that the cognitive vulnerability was most apparent among offspring of the more chronically depressed mothers highlights the heterogeneity of such "high-risk" samples, and is particularly interesting because of its implications regarding how negative cognitive styles might develop. Several possible mechanisms may account for the increased cognitive risk among offspring of chronically depressed mothers. First, more chronically depressed mothers may have a greater genetic vulnerability, which then is inherited by their children. Neuroticism, which tends to be heritable, has been found to predict greater chronicity of depression (Clark et al., 1994). In our sample, we found a significant positive correlation between mothers' neuroticism scores on the Eysenck Personality Inventory and the chronicity of her depression history ($r = .54$, $p < .01$). Thus, the relation between chronic parental depression and children's negative cognitive style could be the result of shared genes for neuroticism that contribute to both.

It also is likely, however, that living with a depressed mother impacts children's developing schema about themselves and their world. We (Garber & Martin, 2002) have proposed that within the psychosocial environment, at least three nonmutually exclusive processes likely contribute to the development of negative cognitions among offspring of depressed parents: modeling, dysfunctional parent–child relationships, and exposure to stressful life events. Of course, these processes themselves are not independent. For example, depressed parents might have negative perceptions of their children, which then can influence how they act toward them. Children likely learn to imitate their parents' cognitions in the context of interactions with them. In addition, negative parent–child interactions can themselves be stressful events.

Through modeling, children may simply copy their depressed parents' expressions of negative beliefs. Whereas some researchers have found a significant mother–child correlations for attributions for negative events (Seligman & Peterson, 1986) and the negative cognitive triad (Stark, Schmidt, & Joiner, 1996), others have failed to find a significant relation between mothers and children on measures of attributional style or perceived self-control (Kaslow, Rehm, Pollack, & Siegel, 1988), or dysfunctional attitudes and self-schema (Oliver & Berger, 1992). In our sample, we (Garber & Flynn, 2001) also found no relation between mothers' and children's general attributional styles. Rather, mothers' attributions about their children's behaviors, in particular, were significantly correlated with children's attributions about the same child behaviors. Thus, children may not simply copy what their parents say in general, but rather might be more inclined to incorporate their parents' cognitions regarding particularly salient events, such as their own behavior. An important caveat, of course, is that correlations between parents' and children's cognitions do not necessarily indicate that they were the result of modeling, or that the direction of the relation is from parent to child. Parental cognitions could influence child cognitions or vice versa, or some shared third variable could contribute to the development of both.

Social cognitions also develop in the context of interpersonal relationships (Beck & Young, 1985; Harter, 1999). Children with caretakers who

are consistently accessible and supportive develop cognitive representations, or "working models," of the self and others as positive and trustworthy, whereas those whose caretakers are unresponsive, inconsistent,
intrusive, or rejecting have insecure attachments and working models characterized by self-criticism and dependency (Bowlby, 1980, 1988). Such dysfunctional parenting has been found to be associated with low self-esteem
(e.g., Litovsky & Dusek, 1985; Parker, 1993), external locus of control (e.g.,
Levenson, 1973; Nowicki & Segal, 1974), self-criticism (e.g., Blatt, Wein,
Chevron, & Quinlan, 1979; Frank, Poorman, & Van Egeren, 1997; Koestner, Zuroff, & Powers, 1991), and helplessness (Rudolph, Kurlakowsky, &
Conley, 2001). Most of these studies, however, have been retrospective or
cross-sectional.

A few studies of depressed mothers, in particular, have shown a link
between parenting and children's negative cognitions (e.g., Goodman et
al., 1994; Radke-Yarrow, Belmont, Nottelmann, & Bottomly, 1990). Garber
and Flynn (2001) examined the extent to which mothers' parenting style
predicted children's self-worth a year later. Controlling for prior levels of
children's perceived self-worth and maternal depression history, parenting
characterized by low levels of acceptance and warmth predicted lower self-
worth a year later. Similarly, maternal psychological control, characterized
by guilt induction, shame, and withdrawal of love, significantly predicted
children's attributional style the following year. Thus, mothers' parenting
style likely contributes to children's developing cognitions about themselves and others.

A third mechanism for developing negative cognitions is through exposure to stressful life events. For example, early loss may create cognitions
of abandonment and the belief that all losses are uncontrollable and irreversible. Subsequent experiences with interpersonal rejection and conflict
likely strengthen existing schema about how fragile relationships can be.
Children also may develop depressive beliefs in response to early trauma or
abuse. Few studies have tested prospectively the relation between stress and
negative cognitions, however. Nolen-Hoeksema et al. (1992) reported that
stressful life events predicted a more depressive explanatory style over time.
Garber and Flynn (2001) similarly found that higher levels of negative life
events significantly predicted more depressive attributions a year later, over
and above prior attributions and maternal depression history. In addition,
self-worth moderated the relation between life events and hopelessness such
that the link between stress and pessimistic cognitions about the future was
greater for children with low as compared to high self-worth. Thus, children
who perceived that they would be less able to handle stressors were more
likely to become hopeless when they encountered negative life events.

Although parental depression is associated with child depression and
negative cognitions, it is not a necessary condition for the development of

negative cognitions (Garber & Martin, 2002). Poor parent–child relationships or stressful life events likely will affect children's beliefs, even in the absence of a depressed parent. Thus, consistent with the goals of developmental psychopathology research, our work with high-risk families highlights how studies of atypical families can inform us about processes that might occur in typical families.

The content and timing of children's cognitive schema likely also are influenced by other child characteristics and other contextual factors. For example, genes, temperament, and level of cognitive development may moderate the extent to which exposure to parents' negative cognitions, dysfunctional parenting, or stressful life events will impact children's developing beliefs. Moreover, although the family environment clearly is important, other contexts such as peers and school can significantly affect children's beliefs about their own competence and their expectations about relationships with others.

Thus, correlational, predictive, and offspring studies have provided evidence of a cognitive style that may be a vulnerability to depressive symptoms and disorders in youth. This cognitive style involves beliefs about the self and explanations about the causes of negative events. The developmental and experiential influences on the emergence of these cognitive tendencies remain an important area of inquiry. One mechanism through which negative cognitions likely contribute to depression is in terms of how such beliefs affect individuals' reactions to stress (i.e., self-regulation and coping) when it occurs.

Self-Regulation. Self-regulation is concerned with an individual's response to stimuli that may be novel, arousing, and/or stressful. Several different constructs have been used to describe individuals' responses to stress including self-regulation, coping, and affect regulation. Although there is debate about the relations among these concepts, self-regulation appears to be the broader term that includes both coping and affect regulation.

Infants are capable of regulating physiological arousal, behavior, and emotions (Gunnar, 1994; Rothbart, 1991). Such regulation is achieved initially through involuntary, biological processes (e.g., Blass & Ciaramitaro, 1994). Thus, some important aspects of self-regulation precede the development of the capacity for the conscious volitional efforts that comprise coping. Individual differences in self-soothing behaviors (Gunnar, 1994) are part of infants' responses to stress that precede coping. Coping is affected by the emergence of cognitive and behavioral capacities for regulation of the self and the environment, including intentionality, representational thinking, language, meta-cognition, and the capacity to delay.

Developmental theorists (e.g., Dahl, 2001; Steinberg et al., 2006) have noted that a very important challenge of the adolescent period is balancing the changes in arousal, affect, and motivation brought on by puberty and the slower development of adolescents' competence to regulate their emotional and behavioral reactions to new contextual demands. That is, there is an increasing need to regulate intense emotional experiences and desires, but an underdeveloped capacity to make conscious and deliberate judgments and decisions. Thus, there is a fundamental disconnect between the biological and emotional changes of puberty and the cognitive capacity to deal with them. Moreover, these changes are occurring at a time when contextual supports and oversight, particularly from parents, likely are diminishing. This mismatch among rapidly changing emotional, biological, and motivational systems and the more gradually emerging systems of self-regulatory control makes adolescence an especially vulnerable period for the development of all forms of psychopathology, particularly depression.

Compas, Connor-Smith, Saltzman, Thomsen, and Wadsworth (2001) suggested that responses to stress are characterized by two sets of processes: automatic and controlled. Automatic processes include physiological and emotional arousal, intrusive thoughts, automatic attentional biases, and impulsive responses. In contrast, controlled responses to stress are reflected in coping that is conscious, volitional efforts to regulate emotion, cognition, behavior, physiology, and the environment in response to stressful events. Automatic and deliberate responses can be further divided into engaged versus disengaged. Engagement coping involves problem-focused coping, cognitive restructuring, positive reappraisal, and distraction, and has been found to be associated with better psychological adjustment. Disengagement responses include avoidance, self-blame, emotional discharge, and rumination, and tend to be linked with poorer outcomes, such as depression and anxiety. Longitudinal studies are needed, however, that examine this coping model developmentally. In particular, what influences the transition from automatic to deliberate regulatory control, and how do the biological, emotional, cognitive, and contextual changes associated with puberty affect the development of these coping processes?

Temperament is one factor that can affect self-regulation. Compas, Connor-Smith, and Jaser (2004) suggested that behavioral inhibition (Kagan & Snidman, 1991), which involves the tendency to experience high levels of arousal in novel, threatening, or stressful situations, may be related to the use of avoidance and withdrawal as coping methods; the capacity for attentional control may be linked to the ability to use coping strategies such as distraction, and negative affectivity may be related to rumination.

Flynn, Garber, and Bradford (2006) found evidence consistent with the view that negative affectivity (NA) is associated with rumination (see Figure 7.5). NA measured in ninth grade with the Positive and Negative Affect Scale (PANAS; Watson, Clark, & Tellegen, 1988) significantly predicted rumination, using the Response Styles Questionnaire (RSQ; Nolen-Hoeksema &

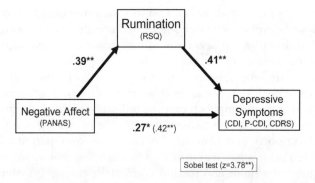

Figure 7.5 Rumination, measured with the Responses to Stress Questionnaire (RSQ), partially mediated the relation between negative affectivity (NA), measured with the PANAS, and depressive symptoms measured with a composite of the Children's Depression Inventory (CDI), the parent version of the CDI, and the revised Children's Depression Rating Scale (CDRS).

Morrow, 1991). Rumination partially mediated the relation between NA and depressive symptoms, which was a composite measure of adolescents' report on the Children's Depression Inventory (CDI; Kovacs, 1985), mothers' report on the P-CDI (parent version of the CDI; Garber, 1984), and clinician ratings on the revised Children's Depression Rating Scale (R-CDRS; Poznanski, Freeman, & Mokros, 1984). These findings are relevant to the part of the model concerned with the relation between the more general trait-like individual diatheses, and specific responses to stress. Individual traits, such as temperament or cognitive style, will influence how the person responds to specific stressors when they occur. One's general cognitive style affects how information about particular stressors is appraised and processed, and then acted on.

Person–Environment Correlations

Individual characteristics also will impact the context in which the person lives. Here, the concept of gene–environment correlations is relevant. Three types of gene–environment correlations have been described: passive, evocative, and active (Rutter & Silberg, 2002; Scarr & McCartney, 1983). We refer here to these as person–environment rather than gene–environment correlations, because our design did not allow us to test the specific contribution of genes. Nevertheless, genes clearly play a role in the "person" component of the person–environment correlation. It is important to examine the person effects on the environment as well as the environmental effects on the person (Rutter, 2002). How does the person's behavior, which could be genetically driven, shape and select experiences, and how do those effects then play a part in developmental continuities and discontinuities over time?

Passive. In passive gene–environment correlations, depressed parents transmit genes directly to their children, and they also create a more adverse rearing environment in which the children live. They do this through generating stress as well as through their behaviors toward their children. Depressed parents provide a stressful family context through problems in their marriage, parenting, job, and other interpersonal relationships (Goodman & Gotlib, 1999). Such high levels of negative life events are not only present when parents are depressed, but also when their depression has remitted (Billings & Moos, 1985). This might be due in part to comorbid personality disorders that are present both during and between depressive episodes. Higher levels of stress have been found in families with a depressed mother compared to families with nondepressed mothers (Adrian & Hammen, 1993). Using a repeated measures analysis of variance (ANOVA), we similarly found significantly higher overall levels of stressful life events in our high-risk group compared to the low-risk group across the 6 years of our study, $[F(4, 188) = 2.92, p < .01]$. Thus, offspring of depressed parents are exposed to consistently high levels of overall stress in the family.

Parental depression also increases stress through more negative interactions with their children. Observational studies of depressed mothers interacting with their children have shown that these mothers are more negative and controlling, less responsive and affectively involved, and communicate more poorly. In a meta-analytic review of 46 observational studies of depressed mothers and their children, Lovejoy, Graczyk, O'Hare, and Neuman (2000) reported that depressed mothers showed significantly more negative and more disengaged behaviors, and significantly less positive maternal behavior than did nondepressed mothers. Only 8 of these 46 studies, however, included children older than age 5, so considerably less is known about the behavior of depressed mothers interacting with older children, especially adolescents.

Consistent with previous studies, Woods, Garber, and Ellis (2006) found that during a laboratory interaction task, depressed mothers were more negative, less positive, and less involved compared to the nondepressed mothers. We also addressed a limitation in this literature regarding the heterogeneity of maternal depression in terms of severity, duration, and recurrence. The few observational studies that have addressed this have produced discrepant results, with one (Gordon et al., 1989) finding that mothers' depression history was not related to her interaction behavior, and another showing a significant association between chronicity and mothers' interaction style (Campbell, Cohn, & Meyers, 1995). In addition, previous studies have been inconsistent in defining "depression," and have not examined the relative contribution of current symptom levels versus previous history of depression to parent–child interactions.

Woods et al. (2006) found that greater chronicity and higher levels of current depressive symptoms were both significantly associated with more negative and less positive and involved maternal behaviors and affect. Comparing the relative contribution of these two aspects of maternal depression, we found that chronicity of maternal depression predicted higher levels of maternal negativity and also lower positivity. Mothers' current depressive symptoms did not contribute additional unique variance to either. In contrast, higher levels of current depression, but not chronicity, were significantly associated with lower levels of involvement in the task. Thus, mothers' chronicity may reflect a long-standing pattern of behaviors toward her child, possibly due in part to personality characteristics such as neuroticism, whereas her level of engagement and involvement in the task was more affected by her current mood and energy level.

Coding of the other mother–child interaction task, which involved problem solving and teaching, again indicated that depressed mothers were significantly more negative and less positive while interacting with their children during a task that was designed to elicit parental behaviors such as helping and teaching (Foster, Garber, & Durlak, 2006). Thus, even in a supposedly positive context, depressed mothers were less able to support and guide their children.

Another way depressed parents affect their children's environment is through their attitudes and expressions of criticism. Expressed Emotion (EE) is thought to reflect the negative emotional atmosphere of the family (Hooley & Gotlib, 2000). Mothers are asked to talk about their child and how they get along together, and this five-minute speech sample (FMSS) then is coded for Expressed Emotion (EE), a construct which includes critical comments and statements that suggest emotional over-involvement. A few studies (Goodman et al., 1994; Nelson, Hammen, Brennan, & Ullman, 2003) have shown that depressed mothers are more likely than well mothers to make critical/hostile comments regarding their children. EE differs from the other measures of parenting in that it consists of observed speech, rather than observed interactions between mothers and their children, although they tend to be related (McCarty, Lau, Valeri, & Weisz, 2004). Frye and Garber (2005) found that depressed mothers were significantly more likely than nondepressed mothers to be coded as high in criticism. Taken together, depressed mothers are described unfavorably by their children, engage in more negative and fewer positive interactions with their children, and express more criticism about their children compared to nondepressed mothers.

Thus, one mechanism through which maternal depression likely affects child outcomes is through their attitudes about and behaviors toward their children. Even if depressed mothers' behaviors are driven, in part, by genes, their resulting interactions with their children may be one indirect, mediating pathway to child maladaptation. For example, Foster et al. (2006) found that the relation between chronicity of maternal depression, a possible marker for higher genetic loading, and children's symptoms was partially mediated through her behaviors measured during the laboratory interaction task.

Evocative. Evocative person–environment correlations reflect that the child's own genetically influenced behaviors elicit responses from others, which in turn, can affect their subsequent interpersonal interactions. Children with behavior problems are particularly likely to elicit negative reactions from others. For example, O'Connor et al. (1998) reported that adopted-away offspring of antisocial biological mothers were more likely to experience negativity from their adoptive parents, although the effects of the children's behaviors on others were similar regardless of their genetic risk. Thus, their behaviors affected others' reactions to them. Although we did not use an adoption design, we have some findings that are consistent with the notion that children can evoke negative reactions from others.

Frye and Garber (2005) assessed maternal expressed criticism with the five-minute speech sample when the children were in both sixth and eighth grades. Children's externalizing symptoms measured in sixth grade significantly predicted maternal criticism in eighth grade, controlling for the chronicity/severity of maternal depression, and sixth-grade maternal criticism. The reverse was not the case, however. That is, maternal criticism in sixth grade did not significantly predict children's externalizing symptoms in eighth grade, once sixth-grade symptoms were controlled. Thus, the children's behaviors likely helped to evoke their mother's expression of criticism and negativity toward them.

Active. Active person–environment correlations involve the tendency of people to put themselves in situations that can produce negative events. That is, the effects of the environment are generated by individuals themselves, rather than the effects they elicit in others. Qualities of the child's behaviors, whether genetically or environmentally influenced, play an active role in selecting and shaping their environment. In particular, something about the way people behave sometimes predisposes them to negative life events. Silberg and colleagues (1999) found a significant genetic contribution to the liability to experience life events, (with a heritability of 49% to 91% across two waves of data). Other studies (Kendler & Karkowski-Shuman, 1997; McGuffin, Katz, & Bebbington, 1987; Silberg et al.,

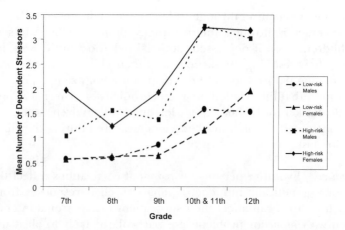

Figure 7.6   Mean number of dependent stressors in high- and low-risk adolescents during high school.

1999; Thapar, Harold, & McGuffin, 1998) have found a significant relation between the liability for both depression and negative life events.

In our high-risk study, we found that adolescents' own behaviors affected their environment, particularly within the interpersonal domain, although we could not determine the extent to which this was the result of genetically influenced behavior. Using our contextual threat interview (LEI-A), we assessed the extent of objective change, threat, or loss that resulted from each event, and rated the event with regard to its independence (e.g., death of a relative, parent gets laid off from a job) or dependence on the person's behavior; that is, events that the child's behaviors affected (e.g., being suspended from school for skipping classes or arguing with a friend). We also categorized events into domains (e.g., interpersonal, achievement), and specific types of stressors (e.g., loss, conflict), and dated the onset and offset of events in order to examine the temporal relation between life events and depression.

We (Grignon, Flynn, & Garber, 2004) found that high-risk youth experienced significantly greater numbers of independent stressors than did low-risk youth, which probably reflects the more disrupted environment in which they live. More pertinent to the issue of active person–environment correlations was the fact that the high-risk teens experienced significantly more dependent stressors than did low-risk youth (see Figure 7.6). Moreover, although dependent stressors were increasing with development for all youth, the trajectory of this growth was steeper for the high-risk teens.

Looking at the different domains of stress, we found that high-risk adolescents experienced significantly more interpersonal stressors than did the low-risk group. Moreover, the generally increasing pattern of interpersonal stress was similar for males and females, although the amount of social stress experienced during adolescence was greater for girls than boys. The patterns of achievement stressors were similar for high-risk and low-risk youth, although the degree of change experienced by high-risk youth over time was greater than that experienced by the low-risk group. Males experienced significantly more achievement stressors than females in the 10th and 11th grade years, which is a time when the academic demands are particularly high.

We also conducted a series of hierarchical linear regression analyses to examine whether stress during the prior year predicted depressive symptoms at Time N, controlling for risk, sex, and depressive symptoms at Time N-1. Total level of stress, but particularly dependent stressors, significantly predicted depressive symptoms at four of the five time points. In contrast, independent stressors did not significantly predict increases in depressive symptoms at any time point.

In addition, we examined specific stressors that have been shown to be associated with either the development of depression or being the offspring of a depressed mother. Conflict, romantic break-ups, and legal problems significantly increased and loss of contact with an important other decreased over adolescence. High-risk youth experienced significantly more of each of these events than low-risk teens, and girls experienced more conflict, romantic break-ups, and loss of contact with an important other, whereas boys had more legal problems and were more likely to be the victim of a crime.

To assess the prospective relation of specific types of stress and diagnoses of depressive disorders, we computed conditional probabilities to indicate the likelihood of an adolescent becoming depressed within 6 months, given that he or she experienced a particular type of stressor. The probability of becoming depressed, given that a teen experienced interpersonal conflict, was 0.31. That is, of all the youth who experienced conflict, 31% became depressed within 6 months of the conflict. The probability of becoming depressed within 6 months of a romantic break-up was 0.29., 0.22 for experiencing less contact with an important person, 0.20 for experiencing legal problems, and 0.22 for having been a victim of a crime. Interestingly, the events that were most associated with the development of depressive diagnoses were conflict and romantic break-up, both largely interpersonal and dependent events. In addition, high-risk youth were significantly more likely to develop a depressive disorder within 6 months of the occurrence of any of these specific stressors than were low-risk youth, and girls were significantly more likely to be diagnosed with depression within 6 months of a romantic break-up than were boys. These results highlight the heterogeneity of stress and the importance of examining the individual's contribution to the negative events they encounter, as well as different domains and specific types of stressors in relation to depression.

Integrated Model

In general, we and others have found some support for each component of the model outlined in Figure 7.1. What is the evidence with regard to integration among these components? The study by Caspi et al. (2003) is an elegant example of how a biological diathesis interacts with stressful life events to predict depression. Specifically, the association between stress and depression was moderated by a polymorphism in the serotonin transporter (5-HTT) gene, thus providing support for the diathesis-stress model of depression. Similarly, the studies by Kendler and colleagues (e.g., Kendler et al., 2002; Kendler, Gatz, Charles, & Pedersen, 2005) have provided evidence of the integration across multiple levels of analysis.

From the Development of Depression Project, we have conducted three studies that combined multiple levels of the model. First, Little and Garber (2005) examined whether child externalizing symptoms generated social stressors (i.e., dependent on the teens' behaviors), which then led to depressive symptoms, controlling for prior levels of depression. We further hypothesized that the personality orientation of interpersonal neediness would moderate the relation between dependent stressors and depression. That is, dependent social stressors, (e.g., peer rejection, conflict with others) would lead to increases in depressive symptoms among those children high in interpersonal neediness, which involves concerns about abandonment, rejection, and loneliness, as measured with the Dependency scale of the Depressive Experiences Questionnaire for Adolescents (DEQ-A; Blatt, Schaffer, Bers, & Quinlan, 1992).

Using structural equation modeling path analyses, we found that among children with high levels of neediness, dependent social stressors partially mediated the relation between externalizing behaviors in sixth grade and depressive symptoms in seventh grade, controlling for sixth-grade depressive symptoms. The test of whether the path from externalizing to depression decreased when the mediator of dependent social stressors was added was significant, providing support for partial mediation. As predicted, this model was not significant for children low in neediness or for nonsocial stressors (dependent or independent), thus showing some specificity.

This short-term longitudinal study showed that among high neediness children, those with higher levels of externalizing problems tended to create more interpersonal problems and, in turn, experienced more depressive symptoms. Although we cannot draw conclusions about causality based on these correlational findings, these prospective data are at least consistent with the broader proposed model of the relations between individual and contextual variables.

In another study, we (Garber, Keiley, & Martin, 2002) explored the relations among cognitions, stress, and depression across a longer time period.

Using latent factor growth modeling, we examined the extent to which variability in growth of depressive symptoms was associated with adolescents' gender, risk (i.e., maternal history of depression), and change in adolescents' attributional style and stressful life events across 6 years. Controlling for gender and risk, changes in attributional styles and initial level of stress were significantly associated with the trajectory of depressive symptoms. Adolescents with a negative attributional style at the initial assessment became more negative over time, had higher initial levels of depressive symptoms, and also had significantly increasing levels of depressive symptoms. In contrast, those with a more positive initial attributional style became more positive over time and had the lowest levels and trajectories of depressive symptoms. In addition, initial levels of stress significantly predicted differences in elevation between the highest and lowest trajectories of depressive symptoms. Thus, both attributional style and stressful life events were related to the levels of depressive symptoms, and growth in attributional style was associated with change in depressive symptoms across adolescence.

The finding of interlocking attributional style and depressive symptom trajectories is consistent with studies that have shown concurrent and predictive relations between attributions and depressive symptoms in adolescents (e.g., Abela, 2001; Hankin, Abramson, & Siler, 2001; Nolen-Hoeksema et al., 1992; Robinson et al., 1995). Prior to this study, however, the relations of growth in these constructs across time had not been explored systematically at the individual level. Using cross-domain growth analysis, this study demonstrated covariation in within-individual growth of attributions and depressive symptoms across adolescence, suggesting possible mutual dependence of the two intraindividual trajectories. Again, conclusions with regard to the direction of causality between attributions and depressive symptoms were not possible from this study. However, it is as plausible that attributional changes precede growth in depressive symptoms as it is that increases in depressive symptoms occur prior to changes in attributional style, or that a common third variable, such as genes or biochemical changes, produces the concurrent intraindividual growth in attributions and depression. Nevertheless, this study also examined the complex relations among individual and contextual variables in relation to depressive symptoms.

Finally, much of what has been discussed here has focused on predicting depressive symptoms. What is known about predicting the first onset of a major depressive episode? Based on the literature and our prior work, we (Garber, Martin, & Keiley, 2002) tested the unique contributions and interactions of chronicity of maternal depression, adolescent gender, negative cognitions, and stress to the prediction of the first onset of MDD during 6th through 12th grades. We used continuous time survival analysis, fitting Cox regression models with continuous data to predict time to first onset of MDD, measured on a weekly basis over approximately 320 weeks. Because we were interested in first onsets, for these survival analyses, seven children who had already had an MDD by the first assessment were excluded, and another 12 participants were eliminated because of missing data, leaving 221 adolescents (120 female, 101 male) in the final analytic sample. By the end of the data collection (about age 18.6 years), 66 (30%) had had a first onset of an MDD. Of these 66, 26 (39%) were males, 40 (61%) were females.

First, we found that the chronicity of maternal depression significantly predicted the first onset of adolescent MDD. The likelihood of not surviving—that is, of having an MDD—was about 1.5 times higher for each increase in level of chronicity of maternal depression. Moreover, by age 17.5, more than half the offspring of the most chronic group had experienced an MDD. These findings are consistent with those reported by Brennan et al. (2000) as well as Keller and colleagues (1986) that chronicity of parental depression is related to greater and earlier maladjustment in offspring.

We next explored whether adolescent gender and negative cognitions incremented the prediction of the onset of adolescent depression beyond chronicity of maternal depression and adolescents' current level of depressive symptoms. The cognitive measures (self-worth, attributions) were time-invariant predictors assessed at the first evaluation, when the children were about 12 years old. The interaction between gender and self-worth significantly improved the prediction of first onset MDD compared to the main effects model. Over time, the difference in the survival rate of first onset of MDD for girls with low self-worth was greater than that for girls with high self-worth, and all boys. By age 17, more than half the girls with low self-worth had not survived, that is, had experienced an episode of MDD. We also tested this same model with regard to attributional style and found a similar pattern, although the interaction with gender was marginally significant.

The final model tested the effect of adding the two time-varying measures of stress: the average level of stress per week and the average level of dependence of stress per week. The simultaneous addition of the two stress variables to the previous model greatly reduced the chi square statistic of the model, and improved the prediction of MDD. Controlling for all else in the model, for a one-unit increase in the average level of stress, the hazard of the onset of depression increased by an estimated 40%. For a one-unit increase in the average dependence of the stressors, the hazard of onset of MDD increased by 29%. In this final model, the effect of chronicity of mothers' depression and the interaction between gender and self-worth remained significant; no other interactions were found.

Thus, stressful life events significantly predicted the first onset of MDD during adolescence, and as the stressors became more dependent on the adolescent's behaviors, the risk of onset of MDD increased further. This is consistent with active person–environment correlations, as well as Hammen's (1991) stress-generation hypothesis, and Coyne's (1976) interpersonal theory of depression, which all emphasize the role of the depressed individual's own behaviors in both initiating and maintaining the stressors they encounter.

CONCLUSIONS AND FUTURE DIRECTIONS

Returning to the overall framework presented in Figure 7.1, there are individual vulnerabilities, both biological (genes, neurobiology) and psychological (temperament, cognitions, self-regulation) that interact with environmental stressors, particularly interpersonal problems, to produce increases in depressive symptoms and the onset of depressive disorder. These vulnerabilities also contribute to how individuals respond to specific stressors when they occur, and these responses mediate the relation between the individual diatheses and depression.

The Development of Depression project found evidence consistent with various aspects of the proposed model. Offspring of depressed mothers were significantly more likely to develop a major depressive episode than were children of psychiatric well mothers. Within the high risk group, those adolescents who developed an MDD were more likely to have a grandparent with depression, particularly a maternal grandparent. Such familial risk is likely a combination of genetic vulnerability as well as suboptimal rearing environments characterized by maladaptive parenting and increased exposure to stressful life events.

Compared to low-risk youth, high-risk offspring of depressed mothers showed significantly greater left frontal hypoactivity, greater levels of negative affectivity (NA), more negative cognitions, and higher levels of stress, particularly dependent and affiliative. NA was significantly associated with negative cognitions. The relation between NA and depressive symptoms was partially mediated by ruminations. Thus, individual characteristics (e.g., personality) are related to how one appraises, processes, and responds to stressors.

Offspring of depressed mothers were exposed to higher levels of stress, particularly dependent stressors. A significant Time by Risk interaction indicated that although the number of dependent events were increasing across time for all adolescents, the increase was significantly greater for the high-risk youth. Moreover, parent–child interactions were significantly more negative and less positive among dyads with depressed mothers, and these negative transactions likely serve as another source of stress for high-risk children.

Finally, with regard to the prediction of the depressive disorders, the conditional probabilities of having a depressive episode given specific events (e.g., conflict, romantic break-ups, legal problems) were significantly greater in the high- versus low-risk teens, and in girls compared to boys for romantic break-ups in particular. Significant predictors of the first onset of a major depressive episode were having a mother with a history of more chronic and severe MDD, being a female with low self-worth, and having high levels of stress, particularly dependent stress.

Limitations of the Development of Depression Project highlight directions for future research:

1. The preferred design for studying psychopathology from a developmental perspective would be a longitudinal, genetically informed investigation of the same children across critical developmental transition periods (Rutter, 2002; Rutter & Silberg, 2002). The program of research that most closely approximates this ideal is the work of Kendler and colleagues (2002), although they started when participants were already adults. The Development of Depression Project did not use such a genetically informed design, nor were measures of neurobiological dysregulation or hormonal measures of puberty included. Future studies need to more thoroughly integrate biological, psychosocial, and contextual factors. For example, how precisely does stress alter the biology of the individual, and how then do such biological changes interact with psychological characteristics to translate into the vegetative, cognitive, motivational, and behavioral symptoms of depression? Interdisciplinary approaches that integrate multiple levels of analysis are needed for a comprehensive understanding of causal mechanisms.

2. All of this work was basically correlational, and thus, definitive conclusions about causality are not possible. Longitudinal designs can address questions of temporal precedence and the direction of the effects. It is likely that bidirectional and transactional relations among variables will be found if examined using appropriate longitudinal designs and data analytic techniques. In addition, prospective studies should explore whether variables that have been found to differentiate high- and low-risk individuals (e.g., left frontal hypoactivity, neuroticism) actually predict the onset of a depressive episode in youth. Experimental studies are needed to show causal relations among the variables of interest. Although laboratory, analogue studies cannot produce the same intensity of depression as found in nature, they still can provide important insights into possible causal relations among variables. Finally, intervention studies that attempt to reduce the likelihood of depression by targeting certain hypothesized mediators are important strategies for identifying potential mechanisms. Preventive interventions in particular can be used to further inform our theoretical models of depression.

3. Although some interesting gender differences were found with regard to left frontal hypoactivity, the number and types of stressors experienced,

and the role of perceived self-worth in predicting onset of depression, the proposed model does not explicitly explain the increase in the rates of depression in girls during adolescence. "Any comprehensive theory about why psychopathology increases in adolescence must be able to account for impressive gender differences in relative rates of certain disorders" (Steinberg et al., 2006, p. 713).

4. The use of a high-risk sample had several advantages such as increasing the likelihood of finding the phenomenon of interest (i.e., depression) in this moderate-sized sample, and greater variability on the measures of interest. It is not possible, however, to generalize these findings to low-risk individuals. Although it is likely that some of the same processes that contribute to depression in offspring of depressed parents will explain depression in representative community samples, this needs to be tested. This is an example of how the study of an atypical sample can help guide studies of more typical samples.

5. Another generalization issue concerns the fact that our sample was predominantly White. The model needs to be examined in ethnically and racially diverse samples. Would we expect the relations among the variables to operate similarly in different cultures and subcultures, and if not, how should the model be altered to reflect these differences?

6. What about fathers? Considerably less is known about the effect of paternal depression on child outcomes (see Connell & Goodman, 2002, and Kane & Garber, 2004, for meta-analytic reviews), and whether the proposed model can explain depression among offspring of depressed fathers. Despite the greater practical barriers to studying fathers, this remains an important area of research.

7. Is the model specific to depression? Whereas several components of the model likely are not unique to depression (e.g., temperament, stress, dysfunctional parent–child relationships), it is likely that the full model as defined by the particular combination of these variables will be specific to depression. It is not necessary for any particular variable to be specific to a disorder for that variable to be part of a unique causal model (Garber & Hollon, 1991).

8. Given that depression is characterized by various subtypes (e.g., melancholic, atypical, seasonal, bipolar), does the proposed model explain these different subtypes? If not, how does the model need to be altered in order to accurately predict subtypes?

9. Although the proposed model is multilevel and intended to be derived from a developmental psychopathology perspective, to what extent is it truly developmental? How well does it explain onset of depression, continuities and discontinuities across time, and the increasing rate of depression during adolescence? The DDP was a longitudinal study that spanned

much of adolescence, but did it start too late or end too early to really witness the developmental unfolding of the risk processes that underlie depression? In general, researchers are constrained by the economic challenges of conducting sufficiently long longitudinal studies in order to really address important developmental questions. Nevertheless, the developmental trajectories of the proposed risk factors, and their relation to depression across time needs to be a focus of study.

Second, how do models of depression need to be modified to reflect the important changes that occur in children's biological, cognitive, and emotional development? For example, evidence that negative cognitions emerge over time and the relation between such cognitions and depression becomes stronger with development, particularly in interaction with stress (Abela, 2001; Nolen-Hoeksema et al., 1992; Turner & Cole, 1994; Weisz, Southam-Gero, & McCarty, 2001), has important implications for defining the developmental boundaries of the components of the cognitive diathesis-stress model. Cognitive theories of depression need to be modified to explain the occurrence of depression in young children, for whom the role of negative cognitions may be less central.

10. What are the implications of the model and related findings for treatment and prevention? On one hand, the complexity of this model makes the challenge of intervention daunting. What are the central processes at which to direct limited intervention resources? Although, ideally, intervening at multiple levels may make the most sense, the expenses in terms of time and money are prohibitive. Therefore, it is important to identify the more proximal processes on which to intervene and thereby reduce the level of symptoms or the risk of developing them. Elsewhere (Garber, 2006), I have outlined the relation between various risk factors and prevention programs targeting these factors.

Briefly, the "Cadillac" prevention program would identify those children and adolescents at greatest risk based on their family history and/or individual characteristics such as personality or cognitive style, or exposure to specific stressors such as divorce. Then, the intervention should teach these youth about how their own behaviors may generate or exacerbate stress, interpersonal communication skills to reduce some of the social stressors they create, engagement rather than disengagement coping, emotion regulation procedures for dampening the intensity and liability of their affect, and cognitive and behavioral strategies for responding to stress including cognitive restructuring, behavioral activation, and problem solving. The specific role of parents in these interventions also needs to be explored. Ideally, we would teach parents about age-appropriate parenting skills, as well as similar communication and cognitive strategies that we teach their children. Of course, each part of the intervention needs to be developmentally appropriate and should consider the cognitive, emotional, and social levels of the children. That is, the role of parents or negative cognitions in the intervention program likely will vary with age.

Once we have a comprehensive program that works, then component studies that identify the most potent ingredients can be conducted. Also, we need to identify who is most likely to respond best to which program and then test the efficacy of matching people to programs. Given that the causes of depression likely are multivariate, prevention approaches will need to focus simultaneously on multiple risk factors. There is a tension between the competing interests of creating the most comprehensive and effective prevention program, while at the same time making it cost effective and feasible for wide-spread dissemination.

ACKNOWLEDGMENTS

This work was supported in part by an Independent Scientist Award (K02 MH66249) from the National Institute of Mental Health. Portions of this work were supported by grants from NIMH (R29-MH45458; R01MH57822; R01MH64735) and the William T. Grant Foundation (173096).

REFERENCES

Abela, J. R. Z. (2001). The hopelessness theory of depression: A test of the diathesis-stress and causal mediation components in third and seventh grade children. *Journal of Abnormal Child Psychology, 29,* 241254.

Abramson, L. Y., Metalsky, G. I., & Alloy, L. B. (1989). Hopelessness depression: A theory-based subtype of depression. *Psychological Review, 96,* 358–372.

Abramson, L. Y., Seligman, M. E., & Teasdale, J. D. (1978). Learned helplessness in humans: Critique and reformulation. *Journal of Abnormal Psychology, 87,* 49–74.

Achenbach, T. M. (1991). *Integrative guide for the child behavior checklist 4–18, youth self-report, and teacher report form profiles.* Burlington: University of Vermont.

Achenbach, T. M., Howell, C. T., McConaughy, S. H., & Stanger, C. (1995). Six-year predictors of problems in a national sample: III. Transitions to young adult syndromes. *Journal of the American Academy of Child and Adolescent Psychiatry, 34,* 658–669.

Adrian, C., & Hammen, C. (1993). Stress exposure and stress generation in children of depressed mothers. *Journal of Consulting and Clinical Psychology, 61,* 354–359.

Akiskal, H. S., & McKinney, W. T. (1975). Overview of recent research in depression: Integration of ten conceptual models into a comprehensive clinical frame. *Archives of General Psychiatry, 32,* 285–305.

Albert, N., & Beck, A.T. (1975). Incidence of depression in early adolescence: A preliminary study. *Journal of Youth and Adolescence, 4,* 301–307.

Allgood-Merten, B., Lewinsohn, P. M., & Hops, H. (1990). Sex differences and adolescent depression. *Journal of Abnormal Psychology, 99,* 55–63.

Alvarez, J. M., Ruble, D. N., & Bolger, N. (2001). Trait understanding or evaluative reasoning? An analysis of children's behavioral predictions. *Child Development, 72,* 1409–1425.

American Psychiatric Association. (1994). *Diagnostic and Statistical Manual of Mental Disorders: DSM-IV* (4th ed). Washington, DC: Author.

Anderson, J. C., Williams, S., McGee, R., & Silva, P. (1987). DSM–III disorders in preadolescent children. *Archives of General Psychiatry, 44,* 69–76.

Angold, A., & Rutter, M. (1992). Effects of age and pubertal status on depression in a large clinical sample. *Development and Psychopathology, 4,* 5–28.

Asarnow, J., Goldstein, M., Carlson, G., Perdue, S., Bats, S., & Keller, J. (1988). Childhood-onset depressive disorders: A follow-up study of rates of rehospitalization and out of home placement among child psychiatric inpatients. *Journal of Child Psychology and Psychiatry, 34,* 129–137.

Avenevoli, S., & Steinberg, L. (2001). The continuity of depression across the adolescent transition. In H. Reese & R. Kail (Eds.), *Advances in child development and behavior* (Vol. 28, pp. 139–173). New York: Academic Press.

Bandura, A. (1977). Self-efficacy: Toward a unifying theory of behavioral change. *Psychological Review, 84,* 191–215.

Barenboim, C. (1981). The development of person perception in childhood and adolescence: From behavioral comparisons to psychological constructs to psychological comparisons. *Child Development, 52,* 129–144.

Baron, R. M., & Kenny, D. A. (1986). The moderator-mediator variable distinction in social psychological research: Conceptual, strategic, and statistical considerations. *Journal of Personality and Social Psychology, 51,* 1173–1182.

Beardslee, W. R., Versage, E. M., & Gladstone, T. R. G. (1998). Children of affectively ill parents: A review of the past 10 years. *Journal of the American Academy of Child and Adolescent Psychiatry, 37,* 1134–1141.

Beck, A. T. (1967). *Depression: Clinical, experimental, and theoretical aspects* (Vol. XI). New York: Harper & Row.

Beck, A. T. (1976). *Cognitive therapy and the emotional disorders.* New York: International Universities Press.

Beck, A. T., & Young, J. E. (1985). Depression. In D. H. Barlow (Ed.), *Clinical handbook of psychological disorders: A step-by-step treatment manual* (pp. 206–244). New York: Guilford.

Bell, R. Q., & Chapman, M. (1986). Child effects in studies using experimental or brief longitudinal approaches to socialization. *Developmental Psychology, 22,* 595–603.

Bennett, D. S., & Bates, J. E. (1995). Prospective models of depressive symptoms in early adolescence: Attributional style, stress, and support. *Journal of Early Adolescence, 15,* 299–315.

Billings, A. G., & Moos, R. (1985). Children of parents with unipolar depression: A controlled 1-year follow-up. *Journal of Abnormal Child Psychology, 14,* 149–166.

Birmaher, B., Dahl, R. E., Williamson, D. E., Perel, J. M., Brent, D. A., Axelson, D. A., et al. (1999). *Growth hormone secretion in children and adolescents at high risk for major depressive disorder.* Paper presented at the Child and Adolescent Depression Consortium, Western Psychiatric Institute and Clinic, Pittsburgh, PA.

Birmaher, B., Kaufman, J., Brent, D. A., Dahl, R. E., Perel, J. M., Al-Shabbout, M., et al. (1997). Neuroendocrine response to 5-hydroxy-l-tryptophan in prepubertal children at high risk of major depressive disorder. *Archives of General Psychiatry, 54,* 1113–1119.

Birmaher, B., Ryan, N, Williamson, D., Brent, D., Kaufman, J., Dahl, R., et al. (1996). Childhood and adolescent depression: A review of the past 10 years. Part I. *Journal of the American Academy of Child and Adolescent Psychiatry, 35,* 1427–1439.

Birmaher, B., Ryan, N.D., Williamson, D.E., Brent, D.A., & Kaufman, J. (1996). Childhood and adolescent depression: A review of the past 10 years. Part II. *Journal of the American Academy of Child and Adolescent Psychiatry, 35,* 1575–1583.

Blass, E. M., & Ciaramitaro, V. (1994). A new look at some old mechanisms in human newborns: Taste and tactile determinants of state, affect, and action. *Monographs of the Society for Research in Child Development, 59,* v–81.

Blatt, S. J., Schaffer, C. E., Bers, S. A., & Quinlan, D. M. (1992). Psychometric properties of the Depressive Experiences Questionnaire for Adolescents. *Journal of Personality Assessment, 59,* 82–98.

Blatt, S. J., Wein, S. J., Chevron, E. S., & Quinlan, D. M. (1979). Parental representations and depression in normal young adults. *Journal of Abnormal Psychology, 88,* 388–397.

Blumenfeld, P. C., Pintrich, P. R., & Hamilton, V. L. (1986). Children's concepts of ability, effort, and conduct. *American Educational Research Journal, 23*(1), 95–104.

Bowlby, J. (1980). *Attachment and loss. Vol 3: Loss, sadness, and depression.* New York: Basic Books.

Bowlby, J. (1988). Developmental psychiatry comes of age. *American Journal of Psychiatry, 145,* 1–10.

Boyce, W. T., Barr, R. G., & Zeltzer, L. K. (1992). Temperament and the psychobiology of childhood stress. *Pediatrics, 90*(3 Pt 2), 483–486.

Brennan, P. A., Hammen, C., Anderson, M. J., Bor, W., Najman, J. M. & Williams, G. M. (2000). Chronicity, severity, and timing of maternal depressive symptoms: Relationships with child outcomes at age 5. *Developmental Psychology, 36,* 759–766.

Brown, G. W., & Harris, T. (1978). *Social origins of depression: A study of psychiatric disorder in women.* New York: Free Press.

Brown, G. W., & Harris, T. O. (Eds.) (1989). *Life events and illness.* New York: Guilford.

Bruder, G. E., Stewart, J. W., Tenke, C. E., McGrath, P. J., Leite, P., Bhattacharya, N., et al. (2001). Electroencephalographic and perceptual asymmetry differences between responders and nonresponders to an SSRI antidepressant. *Biological Psychiatry, 49,* 416–425.

Campbell, S. B., Cohn, J. F., & Meyers, T. (1995). Depression in first-time mothers: Mother–infant interaction and depression chronicity. *Developmental Psychology, 31,* 349–357.

Carlson, G., & Garber, J. (1986). Developmental issues in the classification of depression in childhood. In M. Rutter, C. E. Izard, & P. B. Read (Eds.), *Depression in children: Developmental perspectives* (pp. 399–434). New York: Guilford.

Carlson, G. A. & Kashani, J. H. (1988). Phenomenology of major depression from childhood through adulthood: Analysis of three studies. *American Journal of Psychiatry, 145,* 1222–1225.

Caspi, A., Moffitt, T. E., Newman, D. L., & Silva, P. A. (1996). Behavioral observations at age 3 years predict adult psychiatric disorders: Longitudinal evidence from a birth cohort. *Archives of General Psychiatry, 53,* 1033–1039.

Caspi, A., Sugden, K., Moffitt, T. E., Taylor, A., Craig, I. W., Harrington, H., et al. (2003). Influence of life stress on depression: Moderation by a polymorphism in the 5-HTT gene. *Science, 301,* 386–389.

Cicchetti, D., & Dawson, G. (2002). Editorial: Multiple levels of analysis. *Development and Psychopathology, 14,* 417–420.

Cicchetti, D., & Rogosch, F. A. (1996). Equifinality and multifinality in developmental psychopathology. *Development and Psychopathology, 8,* 597–600.

Cicchetti, D., & Schneider-Rosen, K. (Eds.). (1984). Childhood depression. *New Directions in Child Development,* 5–28. San Francisco: Jossey-Bass.

Cicchetti, D., & Toth, S. L. (1991). A developmental perspective on internalizing and externalizing disorder. In D. Cicchetti & S. L. Toth (Eds.), *Internalizing and externalizing expression of dysfunction* (pp. 1–19). Hillsdale, NJ: Lawrence Erlbaum Associates.

Cicchetti, D., & Toth, S. L. (1998). The development of depression in children and adolescents. *American Psychologist, 53,* 221–241.

Clark, L. A., Watson, D., & Mineka, S. (1994). Temperament, personality, and the mood and anxiety disorders. *Journal of Abnormal Psychology, 103,* 103–116.

Cloninger, C. R. (1987). Genetic principles and methods in high-risk studies of schizophrenia. *Schizophrenia Bulletin, 13,* 515–523.

Cohen, L. H., Burt, C. E., & Bjorck, J. P. (1987). Life stress and adjustment: Effects of life events experienced by young adolescents and their parents. *Developmental Psychology, 23,* 583–592.

Cole, D. A., Martin, J. M., Peeke, L. G., Seroczynski, A. D., & Hoffman, K. (1998). Are cognitive errors of underestimation predictive or reflective of depressive symptoms in children: A longitudinal study. *Journal of Abnormal Psychology, 107,* 481–496.

Cole, D. A., Martin, J. M., Powers, B., & Truglio, R. (1996). Modeling causal relations between academic and social competence and depression: A multitrait-multimethod longitudinal study of children. *Journal of Abnormal Psychology, 105,* 258–270.

Cole, D. A., & Martin, N. C. (2005). The longitudinal structure of the Children's Depression Inventory: Testing a latent trait–state model. *Psychological Assessment, 17,* 144–155.

Cole, D. A., Nolen-Hoeksema, S., Girgus, J., & Paul, G. (2006). Stress exposure and stress generation in child and adolescent depression: A latent trait-state-error approach to longitudinal analyses. *Journal of Abnormal Psychology, 115,* 40–51.

Compas, B. E., Connor-Smith, J., & Jaser, S. S. (2004). Temperament, stress reactivity, and coping: Implications for depression in childhood and adolescence. *Journal of Clinical Child and Adolescent Psychology, 33,* 21–31.

Compas, B. E., Connor-Smith, J. K., Saltzman, H., Thomsen, A. H., & Wadsworth, M. E. (2001). Coping with stress during childhood and adolescence: Problems, progress, and potential in theory and research. *Psychological Bulletin, 127,* 87–127.

Compas, B. E., Grant, K. E., & Ey, S. (1994). Psychosocial stress and child and adolescent depression: Can we be more specific? In W. M. Reynolds & H. Johnston (Eds.), *Handbook of depression in children and adolescents* (pp. 509–524). New York: Plenum.

Conley, C. S., Haines, B. A., Hilt, L. M., & Metalsky, G. I. (2001). The Children's Attributional Style Interview: Developmental tests of cognitive diathesis-stress theories of depression. *Journal of Abnormal Child Psychology, 29,* 445–463.

Connell, A. M., & Goodman, S. H. (2002). The association between psychopathology in fathers versus mothers and children's internalizing and externalizing behavior problems: A meta-analysis. *Psychological Bulletin, 128,* 746–773.

Costa, P. T., & McCrae, R. R. (1980). Influence of extraversion and neuroticism on subjective well being: Happy and unhappy people. *Journal of Personality and Social Psychology, 38,* 668–678.

Costello, E. J., Costello, A. J., Edelbrock, C., Burns, B. J., Dulcan, M. K., Brent, D., et al. (1988). Psychiatric disorders in pediatric primary care. *Archives of General Psychiatry, 45,* 1107–1116.

Coyne, J. C. (1976). Toward an interactional description of depression. *Psychiatry: Journal for the Study of Interpersonal Processes, 39,* 28–40.

Culbertson, F. M. (1997). Depression and gender: An international review. *American Psychologist, 52,* 25–31.

Cyranowski, J. M., Frank, E., Young, E., & Shear, K. (2000). Adolescent onset of the gender difference in lifetime rates of major depression. *Archives of General Psychiatry, 57,* 21–27.

Dahl, R. E. (2001). Affect regulation, brain development, and behavioral/emotional health in adolescence. *CNS Spectrums, 6*(1), 1–12.

Dahl, R. E., Birmaher, B., Williamson, D. E., Dorn, L., Perel, J., Kaufman, J., et al. (2000). Low growth hormone response to growth hormone-releasing hormone in child depression. *Biological Psychiatry, 48,* 981988.

Dahl, R. E., & Ryan, N. D. (1996). The psychobiology of adolescent depression. In D. Cicchetti & S. L. Toth (Eds.), *Rochester symposium on developmental psychopathology, Vol. 7: Adolescence: Opportunities and challenges* (pp. 197–232). Rochester, NY: Rochester University Press.

Davidson, R. J., Pizzagalli, D., Nitschke, J. B., & Putnam, K. (2002). Depression: Perspectives from affective neuroscience. *Annual Review of Psychology, 53,* 545–574.

Dawson, G., Klinger, L. G., Panagiotides, H., Hill, D., & Spieker, S. (1992). Frontal lobe activity and affective behavior of infants of mothers with depressive symptoms. *Child Development, 63,* 725–737.

Devine, D., Kempton, T., & Forehand, R. (1994). Adolescent depressed mood and young adult functioning: A longitudinal study. *Journal of Abnormal Child Psychology, 22,* 629–640.

Digman, J. M. (1989). Five robust trait dimensions: Development, stability, and utility. *Journal of Personality, 57,* 195–214.

Digman, J. M., & Inouye, J. (1986). Further specification of the five robust factors of personality. *Journal of Personality and Social Psychology, 50,* 116–123.

Digman, J. M., & Shmelyov, A. G. (1996). The structure of temperament and personality in Russian children. *Journal of Personality and Social Psychology, 71,* 341–351.

Dinan, T. G. (1998). Neuroendocrine markers: Role in the development of antidepressants. *CNS Drugs, 10,* 145–157.

Dixon, J. F., & Ahrens, A. H. (1992). Stress and attributional style as predictors of self-reported depression in children. *Cognitive Therapy and Research, 16,* 623–634.

DuBois, D. L., Felner, R. D., Brand, S., & George, G. R. (1999). Profiles of self-esteem in early adolescence: Identification and investigation of adaptive correlates. *American Journal of Community Psychology, 27,* 899–932.

Duggal, S., Carlson, E. A., Sroufe, L. A., & Egeland, B. (2001). Depressive symptomatology in childhood and adolescence. *Development and Psychopathology, 13,* 143–164.

Duggal, S., Malkoff Schwartz, S., Birmaher, B., Anderson, B. P., Matty, M. K., Houck, P. R., et al. (2000). Assessment of life stress in adolescents: Self-report versus interview methods. *Journal of the American Academy of Child and Adolescent Psychiatry, 39,* 445–452.

Dweck, C. S., & Leggett, E. L. (1988). A social-cognitive approach to motivation and personality, *Psychological Review, 95,* 256–273.

Eaves, L. J., Silberg, J. L., Maes, H. H., Simonoff, E., Pickles, A., Rutter, M., et al. (1997). Genetics and developmental psychopathology: 2. The main effects of genes and environment on behavioral problems in the Virginia Twin Study of Adolescent Behavioral Development. *Journal of Child Psychology and Psychiatry, 38,* 965–980.

Eley, T. C. (1997). Depressive symptoms in children and adolescents: Etiological links between normality and abnormality: A research note. *Journal of Child Psychology and Psychiatry, 38,* 861–865.

Eley, T. C., Deater-Deckard, K., Fombonne, E., Fulker, D. W., & Plomin, R. (1998). An adoption study of depressive symptoms in middle childhood. *Journal of Child Psychology and Psychiatry and Allied Disciplines, 39,* 337–345.

Eley, T. C., & Stevenson, J. (1999). Using genetic analyses to clarify the distinction between depressive and anxious symptoms in children. *Journal of Abnormal Child Psychology, 27,* 105–114.

Emslie, G. J., Rush, A. J., Weinberg, W. A., Gullion, C. M., Rintelmann, J., & Hughes, C. W. (1997). Recurrence of major depressive disorder in hospitalized children and adolescents. *Journal of the American Academy of Child and Adolescent Psychiatry, 36,* 785–792.

Eysenck, H. J. (1952). *The scientific study of personality.* Oxford, England: Macmillan.

Field, T., Fox, N. A., Pickens, J., & Nawrocki, T. (1995). Relative right frontal EEG activation in 3- to 6-month-old infants of "depressed" mothers. *Developmental Psychology, 31,* 358–363.

Finch, A. J., Saylor, C. F., Edwards, G. L., & McIntosh, J. A. (1987). Children's Depression Inventory: Reliability over repeated administrations. *Journal of Clinical Child Psychology, 16,* 339–341.

Fleming, J. E., & Offord, D. R. (1990). Epidemiology of childhood depressive disorders: A critical review. *Journal of the American Academy of Child and Adolescent Psychiatry, 29,* 571–580.

Fleming, J. E., Offord, D. R., & Boyle, M. H. (1989). Prevalence of childhood and adolescent depression in the community: Ontario Child Health Study. *British Journal of Psychiatry, 155,* 647–654.

Flynn, C. A., Garber, J., & Bradford, L. (2006). *Negative affect, ruminative response style, and adolescent depressive and externalizing symptoms.* Unpublished manuscript.

Forbes, E. E., & Dahl, R. E. (2005). Neural systems of positive affect: Relevance to understanding child and adolescent depression? *Development and Psychopathology, 17,* 827–850.

Foster, C. J. E., Garber, J., & Durlak, J. A. (2006). *Relations among current and past maternal depression, maternal interaction behavior, and adolescents' externalizing and internalizing symptoms.* Manuscript under review.

Frank, S. J., Poorman, M.O., & Van Egeren, L. A. (1997). Perceived relationships with parents among adolescent inpatients with depressive preoccupations and depressed mood. *Journal of Clinical Child Psychology, 26,* 205–215.

Freedman D. C., Wigfield, A., Eccles, J. S., Blumenfeld, P., Arbreton, A., & Harold, R. D. (2000). What am I best at? Grade and gender differences in children's beliefs about ability improvement. *Journal of Applied Developmental Psychology, 21,* 379–402.

Frye, A. A., & Garber, J. (2005). The relations among maternal depression, maternal criticism, and adolescents' externalizing and internalizing symptoms. *Journal of Abnormal Child Psychology, 33,* 1–11.

Furman, W., & Buhrmestor, D. (1985). Children's perceptions of the personal relationships in their social networks. *Developmental Psychology, 21,* 1016–1024.

Garber, J. (1984). The developmental progression of depression in female children. *New Directions for Child Development, 26,* 29–58.

Garber, J. (2006). Depression in children and adolescents: Linking risk research and prevention. *American Journal of Preventive Medicine.*

Garber, J., & Flynn, C.A. (2001). Predictors of depressive cognitions in young adolescents. *Cognitive Therapy and Research, 25,* 353–376.

Garber, J., & Hilsman, R. (1992). Cognitions, stress, and depression in children and adolescents. *Child and Adolescent Psychiatric Clinics of North America, 1,* 129–167.

Garber, J., & Hollon, S. D. (1991). What can specificity designs say about causality in psychopathology research? *Psychological Bulletin, 110,* 129–136.

Garber, J., Keiley, M. K., & Martin, N. C. (2002). Developmental trajectories of adolescents' depressive symptoms: Predictors of change. *Journal of Consulting and Clinical Psychology, 70,* 79–95.

Garber, J., Kriss, M. R., Koch, M., & Lindholm, L. (1988). Recurrent depression in adolescents: A follow-up study. *Journal of the American Academy of Child and Adolescent Psychiatry, 27,* 49–54.

Garber, J., & Martin, N. C. (2002). Negative cognitions in offspring of depressed parents: Mechanisms of risk. In S. H. Goodman & I. H. Gotlib (Eds.), *Children of depressed parents: Mechanisms of risk and implications for treatment* (pp. 121–153). Washington, DC: American Psychological Association.

Garber, J., Martin, N.C., & Keiley, M.K. (2002, September). *Predictors of the first onset of major depressive disorder.* Presented at the Society for Research on Psychopathology, San Francisco, CA.

Garber, J., & Robinson, N. (1997a, April). *The development and validation of the Life Events Interview for Adolescents.* Presented at the biennial meeting of the Society for Research in Child Development, Washington, D.C.

Garber, J., & Robinson, N. S. (1997b). Cognitive vulnerability in children at risk for depression. *Cognitions and Emotions, 11,* 619–635.

Garber, J., Weiss, B., & Shanley, N. (1993). Cognitions, depressive symptoms, and development in adolescents. *Journal of Abnormal Psychology, 102,* 47–57.

Garmezy, N. (1977). On some risks in risk research. *Psychological Medicine, 7,* 1–6.

Garmezy, N., & Streitman, S. (1974). Children at risk: The search for the antecedents of schizophrenia: I. Conceptual models and research methods. *Schizophrenia Bulletin, 8,* 14–90.

Garrison, C. Z., Jackson, K. L., Marsteller, F., McKeown, R., & Addy, C. L. (1990). A longitudinal study of depressive symptomatology in young adolescents. *Journal of the American Academy of Child and Adolescent Psychiatry, 29,* 581–585.

Ge, X., Lorenz, F. O., Conger, R. D., Elder, G. H., & Simons, R. L. (1994). Trajectories of stressful life events and depressive symptoms during adolescence. *Developmental Psychology, 30,* 467–483.

Gershuny, B. S., & Sher, K. J. (1998). The relation between personality and anxiety: Findings from a 3-year prospective study. *Journal of Abnormal Psychology, 107,* 252–262.

Gjerde, P. F. (1995). Alternative pathways to chronic depressive symptoms in young adults: Gender differences in developmental trajectories. *Child Development, 66,* 1277–1300.

Gjone, H., Stevenson, J., Sundet, J. M., & Eilertsen, D. E. (1996). Changes in heritability across increasing levels of behavior problems in young twins. *Behavior Genetics, 26,* 419–426.

Gladstone, T. R. G., & Kaslow, N. J. (1995). Depression and attributions in children and adolescents: A meta-analytic review. *Journal of Abnormal Child Psychology, 23,* 597–606.

Goldberg, L. R.(1992). The development of markers for the Big-Five factor structure. *Psychological Assessment, 4,* 26–42.

Gonzales, L. R., Lewinsohn, P. M., & Clarke, G. N. (1985). Longitudinal follow-up of unipolar depressives: An investigation of predictors of relapse. *Journal of Consulting and Clinical Psychology, 53,* 461–469.

Goodman, S. H., Adamson, L. B., Riniti, J., & Cole, S. (1994). Mothers' expressed attitudes: Associations with maternal depression and children's self-esteem and psychopathology. *Journal of the American Academy of Child and Adolescent Psychiatry, 33,* 1265–1274.

Goodman, S. H., & Gotlib, I. H. (1999). Risk for psychopathology in the children of depressed mothers: A developmental model for understanding mechanisms of transmission. *Psychological Review, 106,* 458–490.

Goodyer, I. M., Herbert, J., Tamplin, A., & Altham, P. M. E. (2000). Recent life events, cortisol, dehydroepiandrosterone and the onset of major depression in high-risk adolescents. *British Journal of Psychiatry, 177,* 499–504.

Gordon, D., Burge, D., Hammen, C., Adrian, C., Jaenicke, C., & Hiroto, D. (1989). Observations of interactions of depressed women with their children. *American Journal of Psychiatry, 146,* 50–55.

Gotlib, I. & Hammen, C. (1992). *Psychological aspects of depression: Toward cognitive and interpersonal integration.* Chichester, England: John Wiley & Sons.

Graber, J., A., Brooks-Gunn, J., & Petersen, A. C. (1996). *Transitions through adolescence: Interpersonal domains and context.* Mahwah, NJ: Lawrence Erlbaum Associates.

Gray, J. A. (1982). *The neuropsychology of anxiety: An enquiry into the functions of the septo-hippocampal system.* New York: Clarendon Press/Oxford University Press.

Graziano, W. G., & Ward, D. (1992). Probing the Big Five in adolescence: Personality and adjustment during a developmental transition. *Journal of Personality, 60*(2), 425–439.

Greene, A. L. (1986). Future-time perspective in adolescence: The Present of things future revisited. *Journal of Youth and Adolescence, 15,* 99–113.

Grignon, D., Flynn, C.A., & Garber, J. (2004, April). *The nature of stressful life events and their relation to depression in offspring of depressed and nondepressed mothers.* Presented at Psychology Day, Vanderbilt University, Nashville, TN.

Gunnar, M. R. (1994). Psychoendocrine studies of temperament and stress in early childhood: Expanding current models. In J. E. Bates & T. D. Wachs (Eds.), *Temperament: Individual differences at the interface of biology and behavior* (pp. 175–198). Washington, DC: American Psychological Association.

Hammen, C. (1988). Self cognitions, stressful events, and the prediction of depression in children of depressed mothers. *Journal of Abnormal Child Psychology, 16,* 347–360.

Hammen, C. (1991). Generation of stress in the course of unipolar depression. *Journal of Abnormal Psychology, 100,* 555–561.

Hammen, C., Adrian, C., & Hiroto, D. (1988). A longitudinal test of the attributional vulnerability model in children at risk for depression. *British Journal of Clinical Psychology, 27,* 37–46.

Hammen, C. L., Adrian, C., Gordon, D., Burge, D., Jaenicke, C., & Hiroto, D. (1987). Children of depressed mothers: Maternal strain and symptom predictors of dysfunction. *Journal of Abnormal Psychology, 96,* 190–198.

Hankin, B. L., & Abramson, L. Y. (1999). Development of gender differences in depression: Description and possible explanations. *Annals of Medicine, 31,* 372–379.

Hankin, B. L., Abramson, L. Y., Moffitt, T. E., Silva, P. A., McGee, R., & Angell, K. E. (1998). Development of depression from preadolescence to young adulthood: Emerging gender differences in a 10-year longitudinal study. *Journal of Abnormal Psychology, 107,* 128–140.

Hankin, B. L., Abramson, L. Y., & Siler, M. (2001). A prospective test of the hopelessness theory of depression in adolescence. *Cognitive Therapy and Research, 25,* 607–632.

Harrington, R. C., Fudge, H., Rutter, M., Bredenkamp, D., Groothues, C., & Pridham, J. (1993). Child and adult depression: A test of continuities with data from a family study. *British Journal of Psychiatry, 162,* 627–633.

Harrington, R., Fudge, H., Rutter, M., Pickles, A., & Hill, J. (1990). Adult outcomes of childhood and adolescent depression: I. Psychiatric status. *Archives of General Psychiatry, 47,* 465–473.

Hart, K. C., Chi, T. C., & Garber, J. (2004). *Familial pattern of psychopathology in offspring of depressed and non-depressed mothers.* Paper presented at the Conference on Human Development, Washington, DC.

Harter, S. (1999). Symbolic interactionism revisited: Potential liabilities for the self constructed in the crucible of interpersonal relationships. *Merrill Palmer Quarterly, 45,* 677–703.

Hilsman, R., & Garber, J. (1995). A test of the cognitive diathesis-stress model of depression in children: Academic stressors, attributional style, perceived competence, and control. *Journal of Personality and Social Psychology, 69,* 370–380.

Hoffman, K. B., Cole, D. A., Martin, J. M., Tram, J., & Seroczynski, A. D. (2000). Are the discrepancies between self- and others' appraisals of competence predictive or reflective of depressive symptoms in children and adolescents: A longitudinal study, Part II. *Journal of Abnormal Psychology, 109,* 651–662.

Hollingshead, A.B. (1975). *Four Factor Index of Social Status.* (Available from A. B. Hollingshead, Department of Sociology, Yale University, P.O. Box 1965, New Haven, CT, 06520).

Holsen, I., Kraft, P., & Vitterso, J. (2000). Stability in depressed mood in adolescence: Results from a 6-year longitudinal panel study. *Journal of Youth and Adolescence, 29,* 61–78.

Hooley, J. M., & Gotlib, I. H. (2000). A diathesis–stress conceptualization of expressed emotion and clinical outcome. *Applied and Preventive Psychology, 9,* 135–151.

Howland, R. H., & Thase, M. E. (1999). Affective disorders: Biological aspects. In T. Millon, P. H. Blaney, & R. D. Davis (Eds.), Oxford textbook of psychopathology (pp. 166–202). New York: Oxford University Press.

Jaenicke, C., Hammen, C., Zupan, B., Hiroto, D., Gordon, D., Adrian, C., et al. (1987). Cognitive vulnerability in children at risk for depression. *Journal of Abnormal Child Psychology, 15,* 559–572.

Johnson, J. H., & McCutcheon, S. M. (1980). Assessing life stress in older children and adolescents: Preliminary findings with the LIfe Events Checklist. In I. G. Sarason & C. D. Spielberger (Eds.), *Stress and anxiety* (Vol. 7, pp. 111–125). Washington, DC: Hemisphere.

Joiner, T. E. (2000). A test of the hopelessness theory of depression in youth psychiatric inpatients. *Journal of Clinical Child Psychology, 29,* 167–176.

Joiner, T. E., & Wagner, K. D. (1995). Attribution style and depression in children and adolescents: A meta-analytic review. *Clinical Psychology Review, 15,* 777–798.

Jorm, A. F., Christensen, H., Henderson, A. S., Jacomb, P. A., Korten, A. E., & Rodgers, B. (2000). Predicting anxiety and depression from personality: Is there a synergistic effect of neuroticism and extraversion? *Journal of Abnormal Psychology, 109,* 145–149.

Kagan, J. (1982). The emergence of self. *Journal of Child Psychology and Psychiatry, 23,* 363–382.

Kagan, J., & Moss, H. A. (1962). *Birth to maturity: A study in psychological development.* New York: Wiley.

Kagan, J., Reznick J. S., & Snidman, N. (1988): Biological bases of childhood shyness. *Science, 240,* 167–171.

Kagan, J., & Snidman, N. (1991). Infant predictors of inhibited and uninhibited profiles. *Psychological Science, 2,* 40–44.

Kandel, D.B., & Davies, M. (1982). Epidemiology of depressive mood in adolescents: An empirical study. *Archives of General Psychiatry, 39,* 1205–1212.

Kandel, D. B., & Davies, M. (1986). Adult sequelae of adolescent depressive symptoms. *Archives of General Psychiatry, 43,* 255–262.

Kane, P., & Garber, J. (2004). The relations among depression in fathers, children's psychopathology, and father–child conflict: A meta-analysis. *Clinical Psychology Review, 24,* 339–360.

Kashani, J. H., & Simonds, J. R. (1979). The incidence of depression in children. *American Journal of Psychiatry, 136,* 1203–1205.

Kaslow, N. J., Rehm, L. P., Pollack, S. L., & Siegel, A. W. (1988). Attributional style and self-control behavior in depressed and nondepressed children and their parents. *Journal of Abnormal Child Psychology, 16,* 163–175.

Kaufman, J., Martin, A., King, R. A., & Charney, D. (2001). Are child-, adolescent-, and adult-onset depression one and the same disorder? *Biological Psychiatry, 49,* 980–1001.

Kazdin, A. E., Rodgers, A., & Colbus, D. (1986). The hopelessness scale for children: Psychometric characteristics and concurrent validity. *Journal of Consulting and Clinical Psychology, 54,* 241–245.

Keating, D. P. (2004). Cognitive and brain development. In R. J. Lerner & L. D. Steinberg (Eds.), *Handbook of adolescent psychology* (2nd ed., pp. 45–84). Hoboken, NJ: Wiley.

Keller, M. B., Beardslee, W. R., Dorer, D. J., Lavori, P. W., Samuelson, H., & Klerman, G. R. (1986). Impact of severity and chronicity of parental affective illness on adaptive functioning and psychopathology in children. *Archives of General Psychiatry, 43,* 930–937.

Keller, M. B., & Boland, R. J. (1998). Implications of failing to achieve successful long-term maintenance treatment of recurrent unipolar major depression. *Biological Psychiatry, 44,* 348–360.

Keller, M. G., Lavori, P. W., Friedman, B., Nielsen, E., Endicott, J., & McDonald-Scott, P. A. (1987). The Longitudinal Interval Follow-up Evaluation: A comprehensive method for assessing outcome in prospective longitudinal studies. *Archives of General Psychiatry, 44,* 540–548.

Keller, M. B., Lavori, P. W., Lewis, C. E., & Klerman, G. L. (1983). Predictors of relapse in major depressive disorder. *Journal of the American Medical Association, 250,* 3299–3304.

Kendler, K. S., Gardner, C. O., & Prescott, C. A. (2002). Toward a comprehensive developmental model for major depression in women. *American Journal of Psychiatry, 159,* 1133–1145.

Kendler, K. S., Gatz, M., Charles O. G., & Pedersen, N. L. (2005). Age at onset and familial risk for major depression in a Swedish national twin sample. *Psychological Medicine, 35,* 1573–1579.

Kendler, K. S., & Karkowski Shuman, L. (1997). Stressful life events and genetic liability to major depression: Genetic control of exposure to the environment? *Psychological Medicine, 27,* 539–547.

Kendler, K. S., Neale, M. C., Kessler, R. C., Heath, A. C., & Eaves, L. J. (1993). The lifetime history of major depression in women. Reliability of diagnosis and heritability. *Archive of General Psychiatry, 50,* 863–870.

Kendler, K. S., Pedersen, N. L., Neale, M. C., & Mathe, A. A. (1995). A pilot Swedish twin study of affective illness including hospital- and population-ascertained subsamples: Results of model fitting. *Behavior Genetics, 25,* 217–232.

Kendler, K. S., Thornton, L. M., & Gardner, C. O. (2000). Stressful life events and previous episodes in the etiology of major depression in women: An evaluation of the "Kindling" hypothesis. *American Journal of Psychiatry, 157,* 1243–1251.

Kim, K. J., Conger, R. D., Elder, G. H., Jr., & Lorenz, F. O. (2003). Reciprocal influences between stressful life events and adolescent internalizing and externalizing problems. *Child Development, 74,* 127–143.

Kochanska, G. (1991). Patterns of inhibition to the unfamiliar in children of normal and affectively ill mothers. *Child Development, 62*(2), 250–263.

Koestner, R., Zuroff, D. C., & Powers, T. A. (1991). Family origins of adolescent self-criticism and its continuity into adulthood. *Journal of Abnormal Psychology, 100,* 191–197.

Kovacs, M. (1985). The Children's Depression Inventory. *Psychophamacology Bulletin, 21,* 995–998.

Kovacs, M. (1996). The course of childhood-onset depressive disorders. *Psychiatric Annals, 26,* 326–330.

Kovacs, M., Devlin, B., Pollock, M., Richards, C., & Mukerji, P. (1997). A controlled family history study of childhood-onset depressive disorder. *Archives of General Psychiatry, 54,* 613–623.

Kovacs, M., Feinberg, T. L., Crouse-Novak, M. A., Paulauskas, S. L., & Finkelstein, R. (1984a). Depressive disorders in childhood. I. A longitudinal prospective study of characteristics and recovery. *Archives of General Psychiatry, 41*, 229–237.

Kovacs, M., Feinberg, T. L., Crouse-Novak, M., Paulauskas, S. L., Pollock, M., & Finkelstein, R. (1984b). Depressive disorders in childhood. II. A longitudinal study of the risk for a subsequent major depression. *Archives of General Psychiatry, 41*, 653–659.

Larson, C. C. (1992). The effects of a cognitive-behavioral education program on academic procrastination. *Dissertation Abstracts International, 53*(5-B), 2530.

Lavoie, F., & Hodgins, S. (1994). Mental disorders among children with one parent with a lifetime diagnosis of major depression. In C. L. S. Hodgins, & M. Lapalme (Eds.), *A critical review of the literature on children at risk for major affective disorders* (pp. 37–82). Ottawa: The Strategic Fund for Children's Mental Health.

Lee-Baggley, D., DeLongis, A., Voorhoeave, P., & Greenglass, E. (2004). Coping with the threat of severe acute respiratory syndrome: Role of threat appraisals and coping responses in health behaviors. *Asian Journal of Social Psychology, 7*, 9–23.

Levenson, H. (1973). Multidimensional locus of control in psychiatric patients. *Journal of Consulting and Clinical Psychology, 41*, 397–404.

Levenson, M. R., Aldwin, C. M., Bosse, R., & Spiro, A. (1988). Emotionality and mental health: Longitudinal findings from the normative aging study. *Journal of Abnormal Psychology, 97*, 94–96.

Lewinsohn, P. M., Allen, N. B., Seeley, J. R., & Gotlib, I. H. (1999). First onset versus recurrence of depression: Differential processes of psychosocial risk. *Journal of Abnormal Psychology, 108*, 483–489.

Lewinsohn, P. M., & Essau, C. A. (2002). Depression in adolescents. In I. H. Gotlib & C. L. Hammen (Eds.), *Handbook of depression* (pp. 541–559). New York: Guilford.

Lewinsohn, P. M., Joiner, T. E., Jr., & Rohde, P. (2001). Evaluation of cognitive diathesis-stress models in predicting major depressive disorder in adolescents. *Journal of Abnormal Psychology, 110*, 203–215.

Lewinsohn, P. M., Roberts, R. E., Seeley, J. R., Rohde, P., Gotlib, I. H., & Hops, H. (1994). Adolescent psychopathology: II. Psychosocial risk factors for depression. *Journal of Abnormal Psychology, 103*, 302–315.

Lewinsohn, P. M., Rohde, P., Klein, D. N., & Seeley, J. R. (1999). Natural course of adolescent major depressive disorder: I. Continuity into young adulthood. *Journal of the American Academy of Child and Adolescent Psychiatry, 38*, 56–63.

Litovsky, V. G., & Dusek, J. B. (1985). Perceptions of child rearing and self-concept development during the early adolescent years. *Journal of Youth and Adolescence, 14*, 373–387.

Little, S. A., & Garber, J. (2005). The role of social stressors and interpersonal orientation in explaining the longitudinal relation between externalizing and depressive symptoms. *Journal of Abnormal Psychology, 114*, 432–443.

Lockhart, K. L., Chang, B., & Story, T. (2002). Young children's beliefs about the stability of traits: Protective optimism? *Child Development, 73*, 1408–1430.

Loeber, R., & Hay, D. (1997). Key issues in the development of aggression and violence from childhood to early adulthood. *Annual Review of Psychology, 48*, 371–410.

Lovejoy, M. C., Graczyk, P. A., O'Hare, E., & Neuman, G. (2000). Maternal depression and parenting behavior: A meta-analytic review. *Clinical Psychology Review, 20*, 561–592.

McCarty, C. A., Lau, A. S., Valeri, S. M., & Weisz, J. R. (2004). Parent–child interactions in relation to critical and emotionally overinvolved expressed emotion (EE): Is EE a proxy for behavior? *Journal of Abnormal Child Psychology, 32*, 83–93.

McCauley, E., Myers, K., Mitchell, J., Calderon, R., Schloredt, K., & Treder, R. (1993). Depression in young people: Initial presentation and clinical course. *Journal of the American Academy of Child and Adolescent Psychiatry, 32*, 714–722.

McConaughy, S. H., Stanger, C., & Achenbach, T. M. (1992). Three-year course of behavioral/emotional problems in a national sample of 4- to 16-year-olds: I. Agreement among informants. *Journal of the American Academy of Child and Adolescent Psychiatry, 31*, 932–940.

McCrae, R. R.,& Costa, P. T. (1987). Validation of the five-factor model of personality across instruments and observers. *Journal of Personality & Social Psychology, 52*(1), 81–90.

McCubbin, H. I., & Patterson, J. M. (1987). Family inventory of life events and changes. In H. I. McCubbin & J. M. Patterson (Eds.), *Family assessment inventories for research and practice* (pp.80–108). Madison, WI: University of Wisconsin Press.

McGuffin, P., Katz, R., & Bebbington, P. (1987). Hazard, heredity and depression: A family study. *Journal of Psychiatric Research, 21,* 365–375.

McGuffin, P., Katz, R., Watkins, S., & Rutherford, J. (1996). A hospital-based twin registry study of the heritability of DSM-IV unipolar depression. *Archives of General Psychiatry, 53,* 129–136.

Merriam-Webster Online Dictionary. (2004). Merriam-Webster, Inc. http://www.m-w.com/ dictionary

Monroe, S. M., & Harkness, K. L. (2005). Life stress, the "kindling" hypothesis, and the recurrence of depression: Considerations from a life stress perspective. *Psychological Review, 112,* 417–445.

Monroe, S. M., & Simons, A. D. (1991). Diathesis-stress theories in the context of life stress research: Implications for the depressive disorders. *Psychological Bulletin, 110,* 406–425.

Moos, R., & Moos, B. (1981). *Family Environment Scale Manual.* Palo Alto: Consulting Psychologists Press.

Murray, C. J. L., & Lopez, A. D. (Eds.). (1996). *The global burden of disease.* Cambridge, MA: Harvard University.

Nelson, D. R., Hammen, C., Brennan, P. A., & Ullman, J. B. (2003). The impact of maternal depression on adolescent adjustment: The role of expressed emotion. *Journal of Consulting and Clinical Psychology, 71,* 935–944.

Newth, S., & Delongis, A. (2004). Individual differences, mood, and coping with chronic pain in Rheumatoid Arthritis: A daily process analysis. *Psychology and Health, 19,* 283–305.

Nicholls, J. G. (1978). The development of the concepts of effort and ability, perception of academic attainment, and the understanding that difficult tasks require more ability. *Child Development, 49,* 800–814.

Nicholls, J. G. (1984). Achievement motivation: Conceptions of ability, subjective experience, task choice, and performance. *Psychological Review, 91,* 328–346.

Nicholls, J. G. (1990). What is ability and why are we mindful of it? A developmental perspective. In R. J. Sternberg & J. Kolligian, Jr. (Eds.), *Competence considered* (pp. 11–40). New Haven, CT: Yale University Press.

Nicholls, J. G., & Miller, A. T. (1984). Reasoning about the ability of self and others: A developmental study. *Child Development, 55,* 1990–1999.

Nolen-Hoeksema, S., & Girgus, J. S. (1994). The emergence of gender differences in depression during adolescence. *Psychological Bulletin, 115,* 424–443.

Nolen-Hoeksema, S., Girgus, J. S., & Seligman, M. E. (1986). Learned helplessness in children: A longitudinal study of depression, achievement, and explanatory style. *Journal of Personality and Social Psychology, 51,* 435–442.

Nolen-Hoeksema, S., Girgus, J. S., & Seligman, M. E. (1992). Predictors and consequences of childhood depressive symptoms: A 5-year longitudinal study. *Journal of Abnormal Psychology, 101,* 405–422.

Nolen-Hoeksema, S., & Morrow, J. (1991). A prospective study of depression and posttraumatic stress symptoms after a natural disaster: The 1989 Loma Prieta earthquake. *Journal of Personality and Social Psychology, 61,* 115–121.

Normandeau, S., & Gobeil, A. (1998). A developmental perspective on children's understanding of causal attributions in achievement-related situations. *International Journal of Behavioral Development, 22,* 611–632.

Nowicki, S., & Segal, W. (1974). Perceived parental characteristics, locus of control orientation, and behavioral correlates of locus of control. *Developmental Psychology, 10,* 33–37.

Nurmi, J. E. (1991). How do adolescents see their future? A review of the development of future orientation and planning. *Developmental Review, 11,* 1–59.

O'Brien, T. B., & DeLongis, A. (1996). The interactional context of problem-, emotion- and relationship-focused coping: The role of the big five personality factors. *Journal of Personality, 64,* 775–813.

O'Connor, T. G., McGuire, S., Reiss, D., Hetherington, E. M., & Plomin, R. (1998). Co-occurrence of depressive symptoms and antisocial behavior in adolescence: A common genetic liability. *Journal of Abnormal Psychology, 107,* 27–37.

O'Connor, T. G., Neiderhiser, J. M., Reiss, D., Hetherington, E. M., & Plomin, R. (1998). Genetic contributions to continuity, change, and co-occurrence of antisocial and depressive symptoms in adolescence. *Journal of Child Psychology and Psychiatry, 39,* 323–336.

Oliver, J. M., & Berger, L. S. (1992). Depression, parent–offspring relationships, and cognitive vulnerability. *Journal of Social Behavior and Personality, 7,* 415–429.

Panak, W. F., & Garber, J. (1992). Role of aggression, rejection, and attributions in the prediction of depression in children. *Development and Psychopathology, 4,* 145–165.

Parker, G. (1993). Parental rearing style: Examining for links with personality vulnerability factors for depression. *Social Psychiatry and Psychiatric Epidemiology, 28,* 97–100.

Perris, C. (1992). Bipolar–unipolar distinction. In E. S. Paykel (Ed.), *Handbook of affective disorders* (pp. 57–75). London: Churchill Livingstone.

Petersen, A. C., Sarigiani, P. A., & Kennedy, R. E. (1991). Adolescent depression: Why more girls? *Journal of Youth and Adolescence, 20,* 247–271.

Piaget, J. (1971). *The construction of reality in the child.* New York: Ballantine.

Pine, D. S., Cohen, P., Gurley, D., Brook, J., & Ma, Y. (1998). The risk for early-adulthood anxiety and depressive disorders in adolescents with anxiety and depressive disorders. *Archives of General Psychiatry, 55,* 56–64.

Plomin, R. (1990). *Nature and nurture: An introduction to human behavioral genetics.* Pacific Grove, CA: Brooks/Cole Publishing Co.

Plotsky, P. M., Owens, M. J., & Nemeroff, C. B. (1998). Psychoneuroendocrinology of depression: Hypothalamic-pituitary-adrenal axis. *Psychiatric Clinics of North America, 21,* 293–307.

Post, R. M. (1992). Transduction of psychosocial stress into the neurobiology of recurrent affective disorder. *American Journal of Psychiatry, 149,* 999–1010.

Poznanski, E. O., Freeman, L. N., & Mokros, H. B. (1984). Children's Depression Rating Scale-Revised. *Psychopharmacology Bulletin, 21,* 979–989.

Prinz, R. J., Foster, S., Kent, R. N., & O'Leary, K. D. (1979). Multivariate assessment of conflict in distressed and nondistressed mother–adolescent dyads. *Journal of Applied Behavior Analysis, 12,* 691–700.

Puig-Antich, J., Lukens, E., Davies, M., Goetz, D., Brennan-Quattrock, J., & Todak, G. (1985). Psychosocial functioning in prepubertal major depressiive disorder II. Interpersonal relationships after sustained recovery from affective episode. *Archives of General Psychiatry, 42,* 511–517.

Radke-Yarrow, M. (1998). *Children of depressed mothers: From early childhood to maturity.* Cambridge: Cambridge University Press.

Radke-Yarrow, M., Belmont, B., Nottelmann, E. D., & Bottomly, L. (1990). Young children's self-conceptions: Origins in the natural discourse of depressed mothers and their children. *Journal of the American Academy of Child and Adolescent Psychiatry, 31,* 68–77.

Rao, U., Hammen, C., & Daley, S. E. (1999). Continuity of depression during the transition to adulthood: A 5-year longitudinal study of young women. *Journal of the American Academy of Child and Adolescent Psychiatry, 38,* 908–915.

Rao, U., Ryan, N. D., Birmaher, B., Dahl, R. E., Williamson, D. E., Kaufman, J., et al. (1995). Unipolar depression in adolescents: Clinical outcome in adulthood. *Journal of the American Academy of Child and Adolescent Psychiatry, 34,* 566–578.

Rehm, L. P. (1977). A self-control model of depression. *Behavior Therapy, 8,* 787–804.

Reid, S. A., Duke, L. M., & Allen, J. J. B. (1998). Resting frontal electroencephalographic asymmetry in depression: Inconsistencies suggest the need to identify mediating factors. *Psychophysiology, 35,* 389–404.

Rende, R. D., Plomin, R., Reiss, D., & Hetherington, E. M. (1993). Genetic and environmental influences on depressive symptomatology in adolescence: Individual differences and extreme scores. *Journal of Child Psychology and Psychiatry, 34,* 1387–1398.

Rholes, W. S., & Ruble, D. N. (1984). Children's understanding of dispositional characteristics of others. *Child Development, 55,* 550–560.

Rice, F., Harold, G., & Thaper, A. (2002). The genetic aetiology of childhood depression: A review. *Journal of Child Psychology and Psychiatry, 43,* 65–79.

Roberts, R. E., Lewinsohn, P. M., & Seeley, J. R. (1991). Screening for adolescent depression: A comparison of depression scales. *Journal of the American Academy of Child and Adolescent Psychiatry, 30,* 58–66.

Roberts, S. B., & Kendler, K. S. (1999). Neuroticism and self-esteem as indices of the vulnerability to major depression in women. *Psychological Medicine, 29,* 1101–1109.

Robertson, J. F., & Simons, R. L. (1989). Family factors, self-esteem, and adolescent depression. *Journal of Marriage and the Family, 51,* 125–138.

Robinson, N. S., Garber, J., & Hilsman, R. (1995). Cognitions and stress: Direct and moderating effects on depressive versus externalizing symptoms during the junior high school transition. *Journal of Abnormal Psychology, 104,* 453–463.

Rosenbaum, J., Biederman, J., Hirshfeld Becker, D. R., Kagan, J., Snidman, N., Friedman, D., et al. (2000). A controlled study of behavioral inhibition in children of parents with panic disorder and depression. *American Journal of Psychiatry, 157,* 2002–2010.

Rothbart, M. K. (1991). Temperament: A developmental framework. In J. Strelau & A. Angleitner (Eds.), *Explorations in temperament: International perspectives on theory and measurement* (pp. 61–74). New York: Plenum Press.

Rudolph, K. D., Kurlakowsky, K. D., & Conley, C. S. (2001). Developmental and social-contextual origins of depressive control-related beliefs and behavior. *Cognitive Therapy and Research, 25,* 447–475.

Ruscio, J., & Ruscio, A. M. (2000). Informing the continuity controversy: A taxometric analysis of depression. *Journal of Abnormal Psychology, 109,* 473–487.

Rutter, M. (2000). Negative life events and family negativity. In T. Harris (Ed.), *Where inner and outer worlds meet: Psychosocial research in the tradition of George W Brown* (pp. 123–149). London: Routledge.

Rutter, M. (2002). Nature, nurture, and development: From Evangelism to science toward policy and practice. *Child Development, 73,* 1–21.

Rutter, M., Bolton, P., Harrington, R., le Couteur, A., MacDonald, H., & Simonoff, E. (1990). Genetic factors in child psychiatric disorders: I. A review of research strategies. *Journal of Child Psychology and Psychiatry, 31,* 3–37.

Rutter, M., Harrington, R., Quinton, D., & Pickles, A. (1994). Adult outcome of conduct disorder in childhood: Implications for concepts and definitions of patterns of psychopathology. In R. D. Ketterlinus & M. E. Lamb (Eds.), *Adolescent problem behaviors: Issues and research* (pp. 57–80). Hillsdale, NJ: Lawrence Erlbaum Associates.

Rutter, M., & Silberg, J. (2002). Gene–environment interplay in relation to emotional and behavioral disturbance. *Annual Review of Psychology, 53,* 463–490.

Rutter, M., & Sroufe, L. A. (2000). Developmental psychopathology: Concepts and challenges. *Development and Psychopathology, 12,* 265–296.

Ryan, N. D., & Dahl, R. (1993). The biology of depression in children and adolescents. In J. J. Mann & D. J. Kupfer (Eds.), *Biology of depressive disorders, Part B: Subtypes of depression and comorbid disorders* (pp. 37–58). New York: Plenum.

Ryan, N. D., Puig-Antich, J., Ambrosini, P., Rabinovich, H., Robinson, D., Nelson, B., et al. (1987). The clinical picture of major depression in children and adolescents. *Archives of General Psychiatry, 44,* 854–861.

Sameroff, A. J., Seifer, R., & Zax, M. (1982). Early development of children at risk for emotional disorder. *Monographs of the Society for Research in Child Development, 47*(7), 82.

Scarr, S., & McCartney, K. (1983). How people make their own environments: A theory of genotype rightwards-arrow environment effects. *Child Development, 54,* 424–435.

Schludermann, E., & Schludermann, S. (1970). Replicability of factors in children's report of parent behavior (CRPBI). *Journal of Psychology, 76,* 239–249.

Scourfield, J., Rice, F., Thapar, A., Harold, G. T., Martin, N., & McGuffin, P. (2003). Depressive symptoms in children and adolescents: Changing aetiological influences with development. *Journal of Child Psychology and Psychiatry, 44,* 968–976.

Segal, Z. V., Williams, J. M., Teasdale, J. D., & Gemar, M. (1996). A cognitive science perspective on kindling and episode sensitization in recurrent affective disorder. *Psychological Medicine, 26,* 371–380.

Seligman, M. E. P., & Peterson, C. (1986). A learned helplessness perspective on childhood depression: Theory and research. In M. Rutter, C. E. Izard, & P. B. Read (Eds.), *Depression in young people: Developmental and clinical perspectives* (pp. 223–250). New York: Guilford.

Seligman, M. E. P., Peterson, C., Kaslow, N. J., Tanenbaum, R. L., Alloy, L. B., & Abramson, L. Y. (1984). Attributional style and depressive symptoms among children. *Journal of Abnormal Psychology, 93,* 235–238.

Silberg, J. L., Pickles, A., Rutter, M., Hewitt, J., Simonoff, E., Maes, H., et al. (1999). The influence of genetic factors and life stress on depression among adolescent girls. *Archives of General Psychiatry, 56,* 225–232.

Silberg, J., & Rutter, M. (2002). Nature–nurture interplay in the risks associated with parental depression. In S. H. Goodman & I. H. Gotlib (Eds.), *Children of depressed parents: Mechanisms of risk and implications for treatment* (pp.13–36). Washington, DC: American Psychological Association.

Singer, D. G., & Revenson, T. A. (1996). *A Piaget primer: How a child thinks.* New York: International Universities Press.

Spence, S. H., Sheffield, J., & Donovan, C. (2002). Problem-solving orientation and attributional style: Moderators of the impact of negative life events on the development of depressive symptoms in adolescence? *Journal of Clinical Child and Adolescent Psychology, 31,* 219–229.

Spitzer, R., Williams, J., Gibbon, M., and First, M., (1990). The Structured Clinical Interview for DSM-III-R (SCID): History, rationale, and description. *Archives of General Psychiatry, 49,* 624–629.

Sroufe, L. A., & Rutter, M. (1984). The domain of developmental psychopathology. *Child Development, 55,* 17–29.

Stark, K. D., Schmidt, K. L., & Joiner, T. E., Jr. (1996). Cognitive triad: Relationship to depressive symptoms, parents' cognitive triad, and perceived parental messages. *Journal of Abnormal Child Psychology, 24,* 615–631.

Steinberg, L., Dahl, R., Keating, D., Kupfer, D., Masten, A., & Pine, D. (2006). Psychopathology in adolescence: Integrating affective neuroscience with the study of context. In D. Cicchetti (Ed.), *Developmental psychopathology, Vol. 2: Developmental neuroscience* (2nd ed., pp. 710–741). New York: Wiley.

Stipek, D. J., & DeCotis, K. M. (1988). Children's understanding of the implications of causal attributions for emotional experiences. *Child Development, 59,* 1601–1610.

Sullivan, P. F., Neale, M. C., & Kendler, K. S. (2000). Genetic epidemiology of major depression: Review and meta-analysis. *American Journal of Psychiatry, 157,* 1552–1562.

Thapar, A., Harold, G., & McGuffin, P. (1998). Life events and depressive symptoms in childhood—shared genes or shared adversity? A research note. *Journal of Child Psychology and Psychiatry, 39,* 1153–1158.

Thapar, A., & McGuffin, P. (1994). A twin study of depressive symptoms in childhood. *British Journal of Psychiatry, 165,* 259–265.

Thase, M. E., & Howland, R. H. (1995). Biological processes in depression: An updated review and integration. In E. E. Beckham & W. R. Leber (Eds.), *Handbook of depression* (2nd ed., pp. 213–279). New York: Guilford Press.

Thase, M. E., Jindal, R., & Howland, R. H. (2002). Biological aspects of depression. In I. H. Gotlib, & C. L. Hammen (Eds.), *Handbook of depression* (pp. 192–218). New York: Guilford.

Tomarken, A. J., Dichter, G. S., Garber, J., & Simien, C. (2004). Resting frontal brain activity: Linkages to maternal depression and socio-economic status among adolescents. *Biological Psychology, 67,* 77–102.

Tomarken, A. J., & Keener, A. D. (1998). Frontal brain asymmetry and depression: A self-regulatory perspective. *Cognition and Emotion, 12,* 387–420.

Tram, J. M., & Cole, D. A. (2004). *A Multimethod Examination of the Stability of Depressive Symptoms in Childhood and Adolescence.* Unpublished manuscript.

Turner, J. E., & Cole, D. A. (1994). Development differences in cognitive diatheses for child depression. *Journal of Abnormal Child Psychology, 22,* 15–32.

van den Oord, E. J., Boomsma, I., & Verhulst, F. C. (1994). A study of problem behavior in 10- to 15-year-old biologically related and unrelated international adoptees. *Behavior Genetics, 24,* 193–205.

van Os, J., Jones, P., Lewis, G., Wadsworth, M., & Murray, R. (1997). Developmental precursors of affective illness in a general population birth cohort. *Archives of General Psychiatry, 54,* 625–631.

Velez, C. N., Johnson, J., & Cohen, P. (1989). A longitudinal analysis of selected risk factors for childhood psychopathology. *Journal of the American Academy of Child and Adolescent Psychiatry, 28,* 861–864.

Vitaro, F., Pelletier, D., Gagnon, C., & Baron, P. (1995). Correlates of depressive symptoms in early adolescence. *Journal of Emotional and Behavioral Disorders, 3,* 241–251.

Wallace, J., Schneider, T., & McGuffin, P. (2002). Genetics of depression. I. H. Gotlib & C. L. Hammen (Eds.), *Handbook of depression* (pp. 169–191). New York: Guilford Press.

Watson, D., Clark, L. A., & Tellegen, A. (1988). Development and validation of brief measures of positive and negative affect: The PANAS scales. *Journal of Personality and Social Psychology, 54,* 1063–1070.

Watson, D., & Tellegen, A. (1985). Toward a consensual structure of mood. *Psychological Bulletin, 98,* 219–235.

Weiner, B., & Graham, S. (1985). An attributional approach to emotional development. In C. E. Izard & J. Kagan (Eds.), *Emotions, cognition, and behavior* (pp. 167–191). New York: Cambridge University Press.

Weiss, B., & Garber, J. (2003). Developmental differences in the phenomenology of depression. *Development and Psychopathology, 15,* 403–430.

Weissman, M. M., Gammon, G. D., John, K., Merikangas, K. R., Prusoff, B. A., & Sholomskas, D. (1987). Children of depressed parents: Increased psychopathology and early onset of major depression. *Archives of General Psychiatry, 44,* 847–853.

Weissman, M. M., Warner, V., Wickramaratne, P., Moreau, D., & Olfson, M. (1997). Offspring of depressed parents: 10 years later. *Archives of General Psychiatry, 54,* 932–940.

Weissman, M. M., Warner, V., Wickramaratne, P., & Prusoff, B. A. (1988). Early-onset major depression in parents and their children. *Journal of Affective Disorders, 15,* 269–277.

Weissman, M. M., Wolk, S., Goldstein, R. B, Moreau, D., Adams, P., Greenwald, S., et al. (1999). Depressed adolescents grown up. *Journal of the American Medical Association, 281,* 1707–1713.

Weisz, J. R., Southam-Gerow, M. A., & McCarty, C. A. (2001). Control-related beliefs and depressive symptoms in clinic-referred children and adolescents: Developmental differences and model specificity. *Journal of Abnormal Psychology, 110,* 97–109.

Weisz, J. R., & Stipek, D. J. (1982). Competence, contingency, and the development of perceived control. *Human Development, 25,* 250–281.

Williamson, D. E., Birmaher, B., Frank, E., Anderson, B. P., Matty, M. K., & Kupfer, D. J. (1998). Nature of life events and difficulties in depressed adolescents. *Journal of the American Academy of Child and Adolescent Psychiatry, 37,* 1049–1057.

Williamson, D. E., Ryan, N. D., Birmaher, B., Dahl, R. E., Kaufman, J., Rao, U., et al. (1995). A case-control family history study of depression in adolescents. *Journal of the American Academy of Child and Adolescent Psychiatry, 34,* 1596–1607.

Woods, K., Garber, J., & Ellis, B. (2006). *Relation of maternal depression and child psychopathology to mother–child interactions.* Unpublished manuscript.

Zahn-Waxler, C., Chapman, M., & Cummings, E. M. (1984). Cognitive and social development in infants and toddlers with a bipolar parent. *Child Psychiatry and Human Development, 15,* 75–85.

Zahn-Waxler, C., Race, E., & Duggal, S. (2005). Mood disorders and symptoms in girls. In D. J. Bell, S.L. Foster, & E. J. Mash (Eds.), *Handbook of behavioral and emotional problems in girls.* (pp. 25–77). New York: Kluwer Academic/Plenum.

Chapter 8

Toward the Application of a Multiple-Levels-of-Analysis Perspective to Research in Development and Psychopathology

Dante Cicchetti
University of Rochester
University of Minnesota

Kristin Valentino
University of Rochester

The gains in scientific knowledge that have accrued over the past several decades have resulted in a dramatic increase in our comprehension of the genetic, neurobiological, biological, psychological, and representational processes in both normal development and psychopathology. One outgrowth of these advances in understanding developmental processes has been that, in order to grasp fully the complexity inherent to the examination of the normal and abnormal human mind, it is important that a multiple-levels-of-analysis approach and an interdisciplinary perspective be incorporated into the research armamentarium of developmental psychopathologists. As the history of science attests, there certainly are problems that are best examined utilizing the conceptual and methodological tools of a single disciplinary perspective. Nonetheless, as many of the chronic mental disorders that confront us today are not as effectively approached by a single investigator or through a single disciplinary model, there are other scientific questions that can be best addressed through an integrative, multidisciplinary framework (Pellmar & Eisenberg, 2000).

Because one of the major goals of a developmental psychopathology approach is to understand individual patterns of adaptation (Sroufe & Rutter, 1984) and to comprehend the "whole organism" (Cicchetti & Sroufe, 1976, 1978; Goldstein, 1939; Zigler, 1973), calls for interdisciplinary research and a multiple-levels-of-analysis approach have been gaining momentum in scientific laboratories across the country (Cacioppo, Berntson, Sheridan, & McClintock, 2000; Cicchetti & Dawson, 2002; Cicchetti & Posner, 2005; Kendler, 2005; Nelson & Bloom, 1997; Nelson, Bloom, Cameron, Amaral, Dahl, et al., 2002). Depending on the questions being addressed in their research, scientists should utilize different levels and methods of analysis (e.g., molecular, cellular, behavioral, and macrosystem levels). Investigators often must direct their energies toward an examination of multiple-levels-of-analysis within the same individual. The sophisticated and comprehensive portrayals of adaptation and maladaptation that ensue will serve not only to advance scientific understanding, but also to inform efforts to prevent and ameliorate psychopathology.

GOALS OF THE CHAPTER

In this chapter, we trace the development of the increasing emphasis that scientists from a variety of disciplines have accorded to the importance of adopting a multiple-levels-of-analysis approach. Next, we utilize the fields of neuroscience and developmental psychopathology as exemplars of this interdisciplinary movement in scientific research. Subsequently, we discuss the increasing support for interdisciplinary, multiple-levels-of-analysis research that has been recommended by the National Institute of Mental Health. We then highlight research from our laboratory on the effects of child maltreatment on maladaptation and psychopathology, as well as on pathways to resilient adaptation. In this section, we illustrate how our research has grown from a predominately single level approach to one increasingly characterized by a progression from a multidomain, within-level perspective to one that is multidomain and multilevel in nature. In the penultimate section, we discuss the importance of translating basic interdisciplinary research into multidomain, multilevel interventions. We conclude by proffering several prescriptions for facilitating interdisciplinary, multidomain, and multilevel research and interventions.

HISTORICAL PERSPECTIVES

The belief in the importance of a multiple-levels-of-analysis approach evolved over the course of the 20th century. For example, the eminent psychiatrist, Adolph Meyer, proffered a psychobiological orientation to normality and psychopathology. For Meyer (1957), the psychobiological approach depicted individuals as integrated organisms such that their thoughts and emotions could affect their functioning all the way down to the cellular and biochemical level, and conversely, that occurrences at these lower biological levels could influence thinking and feeling. Similarly, Hebb (1949, 1958) presented his views on how psychology could become an integrative science. In these and other works, Hebb strove to relate behavioral facts gleaned from experiments to events that occurred within the central nervous system. In his cell assembly theory, Hebb contended that each psychological event—sensation, perception, emotion, or thought—was represented in the nervous system by the flow of activity in a set of interconnected neurons. Hebb argued that synapses could be modified, thereby showing the manner in which neural networks may be organized under the influence of particular experiences.

Relatedly, although he did not include a developmental dimension, Weiss (1959) posited an hierarchically organized system of seven levels (i.e., genes, chromosomes, nucleus, cytoplasm, tissue, organism, and environment) of increasing size, differentiation, and complexity in which each component affects, and is affected by, all the other components, not only at its own level, but at lower and higher levels as well. Thus, for Weiss (1959), levels of influence traverse not only from the gene to the external environment, but also from the external environment through the various levels to the gene.

Influenced by systems theorists in biology, Gottlieb's (1992) newer conceptualization is one of a totally interrelated, fully co-actional system in which the activity of the genes themselves can be affected through the cytoplasm of the cell by events originating at any other level of the system, including the external environment. For example, external environmental factors such as social interactions, traumatic experiences such as domestic violence and child maltreatment, changing day length, and the like, can cause hormones to be secreted, which in turn results in the activation of DNA transcription inside the nucleus of the cell (i.e., "turning genes on"; Cicchetti & Curtis, 2006; Sanchez, Ladd, & Plotsky, 2001).

According to Gottlieb (1991; Gottlieb & Halpern, 2002), outcomes of development, be they organic, neural, or behavioral, occur as a function of at least two specific components of co-action (e.g., person–person, organism–organism, organism–environment, cell–cell, gene–gene, nucleus–cytoplasm). Gottlieb theorizes that the cause of development is the relationship between two or more components, not the components themselves. Accordingly, genes alone do not cause development any more than environmental enrichment by itself can cause development. In Gottlieb's viewpoint, horizontal co-actions take place at the same level of analysis, whereas vertical co-actions occur at different levels of an analysis. As such, and in keeping with Weiss' (1959) notion of the hierarchy of reciprocal influence, vertical co-actions are capable of influencing developmental organization from either lower-to-higher (bottom-up) or higher-to-lower (top-down) levels of the developing system. Thus, epigenesis is viewed as probabilistic rather than predetermined, with the bidirectional and transactional nature of genetic, neural, behavioral, and environmental influence over the life course capturing the essence of probabilistic experiences. Because development is a dynamic process, assertions about causality must include a temporal dimension that specifies and describes when the experience or coactions occurred (Gottlieb & Halpern, 2002). Thus, developmental scientists should adopt a multiple-levels-of-analysis approach as they embark on their investigations of individuals over developmental time.

In a related, but different vein, in his emergence theory, Mayr (1982) stated that complex systems need to be studied at each level of organization (e.g., molecules into cells, cells into tissues, tissues into organs, organisms into their environment). Mayr believed that the characteristics of the whole cannot be deduced from even a thoroughly complete knowledge of its components because of the new and unpredictable characteristics that emerge at each higher level of complexity in hierarchical systems. However, unlike Gottlieb's point of view, Mayr did not believe that the DNA of the organism's genotype entered into the individual's developmental pathway but rather provided a set of instructions.

In a Special Millennium section in *Science*, Lander and Weinberg (2000) stated that 20th-century biology triumphed because of its focus on intensive analysis of the *individual* components of complex biological systems. In contrast, Lander and Weinberg asserted that the 21st-century discipline will focus increasingly on the investigation of entire biological systems, by attempting to understand how component parts collaborate to create a whole. For the first time in approximately a century, reductionists have begun to yield ground to scientists who are striving to obtain a holistic view of cells and tissues.

Finally, a number of scientists have called for psychology to become a more integrated science (see, e.g., Kimble, 1994; Magnusson, 2000; Staats, 1999; Sternberg, 2004). For example, Sternberg and Grigorenko (2001) asserted that psychology must become multiparadigmatic and multidisciplinary rather than remain what they regard as a fragmented discipline. Sternberg and Grigorenko (2001) argue for the importance of utilizing converging measures selected from different levels of analysis instead of the more common use of single methodologies. In addition, Rothbart and Posner (in press) proposed that Hebb's views could be utilized as a basis for reintegrating psychological science. Rothbart and Posner argue that methodological advances in molecular genetics and neuroimaging methods, none of which were available in Hebb's time, permit the understanding of how genes and experience shape the neural networks underlying thoughts, feelings, and actions in humans. Furthermore, Parke (2004), in an assessment of the conceptual and empirical advances that have taken place in the field of child development over the past 70 years, advocated the criticality of adopting an interdisciplinary approach and paying increased attention to interdomain links.

THE FIELDS OF NEUROSCIENCE
AND DEVELOPMENTAL PSYCHOPATHOLOGY
AS HISTORICAL EXAMPLES

The movement toward a multiple-levels-of-analysis perspective is exemplified by work conducted in contemporary neuroscience. Increasingly, neuroscientists have changed their emphasis from a focus on examining single neurons to investigating how the individual neurons that comprise the brain work together in specialized groups (Thelen & Smith, 1998). Systems neuroscience is devoted to the study of these neural networks.

According to this dynamic, neural systems viewpoint, the brain is conceptualized as operating in a plastic, self-organizing fashion and being less constrained by predetermined boundaries than previously thought (Cicchetti & Tucker, 1994). Within this framework, not only can genetic and neurobiological factors exert an impact on psychological processes, but also psychological and social experiences can modify the structure, function, and organization of the brain, as well as affect gene expression (Cicchetti & Tucker, 1994; Eisenberg, 1995; Kandel, 1998).

In the early part of the 20th century (i.e., through the 1920s, 1930s, and 1940s), there were a number of landmark discoveries, each of which made a contribution to one or another of the long established disciplines of neuroanatomy, neurophysiology, and neurochemistry (Cicchetti, 2002a; Cowan, Harter, & Kandel, 2000). None of these seminal discoveries accomplished what has now become the distinguishing feature of neuroscience—its transcendence of traditional disciplinary boundaries. Cowan, Harter, and Kandel (2000) asserted that much of the success and excitement engendered by modern neuroscience can be attributed to the incorporation of several previously independent disciplines into one intellectual framework. This integration took place across three phases:

1. During the 1950s and 1960s, neuroanatomy, neurochemistry, neuropharmacology, and neurophysiology—disciplines that had largely functioned in a separate and distinct fashion— gradually merged into a unified field of neuroscience.

2. The penultimate step in the coalescence of neuroscience occurred in the early 1980s, when neuroscience integrated with molecular biology and molecular genetics. The confluence of these fields enabled scientists to understand the genetic basis of neurological diseases for the first time without requiring foreknowledge of the underlying biochemical abnormalities (Ciaranello et al., 1995).

3. The final phase of the merger of neuroscience into a single discipline took place in the mid-1980s, when cognitive psychology joined with neuroscience, leading to the formation of cognitive neuroscience (Cicchetti & Posner, 2005; Gazzaniga, 2004; Posner & DiGirolamo, 2000).

Albright, Jessel, Kandel, and Posner (2000) attributed the ascendance and coalescence of contemporary systems neuroscience, in part, to the convergence of five critical subdisciplines, each of which made major conceptual or technical contributions to this new field. Albright et al. (2000) contended that the research methodologies and technologies that characterize the fields of neuropsychology, neuroanatomy, neurophysiology, psychophysics, and computational modeling collectively have contributed to an enhanced understanding of the structure, operational mechanisms, and functions of neural systems.

Similar to the historical growth witnessed in neuroscience, developmental psychopathology has evolved as a new discipline that is the product of an integration of various disciplines, including genetics, embryology, neuroscience, epidemiology, psychoanalysis, psychiatry, and psychology, the efforts of which had previously been separate and distinct. Multiple theoretical perspectives and diverse research strategies and findings have contributed to developmental psychopathology. In fact, contributions to this field have come from virtually every corner of the biological and social sciences (Cicchetti & Sroufe, 2000).

As is the case in tracing the pathways to discovery in neuroscience, the influences of these diverse disciplines on the field of developmental psychopathology illustrate the manner in which advances in our knowledge of developmental processes and within particular scientific domains mutually inform each other. These multidisciplinary origins helped to facilitate and forge the emphasis that developmental psychopathologists have begun to place on the importance of examining the processes and pathways to maladaptation, psychopathology, and resilience from a multiple-levels-of-analysis perspective (Cicchetti & Blender, 2004; Cicchetti & Dawson, 2002; Cicchetti & Sroufe, 2000; Moffitt, Caspi, & Rutter, 2005).

In an early statement on the goals of a developmental psychopathology perspective, Cicchetti (1990) stated that such a science should bridge fields of study, span the life cycle, and contribute to reducing the dualisms that exist between the clinical study of and theoretical research into childhood and adult disorders, between the behavioral and biological sciences, between developmental psychology and the study of mental disorders, and between basic and applied research. Thus, work conducted within a developmental psychopathology perspective incorporates theory and research from the field of normal and abnormal development and advocates multidisciplinary and interdisciplinary approaches that examine the biological, psychological, and social-contextual aspects of development (Cicchetti & Sroufe, 2000; Rutter & Sroufe, 2000).

Most of the extant knowledge about the causes, correlates, course, and consequences of psychopathology has been gleaned from investigations that focused on relatively narrow domains of variables. It is apparent from the questions addressed by developmental psychopathologists that progress toward a process-level understanding of maladaptive, psychopathological, and resilient outcomes will necessitate the implementation of research designs and strategies that call for the simultaneous assessment of multiple domains of variables, both within and outside the developing person (Cicchetti & Dawson, 2002). In order to comprehend maladaptation, psychopathology, and resilience fully, all levels of analysis must be examined and integrated. Such research, almost by its very nature, must be interdisciplinary.

Each level of analysis both informs and constrains all other levels of analysis. Moreover, the influence of levels on one another is almost always bidirectional. Because different levels of analysis constrain other levels, as scientists learn more about multiple-levels-of-analysis, researchers conducting their work at each level will need to develop theories that are consistent across all levels. When disciplines function in isolation, they run the risk of creating theories that ultimately will be incorrect because vital information from other disciplines has either been ignored or is unknown. As is characteristic of systems neuroscience, it is crucial that there is an integrative framework that incorporates all levels of analysis about complex systems in the development of psychopathology.

Cacioppo and his colleagues (see, e.g., Cacioppo & Berntson, 1992a, 1992b; Cacioppo, Berntson, Sheridan, & McClintock, 2000) noted that in psychology the term *level of analysis* has been used to refer to several different phenomena, including the level of structural organization, the level of explanation, and the level of processing. In this chapter, we focus on the first usage (i.e., level of structural organization); this conceptualization of level refers to the different scales into which behavior or the brain can be represented. We concur with Cacioppo and colleagues (Cacioppo & Berntson, 1992a; Cacioppo et al., 2000) that the ultimate criterion of what constitutes a level of organization is how useful the posited organization is in elucidating the understanding of a particular biological or psychological phenomenon. Thus, the psychological level can vary in organization from the molecular, to the cellular, to the tissue, to the organ, to the system, to the organism, to the physical environment, to the sociocultural context (cf. Cacioppo et al., 2000). Each of these levels of organization contributes in a dynamic fashion to both the development of normality and psychopathology.

NIMH PRIORITIES FOR BASIC BRAIN AND BEHAVIORAL SCIENCE RESEARCH

The National Advisory Mental Health Council's Workgroup on Basic Sciences has put forth a number of research priorities that reflect the growing impact that a multiple-levels-of-analysis perspective has begun to exert on research on high-risk conditions and mental disorders. The National Advisory Mental Health Council's Workgroup recommended that scientific questions that could elucidate the understanding of the potential causes, treatment, and prevention of mental disorder should be accorded the highest priority given their potential for reducing the burden of serious mental illness.

Recognizing the potential that a multilevel integrative perspective has for augmenting the understanding of mental illness, the members of the Mental Health Council Workgroup further advocated that research that integrates or translates across levels of analysis—from genetic, to molecular, to cellular, to systems, to complex overt behaviors—should be accorded high priority by the NIMH. Importantly, the Mental Health Council Workgroup committee recognized that in order to achieve the aforementioned goals, research and training programs that are interdisciplinary in nature need to be given more emphasis in the NIMH basic science portfolio.

With interdisciplinary research that integrates the biological, behavioral, and social sciences increasingly being viewed as the cutting edge of investigations of maladaptation, psychopathology, and resilience, the NIMH plans to allot more resources for the conduct of interdisciplinary research. Moreover, they will ensure that there is a large enough corpus of properly trained scientists who can work successfully as part of an interdisciplinary them.

Similarly, because recent investigations in the emerging field of epigenetics have demonstrated that it may be possible to examine the effects of environments on behavior at both the molecular and integrative systems levels (Gottesman & Hanson, 2005; Petronis, 2004; Waddington, 1957), the NIMH workgroup advocated for increased resources to be invested in developing the tools of analysis that would permit intensive study of the interaction of the dynamic processes over time that appear to result in the development of mental disorders.

Finally, consistent with the developmental psychopathology framework, the NIMH workgroup stressed that it is essential to reduce the segregation of basic clinical research. Scientists working in each of these levels need to become increasingly familiar with the work at other levels. To achieve this goal, the workgroup should try to create ways of stimulating and supporting translational research and research training.

MOVEMENT TOWARD A MULTIPLE-LEVELS-OF-ANALYSIS APPROACH: ILLUSTRATION FROM RESEARCH ON CHILD MALTREATMENT

As our understanding of the importance of utilizing a multiple-levels-of-analysis perspective has evolved, so, too, has our approach to conducting research. Therefore, in the following sections we draw on the progression of our research at Mt. Hope Family Center over the past several decades to illustrate how our multiple-levels-of-analysis orientation has evolved; over time, we have incorporated this multiple-levels-of-analysis theoretical perspective into our research methodology.

The theoretical framework of an ecological–transactional model (Cicchetti & Lynch, 1995) has guided our research at Mt. Hope Family Center. Accordingly, development is perceived as a progressive sequence of age and stage appropriate issues in which successful resolution of tasks at each developmental level must be coordinated and integrated with the environment, as well as with subsequently emerging issues across the life span. Based on the work of Bronfenbrenner (1979) and Belsky (1980), the ecological–transactional model contains four levels of analysis: the macrosystem, including cultural beliefs and values; the exosystem, including aspects of the community, school, and neighborhood; the microsystem, including within-family factors, and finally ontogenic development, including individual negotiation of stage-salient tasks. Moreover, the growing contribution of neurobiological and genetic research over the past several decades has highlighted the need to incorporate a biological perspective to the study of child maltreatment (Cicchetti, 2002b; Cicchetti & Blender, 2004; DeBellis, 2001). Consequently, our conceptualization of ontogenic development has evolved to include genetic neurobiological and psychological levels (Cicchetti & Valentino, 2006). By studying gene–environment interactions over the course of development, the reciprocal interactions between constitutional and psychosocial factors can be better understood. Although genetic factors are not all expressed at birth, they play a prominent role at each phase of development. The age of onset of disorders is most likely affected by timed biological events (e.g., pruning of the central nervous system, endocrine surges, etc.) as well as by the emergence of stage-salient issues of development.

In applying this view to the study of child maltreatment, the application of a multiple-levels-of-analysis approach is inherently necessary to gain an understanding of the developmental sequelae of child maltreatment.

To this end, our research has utilized a variety of methods ranging from (a) within-level analyses using multiple measures and (b) multimeasure-within-domain analyses to (c) cross-domain analyses and (d) across-level studies.

Within-Level, Multiple Measures

At the level of neurobiological ontogenic development, we have incorporated a wide variety of assessments into our investigations of child maltreatment, each of which has been aimed at the examination of a different biological process. For example, the startle patterns of maltreated children were examined as potentially objective physiological markers of trauma severity. The startle reflex is an obligatory response to sudden or unexpected stimulus (Davis, 1984) and thus may be sensitive to conditions of anxiety and traumatization. Specifically, we assessed acoustic startle to a range of auditory intensities among maltreated and nonmaltreated children in order to ascertain any abnormalities in response magnitude, onset latency, and habituation (Klorman, Cicchetti, Thatcher, & Ison, 2003). Results indicated that maltreated boys' startle responses were smaller in amplitude, slower in onset latency, and were less affected by increasing probe loudness than were those of nonmaltreated boys. These findings suggest that the effects of adverse social experiences, such as child maltreatment, may cause disruptions in basic homeostatic and regulatory processes at the level of brain stem functioning.

Regulatory functioning among maltreated children also has been assessed through the investigation of the neuroendocrine system in our laboratory (Cicchetti & Rogosch, 2001a). Utilizing the context of a summer research day camp program, we were able to collect saliva samples of maltreated and nonmaltreated children twice a day for a week. The saliva samples were assayed for cortisol and then analyzed to determine patterns of neuroendocrine regulation among children with varying subtype configurations of maltreatment in comparison to nonmaltreated children. Reflecting multifinality in the manner by which the experience of maltreatment may alter biological functioning, not all maltreated children exhibited Hypothalomic-Pituitary-Adrenal (HPA) axis dysregulation. Only those who experienced sexual and physical abuse in addition to neglect or emotional maltreatment displayed ongoing high levels of cortisol throughout the camp week, suggesting a pattern akin to hypercortisolism. Additionally, children who experienced physical abuse alone displayed lower levels of cortisol secretion throughout the week than did other subtypes of maltreated children (Cicchetti & Rogosch, 2001a). The pattern exhibited by the youngsters with physical abuse is suggestive of hypocortisolism. Both hypercortisolism and hypocortisolism are harmful to aspects of neurobiological development (Gunnar & Vazquez, in press). Although neuroendo-crine regulation and startle responsiveness are primarily linked to separate neurobiological systems, the pattern of results from both investigations highlights diminished responsiveness among physically abused children.

In addition to basic homeostatic and regulatory processes, cortical func-tioning also has been investigated in our laboratory. In one line of research, we examined event-related potentials (ERP) as a measure of cognitive response to emotional stimuli. Focusing on one particular ERP component, the P300 wave was assessed to illuminate the cognitive processes that might accompany the encoding of salient emotional stimuli and reveal differences in this process between maltreated and nonmaltreated children (Pollak, Cicchetti, Klorman, & Brumaghim, 1997; Pollak, Klorman, Thatcher, & Cic-chetti, 2001). In the first study, maltreated and nonmaltreated school-aged children were presented with happy, angry, or neutral faces, and were asked to respond to either the happy face or the angry face. Analysis of the P300 data revealed that maltreated children had a larger response to the angry faces than to the happy faces. In contrast, the nonmaltreated children did not show a difference in response between the happy and angry condi-tions (Pollak et al., 1997). To clarify the specificity of the relation between the ERP responses of maltreated children and the emotional nature of the stimuli, a second investigation was conducted in which children were pre-sented with happy, angry and fear facial expressions. Consistent with the previous investigation, nonmaltreated children showed equivalent ERPs in response to all of the facial expressions, whereas the maltreated children showed an increased response to the angry faces (Pollak et al., 2001).

In a recent investigation, Cicchetti and Curtis (2005) examined the effect of maltreatment during the first year of life on the neural correlates of pro-cessing facial expressions of emotion in 30-month-old youngsters. Event-related potentials (ERPs) were examined in response to children passively viewing standardized pictures of female models posing angry, happy, and neutral facial expressions. Four ERP waveforms were derived: N150, P260, Nc, and a positive slow wave (PSW). Although maltreated and nonmal-treated toddlers did not differ on the early perceptual negative component (N150), the maltreated youngsters exhibited greater P260 amplitude at frontal leads compared to the nonmaltreated children in response to view-ing angry facial expressions. For the Nc component, the nonmaltreated children displayed greater amplitude while viewing pictures of happy faces compared to angry and neutral faces, whereas the maltreated children exhibited greater Nc amplitude at central sites while viewing angry faces. For the PSW, the nonmaltreated youngsters showed a greater area score in the right hemisphere in response to viewing angry facial expressions com-pared to the maltreated toddlers. Given that the PSW is thought to reflect memory updating of stimuli that are not completely encoded (Nelson &

Monk, 2001), the current findings suggest that anger may be a less familiar stimulus for the nonmaltreated youngsters, and, as such, it requires more effort to be updated in memory.

Taken together, the results of these three ERP investigations suggest that maltreated children have differential processing of emotional information and that this hypervigilance is specific to displays of anger. This pattern of neurophysiological activation might be quite adaptive for coping with the threatening environmental challenges that face maltreated children. However, attentional biases to anger may place maltreated children at risk for maladaptive negotiation of stage salient developmental tasks in contexts outside the home, such as in school, where such a bias is not adaptive for interactions with peers and adults (Rieder & Cicchetti, 1989; Rogosch, Cicchetti, & Aber, 1995).

Within-Domain, Multimeasures

Ontogenic psychological development represents the most extensively studied level within our laboratory. Given the broad nature of psychological development, research has focused on specific domains of functioning within this level; these domains include emotional development, cognitive development, and social development (see, e.g., Cicchetti, 1989; Cicchetti & Toth, 2000). We focus here on cognitive development as an illustration of our research within a single domain.

Consistent with our approach to single-level analysis, our cognitive functioning analyses also utilize multiple measures to assess various aspects of within-domain functioning. Beyond our investigations of attentional mechanisms among maltreated children through the utilization of cognitive event-related potential technology (e.g., Cicchetti & Curtis, 2005; Pollak et al., 1997; Pollak et al., 2001, see previous section), we have conducted research on several additional cognitive processes. For example, language development among maltreated children has been investigated from a number of different perspectives. In an early investigation, Coster, Gersten, Beeghly, and Cicchetti (1989) focused on receptive and expressive language skills among maltreated children. Through this analysis of communicative competence, maltreated children demonstrated shorter mean length utterances and more limited expressive but not receptive language. Also, an assessment of pragmatics during mother–child interactions revealed that maltreated children have developed an interaction style that minimizes the use of language for social or affective exchanges with their mothers in comparison to nonmaltreated children (Coster et al., 1989).

Concentrating on a different aspect of language functioning, Beeghly and Cicchetti (1994) analyzed maltreated preschool children's self-descriptions, use of personal pronouns, and active agency during symbolic play as a reflection of children's self–other differentiation and self-system development. Findings indicated that maltreated children talk less about themselves and their internal states than do nonmaltreated children, are more context-bound when they do so, and show less differentiation in their attributional focus. Utilizing this analysis of internal state language, Beeghly and Cicchetti found support for the notion that maltreated children experience difficulty in developing an autonomous self.

Whereas the previous two studies focused on qualitative or content-based aspects of language, quantitative measures of communicative abilities also have been investigated in our laboratory. Specifically, Eigsti and Cicchetti (2004) examined the syntactic complexity of language among mother–child dyads from maltreating and nonmaltreating families, where they found that child maltreatment was associated with quantitative language delays in both vocabulary and production of syntactic structure. In sum, our analyses of language have assessed a wide variety of skills ranging from basic syntactic development to the development of internal state language and by doing so have informed us of the extent to which maltreatment has exerted an adverse impact on the development of this highly canalized cognitive ability.

A second aspect of cognitive development that has been studied in our laboratory is attention regulation. One method we have applied to the assessment of attention processes among maltreated children is the analysis of cognitive control functioning. The ability for cognitive control refers to the capacity to maintain more differentiated, articulate perceptions of past and external stimuli, and to detect nuances and differences in perceptual stimuli more accurately and readily. When maltreated and nonmaltreated children were presented with aggressive and nonaggressive test stimuli and were instructed to utilize various cognitive strategies in managing information, cognitive controls reorganized differently in each group. In particular, maltreated children recalled a greater number of distracting aggressive stimuli than nonmaltreated children, and they assimilated these aggressive stimuli more readily than nonaggressive stimuli (Rieder & Cicchetti, 1989). Thus, maltreated children demonstrate a relative strength in the processing of negative affect information; however, this attentional bias may occur at the expense of less overall cognitive efficiency and impaired task performance.

Memory processes represent a second area of cognitive functioning that is currently being investigated at Mt. Hope Family Center. Despite the fact that there is considerable interest in the effect of trauma on memory, very little research exists on the prolonged effects of maltreatment on basic memory processes (Eisen, Qin, Goodman, & Davis, 2002; Toth & Cicchetti, 1998). Instead, research has tended to focus on the effect of trauma on memories for the specific traumatic event and whether these memories are more or less susceptible to distortions (e.g., Ceci & Bruck, 1995; Eisen et al., 2002; Howe, 2000; Toth & Cicchetti, 1998). To address this gap in the literature, we are currently conducting a broad assessment of maltreated and nonmaltreated children's basic memory functioning. For instance, in a recent investigation we focused on false memories among maltreated and nonmaltreated low-SES children, as well as middle-SES nonmaltreated children, aged 5 to 7, 8 to 9, and 10 to 12 years. Using the Deese-Roediger-McDermott lists, children were asked to participate in recall and recognition measures. Consistent with the normative literature on memory and development, the results revealed that both true and false memories increased with age. This trend differed as a function of socio-economic class, but contrary to hypotheses, did not differ as a function of maltreatment status (Howe, Cicchetti, Toth, & Cerrito, 2004). Our ongoing research is currently focused on a number of additional aspects of children's memory processes; these include distinctiveness effects, intentional forgetting, and suggestibility. Through the inclusion of multiple measures of memory functioning within this single investigation, we will be able to derive general profiles of memory functioning for the maltreated and non-maltreated children, as well as individual memory profiles based on person-centered data analytic techniques.

Our within domain analyses of cognitive development among maltreated children have encompassed multiple measures of language, attention regulation and memory. By tapping into several areas of cognitive development and applying multi-modal assessments we have been able to obtain a broad understanding of maltreated children's functioning while at the same time gaining specificity in our observations as research findings from distinct paradigms converge. Moreover, we have conducted similar lines of programmatic research in the domains of emotional development and social development. Although we will not describe the details of such research here, in general terms our work on emotional development has focused upon aspects of emotion recognition (i.e., Pollak, Cicchetti, Hornung, & Reed, 2000) and emotion regulation (i.e., Maughan & Cicchetti, 2002; Shields & Cicchetti, 1997, 1998), while our investigations of social development include the study of attachment (i.e., Barnett, Ganiban, & Cicchetti, 1999; Cicchetti & Barnett, 1991), relatedness (i.e., Lynch & Cicchetti, 1991, 1992), and peer relationships (i.e., Rogosch & Cicchetti, 1994; Shields, Ryan, & Cicchetti, 2001).

Undoubtedly, the aforementioned within-level and within-domain research has made a significant contribution to our understanding of the developmental sequelae of child maltreatment. Nonetheless, these investigations limited the type of research questions we were able to address by restricting our focus to a single domain of functioning. Such an approach to research is in stark contrast to the guiding principles of developmental psychopathology, which proffer that adaptation or maladaptation within any level or domain affects and is affected by functioning at all other ecological levels. Therefore, although we continue to advocate the utilization of a single-level approach for the investigation of newly developing foundational areas of research, in order to address the dynamic aspects of the developmental process, we believe that it is necessary to adopt a multiple-levels-of-analysis perspective.

CROSS-DOMAIN STUDIES

As described earlier in this chapter, the field of developmental psychopathology has advocated multidisciplinary approaches that examine the biological, psychological, and social contextual aspects of development. Risk factors tend to occur together rather than in isolation (Rutter, 1987); thus it is important to examine how multiple risk processes may operate collectively to increase the probability for later maladaptation and psychopathology (Cicchetti & Dawson, 2002). In striving to incorporate this theoretical perspective into our empirical research, we pushed beyond within-domain analyses toward studies that measure multiple domains in a single design.

For example, aspects of the cognitive, emotional, and social domains were included in a short-term longitudinal investigation that assessed the role of child maltreatment in early deviations in cognitive and affective processing abilities and later peer relationship problems (Rogosch, Cicchetti, & Aber, 1995). Laboratory assessments of affect understanding (emotional domain) and cognitive control functioning (cognitive domain) were conducted when children were preschool age. Later, peer and teacher assessments of peer relations in the school context (social domain) were conducted when children were school age. Maltreated children demonstrated early aberrations in their understanding of negative affect and immaturity in their cognitive control abilities. In the school setting, maltreated children evidenced lower social effectiveness and higher levels of undercontrolled and aggressive behavior in comparison to their nonmaltreated peers; physically abused children, in particular, were more rejected by their peers. Utilization of multiple domain assessments allowed for mediational analyses across domains where it was found that cognitive control functioning partially mediated the effect of child maltreatment on later social effectiveness. Also, negative affect understanding mediated the relation of maltreatment on maladaptive behavior in the peer setting as well as the effects of physical abuse on later peer rejection. Therefore, this mediational model suggests that child maltreatment contributes to deficits in processing emotional information, which, in turn, results in later problems with peer relationships. Moreover, this investigation illustrates how the inclusion of multiple domains of analyses within a single design provides a rich account of how multiple risk processes contribute to the development of maladaptation among maltreated children over time.

Several additional investigations have examined the interplay between emotional and social processes among maltreated children. For instance, Shields, Cicchetti, and Ryan (1994) examined aspects of emotional and behavioral self-regulation and their relation to the development of social competence among maltreated school-age children. Emotional self-regulation was assessed through observations of maltreated and nonmaltreated children during play interactions. Maltreated children more often displayed maladaptive patterns of emotion regulation, characterized by inflexible or situationally inappropriate affective displays. Maltreated children also expressed impaired behavioral self-regulation, (operationalized as internalizing difficulties). Notably, these emotional and behavioral self-regulatory deficits were found to mediate the effects of child maltreatment on children's social competence with peers. Further support for the role of emotion regulation in peer relationships was provided by a subsequent investigation where emotion dysregulation was found to make a unique contribution toward differentiating maltreated bullies and victims from comparison children who did not evidence bullying/victim problems (Shields & Cicchetti, 2001). Thus, early regulatory difficulties, particularly in the emotional domain, place maltreated children at risk for disturbances in interpersonal relationships.

Expanding this research across social, emotional, and cognitive domains, we examined narrative representations of maltreated and nonmaltreated children (Shields, Ryan, & Cicchetti, 2001). Conceptualizing representations as cognitive-affective mental structures that reflect information about the self, others, and expectations about patterns of social interactions, in this study we focused on representations of caregivers and how these representations might relate to emotion regulation and peer relationships among maltreated children. Findings indicated that maltreated children's representations of their caregivers were more negative/constricted and less positive/coherent than those of nonmaltreated children. Moreover, the association between maladaptive representations and problems with peers suggests one pathway through which disruption of early relationships may place maltreated children at risk for peer rejection. Mediational analysis provided further insight into the mechanisms through which maladaptive representations impact child development such that cognitive-affective representations mediated the effects of maltreatment on children's social problems with peers partly through undermining emotion regulation. This investigation serves as an excellent illustration of the utility of cross-domain research as it highlights the complex interplay among emotional, cognitive, and social domains of child psychological development.

Our research initiatives have not only assessed the influence of risk factors within one domain on another, but also have investigated how risk factors across multiple domains may contribute to maladaptive and/or resilient outcomes among maltreated children. For example, the interplay between attention and emotion dysregulation processes has been examined for their potential contribution to the development of reactive aggression among maltreated and nonmaltreated children within an ecologically valid social context at our summer day camp (Shields & Cicchetti, 1998). Maltreated children showed several deficits in attention processes including distractibility, overactivity, poor concentration, and symptoms of subclinical dissociation. Deficits in emotion regulation also were evident such that maltreated children were more likely to have contextually inappropriate emotional expressions and more lability or negativity in mood. This emotion dysregulation mediated the effects of maltreatment on angry reactivity and aggressive behaviors. Moreover, impaired capacity for attention modulation contributed to emotion dysregulation in at-risk children. Therefore, this investigation expanded our understanding of the role of attentional and emotional processes in the development of maladaptive sequelae among maltreated children by supporting a model whereby emotion dysregulation, fostered by poor attention modulation, was a mechanism of the effects of maltreatment on reactive aggression.

In a separate investigation on the development of maladaptive behaviors among maltreated children, we focused on cognitive and social risk factors to the development of behavioral symptomatology (Toth, Cicchetti, & Kim, 2002). Specifically, the roles of children's attributional style (internal/stable/global or external/unstable/specific) and perceptions of their mothers (positive or negative) were examined in relation to internalizing and externalizing behaviors. Attributional style was found to moderate the effects of maltreatment on externalizing symptomatology; however, with respect to internalizing, only a marginal significance was attained. Toth and her colleagues (2002) discovered that maltreated children with fewer maladaptive attributions demonstrated less externalizing symptomatology than those maltreated children who had more maladaptive attributions. Thus, an adaptive attributional style (internal/stable/global for positive events and external/unstable/specific for negative events) may have served a protective role against the adverse effects of child maltreatment. In contrast to the moderating role of attributional style for externalizing only, children's maternal perceptions operated as a mediator of both internalizing and externalizing behavior problems. Thus, maltreated children were more likely to have negative perceptions of their mother and consequently exhibited greater internalizing and externalizing behavior problems. The findings of this investigation expand our understanding of the mechanisms through which maltreatment may lead to maladaptation by highlighting the contribution of cognitive and social processes to the development of behavior problems, apart from the role of emotion dysregulation.

Consistent with the tenets of developmental psychopathology, it is not only necessary to consider the interrelations among developmental domains and the processes that characterize developmental breakdowns, it is just as important to understand the mechanisms through which these systems interact to eventuate in self-righting tendencies and adaptation. Such is the focus of the study of resilience, where we strive to explain the pathways through which individual children show the capacity for successful adaptation and competent functioning despite experiencing chronic stress, adversity, and exposure to prolonged trauma (Cicchetti & Rogosch, 1997; Cicchetti, Rogosch, Lynch, & Holt, 1993; Flores, Cicchetti, & Rogosch, 2005; Luthar, Cicchetti, & Becker, 2000). In our initial investigation, carried out within the context of a summer day camp, we examined maltreated and nonmaltreated children's functioning in several areas that are relevant to successful adaptation among school-age children. Multiple measures were included to assess areas of both strength and vulnerability across domains. We employed explicit indices of competence, investigated cognitive, emotional, and social areas of functioning, and utilized multiple raters and informants. For example, we included a variety of self-report measures of self-system functioning, assessments of intellectual functioning, peer rating measures, counselor measures of behavior, and school measures of academic risk. Integrating information from the children, peers, counselors, and school district records, we derived seven indicators of competent adaptation, which were then summed to form a composite score of adaptive functioning across domains of analysis. In addition, personality dimensions and personal resources were evaluated as mechanisms to promote individual differences in successful adaptation. These personality constructs included cognitive maturity, self-esteem, ego-resiliency and ego-control.

Results from this cross-sectional analysis indicated that, as a group, maltreated children had fewer areas of adaptive functioning than their nonmaltreated age-mates. Although a comparable percentage of competent maltreated and nonmaltreated children emerged at medium and high levels of competence, there were a significantly larger percentage of maltreated children in the lowest level, where children evidenced few signs of competence (Cicchetti et al., 1993). Ego-resiliency, ego-control, and self-esteem were each predictors of individual differences in competent functioning; however, ego-control promoted competence differentially between the maltreated and nonmaltreated groups. Whereas ego-control, in addition to ego-resiliency and self- esteem, was an important predictor of successful adaptation among maltreated children, it did not emerge as a significant contributor to competence among nonmaltreated children. Such findings highlight the importance of self-striving processes to resilient functioning among maltreated children.

To further examine pathways to resilience among maltreated children, we conducted a second investigation of adaptive functioning over a 3-year time period (Cicchetti & Rogosch, 1997). Set once again within the context of a summer day camp, the measurement battery allowed for a multiple domain and multiple informant analysis of child adaptive and personality functioning over the 3 years of assessment. As in our previous design, measures included child self-report, peer evaluations, and counselor ratings of both individual and group processes, where all raters were unaware of the children's maltreatment histories. Also, school assessments for each child were obtained from annual school district records to provide an ecologically valid measure of scholastic functioning. In accord with our prior investigation, a higher percentage of maltreated children consistently exhibited functioning in the low adaptive range across the 3 years of assessment, and differential predictors of resilience were found for maltreated and nonmaltreated children. Whereas relationship features were important for the resilient functioning among nonmaltreated children, positive self-esteem, ego-resilience and ego overcontrol were the strongest predictors of resilient functioning among maltreated children. In sum, nonmaltreated children seem to be able to utilize resources within the social domain in particular to promote adaptive functioning across domains, whereas maltreated children, who likely have a poverty of positive social relationships, have developed a reliance on self-striving and self-determination to exhibit resilient functioning across domains.

Although these initial attempts at multiple analysis designs focused within the psychological ontogenetic (behavioral) level, they represented an important advance in our ability to integrate variables across domains. Moreover, cross-domain research designs have afforded us the opportunity to achieve a more in-depth understanding of psychological ontogenic development. The development of this extensive body of knowledge was necessary to provide a foundation on which subsequent research initiatives could emerge to incorporate the psychological ontogenic level into multiple-levels-of-analysis research programs. Thus, the incorporation of multiple levels of analysis within a single study represents the final methodological shift in our approach to conducting research on the effects of child maltreatment on child adaptation and maladaptation.

CROSS-LEVEL STUDIES

Consistent with the central thesis of this chapter, our own growing understanding of the significance of a multiple-levels-of-analysis approach for informing the field of developmental psychopathology has guided the translation of this theoretical perspective into our research designs. Our earliest foray into multiple levels research focused on exosystem influences in relation to child maltreatment, and its effect on children's ontogenic functioning over a 1-year time period (Lynch & Cicchetti, 1998a). Specifically, exposure to community violence was assessed as an exosystem risk factor among 7- to 12-year-old maltreated and nonmaltreated children. Highlighting the additive effects of child maltreatment and exposure to community violence on children's traumatic stress reactions, maltreated children from high-violence neighborhoods exhibited higher levels of depressive, externalizing, and traumatic stress symptomatology than nonmaltreated children from low-violence neighborhoods. Victimization by community violence significantly predicted children's traumatic stress symptoms 1 year later. Moreover, exposure to community violence was related to children's functioning over and above the effects of a more proximal contextual feature (maltreatment). Therefore, this investigation provides evidence of how children and their contexts, or risk factors at multiple levels of ecology, mutually influence each other over time.

Extending the findings of this investigation, we conducted a second investigation to examine the joint impact of child maltreatment and community violence on children's memory processes and representational models (Lynch & Cicchetti, 1998b). Utilizing an incidental recall task among 8- to 13-year-old maltreated and nonmaltreated children, we assessed the links between trauma, maternal representations, and memory for mother-relevant information. The results suggest that experiences of trauma influence the representational models children develop about their mothers. These cognitive-affective models then moderate the effects of trauma on memory. In particular, there was an interaction between traumatic experience and security of maternal representations in predicting children's recall for maternal attribute words such that victimized children with insecure models recalled the highest proportion of negative maternal stimuli. Thus, this investigation demonstrates evidence for multiple pathways from the experience of trauma (resulting from both victimization by community violence and by maltreatment) that are associated with differences in the security of children's mental representations. The inclusion of both exosystem and ontogenic measures in this investigation has brought light to yet another example of the complex interplay among dynamic levels, which can only be discovered through multiple-levels-of-analysis research designs.

By far, our most active area of cross-level research has focused on the reciprocal coactions between neurobiological/physiological and psychological processes in relation to the experience of child maltreatment. For example, we have conducted several analyses on the relationship between neuroendocrine functioning, child maltreatment, and various developmental outcomes ranging from social competence to internalizing and externalizing symptomatology (Hart, Gunnar, & Cicchetti, 1995, 1996; Cicchetti & Rogosch, 2001b). First, we examined the relationship between HPA activity and socioemotional functioning among maltreated and nonmaltreated children in a preschool setting (Hart et al., 1995). HPA system functioning was assessed through the analysis of cortisol, assayed from saliva samples that were obtained during the normal preschool day at the same time, over multiple days. Two aspects of cortisol levels were examined: basal cortisol activity, defined as the median of each child's cortisol levels over several weeks, and reactivity, defined as the tendency to produce cortisol levels significantly higher than one's basal level. Children's behaviors were assessed through teacher report, and were additionally recorded by trained observers. Three behavioral scales were then constructed to reflect acting out/ externalizing behavior, shy/internalizing behavior, and social competence. Results indicated that whereas median cortisol was not related to measures of social behavior, neuroendocrine reactivity was positively correlated with social competence and negatively related to shy/internalizing behavior. Maltreated children demonstrated less neuroendocrine reactivity than did comparison children, and scored lower in social competence and higher in shy/internalizing behaviors. Social competence was positively correlated with cortisol levels on high-conflict preschool days among nonmaltreated children. In contrast, maltreated children failed to exhibit elevations in cortisol on high-conflict compared to low-conflict days. Taken together, the reduction in neuroendocrine reactivity among maltreated children suggests that the experience of maltreatment may eventuate in deviant HPA functioning. Moreover, social competence, a psychological ontogenic developmental skill that is impaired among maltreated children, appears to be related to the reactivity of the HPA system, a marker of neuroendocrine system function.

Expanding the analysis of neuroendocrine activity among maltreated children to the development of psychopathology, a second investigation examined the effects of stressful social environments on physiological and affective functioning among maltreated and nonmaltreated school-aged children who attended our summer day camp program (Hart et al., 1996). The camp represented a novel experience for all children, and thus represented a socially challenging context. As noted earlier in this chapter, the structure of the camp day also allowed for standard collection of salivary cortisol twice daily. Psychopathology variables included depression, measured using the Child Depression Inventory (CDI; Kovacs, 1992), as well as clinical level Internalizing and Externalizing symptomatology, assessed through the Teacher Report Form of the Child Behavior Checklist (TRF-CBCL; Achenbach, 1991) from children's camp counselors.

Results indicated that maltreated children had slightly elevated afternoon cortisol levels; however, their morning cortisol concentrations did not significantly differ from the nonmaltreated comparison children. Thus, at this single level of analysis, maltreated and nonmaltreated children did not appear to evidence differential functioning. In addition, neither internalizing symptoms, externalizing symptoms, or depression were predictive of afternoon cortisol concentrations. However, when we simultaneously considered psychopathology and its relation to neuroendocrine functioning, an interesting pattern of results emerged. Specifically, the presence of depression among maltreated children was associated with deviations in HPA functioning; these depressed maltreated children demonstrated lower morning cortisol concentrations than nondepressed maltreated children and were more likely to show a rise, rather than a normative decrease, in cortisol from morning to evening. This pattern of diurnal cortisol activity was unique to the depressed maltreated group; the depressed nonmaltreated children did not demonstrate a similar pattern in comparison to nonmaltreated children without depression (Hart et al., 1996). Therefore, the incorporation of multiple-levels-of-analysis to this research design allowed us to clarify the interrelations between child maltreatment and depression on neuroendocrine regulation, and to identify depressed nonmaltreated children, in particular, as a high-risk group for HPA dysregulation.

Although a relationship between clinical-level internalizing, maltreatment, and neuroendocrine dysregulation seemed clear, we conducted a further study to clarify the complex relationships between child maltreatment and externalizing symptomatology on neuroendocrine functioning, as well as the effects of comorbid clinical-level internalizing and externalizing symptomatology on the HPA functioning of maltreated and nonmaltreated children (Cicchetti & Rogosch, 2001b). Also conducted within the context of a research summer day camp, a large sample of maltreated ($n = 167$) and nonmaltreated ($n = 204$) boys and girls were assessed for the presence of clinical-level internalizing and externalizing symptomatology through self-report and adult evaluation. Children with clinical-level internalizing only, externalizing only, and comorbid clinical-level internalizing and externalizing symptomatology were identified. On average, clinical-level cases were more prevalent among the maltreated children. Independent of gender, maltreated children with clinical-level internalizing problems evidenced higher morning, afternoon, and average daily cortisol levels than nonmaltreated children with clinical-level internalizing problems. In contrast, nonmaltreated boys with clinical-level externalizing problems were distinct in that they demonstrated the lowest levels of morning and average daily levels of cortisol of any group. Moreover, maltreated children with comorbid clinical-level internalizing and externalizing problems were more likely to not show the normative diurnal decrease in cortisol. Thus, this investigation demonstrates the multifinality of the experience of child maltreatment in relation to neuroendocrine regulation, and has suggested that the presence of maltreatment may moderate the impact of internalizing problems on adrenocortical regulation. Clearly, the neurobiological functioning of all maltreated children is not effected uniformly by the experience of maltreatment. Therefore, it is imperative for researchers to investigate potential mediators and moderators of child maltreatment in order to better delineate developmental pathways. It is for this reason that multiple-levels-of-analysis research is essential; it allows for the examination of cascading effects of risk processes across developmental stages and levels of ecology, and promotes the identification of protective processes that might alter the course of child development.

Another rapidly growing area of multilevel research in our laboratory is molecular genetics, which was developed for the specific purpose of conducting multilevel gene–environment interaction research. Multiple-levels-of-analysis research that incorporates genetic information may allow us to identify genes that are associated with maladaptive developmental outcomes as well as genes that may serve a protective function for individuals in the face of adversity (Cicchetti & Blender, 2004). To that end, we have been collecting DNA samples from maltreated and nonmaltreated children as well as from their parents over the past several years. Using buccal cells obtained through a simple oral cheek swab procedure, we are able to extract and purify DNA. We utilize the gene sequencer in our laboratory to genotype the particular genes at regions of interest. We may then examine how genetic factors may interact with the experience of maltreatment to further our understanding of the development of psychopathology (see, e.g., Caspi et al., 2002; Foley et al., 2004). For example, a current investigation is focusing on two particular genes and their relation to the development of psychopathology among maltreated and nonmaltreated children (Blender & Cicchetti, in preparation). Specifically, we are investigating the gene that encodes the neurotransmitter metabolizing enzyme monoamine oxidase A (MAOA), as well as the promoter region of the serotonin transporter gene (5-HTT), each of which has been demonstrated to moderate the effect of maltreatment on the development of psychopathology (Caspi et al., 2002; Caspi et al., 2003). No study to date, however, has analyzed both of these genes in a single investigation. Thus, our study represents an advance in gene–environment interaction research in relation to child maltreatment by incorporating multiple genes into a multilevel investigation.

These genes are of particular interest because their functionality is determined in large part by polymorphisms in the promoter regions. This is important methodologically because it allows for a good estimate of the activity of these genes by merely genotyping the individual's non-invasively collected DNA, rather than requiring the considerably more invasive mRNA collection. This research is designed to probe the role of gene–environment interaction in the development of externalizing behavior problems and conduct disorder. The findings will be able to elucidate the extent of risk associated with variation in specific genes, the combined effects of variation in two genes, the independent effect of extreme childrearing experience (i.e., child maltreatment), and the interactive effects of genetic features and maltreatment history. We anticipate that individuals with particular genetic configuration will be more vulnerable to the effects of child maltreatment. Alternatively, different genetic configurations may confer a protective influence over the impact of adverse family experience on the development of externalizing behavior problems (cf. Caspi et al., 2002; Cicchetti & Blender, 2004; Curtis & Cicchetti, 2003).

Finally, one of our most comprehensive multiple-levels-of-analysis research initiatives is carried out through our summer day camp research. The summer camp serves as an ecologically valid context to assess child functioning as well as peer interactions. Maltreated and nonmaltreated children attend the camp from 9 a.m. to 4 p.m. daily for 1 week. Children are assigned to recreational groups of same age, same sex peers, within which there are equal numbers of maltreated and nonmaltreated children. Each group is run by three trained counselors who are unaware of children's maltreatment status. These counselors provide multiple raters to assess child behaviors following 35 hours of interaction over the course of the camp week. While at camp, children participate in a wide variety of research assessments that are conducted on an individual basis in separate lab and interview rooms. The camp context also allows for assessment of how children are perceived by their peers, and additionally, provides an ideal structure for cortisol collection. Given the time-sensitive nature of adrenocortical functioning, our ability to consistently collect salivary samples for all children at the same times each day of the week allows our sampling to be highly controlled. Due to the diurnal variation that characterizes hormone secretion, our ability to collect saliva samples in such a uniform manner is a major asset of the camp context.

Our measurement battery for the summer camp reflects our goal of obtaining measures of child functioning at multiple-levels-of-analysis. Although our measures also assess aspects of the microsystem (i.e., school, parenting, dimension of maltreatment, etc.), we focus here on the levels of neurobiological and psychological ontogenic functioning. Individual features of the child that are assessed include molecular genetics, acoustic startle, neuroendocrine regulation, EEG asymmetry and coherence, emotion regulation, attention networks, executive functions, and intelligence. Child personality, psychopathology, and substance use also are examined.

The neurobiological assessments included at camp involve several of the measures previously described. For example, genetic samples are being collected among the children who attend our camp program. Using the oral buccal swab technique, this simple, noninvasive procedure enables DNA to be extracted and purified from cells that line children's inner cheeks. Once the DNA has been isolated, specific regions of interest can be identified and genotyped (see the earlier discussion of molecular genetics). We are also examining the acoustic startle reflex and neuroendocrine regulation among maltreated and nonmaltreated children (see section on within-level, multiple measures). Although our previous investigations of adrenocortical functioning among maltreated children were able to assess diurnal changes in cortisol concentrations, we were limited to testing linear patterns because only two samples of cortisol were collected throughout the camp day. Presently, salivary samples are being collected at three times during the camp day: on arrival at 9 a.m., before lunch at 12 p.m., and prior to departure at 4 p.m. The inclusion of a midday salivary cortisol collection allows us to evaluate curvilinear functions of neuroendocrine regulation among maltreated and nonmaltreated children. Additionally, we are now assaying saliva samples for concentrations of testosterone and DHEA, two other measures of neuroendocrine functioning. Similar in theory to our multigene by environment interaction studies, we are collecting several hormones so that we might investigate multihormone–environment interactions.

Patterns of electroencephalogram (EEG) activity are also assessed in children who attend our summer research day camp. Over the past two decades, several lines of research employing quantitative electroencephalography have established a consistent relation between individual difference in resting frontal alpha asymmetry and emotion with normative populations of adults, children, and infants. This growing body of evidence has indicated differential roles for left and right prefrontal cortex in emotion (Hugdahl & Davidson 2003). In general, it appears that the left hemisphere participates in approach emotions (e.g., happiness or interest), whereas the right hemisphere mediates withdrawal-directed emotional responses, (e.g., sadness; Davidson, 2000).

Such characteristic patterns of lateralized brain activity have been associated with emotion-related individual differences in normative populations across development. For example, hemispheric asymmetries reliably predict infants' responses to maternal separation (Davidson & Fox, 1989), and are associated with social competence in toddlers (Fox et al., 1995). Other studies of infants have generally found increased right frontal EEG activity during the expression of emotions such as crying and sadness, and increased left frontal activation during the expression approach emotions, such as happiness (e.g., Bell & Fox, 1994; Dawson, Panagiotides, Klinger, & Hill, 1992).

Induced positive and negative affective states can reliably shift hemispheric EEG asymmetry, with the presentation of negatively toned stimuli being associated with increased relative right prefrontal activation and viewing positive stimuli associated with increased left prefrontal activation. Furthermore, an association between dispositional affective style and baseline levels of asymmetric EEG activation in the prefrontal cortex has been found, with individuals showing greater left frontal activation reporting more positive affect than those with greater right frontal activation (Davidson, 2000). Other work has shown that individuals who vary in resting prefrontal EEG activation asymmetry respond differently to positive and negative emotional stimuli (e.g., Davidson, 2000; Tomarken, Davidson, & Henriques, 1990). Individuals with greater relative left hemisphere EEG activation reported more positive affect when viewing positively toned film clips and less negative affect after viewing negatively toned film clips. Given that negative social experience such as child maltreatment can exert a negative impact on neurobiological development and functioning, we expect to find that maltreated children will predominantly display right hemispheric asymmetry more than their demographically comparable nonmaltreated age-mates.

To gain a more comprehensive understanding of the extent to which the experience of child maltreatment may affect cortical functioning, neuropsychological assessments have been incorporated into the camp battery. Working memory processes and inhibitory control are associated with the dorsolateral prefrontal cortex, whereas other neuropsychological abilities such as temporal order memory or recognition memory are associated with the temporal areas of the cortex (Luciana & Nelson, 2002). To evaluate a range of these processes and their associated neural substrates, the Cambridge Neuropsychological Testing Automated Battery (CANTAB; Sahakian & Owen, 1992) is currently being used to better characterize different aspects of prefrontal and medial temporal functioning among maltreated children. Notably, the prefrontal cortex and medial temporal lobe have high concentrations of glucocorticoid receptors. Given the atypical patterns of neuroendocrine functioning that have been demonstrated among maltreated children (Cicchetti & Rogosch, 2001a, 2001b), we are interested in determining how this atypical regulation may impair executive functions that are dependent on these brain regions (Teicher, Anderson, Polcari, Anderson, Navalta, et al., 2003).

The CANTAB is comprised of several subtests that tap features of memory, attention, and planning ability; these subtests include assessments of visual memory (delayed matching to sample, pattern recognition, spatial recognition), visual attention (set shifting), and planning/working memory (spatial memory span, spatial working memory, stockings of Cambridge). We are interested in determining how maltreatment may impair these cognitive processes and potentiate the development of psychopathology.

In terms of the psychological ontogenic level, attention abilities are measured through the use of the Attention Network Test (ANT; Fan, McCandliss, Sommer, Raz, & Posner, 2002). This computer-administered paradigm assesses three aspects of attention: alerting, orienting, and executive control. Alerting refers to the ability to achieve and maintain sensitivity to incoming stimuli, orienting involves the ability to select and focus on specific sensory input, and executive control involves monitoring and resolving conflict among thoughts, feelings, and behavioral output. These three areas of attention are associated with different brain regions (Posner & Peterson, 1990); thus, we are interested in ascertaining how the experience of child maltreatment might alter the neural development of these separable attention networks.

Intelligence is assessed through the Wechsler Intelligence Scale for Children-IV (WISC-IV; Wechsler, 2003). Eight subtests (four from the Verbal Scale and four from the Performance Scale) are administered to derive a Verbal IQ, Performance IQ and a Full Scale IQ. Intelligence may serve a protective function for maltreated children. Alternatively, the experience of chronic maltreatment might impair intelligence. In addition, measurement of IQ is essential so that it can be used as a covariate in analyses involving attention and executive functioning abilities so that we may determine their contributions to prediction beyond general intelligence level.

Children also are given a series of self-report measures to determine their own appraisal of their affective experience, psychological symptomatology, and involvement with substance use. For example, the Children's Depression Inventory (CDI; Kovacs, 1985), the Revised Child Manifest Anxiety Scale (RCMAS; Reynolds & Richmond, 1985), and the Positive and Negative Affect Scale for Children (PANAS-C; Laurent et al., 1999) are among the self-report measures collected. Children also participate in peer ratings on the last day of camp. After children have interacted with each other for the camp week, they evaluate the interpersonal characteristics of their peers (from within their camp group) using a peer rating method (Coie & Dodge, 1983). Each child is asked to rate every other child from their group on the extent to which the peer exhibited different descriptions of social behaviors. Thus the child self-report measures provide us with information regarding children's emotional and social domains.

Child self-report and peer ratings are used in conjunction with counselor and teacher assessments to derive more rigorous constructs of children's behavior and symptomatology. For example, at the end of the camp week, the three counselors from each group, who are unaware of children's maltreatment status, independently complete the Teacher Report Form of the Child Behavioral Checklist (TRF; Achenbach, 1991); the California Q-Set (CCQ; Block & Block, 1980) and the Five Factor Model Rating Scale (FFMRS; Hagekull & Bohlin, 1998) for each child in their group. Thus children are assessed on features of psychopathology, emotion regulation, interpersonal behavior, and personality.

In order to have a more detailed understanding of the environment within which the children who participate in camp are developing, we additionally administer a wide range of measures to the primary caregiver of every child who attends camp. This parent battery, completed by the child's mother, includes assessments that primarily focus on microsystem and exosystem factors. For example, to obtain an account of exosystem influences, we ask mothers to complete measures pertaining to their neighborhood, experiences of community violence, and their personal feelings of religiosity. In terms of microsystem influences, mothers report on domestic violence, socioeconomic status, perceived social support, and perceived stress, as well as aspects of their parenting and conflict resolution strategies. Additionally, we assess current psychopathology (including depression, substance abuse, PTSD, dissociation, and antisocial behavior) among the mothers, as well as childhood trauma and perceptions of their own attachment relationships. Finally, we collect buccal samples from the mothers as we look toward analyzing the contribution of genetic factors to the intergenerational transmission of risk for child maltreatment.

The multidomain, multilevel measurement battery employed in our camp research also enables us to investigate both biological and psychological correlates of, and contributors to, resilience. To date, the investigation of pathways to resilience has been predominantly characterized by psychological approaches. The incorporation of a multiple-levels-of-analysis perspective into the study of resilience will result in a more precise understanding of the mediators and moderators underlying this dynamic developmental construct (Curtis & Cicchetti, 2003; Luthar, Cicchetti, & Becker, 2000).

Furthermore, the incorporation of biological measures to research that strives to differentiate between individuals who function well in adversity and those who function well without adversity may reveal differential neurobiological correlates of and contributors to resilience and positive adaptation, respectively. If distinctions between these two constructs can be made at both the neurobiological and behavioral levels, then there would be strong evidence for the distinctiveness of positive adaptation and resilience (see Curtis & Cicchetti, 2003; Masten, 2001).

The incorporation of a biological perspective into research on resilience still requires adherence to a dynamic, transactional view that respects the importance of context (Sameroff, 2000). As Curtis and Cicchetti (2003) asserted:

> Omitting biology from the resilience equation is tantamount to omitting psychology . . . If we are to grasp the true complexity of the concept of resil-

ience, then we must investigate it with a commensurate level of complexity. (p. 803)

In sum, the extensive measurement battery that we are currently implementing through our summer day camp allows us to examine the effects of child maltreatment from numerous perspectives and levels of ecology. Given the breadth of our assessments, we are able to evaluate mediators and moderators at both the neurobiological and psychological levels, and within levels we are able to assess multiple domains. Moreover, the use of multiple informants allows us to derive robust measures of children's functioning across multiple viewpoints. Therefore, our summer camp serves as an example of the culmination of our theoretical perspective into a functional research design.

TRANSLATION INTO INTERVENTIONS/PREVENTIONS

Beyond informing research designs, it is critically important to translate our multilevel approach to the development and implementation of theoretically informed intervention and prevention programs. In recent years, the National Institute of Mental Health (NIMH) has become greatly interested in fostering and supporting translational research on the behavioral and social sciences (Cicchetti & Toth, 2000, in preparation). As funding decisions at the NIMH increasingly become tied to reducing the burden of mental illness and to the real world application of research findings, investigators will need to devise and implement policy-relevant investigations. In a report of the National Advisory Mental Health Council on Behavioral Sciences (2000) entitled *Translating Behavioral Science Into Action,* strategies for enhancing contributions of behavioral science to society more broadly are proposed. The report of the workgroup concludes:

> At present too few researchers are attempting to bridge across basic, clinical, and services research, and not enough are working with colleagues in related allied disciplines to move research advances out of the laboratory and into clinical care, service delivery, and policymaking. (p. v)

In this report, "translational research is defined as research designed to address how basic behavioral processes inform the diagnosis, prevention, treatment, and delivery of services for mental illness, and, conversely, how knowledge of mental illness increases our understanding of basic behavioral processes" (p. iii). This formulation of translational research is in direct accord with two of the key tenets of a developmental psychopathology perspective, namely the reciprocal interplay between basic and applied research, and between normal and atypical development (Cicchetti & Toth, 1991, 2006).

The parameters of developmental psychopathology lend themselves to fostering translational research that has implications for society, policy-makers, and individuals with mental disorders and their families. The very subject matter of the field, which encompasses risk and resilience, preven-tion and intervention, the elucidation of precipitants of mental illness, the mediating and moderating processes that contribute to or mitigate against the emergence and maintenance of psychopathology, a multiple-levels-of-analysis approach, and the incorporation of principles of normal develop-ment into the conduct of empirical investigations, necessitates thinking clearly about the implications of the work and devising strategies to remedy the problems being studied.

Preventive interventions that take into account multiple levels of influ-ence present a means of reducing the schisms that often exist between academic researchers and clinicians. A central tenet of developmental psy-chopathology is that the understanding of atypical development can inform the understanding of normal development, and vice versa, as long as appro-priate consideration is given to contextual variables and developmental principles in the explanation of how the process of development can go awry. We extend this assertion through our contention that methodologi-cally rigorous prevention and intervention science can provide a unique lens through which the process responsible for the development, mainte-nance, and alteration of both typical and atypical patterns can be discerned (Cicchetti & Hinshaw, 2002; Hinshaw, 2002; Kellam & Rebok, 1992).

The dearth of attention to biological processes in prevention evaluation may stem in part from beliefs that biological processes are not malleable or less amenable to positive change as a result of experience. Evidence for neurobiological change in response to changes in the environment may be less apparent in normative populations where there is likely greater stability in supportive milieus. Although adversity and trauma are known to be det-rimental to biological systems, how preventive interventions may contribute to recovery or repair of biological sequelae is little understood. A dynam-ics systems view posits bidirectional transactions between different levels of organismic organization, and in so doing, it must be recognized that expe-rience influences biology (Cicchetti & Tucker, 1994; Eisenberg, 1995; Kan-del, 1998). Thus, it is important to consider how changes in experience and behavioral functioning resulting from preventive interventions may alter biological processes.

The concept of neural plasticity offers a valuable heuristic for conceptu-alizing how preventive interventions may affect brain structure and func-tion, contributing to resilience among individuals confronted with adversity (Curtis & Cicchetti, 2003). Analogous to recovery from physical injury to the brain, neural plasticity also may involve recovery from the damaging effects of trauma and extreme stress. Adverse environmental experience can induce physiological changes in the brain, and conversely, experiences to ameliorate and safeguard against severe adversity may similarly produce physiological changes that are advantageous to the central nervous system (Cicchetti & Tucker, 1994; Nelson, 1999). Greenough and colleagues (Black, Jones, Nelson, & Greenough, 1998; Greenough & Black, 1992; Greenough, Black, & Wallace, 1987) identify two forms of neural plasticity in mammalian brains, including experience-expectant and experience-dependent plasticity. Most notably in early development, the brain "expects" to receive particular forms of information from the environment, and based on input, an early overabundance of neurons is pruned and new neuronal connections are formed as brain development proceeds. Appropriate timing and quality are important for optimal brain development, whereas deprivation and atypical experience may lead to detrimental consequences for brain neurobiological development (Cicchetti & Cannon, 1999a, 1999b). Given the rapid rate of growth and organization occurring during the early years of life, early interventions that alter adverse and stressful environments may influence the type of brain that emerges during this important period of neurobiological epigenesis. In contrast to experience-expectant plasticity, experience-dependent plasticity occurs in later periods of development as the established yet evolving brain responds to new experience through the formation of new neural connections. Thus, for high-risk individuals who are confronted with multiple environmental stresses, the positive effects of preventive interventions may occur in part through alterations that are set in motion in the structure and functioning of neurobiological systems.

In broad terms, many preventive interventions strive to reduce stress experienced by children exposed to social adversity and multiple risk factors. Accordingly, inclusion of physiological stress measurements in preventive trial measurement batteries would greatly augment knowledge regarding physiological responses to preventive interventions, in tandem with changes in psychological functioning. Much attention has been given in recent years, in rodents, nonhuman primates, and humans, to effects of stress and social adversity on the neuroendocrine system (Gunnar & Vazquez, 2006; Meaney, 2001; Sanchez, Ladd & Plotsky, 2001; Sapolsky, 1992, 1996). The activation of the hypothalamic-pituitary-adrenal (HPA) axis in response to stress is an adaptive mechanism serving a protective function for the organism (McEwen, 1998). However, extreme and prolonged stress may dysregulate neuroendocrine functioning, resulting in damaging effects to neurons. Measuring the stress hormone cortisol through saliva sampling has provided an easily accessible window into neuroendocrine regulation in biobehavioral studies. In preventive intervention trials, measurements of average basal cortisol levels and cortisol reactivity in response to stress could readily be incorporated into pre- and postintervention and follow-up assessment batteries. In so doing, improvements in neuroendocrine functioning and concomitant relations to behavioral change could be articulated for a more complete appraisal of the range of impact of the prevention trial and processes through which its effects are achieved.

Other technologies utilized in investigations of brain structure and function also could be applied to understanding preventive intervention effects. For example, psychophysiological studies of neurological processing of discrete stimuli using EEG recordings of event-related potentials (ERP's) allow for monitoring of neural activity as it occurs. As previously discussed, ERP differences in response to anger stimuli have been observed in maltreated children (Cicchetti & Curtis, 2005; Pollak et al., 1997, 2001). As a preventive trial measurement, the extent to which there is a normalization of ERP waveform profiles as a result of intervention could be investigated. In addition, altering patterns of hemispheric activation asymmetries could accompany positive outcomes in maltreated children's processing and emotion regulation resulting from intervention. Moreover, the dynamic interrelations between brain and behavioral systems would be clarified, particularly in terms of the multiple levels at which intervention effects may occur. Furthermore, the inclusion of measures of neuropsychological abilities and executive functions could identify improvements in, for example, attention, inhibition, memory, and logical planning resulting from a preventive intervention. Similarly, atypicalities in the startle reflex have been observed in adults with PTSD, including combat veterans and women who were sexually assaulted (Morgan, Grillon, Lubin, & Southwick, 1997; Orr, Lasko, Shalev, & Pitman, 1995), as well as children with PTSD (Ornitz & Pynoos, 1989) and maltreated children (Klorman et al., 2003). By including assessments of the startle reflex, preventive interventions designed to reduce the risk for anxiety disorders due to trauma could determine whether the effects of the intervention also occurred at the physiological level.

Thus, the incorporation of a neurobiological framework into the conceptualization of preventive interventions holds considerable promise for expansion of knowledge regarding the complexity of the developmental process. By basing preventive trials on more comprehensive, integrative developmental theories of psychopathology, prevention research offers the opportunity to conduct developmental experiments that alter environment and experience in efforts to promote resilience among individuals faced with adversity. Determining the multiple levels at which change is engendered through preventive trials will provide more in-depth insights into the mechanisms of change, the extent to which neural plasticity may be promoted, and the interrelations between biological and psychological processes in risk, resilience, and psychopathology (Curtis & Cicchetti, 2003).

In our ongoing preventive intervention with 12-month-old maltreated infants and their mothers, we have included a number of biological parameters at both the baseline (pre-intervention) and postintervention assessment periods. Stress-reactivity paradigms are included at the inception of the intervention and at the conclusion of the intervention, 12 months later. Additionally, neuroendocrine regulation is assessed through obtaining saliva samples at uniform morning and afternoon times, both at the initiation and conclusion of the intervention. Moreover, EEG hemispheric activation asymmetries are measured both at pre- and postintervention. Finally, buccal cells are collected and DNA is purified and extracted for future molecular genetic G × E interaction analyses.

In this randomized clinical trial intervention, maltreated babies and their caregivers are assigned to one of three interventions: (a) a didactic Psychoeducational Parenting Intervention (PPI) that focuses on improving parenting and maternal knowledge of normative child development, as well as increasing maternal social networks, decreasing mothers' stress, and enhancing maternal coping; (b) an attachment-theory informed intervention, Infant-Parent Psychotherapy (IPP), that focuses on expanding the mother's empathic responsiveness, sensitivity, and attachment to the infant stemming from negative maternal representational models of relationships; and (c) a Community Standard (CS) intervention, in which maltreating mothers receive whatever intervention is provided by the social worker assigned to their case by the local Department of Health and Human Services. A final group of infants, who have not experienced maltreatment and who were drawn from a comparable low-SES background, serve as the Nonmaltreated Comparison (NC) group.

Through employing a multiple-levels-of-analysis approach to the evaluation of the efficacy of this randomized clinical trial intervention with maltreated infants, we are in a position to discover if behavior, physiology, and gene expression are modified as a function of each of the interventions provided. Moreover, we will be in a position to ascertain which levels of analysis serve as mediators or moderators of intervention efficacy. Finally, the more comprehensive portrayal of the person that will eventuate from a multiple-levels-of-analysis framework may aid in the development of interventions that are best suited for particular types of individual structural organizations.

CONCLUSION

In this chapter, we argued that it is imperative that researchers in developmental psychopathology adapt a multiple-levels-of-analysis approach to the study of both deviant and adaptive functioning. Moreover, by describing the progression of our research on child maltreatment, we illustrated how the inclusion of multiple-levels-of-analysis afforded us the opportunity to gain an understanding of the emergence of psychopathological, as well as resilient, development that would not have been possible with a single-level approach (e.g., Cicchetti & Rogosch, 2001b; Hart et al., 1996). New programs of research must take into account both normal and abnormal developmental processes in examining psychopathology, and intervention studies must be undertaken in order to more fully establish the characteristics of and processes underlying the relation among genetics, biology, and psychopathology. Such multiple-levels-of-analysis research programs must be supported by funding agencies, many of which still view multiple-levels-of-analysis approaches as too risky to merit financial support. Additionally, journal editors should encourage such research by increasing their willingness to publish papers that investigate a phenomenon across multiple-levels-of-analysis, some of which might fall outside the purview of the particular journal. Furthermore, research in developmental psychopathology that is driven by broadly based theory incorporating multiple-levels-of-analysis must be increasingly encouraged by faculty in the context of graduate and medical training.

In order to ensure that future generations of scholars in developmental psychopathology are exposed to a dynamic systems-based, multiple-levels-of-analysis perspective, undergraduate, graduate, and medical school programs in clinical and developmental psychology, neuroscience and molecular genetics, and psychiatry should encourage students to take courses in a broad spectrum of areas (Cicchetti & Toth, 1991; Pellmar & Eisenberg, 2000). These might include courses in basic neurobiology, neuroendocrinology, immunology, molecular genetics, and developmental processes, as well as courses on brain imaging technologies, molecular genetic laboratory methods, neuroendocrine and immunological assay techniques, and other tools involved in assessing neurobiological and genetic processes.

Finally, students in basic science areas such as neuroscience or molecular genetics should be encouraged to gain exposure to the fundamentals of normative and atypical developmental processes. Furthermore, specific interdisciplinary programs, for both students and faculty, spanning interest areas from clinical intervention to basic neuroscience, would help to foster communication and collaborative research endeavors among the fields of molecular genetics, developmental neuroscience, and developmental psychopathology (see, e.g., Cicchetti & Posner, 2005). The power embodied by cross-disciplinary collaborations that utilize multiple-levels-of-analysis methodologies promises to significantly strengthen our capacity to decrease the burden of mental illness for individuals as well as for society at large.

ACKNOWLEDGMENTS

We acknowledge the support of grants from the NIMH (MH54643) and from the Spunk Fund, Inc.

REFERENCES

Achenbach, T. M. (1991). *Manual for the Child Behavior Checklist — teacher's report form*. Burlington, VT: University of Vermont.

Albright, T. D., Jessell, T. M., Kandel, E. R., & Posner, M. I. (2000). Neural science: A century of progress and the mysteries that remain. *Cell, 100,* S1–S55.

Barnett, D., Ganiban, J., & Cicchetti, D. (1999). Maltreatment, negative expressivity, and the development of Type D attachments from 12- to 24-months of age. *Society for Research in Child Development Monograph, 64,* 97–118.

Beeghly, M., & Cicchetti, D. (1994). Child maltreatment, attachment, and the self system: Emergence of an internal state lexicon in toddlers at high social risk. *Development and Psychopathology, 6,* 5–30.

Bell, M. A., & Fox, N. A. (1994). Brain development over the first year of life: Relations between EEG frequency and coherence and cognitive and affective behaviors. In G. Dawson & K. Fischer (Eds.), *Human behavior and the developing brain* (pp. 314–345). New York: Guilford.

Belsky, J. (1980). Child maltreatment: An ecological integration. *American Psychologist, 35,* 320–335.

Black, J., Jones, T. A., Nelson, C. A., & Greenough, W. T. (1998). Neuronal plasticity and the developing brain. In N. E. Alessi, J. T. Coyle, S. I. Harrison, & S. Eth (Eds.), *Handbook of child and adolescent psychiatry* (pp. 31–53). New York: Wiley.

Blender, J.A., & Cicchetti, D. (in preparation). The influence of specific maltreatment experiences, gender and the MAOA-uVNTR and 5-HTTLPR polymorphisms on conduct disorder symptoms: A multi-gene by environment interaction. (Available from the authors).

Block, J., & Block, J. H. (1980). The role of ego-control and ego-resiliency in the organization of behavior. In W. A. Collins (Ed.), *The Minnesota symposia on child psychology: Development of cognition, affect, and social relations* (Vol. 13, pp. 39–101). Hillsdale, NJ: Lawrence Erlbaum Associates.

Bronfenbrenner, U. (1979). *The ecology of human development: Experiments by nature and design.* Cambridge, MA: Harvard University Press.

Cacioppo, J. T., & Berntson, G. G. (1992a). The principles of multiple, nonadditive, and reciprocal determinism: Implications for social psychological research and levels of analysis. In D. Ruble, P. Costanzo, & M. Oliveri (Eds.), *The social psychology of mental health* (pp. 328–349). New York: Guilford.

Cacioppo, J. T., & Berntson, G. G. (1992b). Social psychological contributions to the decade of the brain: The doctrine of multilevel analysis. *American Psychologist, 47,* 1019–1028.

Cacioppo, J. T., Berntson, G. G., Sheridan, J. F., & McClintock, M. K. (2000). Multilevel integrative analysis of human behavior: Social neuroscience and the complementing nature of social and biological approaches. *Psychological Bulletin, 126,* 829–843.

Caspi, A., McClay, J., Moffitt, T., Mill, J., Martin, J., Craig, I. W., et al. (2002). Role of genotype in the cycle of violence in maltreated children. *Science, 297,* 851–854.

Caspi, A., Sugden, K., Moffitt, T. E., Taylor, A., Craig, I. W., Harrington, H. L., et al. (2003). Influence of life stress on depression: Moderation by a polymorphism in the 5-HTT gene. *Science, 301,* 386–389.

Ceci, S. J., & Bruck, M. (Eds.). (1995). *Jeopardy in the courtroom: A scientific analysis of children's testimony.* Washington, DC: American Psychological Association.

Ciaranello, R., Aimi, J., Dean, R. S., Morilak, D., Porteus, M. H., & Cicchetti, D. (1995). Fundamentals of molecular neurobiology. In D. Cicchetti & D. J. Cohen (Eds.), *Developmental psychopathology: Theory and method* (Vol. 1, pp. 109–160). New York: Wiley.

Cicchetti, D. (1989). How research on child maltreatment has informed the study of child development: Perspectives from developmental psychopathology. In D. Cicchetti & V. Carlson (Eds.), *Child maltreatment: Theory and research on the causes and consequences of child abuse and neglect* (pp. 377–431). New York: Cambridge University Press.

Cicchetti, D. (1990). A historical perspective on the discipline of developmental psychopathology. In J. Rolf, A. Masten, D. Cicchetti, K. Nuechterlein, & S. Weintraub (Eds.), *Risk and protective factors in the development of psychopathology* (pp. 2–28). New York: Cambridge University Press.

Cicchetti, D. (2002a). How a child builds a brain: Insights from normality and psychopathology. In W. W. Hartup & R. A. Weinberg (Eds.), *The Minnesota symposia on child psychology: Child psychology in retrospect and prospect* (Vol. 32, pp. 23–71). Mahwah, NJ: Lawrence Erlbaum Associates.

Cicchetti, D. (2002b). The impact of social experience on neurobiological systems: Illustration from a constructivist view of child maltreatment. *Cognitive Development, 17,* 1407–1428.

Cicchetti, D., & Barnett, D. (1991). Attachment organization in pre-school-aged maltreated children. *Development and Psychopathology, 3,* 397–411.

Cicchetti, D., & Blender, J. A. (2004). A multiple-levels-of-analysis approach to the study of developmental processes in maltreated children. *Proceedings of the National Academy of Sciences, 101*(50), 17325–17326.

Cicchetti, D., & Cannon, T. D. (1999a). Neurodevelopment and psychopathology [Special Issue]. *Development and Psychopathology, 11*(3), 375–654.

Cicchetti, D., & Cannon, T. D. (1999b). Neurodevelopmental processes in the ontogenesis and epigenesis of psychopathology. *Development and Psychopathology, 11,* 375–393.

Cicchetti, D., & Curtis, W. J. (2005). An event-related potential (ERP) study of processing of affective facial expressions in young children who have experienced maltreatment during the first year of life. *Development and Psychopathology, 17*(3).

Cicchetti, D., & Curtis, W. J. (2006). The developing brain and neural plasticity: Implications for normality, psychopathology, and resilience. In D. Cicchetti & D. Cohen (Eds.), *Developmental Psychopathology* (2nd ed.).: *Developmental neuroscience* (Vol. 2). New York: Wiley.

Cicchetti, D., & Dawson, G. (Eds.). (2002). Multiple levels of analysis [Special Issue]. *Development and Psychopathology, 14*(3), 417–666.

Cicchetti, D., & Hinshaw, S. P. (2002). Editorial: Prevention and intervention science: Contributions for developmental theory. *Development and Psychopathology, 14,* 667–671.

Cicchetti, D., & Lynch, M. (1995). Failures in the expectable environment and their impact on individual development: The case of child maltreatment. In D. Cicchetti & D. J. Cohen (Eds.), *Developmental psychopathology: Risk, disorder, and adaptation* (Vol. 2, pp. 32–71). New York: John Wiley & Sons.

Cicchetti, D., & Posner, M. I. (Eds.). (2005). Integrating cognitive and affective neuroscience and developmental psychopathology [Special Issue]. *Development and Psychopathology, 17*(3), 569–891.

Cicchetti, D., & Rogosch, F. A. (1997). The role of self-organization in the promotion of resilience in maltreated children. *Development and Psychopathology, 9,* 799–817.

Cicchetti, D., & Rogosch, F. A. (2001a). Diverse patterns of neuroendocrine activity in maltreated children. *Development and Psychopathology, 13,* 677–694.

Cicchetti, D., & Rogosch, F. A. (2001b). The impact of child maltreatment and psychopathology upon neuroendocrine functioning. *Development and Psychopathology, 13,* 783–804.

Cicchetti, D., Rogosch, F. A., Lynch, M., & Holt, K. (1993). Resilience in maltreated children: Processes leading to adaptive outcome. *Development and Psychopathology, 5,* 629–647.

Cicchetti, D., & Sroufe, L. A. (1976). The relationship between affective and cognitive development in Down's syndrome infants. *Child Development, 47,* 920–929.

Cicchetti, D., & Sroufe, L. A. (1978). An organizational view of affect: Illustration from the study of Down's syndrome infants. In M. Lewis & L. Rosenblum (Eds.), *The development of affect* (pp. 309–350). New York: Plenum.

Cicchetti, D., & Sroufe, L. A. (2000). Editorial: The past as prologue to the future: The times they've been a changin'. *Development and Psychopathology, 12,* 255–264.

Cicchetti, D., & Toth, S. L. (1991). The making of a developmental psychopathologist. In J. Cantor, C. Spiker, & L. Lipsitt (Eds.), *Child behavior and development: Training for diversity* (pp. 34–72). Norwood, NJ: Ablex.

Cicchetti, D., & Toth, S. L. (2000). Developmental processes in maltreated children. In D. Hansen (Ed.), *Nebraska Symposium on motivation: Child maltreatment* (Vol. 46, pp. 85–160). Lincoln, NE: University of Nebraska Press.

Cicchetti, D., & Toth, S. L. (2006). A developmental psychopathology perspective on preventive interventions with high risk children and families. In A. Renninger & I. Sigel (Eds.), *Handbook of child psychology* (6th ed., pp. 497–547). New York: John Wiley & Sons.

Cicchetti, D., & Toth, S. L. (in preparation). Translational research and developmental psychopathology [Special Issue]. *Development and Psychopathology, 18*(3).

Cicchetti, D., & Tucker, D. (1994). Development and self-regulatory structures of the mind. *Development and Psychopathology, 6,* 533–549.

Cicchetti, D., & Valentino, K. (2006). An ecological transactional perspective on child maltreatment: Failure of the average expectable environment and its influence upon child development. In D. Cicchetti & D. J. Cohen (Eds.), *Developmental psychopathology (2nd ed.).: Risk, disorder, and adaptation* (Vol. 3). New York: Wiley.

Coie, J. D., & Dodge, K. A. (1983). Continuities and changes in children's social status: A five-year longitudinal study. *Merrill-Palmer Quarterly, 29,* 261–282.

Coster, W. J., Gersten, M. S., Beeghly, M., & Cicchetti, D. (1989). Communicative functioning in maltreated toddlers. *Developmental Psychology, 25,* 1020–1029.

Cowan, W. M., Harter, D. H., & Kandel, E. R. (2000). The emergence of modern neuroscience: Some implications for neurology and psychiatry. *Annual Review of Neuroscience, 23,* 343–391.

Curtis, W. J., & Cicchetti, D. (2003). Moving research on resilience into the 21st century: Theoretical and methodological considerations in examining the biological contributors to resilience. *Development and Psychopathology, 15,* 773–810.

Davidson, R. J. (2000). Affective style, psychopathology, and resilience: Brain mechanisms and plasticity. *American Psychologist, 55,* 1196–1214.

Davidson, R. J., & Fox, N. A. (1989). Frontal brain asymmetry predicts infants' response to maternal separation. *Journal of Abnormal Psychology, 98*(2), 127–131.

Davis, M. (1984). The mammalian startle response. In R. C. Eaton (Ed.), *Neural mechanisms of startle behavior* (pp. 287–351). New York: Plenum.

Dawson, G., Panagiotides, H., Klinger, L. G., & Hill, D. (1992). The role of frontal lobe functioning in the development of self-regulatory behavior in infancy. *Brain and Cognition, 20,* 152–175.

DeBellis, M. D. (2001). Developmental traumatology: The psychobiological development of maltreated children and its implications for research, treatment, and policy. *Development and Psychopathology, 13,* 539–564.

Eigsti, I. M., & Cicchetti, D. (2004). The impact of child maltreatment on expressive syntax at 60 months. *Developmental Science, 7,* 88–102.

Eisen, M. L., Qin, J., Goodman, G. S., & Davis, S. L. (2002). Memory and suggestibility in maltreated children: Age, stress arousal, dissociation and psychopathology. *Journal of Experimental Child Psychology, 83,* 167–212.

Eisenberg, L. (1995). The social construction of the human brain. *American Journal of Psychiatry, 152,* 1563–1575.

Fan, J., McCandliss, B. D., Sommer, T., Raz, M., & Posner, M. I. (2002). Testing the efficiency and independece of attentional networks. *Journal of Cognitive Neuroscience, 14*(3), 340–347.

Flores, E., Cicchetti, D., & Rogosch, F. A. (2005). Predictors of resilience in maltreated and nonmaltreated Latino children. *Developmental Psychology, 41*(2), 338–351.

Foley, D. L., Eaves, L. J., Wormley, B., Silberg, J. L., Maes, H. H., Kuhn, J., et al. (2004). Childhood adversity, monoamine oxidase: A genotype, and risk for conduct disorder. *Archives of General Psychiatry, 61*(7), 738–744.

Fox, N. A., Rubin, K. H., Calkins, S. D., Marshall, T. R., Coplan, R. J., Porges, S. W., et al. (1995). Frontal activation asymmetry and social competence at four years of age. *Child Development, 66*(6), 1770–1784.

Gazzaniga, M. S. (Ed.). (2004). *The cognitive neuroscience: III* (3rd ed.). Cambridge, MA: MIT Press.

Goldstein, K. (1939). *The organism.* New York: American Book Company.

Gottesman, I. I., & Hanson, D. R. (2005). Human development: Biological and genetic processes. *Annual Review of Psychology, 56,* 263–286.

Gottlieb, G. (1991). Experiential canalization of behavioral development: Theory. *Developmental Psychology, 27,* 4–13.

Gottlieb, G. (1992). *Individual development and evolution: The genesis of novel behavior.* New York: Oxford University Press.

Gottlieb, G., & Halpern, C. T. (2002). A relational view of causality in normal and abnormal development. *Development and Psychopathology, 14*(3), 421–436.

Greenough, W., & Black, J. (1992). Induction of brain structure by experience: Substrates for cognitive development. In M. Gunnar & C. A. Nelson (Eds.), *Developmental behavioral neuroscience: The Minnesota Symposia on Child Psychology* (Vol. 24, pp. 155–200). Hillsdale, NJ: Lawrence Erlbaum Associates.

Greenough, W., Black, J., & Wallace, C. (1987). Experience and brain development. *Child Development, 58,* 539–559.

Gunnar, M. R., & Vazquez, D. M. (in press). Stress neurobiology and developmental psychopathology. In D. Cicchetti & D. Cohen (Eds.), *Developmental psychopathology (2nd ed.): Developmental neuroscience* (Vol. 2). New York: Wiley.

Hagekull, B., & Bohlin, G. (1998). Preschool temperament and environmental factors related to the Five-Factor Model of personality in middle childhood. *Merrill-Palmer Quarterly, 44,* 194–215.

Hart, J., Gunnar, M., & Cicchetti, D. (1995). Salivary cortisol in maltreated children: Evidence of relations between neuroendocrine activity and social competence. *Development and Psychopathology, 7,* 11–26.

Hart, J., Gunnar, M., & Cicchetti, D. (1996). Altered neuroendocrine activity in maltreated children related to depression. *Development and Psychopathology, 8,* 201–214.

Hebb, D. O. (1949). *Organization of behavior: A neuropsychological theory.* New York: John Wiley & Sons.

Hebb, D. O. (1958). *A textbook of psychology.* Philadelphia: Saunders.

Hinshaw, S. P. (2002). Prevention/intervention trials and developmental theory: Commentary on the Fast Track Special Section. *Journal of Abnormal Child Psychology, 30,* 53–59.

Howe, M. L. (2000). *The fate of early memories: Developmental science and the retention of childhood experiences.* Washington, DC: American Psychological Association.

Howe, M. L., Cicchetti, D., Toth, S. L., & Cerrito, B. M. (2004). True and false memories in maltreated children. *Child Development, 75*(5), 1402–1417.

Hugdahl, K., & Davidson, R. J. (Eds.). (2003). *An asymmetrical brain*. Cambridge, MA: MIT Press.

Kandel, E. R. (1998). A new intellectual framework for psychiatry. *American Journal of Psychiatry, 155*, 475–469.

Kellam, S. G., & Rebok, G. W. (1992). Building developmental and etiological theory through epidemiologically based preventive intervention trials. In J. McCord & R. E. Tremblay (Eds.), *Preventing antisocial behavior: Interventions from birth through adolescence* (pp. 162–195). New York: Guilford.

Kendler, K. S. (2005). Toward a philosophical structure for psychiatry. *The American Journal of Psychiatry, 162*(3), 433–440.

Kimble, G. A. (1994). A frame of reference for psychology. *American Psychologist, 49*, 510–519.

Klorman, R., Cicchetti, D., Thatcher, J. E., & Ison, J. R. (2003). Acoustic startle in maltreated children. *Journal of Abnormal Child Psychology, 31*, 359–370.

Kovacs, M. (1985). The children's depression inventory. *Psychopharmacology Bulletin, 21*, 995–998.

Kovacs, M. (1992). *Children's depression inventory manual*. N. Tonawanda, NY: Multi-health Systems.

Lander, E. S., & Weinberg, R. A. (2000). Genomics: Journey to the center of biology. *Science, 287*, 1777–1782.

Laurent, J., Catanzaro, S. J., Joiner, E., Rudolph, K. D., Potter, K. I., Lambert, S., et al. (1999). A measure of positive and negative affect for children: Scale development and preliminary validation. *Psychological Assessment, 11*, 325–338.

Luciana, M., & Nelson, C. A. (2002). Assessment of neuropsychological function through use of the Cambridge Neuropsychological Testing Automated Battery: Performance in 4- to 12-year-old children. *Developmental Neuropsychology, 22*, 595–624.

Luthar, S. S., Cicchetti, D., & Becker, B. (2000). The construct of resilience: A critical evaluation and guidelines for future work. *Child Development, 71*, 543–562.

Lynch, M., & Cicchetti, D. (1991). Patterns of relatedness in maltreated and nonmaltreated children: Connections among multiple representational models. *Development and Psychopathology, 3*, 207–226.

Lynch, M., & Cicchetti, D. (1992). Maltreated children's reports of relatedness to their teachers. *New Directions for Child Development, 57*, 81–107.

Lynch, M., & Cicchetti, D. (1998a). An ecological-transactional analysis of children and contexts: The longitudinal interplay among child maltreatment, community violence, and children's symptomatology. *Development and Psychopathology, 10*, 235–257.

Lynch, M., & Cicchetti, D. (1998b). Trauma, mental representations, and the organization of memory for mother-referent material. *Development and Psychopathology, 10*, 739–759.

Magnusson, D. (2000). Developmental science. In A. E. Kazdin (Ed.), *Encyclopedia of psychology* (Vol. 3, pp. 24–26). Washington, DC: American Psychological Association; London: Oxford University Press.

Masten, A. S. (2001). Ordinary magic: Resilience processes in development. *American Psychologist, 56*, 227–238.

Maughan, A., & Cicchetti, D. (2002). The impact of child maltreatment and interadult violence on children's emotion regulation abilities. *Child Development, 73*, 1525–1542.

Mayr, E. (1982). *The growth of biological thought*. Cambridge, MA: Harvard University Press.

McEwen, B. S. (1998). Protective and damaging effects of stress mediators. *Seminars in Medicine of Beth Israel Deaconess Medical Center, 338*, 171–179.

Meaney, M. J. (2001). Maternal care, gene expression, and the transmission of individual differences in stress reactivity across generations. *Annual Review of Neuroscience, 24*, 1161–1192.

Meyer, A. (1957). *Psychobiology: A science of man*. Springfield, IL: Charles C. Thomas.

Moffitt, T. E., Caspi, A., & Rutter, M. (2005). Strategy for investigating interactions between measured genes and measured environments. *Archives of General Psychiatry, 62*(5), 473–481.

Morgan, C. A., Grillon, C., Lubin, H., & Southwick, S. M. (1997). Startle abnormalities in women with sexual assault related PTSD. *American Journal of Psychiatry, 154,* 1076–1080.

National Advisory Mental Health Council. (2000). *Translating behavioral science into action: Report of the National Advisory Mental Health Counsel's behavioral science workgroup* (No. 00–4699). Bethesda, MD: National Institutes of Mental Health.

Nelson, C. A. (1999). Neural plasticity and human development. *Current Directions in Psychological Science, 8,* 42–45.

Nelson, C. A., & Bloom, F. E. (1997). Child development and neuroscience. *Child Development, 68,* 970–987.

Nelson, C. A., Bloom, F. E., Cameron, J. L., Amaral, D., Dahl, R. E., & Pine, D. (2002). An integrative, multidisciplinary approach to the study of brain–behavior relations in the context of typical and atypical development. *Development and Psychopathology, 14,* 499–520.

Nelson, C. A., & Monk, C. S. (2001). The use of event related potentials in the study of cognitive development. In C. A. Nelson & M. Luciana (Eds.), *Handbook of developmental cognitive neuroscience* (pp. 125–136). Cambridge, MA: MIT Press.

Ornitz, E. M., & Pynoos, R. S. (1989). Startle modulation in children with posttraumatic stress disorder. *American Journal of Psychiatry, 146,* 866–870.

Orr, S. P., Lasko, N. B., Shalev, A. Y., & Pitman, R. K. (1995). Physiological responses to loud tones in Vietnam veterans with posttraumatic stress disorder. *Journal of Abnormal Psychology, 104,* 75–82.

Parke, R. D. (2004). The Society for Research in Child Development at 70: Progress and promise. *Child Development, 75*(1), 1–24.

Pellmar, T. C., & Eisenberg, L. (Eds.). (2000). *Bridging disciplines in the brain, behavioral, and clinical sciences.* Washington, DC: National Academy Press.

Petronis, A. (2004). The origin of schizophrenia: Genetic thesis, epigenetic antithesis, and resolving synthesis. *Biological Psychiatry, 55,* 142–146.

Pollak, S. D., Cicchetti, D., Hornung, K., & Reed, A. (2000). Recognizing emotion in faces: Developmental effects of child abuse and neglect. *Developmental Psychology, 36,* 679–688.

Pollak, S. D., Cicchetti, D., Klorman, R., & Brumaghim, J. (1997). Cognitive brain event-related potentials and emotion processing in maltreated children. *Child Development, 68,* 773–787.

Pollak, S. D., Klorman, R., Thatcher, J. E., & Cicchetti, D. (2001). P3b reflects maltreated children's reactions to facial displays of emotion. *Psychophysiology, 38,* 267–274.

Posner, M. I., & DiGirolamo, G. I. (2000). Cognitive neuroscience: Origins and promise. *Psychological Bulletin, 126,* 873–889.

Posner, M. I., & Peterson, S. E. (1990). The attention system of the brain. *Annual Review of Neuroscience, 13,* 25–42.

Reynolds, C. R., & Richmond, B. O. (1985). *Revised children's manifest anxiety scale (RCMAS) manual.* Los Angeles, CA: Western Psychological Services.

Rieder, C., & Cicchetti, D. (1989). Organizational perspective on cognitive control functioning and cognitive–affective balance in maltreated children. *Developmental Psychology, 25,* 382–393.

Rogosch, F. A., & Cicchetti, D. (1994). Illustrating the interface of family and peer relations through the study of child maltreatment. *Social Development, 3,* 291–308.

Rogosch, F. A., Cicchetti, D., & Aber, J. L. (1995). The role of child maltreatment in early deviations in cognitive and affective processing abilities and later peer relationship problems. *Development and Psychopathology, 7,* 591–609.

Rothbart, M. K., & Posner, M. I. (in press). Temperament, attention, and developmental psychopathology. In D. Cicchetti & D. Cohen (Eds.), *Developmental Psychopathology (2nd ed.): Developmental Neuroscience* (Vol. 2). New York: Wiley.

Rutter, M. (1987). Psychosocial resilience and protective mechanisms. *American Journal of Orthopsychiatry, 57,* 316–331.

Rutter, M., & Sroufe, L. A. (2000). Developmental psychopathology: Concepts and challenges. *Development and Psychopathology, 12,* 265–296.

Sahakian, B. J., & Owen, A. M. (1992). Computerized assessment in neuropsychiatry using CANTAB. *Journal of the Royal Society of Medicine, 85,* 399–402.

Sameroff, A. J. (2000). Developmental systems and psychopathology. *Development and Psychopathology, 12*(3), 297–312.

Sanchez, M. M., Ladd, C. O., & Plotsky, P. M. (2001). Early adverse experience as a developmental risk factor for later psychopathology: Evidence from rodent and primate models. *Development and Psychopathology, 13,* 419–450.

Sapolsky, R. M. (1992). *Stress, the aging brain, and the mechanisms of neuron death.* Cambridge, MA: MIT Press.

Sapolsky, R. M. (1996). Stress, glucocorticoids, and damage to the NS: The current state of confusion. *Stress, 1,* 1–19.

Shields, A., & Cicchetti, D. (1997). Emotion regulation among school-age children: The development and validation of a new criterion Q-sort scale. *Developmental Psychology, 33,* 906–916.

Shields, A., & Cicchetti, D. (1998). Reactive aggression among maltreated children: The contributions of attention and emotion dysregulation. *Journal of Clinical Child Psychology, 27,* 381–395.

Shields, A., & Cicchetti, D. (2001). Parental maltreatment and emotion dysregulation as risk factors for bullying and victimization in middle childhood. *Journal of Clinical Child Psychology, 30,* 349–363.

Shields, A., Cicchetti, D., & Ryan, R. M. (1994). The development of emotional and behavioral self-regulation and social competence among maltreated school-age children. *Development and Psychopathology, 6,* 57–75.

Shields, A., Ryan, R. M., & Cicchetti, D. (2001). Narrative representations of caregivers and emotion dysregulation as predictors of maltreated children's rejection by peers. *Developmental Psychology, 37,* 321–337.

Sroufe, L. A., & Rutter, M. (1984). The domain of developmental psychopathology. *Child Development, 55,* 17–29.

Staats, A. W. (1999). Unifying psychology requires new infrastructure, theory, method, and a research agenda. *Review of General Psychology, 3,* 3–13.

Sternberg, R. J. (2004). *Unity in psychology: Possibility or pipedream?* Washington, DC: American Psychological Association.

Sternberg, R. J., & Grigorenko, E. L. (2001). Unified psychology. *American Psychologist, 56*(12), 1069–1079.

Teicher, M. H., Anderson, S. L., Polcari, A., Anderson, C. M., Navalta, C. P., & Kim, D. M. (2003). The neurobiological consequences of early stress and childhood maltreatment. *Neuroscience and Biobehavioral Reviews, 27,* 33–44.

Thelen, E., & Smith, L. B. (1998). Dynamic systems theories. In W. Damon & R. Lerner (Eds.), *Handbook of child psychology: Volume 1. Theoretical models of human development* (pp. 563–634). New York: John Wiley & Sons.

Tomarken, A. J., Davidson, R. J., & Henriques, J. B. (1990). Resting frontal activation asymmetry predicts emotional reactivity to film clips. *Journal of Personality and Social Psychology, 59,* 791–801.

Toth, S. L., & Cicchetti, D. (1998). Remembering, forgetting, and the effects of trauma on memory: A developmental psychopathology perspective. *Development and Psychopathology, 10,* 589–605.

Toth, S. L., Cicchetti, D., & Kim, J. E. (2002). Relations among children's perceptions of maternal behavior, attributional styles, and behavioral symptomatology in maltreated children. *Journal of Abnormal Child Psychology, 30,* 478–501.

Waddington, C. H. (1957). *The strategy of genes.* London: Allen & Unwin.

Wechsler, D. (2003). *Wechsler Intelligence Scale for Children.* San Antonio, TX: The Psychological Corporation.

Weiss, P. (1959). Cellular dynamics. *Review of Modern Physics, 31,* 11–20.

Zigler, E. (1973). The retarded child as a whole person. In D. Routh (Ed.), *The experimental study of mental retardation* (pp. 231–322). Chicago: Aldine.

Chapter 9

The Place of Development
in Developmental Psychopathology

L. Alan Sroufe
University of Minnesota

When Michael Rutter was asked at a meeting 25 years ago for his definition of "developmental psychopathology," he said that it is, as the name says, first and foremost about development. And so it remains today. After all, "the process of development constitutes the crucial link between genetic . . . and environmental variables, between sociology and individual psychology, and between physiogenic and psychogenic causes" (Rutter, 1980, p. 1).

The chapters in this book are remarkable, each beautifully written and informative. Moreover, they are in accord in making two points of profound importance for developmental psychopathology. First, repeatedly and convincingly, they make the point that developmental psychopathology is necessarily a multidisciplinary field. The argument was for *multiple* levels of analysis, not simply different levels. No one argued that the level of focus in his or her chapter was more important than some other level, but rather that it gained in importance when considered in concert with another level of analysis. Thus, for example, the role of environment is not diminished when considered in concert with genes, but amplified. Determining the true nature of development is not a zero-sum game. The second point is closely related. Behavior, disorder, and development are always the result of interdependence, codetermination, or co-actions among multiple levels of influence (see also Gottlieb & Halpern, 2002). Although the terms may have been somewhat different, all authors in this book described an adaptational process wherein child influences environment and environment influences child in an ongoing way. All recognized the inappropriateness of linear causal models in which some single pathogen is linked ineluctably to a singular outcome or in which there is an artificial separation of mind and body, genes and experience, or child and surrounding context. As Rutter (chapter 1) put it, for example: ". . . the traditional neat and tidy subdivision into genetic effects and environmental effects has broken down" (p. 20).

In addition, each of the chapters provided important examples of the place of development in a multilevel approach to psychopathology. Rutter (chapter 1) provides a complex model of development in medicine, wherein, for example, changes that in themselves are benign initiate a course of development that leads to disease (as in malignant tumors), or where there is heterotypic continuity in development, in which distinctly different risk factors are potent at different points in the developmental process (as in heart disease). He also gives numerous examples of co-action, including the classic studies of Cadoret and Tienari, which show that the conjoint effects of genetic and environmental liability are far beyond those of either alone (Cadoret, Troughton, Merchant, & Whitters, 1990; Tienari et al., 1990). Finally, he provides examples from his work that even disorders widely believed to have genetic involvement, such as schizophrenia, are subject to notable environmental influence.

In chapter 2, Hanson and Gottesman enliven the once more static concepts of "reaction range" and "diathesis-stress" through use of the developmental concept of adaptation. Neither diathesis nor potentials are set at birth, and the reaction range becomes a "reaction surface" in this evolved view. "Human development is more than an interaction term in an analysis of genetic and environmental variances" (p. 32). The dynamic concept of epigenesis continues to evolve and now includes environmental effects at every level. These authors, as well as Rutter (chapter 1) and Boyce (chapter 3), discuss the exciting new research on methylation that shows that early experience can have lasting effects, not only on behavior but also on the physiological stress reactivity system and on the turning on and off of the glucocorticoid receptor genes themselves. "The previously spurned concept of the inheritance of acquired characteristics is resurfacing at the molecular level . . . but now based on credible data" (p. 32).

Boyce (chapter 3) presents a general model in which reactive children in high stress environments are placed on long-term trajectories toward physical and mental health problems. Thus, genetic vulnerability would increase the salience of environmental adversity, not reduce it. Moreover, the model is even more complex than first implied because "biological sensitivity to context may not only moderate associations between social context and health, but may be itself a product of early social contextual influences" (p. 63). Biological sensitivity to context is not simply a cause but is an outcome as well.

Such thinking is consistent with the nonlinear, systemic thinking that runs throughout this book.

Egeland (chapter 4) uses longitudinal data from the Minnesota Parent–Child Project to illustrate the "organized" nature of development. Pathology and resilience are viewed as dynamic constructs, being based not just on current individual characteristics or current circumstances, but on foundations established through prior experience and early adaptation. In addition, change in problem behavior is linked to change in parental stress or parental depression. Such change data make clear that links between parent problems and child behavior are not simply due to genetics. As do other chapters in the volume, the Egeland chapter also illustrates pathways concepts; here, for example, a pathway from maltreatment to alienation to conduct problems. Finally, Egeland provides critical data on the importance of timing. He shows, for example, that early trauma may predict adult problems, such as dissociation, even after accounting for middle childhood problems, and that early trauma is a more powerful predictor of adolescent and adult dissociation than is later trauma, likely because of the young child's lesser capacity to integrate disparate and challenging aspects of experience.

In chapter 5, Fiese and Spagnola adopt many of the same perspectives used by Egeland to look at the level of the total family. Thus, it is family features that are risk or promotive factors, and it is family practices and rituals that are interiorized by the child, in addition to dyadic, parent–child factors. Reciprocal influences between child and family are described. Serious illness of the child (asthma is their example) clearly represents a challenge to the family, but different families are organized differently to respond to this challenge. When routine and affectively positive family practices can be continued and the positive family representation can accommodate an ill child, necessary medical regimens are followed and fewer internalizing disorders result. In contrast, "in cases where the family perceives daily care as a drain on personal resources, children worry more about their asthma symptoms (and) report . . . that their daily activities are often interrupted by health symptoms" (pp. 134–135).

Dishion and Piehler (chapter 6) present an exquisite example of developmental process, wherein children with established problem behavior develop associations with deviant peers, which then create a progressive amplification or cascade of antisocial problems. The work is important for the field both because it illustrates the importance of understanding normal developmental phenomena (here, friendships and peer networks) and because such change in problem behavior cannot be readily assimilated to a simple causal model. A true transaction is illustrated. There is no question that antisocial children increasingly associate with deviant peers, that such friendships operate in distinctive ways, and that over time they promote increased individual problems, which in turn consolidate deviant peer associations. A simple defect model is not adequate because level of social skills and the capacity for mutual influence seem equivalent for deviant and non-deviant peer friendships. But in this case mutuality, through mutual support of deviance, promotes escalating antisocial behavior.

Garber (chapter 7) recapitulated many of these themes in adopting a multilevel view of a particular disorder, depression. She illustrates clearly that depression in not appropriately considered as simply an organic disorder, but rather is best understood in light of physiological, cognitive, and social features. As Rutter (chapter 1) said, "a subdivision of mental disorders into those that are 'medical' and those that are 'social' is totally meaningless" (p. 5).

A comprehensive overview of the potential role for every level of analysis in understanding pathways to psychopathology is presented by Cicchetti and Valentino (chapter 8). Levels considered range from molecular genetics, acoustical startle, and neuroendocrine regulation, to emotional regulation, attention, memory and language, to self-representations, social relationships, and community. Their data reveal co-actions, such as powerful joint effects on problem behavior of parental maltreatment and living in violent neighborhoods, and the interplay of maltreatment, neuroendocrine regulation, and depression. Such multilevel analysis is used to explain diverging pathways associated with maltreatment over time. Their work also reveals developmental mediation effects. For example, the link between maltreatment and later peer problems was mediated by assessed cognitive control or understanding of negative affect. Complex paths also were shown, wherein negative representations undermined emotion regulation, which then compromised peer functioning.

In light of these splendid chapters, which move the field forward so nicely, what more then is there for a commentator to say? In this case, only to go further and to do so in a particular way; namely, by adopting an even more thoroughgoing developmental perspective. The bulk of this final chapter is devoted to laying out what this would mean and what the implications of a more thorough developmental view would be for thinking about and understanding psychopathology. Before doing that, I make some initial comments about the nature of development and its place in explaining behavior.

THE NATURE OF DEVELOPMENT

All students are now taught that development and all behavior, whether normal or abnormal, results from the interaction of genes and environment. This marks an important advance over simpler ideas that genes cause behavior or that the environment simply washes over a passive organism. And yet it does not really capture the full complexity of development.

There is a critical third ingredient that is not yet fully appreciated. It is not just genes and environment, but genes, environment, and past development that set the stage for future development.

The necessity of this altered viewpoint is readily illustrated by examples from prenatal development (Arms & Camp, 1987; Kuo, 1967). For example, consider an early stage in the development of the chick embryo, when buds that will become legs and wings are just emerging. If one surgically removes a tiny piece of tissue from an area that would otherwise develop into thigh tissue and places it at the tip of the wing bud, it can become a normal part of the wing tip. The surrounding cells, it is argued, "induce" it to become wing tissue. Timing is crucial; the tissue must not yet be "committed" to becoming leg tissue. This is, of course, another example of genes being turned off and on, as discussed by Rutter, Hanson & Gottesman, and Boyce (this volume). But because of the timing issue, one also already sees a role for past development. If one does this transfer too late, a glob of anomalous tissue at the tip of the wing results. More remarkably, if one does the transfer at a very particular point, not as early as in the first experiment and not too late, an amazing result is possible. One gets not thigh tissue at the tip of the wing and not normal-looking wing tissue, but a *claw*. How can this be? Apparently, the transferred tissue already was committed to (differentiated toward) becoming leg tissue, but not fully committed to becoming thigh tissue. Thus, the surrounding wing-tip tissues (the surrounding context) could not alter it away from becoming a leg part; yet the new context could induce it to become a tip, so it becomes the tip of a leg—a claw.

In this example, we of course continue to see an important role for genes. After all, it does not become a fin. We also see a crucial role for the environment (here, surrounding tissues) and for the interaction of the two. But there is a critical role for development as well. The intervening event has a notably different impact depending on when it happens; that is, depending on the prior development of the organism.

These examples from prenatal life are not simply a metaphor for the nature of development. Rather, this is the way development always works. There is no reason to think that things progress any differently whether we are talking about the development of tissue, the brain, a cognitive capacity, temperament, or the personality. Once we realize the importance of the time dimension, of development itself, we can never see genes and environment in the same way again. Except perhaps for a micromoment in time in the very beginning of development, it is not gene–environment interaction that concerns us when we study whole, living systems. In the embryonic example just cited, it really was tissue–environment interaction. Most often, in developmental psychology, it is organism–environment interaction or person–environment interaction (Sroufe, Egeland, Carlson, & Collins, 2005). The organism is, after all, Genes × Environment × Time. Once time is entered, there is organism, and it is the organism that then interacts with environment. Following birth, with development, there is the person, and it is the person that interacts with the environment. The cumulative history of the person in part determines the environment (through what the person engages, reacts to, elicits, and processes) and even, at least in part, the genes that are active and inactive at a given time. "Child effects" are not gene effects but person effects. Person–environment correlations come to the fore, not gene–environment correlations. All of this derives from the inclusion of development as not just an outcome but as also a critical feature of a causal system.

This embryology example not only makes clear the three ingredients of development, but it reveals the very nature of development as well. Development is lawful and orderly in a particular way; namely it is "hierarchically integrated" (Werner, 1948) or *cumulative*. This means that development always entails everything that went before and something more. The "something more" is the emerging complexity resulting from the co-actions of organism and environment. The emerging complexity is not specified by prior features, yet it is founded on them (Sroufe et al., 2005). Acquired capacities are retained yet changed in meaning when new capacities are acquired and organized with them into more complex wholes. Future development, however complexly transformed, builds on what was already there. The tissue, organism, or person reacts differently to what appears to be the same environmental circumstance at different points in development. And individuals react differently because of their individual histories. As Freud is reported to have said: "The human mind is from start to finish incapable of separating itself from its own experience but can only build upon that" (Rosen, 1989, p. 126).

Development is an ongoing transactional process—the organism (person) as developed to that point in time engages the environment in particular ways (selecting, "interpreting," reacting to, and eliciting), while at the same time the current context (including the engaged environment) transforms the organism. In a cyclical way, the further developed person now engages the environment in altered ways and continually is further influenced by the engaged environment.

Our evolving view of development is that although genetic endowment is never lost, it is never the same following the early organizations of the organism. Likewise, although any inborn physiological and behavioral tendencies are not lost, they are never the same once the person begins interacting with the surrounding environment. As Werner (1948) argued:

> The development of biological forms is expressed by an *increasing differentiation* of parts and an increasing subordination or *hierarchization*. Such a process of hierarchization means that for any organic structure the organization of the differentiated parts is a closed totality, an ordering and grouping of parts in terms of the whole organism. (p. 41)

IMPLICATIONS OF A DEVELOPMENTAL VIEWPOINT

Adopting a thoroughgoing developmental viewpoint has widespread implications for the study of psychopathology, altering all aspects of our enterprise. It would change our language—the way we describe phenomena and conceptualize the origins and course of disorder. It would change how we interpret and explain research findings. And it would profoundly change the research agenda.

The Language We Use

Linear, reductionistic thinking is deeply ingrained in all of us, and we readily slip into describing cause in terms of individual traits rather than developmental systems. At the outset, I want to adopt the curved finger of accusation and say that attachment theorists, such as myself, are equally vulnerable to this problem. Frequently, we slip into using terms such as "securely attached child" when we know that attachment is really a relationship term, and the proper description would be "a child with a history of a secure relationship with the primary caregiver." We don't do it because this is unwieldy, and I think that often explains why we use, as well, terms such as "inherent," "predisposition," and "largely genetic." Such terms are not developmental constructs and although, generally, we don't mean it, these terms imply a linear, not thoroughly developmental view. We know genes are modified by environment and that temperament is subject to transformation and is developing from the start, but in our language we sometimes gloss over this.

In a developmental viewpoint, we would not use the term *heritable* as though we had explained the cause of something, even in part. Heritability estimates would not be taken to imply genetic cause. Following Turkheimer (1998), we know that all we really can conclude is that H squared is not 0. When we say something like, "The heritability of ADHD is .70" and imply or say that this problem is then largely genetic, we are forgetting about development. Heritability estimates always would fluctuate depending on the variation in environments sampled. With one member of monozygotic twin pairs reared in a group-care Romanian orphanage and the other in a stable, supportive family, with an extensive social support network, heritability of almost any psychological characteristic would be very low. Moreover, the genetic term in these computations also includes the interaction with environment, and generally it is not possible to extract the effect that is purely due to genes. As Piaget (1952) said regarding cognition and affect, the workings of genes and environment are "non-dissociable." Finally, in the case of ADHD, heritability estimates very widely, being about .70 for parent report, .50 for teacher report, and .20 for observational data. Our own prospective data on onset and course of ADHD (e.g., Carlson et al., 1995) make clear that there is a critical role for environment in this problem (see Research Agenda, later in this chapter). Genes are important. Environment is important. We cannot say one is more important than the other.

Cicchetti and Cannon (1999) make this same point when they say, "No component, subsystem, or level of organization possesses causal privilege in the developmental system . . ." (p. 377). Yet we often do slip into granting privileged causal status to biological features. Authors who at times provide elegant statements regarding the co-active, integrative, and systemic nature of disturbance will at the same time speak of genetic *influences,* speak of biological *predispositions,* and use temperament as a causal construct. We seem to more readily accept circular statements such as, "She is shy because she has a behaviorally inhibited temperament" than "She is shy because she has an unresponsive caregiver." We treat neurobiological explanations as more basic, fundamental, and important. They are basic, fundamental, and important, but not more so than other levels of explanation.

One concluding example of how use of language impacts our thinking comes from the important work by Boyce (chapter 3). He describes the compelling and clearly developmental idea that children are differentially sensitive to stressful environments; that is, that there is an interaction between individual stress reactivity and context. And all would agree that biological features would be an important consideration in such sensitivity. However, choosing to describe the phenomenon as "biological sensitivity to context" has the consequence of moving his exquisite developmental view into and out of focus. On one hand, he points out that "biological" sensitivity to context may be itself an outcome of early social contextual influences and that "*all* children are vulnerable in settings of . . . deprivation" (p. 62). These statements make clear his understanding of the transactional, systemic nature of development. On the other hand, in the same chapter, he refers to "inherent individual susceptibility" and to "dandelion children" who "survive and even thrive in whatever circumstances they encounter (p. 61)." They are "resilient," he argues, because they are low on biological sensitivity to context. In fact, there are no dandelion children in this sense. Resilience is a product of a complexly evolved foundation of prior development and presence of current supports that offset challenges (Sroufe et al., 1999; see also Egeland, chapter 4, this volume). Studies of high early risk, such as the Rochester study (Sameroff, 2000), show that when eight or nine of the potent risk variables are present, there are no resilient children. Resilience, like sensitivity to context, develops, and defining resilience in terms of inherent characteristics moves us away from developmental analysis. I clarify this further in discussing research findings.

How We Interpret Research

A thoroughgoing developmental approach would not just change our descriptive language, but the way we interpret research findings. One recent example is the important research by Caspi et al. (2002) on an interaction effect between maltreatment and the MAO-A gene on conduct problems. It should, of course, be obvious with any interaction that both components must matter; yet it is striking how often this finding is interpreted to mean (and only mean) that maltreatment has an effect *only* on genetically vulnerable children. Oddly, it is often suggested that maltreatment per se does not matter; that is, it only matters if the genetic *defect* is present. It is not similarly concluded that genes do not matter. This widespread interpretation is doubly ironic. First, it is ironic because the graphed data reveal a classic crossover interaction. Thus, it is just as valid to conclude that the genetic variation only has its negative effect when children are maltreated, and even that the same genetic anomaly may have a positive effect in a nurturing environment (see also Suomi, 2002, for more compelling data on such phenomena with monkeys). The idea of a genetic "defect" should be called into question and the more developmentally friendly concept of genetic "feature" should be put forward. The frequent, overly simplified explanation is also ironic because a larger replication study found no main effect for gene but did find evidence for an interaction, *and* for a main effect for maltreatment (Foley et al., 2004). The implication that maltreatment only matters sometimes was misguided, especially given that it is a risk factor for diverse problems beyond conduct disorders. Maltreatment *always* matters (as do genes, even if their contribution is indirect).

Werner's classic, vitally important work (e.g., Werner & Smith, 1992) on resilience provides another example. In virtually every textbook, and in other scholarly writing, one conclusion almost always put forward from this study is that temperamental robustness enables some children to be resilient in the face of even overwhelming adversity. By this it is meant that some children have inherent, endogenous qualities that promote resilience. A close reading of the Werner work, however, reveals that significant results were for *one* (of numerous) temperamental variable at *one* age period, and this variable was the mother's description of her child as "loveable" at age 2 years. It is a stretch to interpret this variable, assessed in this way, as reflecting inherent child variation. Such a variable plausibly reflects more than endogenous child characteristics. It could be viewed as reflecting parental perceptions and attitudes as well, and is most prudently interpreted as a complex developmental outcome itself. Although this is an obvious case, showing how readily temperament as cause is accepted, the same considerations apply to other cases as well.

It is when temperament constructs are used causally (as endogenous variation that explains later functioning), rather than descriptively, that developmental thinking erodes. Many constructs currently discussed by temperament researchers are vitally important to developmental psychopathology. These certainly include "effortful control" and "emotion regulation." Such characteristics are central in current definitions of disorder (Cole et al., 1994), and they are deeply important developmental constructs. But that is the point. Effortful control and emotion regulation are capacities that develop, as do sensitivity to stimulation, biological vulnerability, and other important characteristics subsumed by temperament researchers. That such capacities may be linked to measures of brain functioning goes without saying. How could it be otherwise? Whatever the role of environment or of past development, such capacities would be reflected in brain activity. This is reductionism in the good sense that Rutter (chapter 1) describes. But such a link does not remove the need to understand development, and it does not mean that variations in such capacities are genetic or inborn.

Temperament as a term used to described individual variation has an important place in developmental study, but temperament as a causal concept obfuscates developmental understanding. When complex constructs such as emotion regulation are defined as temperamental differences, as though that explains something, we have left development behind and moved ourselves further from understanding. What we want to understand are the array of co-actions involving numerous levels across time that lead to differences in such capacities. There is at present extraordinarily little evidence, based on direct observations made early in the first year, that any temperamental dimension taken by itself has long-term predictive significance for psychopathology. In our own study, unprecedented with regard to its starting point, density of observations, comprehensiveness, and long-term follow-up, we do find evidence of interaction effects involving early emerging individual variation and experiential variables, but virtually no main effects for temperament (Sroufe et al., 2005).

There is a general tendency in the field to take "child effects" as implying causality based on inherent, endogenous, physiological variation. "Bidirectionality" of effects is a reality; children impact as well as are influenced by their parents. But demonstrations that different children elicit different reactions from parents and others, rather than giving an answer about the role of biology, raises a question about development. How do children come to do this? When the phenomenon is looked at developmentally, one discovers that child effects actually increase with age, which could be explained in a variety of ways (Sroufe et al., 2005). The child is an increasingly powerful influence with development. Also, one may predict varying environmental reactions to different children ("child effects") from knowledge of varied prior experience, as well as or better than from knowledge of early temperament (Sroufe et al, 2005). Furthermore, there is a dramatically greater predictability of later disturbance from assessed child behavior after age 3 years than before age 3.

Likewise, individual variation on any characteristic in and of itself does not mean genetic variation or inborn variation or inherent variation. The fact that some children show persistent, stable conduct problems, with early onset, is not best simply taken as evidence of neurobiological disorder but, rather, as posing a developmental question. How does this come about? At the least, in addition to endogenous variation, one would wish to examine how this pattern of adaptation elicits perpetuating feedback from environmental encounters in an ongoing way. This is what Dishion and Piehler show with their work on deviant peer associations. Prospective, early beginning studies show that, in fact, the demonstrated verbal deficits of these children in general emerge subsequent to initiation of the conduct problem pathway and do not precede it; nor do newborn assessments of temperament or neurological status predict it (Aguilar et al., 2000).

Our tendency to attribute causal status to temperament is most obvious in studies beyond infancy. Such studies can show how readily we lose hold of developmental thinking even in the midst of exquisite studies of developmental process. In their wonderful chapter in this volume, Dishion and Piehler demonstrated an intriguing interaction between self-regulation capacity and deviant peer group membership; namely, that for those assessed as high on self-regulation, deviant peer membership was less predictive of increased behavior problems. This is an important finding and would immediately lead to the question of how self-regulation develops and how we can promote this capacity. But not when self-regulation is simply defined as temperament (and implied to be endogenous). The quest for understanding is ended when temperament is taken as explanation. The case for doing so is not strong. Using an instrument, a form of which has been used in infancy, and constructs that other investigators label as "temperament," does not make something a measure of temperament in anything other than a descriptive sense. It is not even clear yet whether parental descriptions in infancy of these constructs reflect endogenous variation, and there is no data to support the stability of these constructs, independently assessed, from infancy to adolescence. It is a strength that Dishion and Piehler use both parent and child report (although these did not agree with their experimental measure) and that other data sources were independent. This often is not the case. The main point is that by defining "capacity for self-regulation" as temperament (and using the term causally), the investigators moved away from a thoroughgoing developmental view.

Research Agenda

The research agenda within a thoroughgoing developmental approach to disturbance would be quite different from the apparent agenda today.

> Within a developmental perspective, maladaptation is viewed as evolving through the successive adaptations of persons in their environment. It is not something a person "has" or an ineluctable expression of an endogenous pathogen. It is the result of a myriad of risk and protective factors operating over time. (Sroufe, 1997, p. 251)

Therefore, within this perspective, key research questions are focused on the factors that initiate and maintain maladaptive developmental processes.

The bulk of research in the current psychiatric literature is two-group research (those with and without some disorder), and the focus is on establishing correlates of disorder once established. Mostly, the search is for neurophysiological concomitants or, more recently, specific gene loci. The clear implication is that cause is understood once these correlates are discovered. Much of this work seems to spring from a belief in the inherent and fixed nature of disorder. The fallacy of this logic is obvious. The physiological differences may be results of the disorder, reflections of complex causal features that led to the disorder, or, if genuine antecedents, themselves the results of developmental processes. Now, even genetic effects are known to be subject to experiential influence through methylation, Moreover, establishing a role for genes still leaves open questions of mechanisms and process. Thus, the current agenda is restrictive.

The broader agenda of a developmental approach is concerned with at least three foci (Sroufe, 1997). The first focus is on understanding the array of factors and combination of factors that coalesce to initiate individuals onto a pathway that is probabilistically related to later disorder. Central here is discovering early patterns of adaptation that are precursors to disorder. They are themselves not pathological but are markers of pathways to disorder when subsequent developmental challenges are faced, if surrounding structures of support and liabilities are not altered. There will be critical clues here for prevention.

The second and third issues concern understanding features of the developmental landscape that serve to maintain individuals on a pathway and guide them to one outcome or another (cf. Dishion & Piehler, chapter 6), and discovering factors and processes that help deflect individuals away from pathways toward disorder, back toward health or vice versa. It is understood that factors that initiate a pathway may not be the same as those that maintain or deflect individuals from the pathway. Discovering mechanisms and processes of change comes to the fore, and a more dynamic view of disorder results. When, for example, one sees ADHD in terms of a pathway a child is *on,* rather than a condition a child *has,* change processes become central. The attention and control problems of these children, in fact, fluctuate (e.g., Sroufe et al., 2005), and changes in family stress and social support in part account for such changes (Carlson et al., 1995). Even with disorders that are quite stable, numerous developmental questions arise. What governs this stability? What determines when it becomes relatively stable?

The complete developmental question is not just whether some marker, characteristic, or experience is associated with later disorder, but how did this feature arise or have the impact it did and how does this process vary when other features are present. The discovery of particular genetic loci is important within this view as well, but in a very different way. Genes do not have the status of explanations, and they never will, but they may be starting points for developmental inquiry. Like other risk factors, they may serve to focus our work on developmental processes by pointing to key aspects of development that may go awry or at least by defining groups where more individuals might be expected to ultimately manifest the disorder in question. This would increase research efficiency. It is no accident that genetic work where there has been most promise concerns genes where something about developmental process is understood.

The agenda centered on understanding developmental pathways has radical effects on all aspects of our work. With all disorders, we want to know the differing array of features that are associated with onset at one point in development versus another. For example, early onset of depression and of conduct disorders is associated more with early adversity than is adolescent onset (Aguilar et al., 2000; Duggal et al., 2001).

A developmental approach also has implications for classification. Classification based on current manifest behaviors alone ignores the potential meaningfulness of different pathways to the same problem and different prognoses depending on foundations established before the period of difficulty. Moffitt's (1993) work represents an important beginning for this type of work. Dividing adolescents with conduct problems into those whose problems began very early and were persistent and those whose problems began in adolescence appears to have etiological and prognostic significance. Early onset is more heavily associated with harsh treatment than is adolescent onset, and adolescent onset cases more likely desist in early adulthood. These pathways considerations add to our understanding far beyond that granted by a symptom portrait in adolescence. In this case and more generally, developmental pathways considerations may help resolve the vexing problems of heterogeneity and of multiple disorders (comorbidity) that plague the current DSM system. We have yet to begin in earnest research in which we proceed forward in time from early patterns of adaptation and maladaptation and their later manifestations in disturbed or healthy behavior, rather than proceeding backwards from presumed disorders in later life to antecedents.

CONCLUSION

The chapters in this book are sophisticated and thoughtful, and in addition to underscoring the value of a multilevel approach, they point toward a comprehensive developmental perspective on psychopathology. When this perspective is taken further, and development is put fully at the forefront of our endeavors, several conclusions are reached.

First, development (of anything) is not just the product of genes and environment in interaction, but genes, environment, and past development. From the first cell division forward, there is no outcome that does not entail development.

Second, it more properly is the organism or person that interacts with environment or context, not genes. Given development, the interaction between genes and environment is only indirect. From this perspective, it actually makes more sense to talk about genes as part of the total context within which the person is acting.

Third, everything develops—including irritability, EEG asymmetry, stress reactivity, effortful control of attention, cognitive biases, resilience and psychopathology itself. None of them are givens. "There is no aspect, activity, function, or structure of the psyche that is not subject to development" (Spitz, Emde, & Metcalf, 1970, p. 417). Heterogeneity of reaction to the environment is not evidence of genetic effects, but of development (although genes, of course, are presumed to play a role). Parent reactions to children likewise are developmental outcomes.

Not only is it inappropriate to speak of gene or environmental effects as independent of one another, it also is inappropriate to speak of genes and environment as independent of development. To paraphrase the remarkable insight of developmentalist René Spitz, writing decades ago (e.g., Spitz et al., 1970): Where we once saw maturation and experience, genes and environment, brain and mind, body and psyche, now there is only development.

REFERENCES

Aguilar, B., Sroufe, L. A., Egeland, B., & Carlson, E. (2000). Distinguishing the early-onset/persistent and adolescent-onset anti-social behavior types: From birth to 16 years. *Development and Psychopathology, 12,* 109–132.

Arms, K., & Camp, P. (1987). *Biology* (3rd ed.). Philadelphia: Saunders.

Cadoret, R., Troughton, E., Merchant, L., & Whitters, A. (1990). Early life psychosocial events and adult psychosocial symptoms. In L. Robins & M. Rutter (Eds.), *Straight and devious pathways from childhood to adulthood* (pp. 300–313). Cambridge, England: Cambridge University Press.

Carlson, E. A., Jacobvitz, D., & Sroufe, L. A. (1995). A developmental investigation of inattentiveness and hyperactivity. *Child Development, 66,* 37–54.

Caspi, A., McClay, J., Moffitt, T. E., Mill, J., Martin, J., & Craig, I. W. (2002). Role of genotype in the cycle of violence in maltreated children. *Science, 297,* 851–854.

Cicchetti, D., & Cannon, T. D. (1999). Neurodevelopmental processes in the ontogenesis and epigenesis of psychopathology. *Development and Psychopathology, 11,* 375–393.

Cole, P. M., Michel, M. K., & O'Connell-Teti, L. (1994). The development of emotion regulation and dysregulation: A clinical perspective. *Monographs of the Society for Research in Child Development, 59* (2–3, Serial No. 240).

Duggal, S., Carlson, E. A., Sroufe, L. A., & Egeland, B. (1998). Depressive symptomatology in childhood and adolescence. *Development and Psychopathology, 13,* 143–164.

Foley, D., Eaves, L., Wormley, B., Silberg, J., Maes, H., Kuhn, J., et al. (2004). Childhood adversity, monoamine oxidase: A genotype, and risk for conduct disorder. *Archives of General Psychiatry, 61*(7), 738–744.

Gottlieb, G., & Halpern, C. T. (2002). A relational view of causality in normal and abnormal development. *Development and Psychopathology, 14*(3), 421–435.

Kuo, Z. (1967). *The dynamics of behavior development.* New York: Random House.

Moffitt, T. (1993). Adolescence-limited and life-course-persistent antisocial behavior: A developmental taxonomy. *Psychological Review, 100,* 674–701.

Piaget, J. (1952). *The origins of intelligence in children.* New York: Norton.

Rosen, N. (1989). *John and Anzia: An American romance.* New York: Dutton.

Rutter, M. (1980). Introduction. In M. Rutter (Ed.), *Scientific foundation of developmental psychiatry* (pp. 1–7). London: Heinemann.

Sameroff, A. (2000). Dialectical processes in developmental psychopathology. In A. Sameroff, M. Lewis & S. Miller (Eds.), *Handbook of developmental psychopathology* (2nd ed., pp. 23–40). New York: Plenum.

Spitz, R., Emde, R., & Metcalf, D. (1970). Further prototypes of ego formation. *The Psychoanalytic Study of the Child, 25,* 417–444.

Sroufe, L. A. (1997). Psychopathology as an outcome of development. *Development and Psychopathology, 9,* 251–268.

Sroufe, L. A., Carlson, E. A., Levy, A. K., & Egeland, B. (1999). Implications of attachment theory for developmental psychopathology. *Development and Psychopathology, 11,* 1–13.

Sroufe, L. A., Egeland, B., Carlson, E., & Collins, W. A. (2005). *The development of the person: The Minnesota Study of Risk and Adaptation from Birth to Adulthood.* New York: Guilford.

Suomi, S. (2002). Parents, peers, and the process of socialization in primates. In J. Borkowski, S. Ramey & M. Bristol-Power (Eds.), *Parenting and your child's world* (pp. 265–282). Hillsdale, NJ: Lawrence Erlbaum Associates.

Tienari, P., Lahti, I., Sorri, A., Naarala, M., Moring, J., Kaleva, M. et al. (1990). Adopted-away offspring of schizophrenics and controls: The Finnish adoptive family study of schizophrenia. In L. Robins & M. Rutter (Eds.), *Straight and devious pathways from childhood to adulthood* (pp. 365–379). Cambridge, England: Cambridge University Press.

Turkheimer, E. (1998). Heritability and biological explanation. *Psychological Review, 105*(4), 782–791.

Werner, E. E., & Smith, R. S. (1992). *Overcoming the odds.* New York: Cornell University Press.

Werner, H. (1948). *The comparative psychology of mental development.* New York: International Universities Press.

Author Index

Subject Index